James Whitcomb Riley

JAMES
WHITCOMB
RILEY
A Life

Elizabeth J. Van Allen

Indiana University Press   Bloomington and Indianapolis

This book is a publication of

Indiana University Press
601 North Morton Street
Bloomington, Indiana 47404-3797 USA

www.indiana.edu/~iupress

Telephone orders 800-842-6796
Fax orders 812-855-7931
e-mail orders iuporder@indiana.edu

The paper used in this publication meets the minimum
requirements of American National Standard for Information
Sciences—Permanence of Paper for Printed Library
Materials, ANSI Z39.48–1984.

Manufactured in the United States of America

Library of Congress Cataloging-Publication Data

Van Allen, Elizabeth J.
    James Whitcomb Riley : a life / Elizabeth J. Van Allen.
        p.   cm.
    Includes bibliographical references (p.   ) and index.
    ISBN 0-253-33591-4 (cloth : alk. paper)
    1. Riley, James Whitcomb, 1849–1916. 2. Poets,
American—19th century Biography. 3. Poets, American—
Indiana Biography.   I. Title.
PS2706.V36   1999
811'.4—dc21
    [B]   99-40585

1   2   3   4   5   04   03   02   01   00   99

To Omer H. Foust

CONTENTS

Illustrations follow page 194.

PREFACE

At the time of his death in 1916, James Whitcomb Riley was the most popular and successful poet in America. In his home state, he had reached a status approaching sainthood. Through the years, however, his reputation has fallen so far that he has become a caricature to many. Today, literary scholars characterize him as a drunken poet who composed rural doggerel, while his remaining popular audience pictures him as a kindly old poet who wrote about nature and children. Whether he is depicted as a saint or as a minor literary figure, neither image is fair or accurate, and both, from opposite perspectives, minimize his complexity and significance. Past Riley biographers have only reinforced these distortions. For this reason, on the occasion of the sesquicentennial of his birth, the life of Riley deserved a fresh look, one that avoided such simple iconography. My challenge, therefore, as his biographer, was to attempt to correct these distortions that have pervaded our perceptions of Riley and to present as complete and accurate a picture of the man and his character as I could.

Shortly after Riley's death, Hoosier author Booth Tarkington, who had known Riley since he was a child, stated one of the principal difficulties of describing the poet's life. In a *Collier's Magazine* article published in December 1916, he said, "We are so naively ready to confuse [Riley] the artist with his work."[1]

Before I started doing research on Riley, I was one of those guilty of such confusion. I had the same experience with Riley that most native Hoosiers have had. I read "Little Orphant Annie," "When the Frost Is on the Punkin," "The Raggedy Man," and "The Bear Story" in grade school. I visited his Indianapolis home on Lockerbie Street on school field trips. After grade school, he never surfaced again. He was never mentioned in any literature classes I took in high school or college. As a Hoosier, I was aware of Riley as a beloved native of the state. I thought of him, however, as an almost one-dimensional figure—a backwoods poet who wrote from his homes in Indianapolis and Greenfield.

I was barely aware that the only children's hospital in the state was named after him, and I certainly had no idea of the reason why. Furthermore, I had no idea that the James Whitcomb Riley Memorial Association (RMA), dedicated to honoring the poet by helping sick and disabled children, even existed. Then, Omer H. Foust, who had previously served as this organization's Executive Director, approached me about coming to work with him on a history project to celebrate the Riley Memorial Association's 75th anniversary. My entire perspective on the Hoosier poet was soon to change.

I must admit that, as a social historian, I initially was most interested in the history and evolution of the James Whitcomb Riley Hospital and its long-standing association with the Indiana University School of Medicine. However, early in my employment, Robert Baxter, who was then President of the association, asked me to create an exhibit about Riley for the hospital so that patients, parents, and hospital staff might become more conscious of the man after whom the institution was named.

To do this, I received special permission to look at photographs in a collection of materials that had been acquired by the Indiana Historical Society (IHS) a short time before. In this collection, which at that point was being processed so that it might be easily used by library patrons, there were many photographs of a young man with a large mustache. The IHS staff member who was doing the preprocessing evaluation of the material had marked many of the photographs with the query, "Who is this?" Staring down at each one, I realized that this young man was none other than the poet himself. Suddenly, I knew that there was much more to Riley than I had ever imagined. Thus my odyssey began.

Because of my increasing interest in the poet and because I needed more information for the hospital display and related education material which was distributed by RMA to Indiana elementary schools, I began my investigation of Riley's life. As work on the history of RMA reached its conclusion, John Gallman, Director of Indiana University Press, approached me to write this biography to be released during the poet's sesquicentennial year. After the contract was signed, my serious research on the life and work of Riley intensified.

Fortunately, James Whitcomb Riley was a compulsive saver. He thought that throwing away letters would bring him bad luck. As fame came, early in his career, his friends and family followed suit. Therefore, in many instances, I was able to read both sides of his correspondence, allowing for unusual insight into the man and his relationships. These letters were a source of much of the primary research for this biography.

Because he corresponded with some of the nation's top literati, Riley's letters are scattered in the special collections of libraries across the nation. They are in the Henry E. Huntington Library in San Marino, California, the New York Public Library, and the Alderman Library at the University of Virginia, just to name a few.

In my research, I also used collections at the Indiana State Library and the Indiana Historical Society as well as from the Indiana State Archives. However, it is largely thanks to Marcus Dickey, one of Riley's personal managers and secretaries and his first biographer, who accumulated a wealth of material, and Indianapolis philanthropist J. K. Lilly, who acquired this material from Dickey, that the Lilly Library at Indiana University, Bloomington, has the largest collection of manuscripts and published information about the poet. It was there that I spent most of my time looking into the life and character of this complicated and fascinating man.

The research revealed a man much different from my earlier perceptions of him, and, certainly, from almost everyone else's as well. In this volume, I have tried to describe the real man and to dispel the many myths about him. I hope that I have provided a means for a new appreciation of Riley and of his significance to the American culture of the late nineteenth and early twentieth centuries.

This book would not have been possible if not for the financial support of the James Whitcomb Riley Memorial Association and Lilly Endowment, Inc. I am grateful for the encouragement and support of Omer H. Foust, past Executive Director of the Riley Memorial Association; Robert R. Baxter, Past President and current member of the association's Board of Governors; and Morris Green, MD, also a current member of this institution's Board of Governors. I also must thank D. Susan Wisely, Program Evaluation Director of the Endowment.

Special thanks also go to John Gallman, of the Indiana University Press, for helping to institute the project and for his patience, and to my editor, Roberta Diehl.

I also express my appreciation to all the repositories that facilitated my research. These include, of course, the Lilly Library, Indiana University, Bloomington. I owe a debt of special gratitude to Lisa Browar, Lilly Librarian, and to the following personnel of the Lilly Library Public Services Department: Becky Cape, Cinda May, Elizabeth Powers, Sue Presnell, and especially Helena Walsh.

I must also thank Bruce Johnson, Director, and Susan Sutton, Visual Collections Coordinator, of the William Henry Smith Library of the Indiana Historical Society.

My gratitude also goes to David J. Bodenhamer, Douglas E. Clanin, and Robert M. Taylor, Jr., for reading portions or all of my manuscript and for their overall support.

Finally, my thanks go to Mom and Dad, Mary and Arthur Van Allen, for manuscript reading and for pitching in wherever necessary, and to John Bates for his patience and support.

James Whitcomb Riley

Prologue

A Poet for His Time

On 23 July 1916, the news of the sudden death of James Whitcomb Riley, one of the most beloved literary figures in America, shocked the nation. In Indianapolis, where this popular poet had lived over one-half of his life, his death made newspaper headlines. Although members of the local press had been informed that Riley had suffered a "violent stroke" in his home the previous morning and that "members of his household" had been "greatly alarmed" by the state of his health, by that same evening, they had been told that his personal physician believed that he was in no immediate danger. Riley had even been able to receive friends and relatives "with whom he chatted and joked." However, just hours later "the great Hoosier poet" was dead at the age of sixty-six.[1]

Few literary figures ever reached such heights of fame during their lifetimes as did James Whitcomb Riley. When schools throughout the state of Indiana first celebrated his birthday on 7 October 1911, he was only sixty-two. By his sixty-fifth birthday, in 1915, the celebration had become a national affair. Children throughout the nation paid homage to Riley, and the citizens of Indianapolis organized a day full of events, including a dinner attended by national as well as local dignitaries.[2] Less than one year later, news of Riley's death brought an outpouring of grief rarely seen.

The underlying messages about traditional values and virtues in Riley's poems spoke to a public yearning to recapture what it perceived to have been a simpler, more moral past. Riley is best known for the poetry he wrote in what in common parlance came to be called "Hoosier dialect"—poems such as "The Raggedy Man," "Little Orphant Annie," "The Old Swimmin'-Hole," and "When the Frost Is on the Punkin." With these poems and others about nature and the memories of childhood, Riley captured the mood of the country at the end of the nineteenth century.

Riley was admired and respected by some of America's top literary figures, such as Samuel L. Clemens and William Dean Howells. He received honorary degrees from Yale, the University of Pennsylvania, Indiana University, and Wabash College. He was elected to the National Institute of Arts and Letters in 1908, and the National Academy of Arts and Letters awarded him its medal for distinction in poetry in 1912. Riley attended many events at the White House, meeting and reciting poetry for every president from Grover Cleveland to Woodrow Wilson. He was a friend of President Benjamin Harrison and Vice Presidents Thomas R. Marshall and Charles W. Fairbanks. Yet Riley was beloved, first and foremost, as a friend of the people.

On the day following his death, telegrams and letters of condolence, expressing deep regret and sorrow, poured in to Riley's home on Lockerbie Street. Among these letters was one from Samuel M. Ralston, then governor of Indiana. Because "Riley was loved by the people of the State of Indiana as was no other man," Ralston requested that the poet's relatives allow Riley's body to lie in state in the rotunda of the state Capitol. "In an exceptionally tender sense," Ralston observed, "the people of his native state felt and believed that he belonged to them, and they mourn—bitterly mourn—his passing."[3]

The honor of lying in state in the rotunda had been given to few men. Before Riley only two others, Abraham Lincoln and General Henry W. Lawton (a Hoosier who led U.S. forces in the Philippines during the Spanish American War), had ever had such tribute paid to them. Not even President Benjamin Harrison, also from Indiana, was honored after his death in this way. It was truly remarkable that Riley, neither a soldier nor a statesman, received such recognition.

On 24 July 1916, in the middle of the afternoon, a funeral cortege composed of forty members of the local police drill squad and sixteen mounted policemen escorted Riley's body slowly through the streets of downtown Indianapolis toward the Capitol. Also joining the procession were Governor Ralston and Joseph E. Bell, the city's mayor. As the cortege approached the south entrance to the State House, the huge throng of people who patiently waited in the hot July afternoon sun to view the body parted to allow it to pass. Thirteen policemen, acting as pallbearers, removed Riley's massive bronze coffin, which weighed about twelve hundred pounds, from a hearse and staggered under its weight as they carried it up the stairs to the rotunda.[4]

At 3:00 P.M. the doors of the Capitol were opened. Within the first hour, over four thousand people passed by the poet's casket, and they continued at that rate throughout the afternoon and evening. Policemen outside lined the streets to keep the crowd moving. The newspapers reported that "people from every walk of life" came to see Riley one last time. Early in the afternoon, the crowd was dominated by mothers and their children. After 5:00 P.M., professionals and office workers came. Men and women from the factories followed. Shortly after 7:00 P.M., a large group that had chartered two interurban railway cars arrived from Riley's hometown of Greenfield to bid farewell to the poet.

Many in the crowd were tearful, but their voices were hushed. Only the sound of footsteps could be heard in the Capitol rotunda. Some of the children were barely tall enough to peer into the coffin. Policemen in attendance lifted many of them up so that they could see the man they loved so much for writing such poems as "Little Orphant Annie."

At 9:00 P.M., when the viewing was scheduled to end, the line outside was still several blocks long. Because the crowd had not diminished, the doors of the Capitol were kept open for an extra hour. Finally, at 10:00, Riley's casket was removed from the rotunda and was returned to his home on Lockerbie Street, where a private funeral was scheduled to take place the next day. Within seven hours, thirty-five thousand people had personally paid their last respects to "the Hoosier poet."[5] Only two days later, some of Indiana's foremost citizens announced that they were making plans for a permanent memorial. These plans culminated in the establishment of the James Whitcomb Riley Memorial Association, Riley Hospital for Children, and, eventually, Camp Riley for Youth with Physical Disabilities, all of which still operate in the poet's name. Riley's body was eventually interred at the point of highest elevation in Marion County in Crown Hill Cemetery.[6]

Riley reached the height of his popularity as the United States made its transition from being rural and agricultural to being urban and industrial. When Riley was born in Greenfield, Indiana, in 1849, the United States was primarily a rural society that possessed a few important cities. By 1900, it had become an urban, industrial nation. Many areas of the country previously classified as frontier territory were quickly being settled. In 1893 at a meeting of the American Historical Association in Chicago, the historian Frederick Jackson Turner gave his famous address on the closing of the American frontier, which "would become the most vital interpretation of the United States for at least the next fifty years." Turner stated that, although the story of the frontier had reached an end, the result of this experience remained a dominant factor in defining the American character.[7]

The closing of the frontier was just as symbolic as it was real. The "psychological element was fully as important as the geographical, for the frontier had always been a state of mind as much as a state of anything else." Psychologically, the "symbolism of the vanishing frontier" proved more traumatic than its reality. Almost everyone agreed that its passing portended a great change in the American way of life; and many people believed that this change would not be for the better. Those who predicted decline thought that America's best days were already behind it. As a consequence, much of the nation's population was seized with a spirit of nostalgia. Many men and women looked back to the past with longing, wanting to recapture the days when the country was young and the land beyond the Alleghenies was wild. They clung to the idea of a mythic, peaceful New World garden in the West, inhabited by hardy, resourceful, and independent pioneers.[8]

Riley too lamented the loss of the country's frontier traits and idealized the Indiana he knew in his boyhood. Much of his verse describes sturdy pioneer ancestors who, in the face of many hardships, brought civilization to the frontier. Riley won affection and praise from a vast audience because he elevated the common sense and wisdom of this pioneer type over the sophistication of the big-city Easterner. He seemed to express the ideas of these common, ordinary men and women in their own words, keeping alive impressions of how life had been in an America that was vanishing.[9]

According to Howells, Riley knew "how to endear himself to a wider range of American humanity than any other American poet."[10] Riley's poems interested "the lettered as well as the unlettered" and were read more than even those written by Henry Wadsworth Longfellow and John Greenleaf Whittier. Howells saw this as no small accomplishment in an era when poetry was generally not being read as much as it had been. For just this reason, Riley had earned some admiration from this nineteenth-century literary lion, but he also had earned his respect. Howells valued Riley as "a very great artist" who possessed "subtle insight" into human character. Moreover, Howells saw in Riley's poetry the expression of what was truly American: "his primacy is significant of a more entire liberation to our native genius than we have yet realized; at the least and the lowest, here is a poet who could have come in no other time or place than ours; and quite so much could not have been said of any American poet before."[11]

Riley's poetry met Howells's standards for realism in literature. Riley delighted in truthfully depicting lower-class characters, and he permitted them to speak "the dialect, the language . . . of unaffected people."[12] While Howells and Riley felt that literature should not lie about life, they also believed that literature should be morally uplifting. Both Riley and Howells wanted to make the human race better and kinder through their literary efforts and believed that American society was governed ultimately by a moral universe. "In all genuine poetry," Riley said, "there is a poignant quality that strikes to the center of the human heart, and quivers there and thrills us through and through with gentler emotions, higher purposes and yearnings to be better than we are."[13]

When asked in a 1901 interview what he thought about realistic novels written by such authors as fellow Hoosier Theodore Dreiser, Riley responded: "There is no call for this problem writing. Why don't these people look around them and see the beautiful things given for their admiration. All this feverish nasty stuff has no right to exist." Riley thought that the "path of mankind . . . [was] rough enough and stern enough without artificial aid to make it worse." He wanted his poems to "lead the human [being] in pleasant places, cheer him by holding up to him only the bright the beautiful and the good."[14]

Thus, the realism in Riley's work was often flawed by his inability to abandon middle-class standards of social respectability and propriety. Riley thought that every subject would reveal "a gem of glory," if approached in "the right spirit," no matter how rough and crude it appeared on the surface.[15] Riley even found innate goodness and wholesomeness in such social marginals as the rag man or tramp, ignoring the character's inherent potential for committing crime, not to mention issues of social injustice. Indeed, Riley's poetry drew attention away from social rifts in society, away from such agents of cultural and social change as urbanization and industrialization. It sought "the universal in the individual rather than the social interests."[16]

Despite this, Riley was a close friend of the American Socialist and labor radical Eugene V. Debs. Debs had been a friend of Riley's since both men had been in their twenties, and he held Riley in high regard although the Greenfield poet "did not attempt, as did Shelley and Burns, to incite . . . [the poor] to revolt against their exploiters and despoilers." Debs knew that it never occurred to his friend "that poverty, in the . . . [industrial] age of marvelous machinery and rapid production, was an unnecessary evil." Although Debs believed that such tolerance of labor exploitation "was scarcely less than a social crime," he forgave Riley this lapse because the poet "had the profoundest respect for and sympathy with honest toil and in many poems he paid sincere tribute to the working class."[17] A popular writer, Clara E. Laughlin, another of Riley's admirers, thought that Riley's poetry created greater sympathy for "the . . . hungry man or homeless cur or crippled child."[18]

Today, most serious readers of poetry are not so forgiving of Riley's unwillingness to confront serious social issues. Many classify him as a minor literary figure who wrote overly sentimental Victorian doggerel. Nevertheless, in Riley's own time, Howells was not the only important literary figure who highly regarded his work. In Henry Augustin Beers's essay "The Singer of the Old

Swimmin' Hole," this eminent literary critic and Yale University English professor compared Riley with Walt Whitman.[19] Modern English professors and literary critics find such a comparison unthinkable and an insult to the reputation of Whitman; but Beers, along with his colleague William Lyon Phelps, considered Riley a great poet, and they were primarily responsible for Yale's decision to confer an honorary degree upon him in 1902.

Although Beers stated that Whitman "had an extraordinary feeling of the bigness of America with its swarming multitudes," he underestimated Whitman's greatness as a poet by calling him "the idol of a literary *culte*" and proclaimed Riley the true poet of the American people. Beers admitted that in some ways Riley's poems are provincial. He believed them to be "intensely true to local conditions, local scenery and dialect, childish memories and the odd ways and characters of little country towns." Yet, at the same time, Beers felt that Riley was more than just "the Hoosier poet"—he was "a national poet." Beers thought that the conditions in which people lived "far away from the Wabash" were not so different from those that Riley described and that his poems embodied the essence of the American character in a way in which Whitman's did not: "America . . . is a land of homes: of dwellers in villages, on farms, and in small towns. We are a common people, middle-class people, conservative, decent, religious, tenacious of old ways, home-keeping and home loving. We do not thrill to Walt Whitman's paeans to democracy in the abstract; but we vibrate to every touch on the chord of family affections, of early friendships, and of dear old homely things that our childhood knew. Americans are sentimental and humorous; and Riley abounds in sentiment—wholesome sentiment—and natural humor, while Whitman had little of either."[20]

Beers criticized Whitman for his failure "to discriminate among individuals and characterize them singly." He complained that Whitman described America's "millions of plain people . . . in the mass." Beers stated that the people in Whitman's poems "are all alike, all 'leaves of grass.'"[21] In this essay, Beers did not recognize that Whitman knew that America was a diverse land full of differences and contrasts: "ONE'S-SELF I sing, a simple separate person, / Yet utter the word Democratic, the word En-Masse."[22] Whitman acknowledged the tensions in American society between the multitudes of opportunities it offered people to express themselves, to realize their potentials and the hidden pressures for conformity. Because the country's founding forefathers rejected Old World social conventions that helped to guarantee social order, Americans have often attempted, unconsciously and not so unconsciously, to minimize diversity to compose a more coherent and unified identity. In *Leaves of Grass,* Whitman asked how personal separateness could be retained in the quest for shared experience in a nation of equals.[23]

No such paradoxes of the American experience troubled Riley. Although Riley's characters were often from the lower classes, they assumed the attitudes and mores of the predominant Protestant middle class. Because Riley's poems portrayed a nation that Beers and many others wanted to believe still existed, they simply accepted that the experiences and emotions Riley described were essentially universal: "To all Americans who were ever boys; to all, at least who have had the good luck to be country boys and go barefoot; whether they dwell in the prairie states of the Middle West, or elsewhere, scenes and characters of Riley's poems are familiar."[24]

Many people, such as Beers, believed that life in the Midwest, and especially life in Indiana, was more typically American than it was elsewhere in the United States. Indiana was thought to approximate "an average of America."[25] In 1900, Indiana was at the imaginary center of the United States population. It had "fewer of the very rich, . . . fewer of the very poor, . . . fewer of the foreign born, . . . [and] a larger proportion of the home born than most . . . other States."[26] Because much of Indiana's population was native, Beers and many of his contemporaries believed that the state's inhabitants had developed a particularly American culture.[27]

In the American imagination, the Midwest still represents the most typical region of the United States. In the literary world, it is "a middling region in a country whose literary genius has been given to the portrayal of middling life."[28] Between 1871 and 1920, Hoosiers produced a large amount of the literature coming from the Midwest. Riley was mentor or colleague to a number of them. Not only did Riley produce the most popular poetry of his age, but his friends, including Booth Tarkington, Lew Wallace, and Meredith Nicholson, also wrote some of the top-selling novels of the era.[29]

However, Theodore Dreiser, Edgar Lee Masters, Sherwood Anderson, Willa Cather, and Sinclair Lewis are the authors who are still considered to be important, not the "Hoosier romancers" from the so-called Golden Age of Indiana Literature. While the latter group appealed to a public who wanted to escape from the social problems and theories of the day by turning to romance, the former depicted grim social realities. Their work endures because they showed the limitations, the desperation, and the futility of life on the farm and in the small town rather than displaying a wistful, folksy, and homespun charm. They revealed "a state of mind of people born where they do not want to live."[30]

Riley and his friends, on the other hand, felt deep affection for and were deeply loyal to the people of the Midwest and their home state. Although Riley briefly contemplated moving to New York when he was a young man, he soon thought better of it.[31] In 1891, the Kentucky poet Madison Julius Cawein wrote to Riley that he was considering a move to the East Coast to pursue his literary career. Riley, the older of the two men, strongly advised him against it: "Is it so, you're contemplating going East to work? O *don't* do that, I beg. You're right in the country you belong in—so, at least, stay loyal to it, and let 'em *send* their work to you.—You'll be the better for it everyway." He told Cawein that no money could ever tempt him to quit his home and that he was sorry "that . . . even in youthful thought" he was ever disloyal to his own.[32]

Remaining faithful to his "home folk," therefore, was important to Riley. He felt no need to hunt for themes from the past or "in foreign lands" for his work. He believed that modern poetry should celebrate the deeds that happen every day. Local customs, traits, scenery, and romantic episodes "daily chronicled in the papers" inspired his poems. His subjects were "at his feet" and about him at home: "I see them in the green fields as I ride along the road. I meet them on the train and in my daily intercourse with my fellow-men. I often gather inspiration from some pathetic episode from . . . real life." Riley stayed in Indiana because he believed that he best found his muse surrounded by his native countryside, where he could record as accurately as possible the ordinary experiences and language of everyday life.[33]

Above all, Riley tried "to avoid exaggeration and to follow nature as closely as possible." He agreed with his friend the Hoosier painter T. C. Steele that the nearer "one draws to the heart of nature, and the more fully and truthfully he is enabled to embody his impressions, the more powerful does his work become."[34] For Riley, the voice of poetry was "nature's voice refined into echo form." He did not find that voice among people living in America's great cities but in her "interior . . . among the plain people," who were "earnest, honest, self-reliant. . . , [and] simple in their tastes and without any over-weaning vanities, conceits or ambitions to make their lives miserable."[35]

According to Riley, the innocence of the civilized and educated urban dweller was destroyed by the sophistication and artifice of the city: "We who are educated and civilized are in fact farther away from nature—which should be the fundamental basis of our lives—than are the ones who toil away in the humbler walks of life."[36] These humble folk allowed nature's moral and divine order to rule their existence. They "seem[ed] to feel and recognize fully that their destiny . . . [was] perforce to be wholesome and happy, with patient prosperity to compensate for their everyday lives and duties."[37] Riley refused to acknowledge the dreariness or the quiet desperation of life in the small town and on the farm in middle America. He only saw the wholesome and solid, Protestant, middle-class values that he believed made the nation great. He so accepted those values that he presented them as a natural part of the moral and social order.

With the encroachment of industrialization and urbanization, Riley believed it his duty to record for the ages how these modest, plain people spoke. He thought that he was recording a vanishing culture and way of speech. Riley did not feel he should have to apologize for writing in dialect. He complained that it was "a great mistake to think that dialect consists in bad spelling, bad grammar, carelessness in speech, and above all vulgarity." For Riley, this was not dialect. Instead, he said, "Dialect and the purest English come from a faultless heart." He claimed that dialect, properly used, involved "an effort to represent people just as they are." In the hands of an author who used it well, he believed that it enriched literature.[38] When Riley wrote in dialect, he always demanded "absolute clearness and fidelity of utterance": "Especially in the dialect of my native region and people this has been, and is, my conscientious effort always to write words exactly as they were pronounced."[39]

Riley not only wrote about the people of Indiana, he wrote for them. However, Riley preferred to associate himself with the whole of the literature of the American West. Unlike some people he knew who started to believe that "the hub of the literary universe . . . [was] no longer Boston, but Indianapolis," Riley did not regard his home city "as a modern Athens or Indiana as anything uncommon" because of the number of popular books that were being written there.[40] Indeed, he saw nothing unique about Hoosier literature: "The whole West produces, and what is produced has the tang and flavor of the community from which it comes."[41] He placed himself in the company of a large number of authors from all over the western United States who were turning out fresh and exciting work that was true to the regions about which it was written.

While contemporary literary critics such as Howells and Beers said that Riley should be categorized with these authors who were thought to be masters of "realistic art," other critics disagreed as to the quality of his verse and were undecided as to what place to give him among poets. Some believed that Riley could not be considered a great poet because his subjects were not serious enough, and yet others refused to classify him as a poet at all. Instead, they defined him merely as either a "jingler," "trick rhymster," or worse.[42]

For example, the poet, journalist, and critic Ambrose Bierce called Riley's poetry "dreary illiterature." Although Bierce stated that poetry could legitimately deal "with the lives and sentiments, the deeds and emotions, of common people . . .[,] in the dirt of . . . [Riley's] 'dialect' . . . [Bierce found] no grain of gold." He thought that Riley's "pathos . . . [was] bathos, his sentiment sediment, his 'homely philosophy' brute platitudes." In fact, Riley knew "nothing of poetry" and had neither "written a line of it, nor of anything resembling it."[43]

According to Bierce, Riley's "raucous" lines of verse showed that he lacked a true understanding of the poetic. He could not praise Riley's poems in dialect as "a direct expression of the life of American people," as did Bliss Perry, who served as editor of the *Atlantic Monthly* between 1899 and 1909. In Bierce's opinion, Riley's poems were a disgraceful butchering of the English language, if the dialect Riley used could be classified as English at all, and his work was devoid of the style, technique, and language necessary to make his writings true poetry.[44]

As Ronald Weber states in *The Midwestern Ascendancy in American Writing,* early realists have been criticized often for forsaking all considerations of "style, form, and technique in general" to create a faithful and accurate depiction of the subjects they undertook. With the advent of realism, writers who had little formal education could legitimately use their own personal experiences as subjects without concern about having much knowledge of literary conventions. Riley can easily be placed in context with a group of early realists, such as Joseph Kirkland, E. W. Howe, and Hamlin Garland, who did not possess much literary background but who were able to write about the farms and little towns they knew because the new doctrine of realism gave them license to do so.[45]

In fact, Riley dismissed the need to study past literary masterpieces. After reading some acclaimed and notable pieces of literature, he concluded that all good writing simply involved the truthful rendering of time and place: "When I commenced first I knew I hadn't much of a fund of scholarship, and so wondered what I could put in its stead. I looked up the early works, which are so great, and found they merely treated of the environment of their several times. They have become classic by the lapse of time. So I didn't trouble myself about scholarship any more, but I set to work to dig in that which was about me."[46]

Over time, Riley also troubled himself less and less with what critics said. Rather than pleasing himself or a small coterie of people of elite literary standing, Riley placed increasing importance on winning and holding the high esteem and favor of a general audience. He said that he wrote dialect verse not from choice "but because . . . [he] found that the public wanted it." Although critics continually told him "to write serious verse," and although personally he would have preferred "a reputation with a little more dignity attached to it," he found that "the more serious and earnest" he became, the less his writings were liked. The public, however, were willing to pay for his dialect poems, and Riley was "very grateful and more than willing to oblige them." Having no independent sources of income, he could not afford to ignore the inclinations of the popular market. In an 1888 interview, Riley explained: "You see I have to use a little money occasionally, as I go along; I need it, even in my business."[47]

Reflecting the commercialization of the publishing industry, Riley characterized the professional writer as a "literary worker," much in the same way that Howells pictured "The Man of Letters as a Man of Business."[48] Riley acknowledged that although he did not "like the hard business world" it had been necessary for him "to learn its lessons." He admonished authors to consider a broader market of readers as they wrote and told those who carefully crafted their work only to please themselves and their literary friends to abandon their "Boston habit." Instead of being ruled by what the Eastern critics of literature living in Boston or New York said, Riley strongly believed that authors should let "the public be the judge" of the value of what they produced.[49]

Therefore, Riley thought that the discerning author should write books "to please the masses." To do that, according to Riley, the writer had to get down among the people. He could not stand aloof or think that he was superior: "The writer must not be too good for human nature and human provender. He must live with the people mentally and eat what they eat. He'll find that as a rule the people live in a good healthy wholesome fashion both intellectually and physically, and that what's good enough for them is good enough for anybody."[50] For Riley, writing to please the popular market did not exclude the resulting product from being classified as serious literature. He believed that books written with the tastes of common people in mind were the ones that, in the end, would receive acclaim.[51]

Although there was "an increasing stratification of readership evolving in the United States by social class, by level and interest," making it impossible for writers to establish "any single literary mode" as the general fashion, Riley held to the ideal that ultimately a consensus of ideas and opinions—a homogeneity of American tastes—would emerge.[52] Like other members of his generation, he did not foresee that the socioeconomic world would continue to fragment, creating more distinctions between a "high" and a "mass" culture, "whereby a single, approved group of texts could pass for High Culture, while the kinds of works enjoyed by the majority of the people were dismissed as worthless."[53]

Because of his broad appeal, Riley saw his own work as evidence of a reversal of this trend. He maintained that his poetry's widespread popularity, even among the nation's intelligentsia, revealed that a cultural middle ground still existed and had faith that it would only grow stronger as democracy in America continued to develop. He believed that the possibilities offered by democracy encourage and inspire the nation's "common intelligence—the minds of all . . . people, in whatever humble walk of life" to strive for excellence. The fact that America had produced such men as Abraham Lincoln, Thomas Edison, and John Greenleaf Whittier demonstrated to Riley that it was possible for some of "the greatest . . . masters in literature and science" to emerge even from ordinary environments. He thought that even the most common people of the country had a general tendency toward the "natural graces of education, refinement, art, and literature."[54]

Moreover, because Riley believed that all American people had the tendency to acquire naturally "the unconscious exercise of taste," the public could legitimately establish the worth of any literary work as art simply by purchasing it.[55] All literary forms, even poetry, could simultaneously be considered as art and commodity. Scholars have focused on novels and novelists, not poetry and poets, in exploring the commercial development of the publishing industry in the United States following the Civil War. They have concluded that poetry was "a place kept pure, the locus of 'art for art's sake,' uncontaminated by the profit motive or by the vulgar requirements of the popular market."[56] Riley presents a noteworthy exception.

However, Riley did not conceive his conscious desire to appeal to a wide audience as a vulgarization of his work as an artist. He did not subscribe to the idea that poetry was a literary genre that was intelligible only to an elite, high culture. He believed that a great poet "does not require educated classes to understand him." If an artist's "words have poetic strength, if they are fervid, sublime, if they stir the heart, excite the emotions, burn with scorn[,] thrill with hope and promise," then Riley claimed, he or she can be "sure of an audience."[57] Riley trusted the opinion of the general public respecting literature without reservation: "What they do not take to, and you think so fine, will prove to be false, factitious, unhuman documents."[58]

Because he had such faith in their native intelligence, because he was so able to touch their hearts and to ennoble their lives through his poetry, Riley can be called a "poet of the common people." Riley knew that his late nineteenth century audience wanted "smiles and wholesome cheer and heartening words" rather than "sobs and tears and agony." His poetry always showed people in the best light. Always very sympathetic, it depicted ordinary men, women, and children in a way in which they would have liked to depict themselves.[59]

With the onslaught of increasing industrialization and urbanization, Riley's poetry hearkened back to times that his readers perceived to have been simpler and more virtuous. His work's underlying messages about traditional values also offered reassurance to the dominant middle classes by reinforcing the idea that their way of life was right and true at a time when the very foundations of society itself seemed threatened by tumultuous social and economic change. In the face of widespread urban violence and social unrest at the end of the nineteenth century, many believed that the United States was on "the ragged edge of anarchy." At this time, Riley's voice served as a voice of social reconciliation. Riley showed the American public that men and women from different stations in life were really not so very different from each other. He demonstrated "the truth of elemental emotion," the truth of "common and universal life." "He believed in man's faith in man" and had a way of making all humankind feel "akin."[60]

Riley so captured the spirit of his age that shortly after his death one newspaper reporter was moved to write: "He was nearer to us than any other [poet]; more than any other he cheered us; more than any other he expressed the conscience of the true American, of the true man anywhere beneath the skies."[61] For the men and women of his era, Riley, not Whitman, was "the poet of democracy." Riley interpreted "the life, not of the select few for the select few, but the life of the multitude, of the lowly, of the uncouth and of the children. And these classes, and many more—including even the academic gentlemen— recognize Mr. Riley as their poet, . . . [while] most of them turned away from Whitman with an utter lack of comprehension."[62]

In the 1855 preface to *Leaves of Grass,* Whitman had written, "The proof of the poet is that his country absorbs him as affectionately as he has absorbed it." Indeed, at the turn of the century, Riley seemed to have passed this test while Whitman appeared to have failed it. As Beers pointed out, "there is no record elsewhere in our literary history of a tribute so loving and so universal to a mere man of letters, as the Hoosier State" paid annually to Riley on his birthday. As previously stated, this celebration of Riley started in 1911; in 1915, U.S. Secretary of the Interior Franklin K. Lane asked for a national observance of Riley Day, calling attention to the fact that Riley and Howells were "the last of a generation of great literary men who were distinctly American."[63]

Riley, more than any other literary figure, gave the state of Indiana pride of place. As the text at the beginning of the film celebrating Indiana's centennial of statehood proclaimed, Riley "revealed the Hoosiers to themselves and to the world."[64] His poetry sets Midwesterners, and especially Hoosiers, apart from Southerners and Easterners, defends their regional culture, and gives them their own identity. Moreover, in the state of his birth, the poet's legacy lives on in the institutions that bear his name—most notably Riley Hospital for Children, located in Indianapolis.

When Riley died in 1916, many believed that the appeal of his poems would be universal and lasting—"like fadeless roses," they would "bloom eternal."[65] Although their reputation has faded in many circles, they and their author nevertheless still offer a unique window on the past. His life and work reflect the longings and anxieties of his age. His poems express a timeless yearning for an idyllic, rural, and preindustrial world, untroubled by the problems and complications of modern, everyday life problems and complications from which Riley himself could not escape. In an increasingly mobile and anonymous society, the poet discovered relatively early the potential for self-transformation. After he left home in his youth, he learned to manipulate appearances and to reinvent himself. The Hoosier poet emerges as a self-made man who carefully constructed the image he wanted people to have of him. For this reason, in contrast to the way he has usually been portrayed, Riley's true character is elusive. Ironically, his poems describe a static world where stability and certainty reign, while his life demonstrates how mutable reality in modern society can be.

A Child-World

Toward the end of his life, Riley expressed his fears about the disappearance of rural America in a letter to a friend, the poet Edith M. Thomas: "Is the real rural scene and people vanishing there, as here? Indeed I feel that all Country life is doomed, and that very soon it will be ground and powdered under the wheels of the Interurban." An increasingly urban and industrial audience, he feared, would not appreciate his poetry: "Then what's to become of the already waning fortunes of the poet, in his literary overalls, who for so long has been earning his board by the sweat of his dialect."[1] In her reply, Thomas reassured Riley that although life was *"being syndicated,"* he had no need to "discard the 'literary overalls' as yet; for the more the rustic, and his 'outfit,' recedes, the more curiosity will there be about him, and the more relish of his preserved quaintness of dress & speech."[2]

In retrospect, Riley's conclusions about the fate of his poetry seem more prophetic than Thomas's. However, his fears about the future did not deter him in his attempt to record for posterity the customs, manners, and speech of the people whom he knew in his boyhood. Riley lamented the disappearance of "the real rural scene and people."[3] When he was a child, Indiana was still predominantly an agricultural state. Life in some areas continued as it had in the pioneer era. However, starting in the 1850s, railroads vastly improved transportation and began the breakdown of rural isolation. Corporate-capitalist development further eroded local autonomy; and expanding marketing networks emerged, destroying older agrarian and artisanal relationships. Although farming remained an important part of the economy, the percentage of Indiana's population engaged in agricultural labor decreased markedly during the last decades of the nineteenth century. In 1880, 52.2 percent of the state's labor force held agricultural occupations. By the time Riley was writing his letter to Thomas, the number of workers involved in farming had dropped to 38.1 percent. With burgeoning industrial growth, a fairly militant organized labor movement emerged; and, although a majority of the new industrial laborers in Indiana were native-born Americans, immigrants from southern and eastern Europe began to arrive, especially in the Calumet region to the northwest.[4]

As the "rural scene" disappeared, Riley feared that all of the fundamental values that had made the nation great were being lost. In his poetry, he wanted to foster all the virtues of this vanishing way of life—"all the *child* elements of it in particular."[5] His writings captured the innocence and genuineness of a people who were seemingly unspoiled by the evils of civilization. For Riley, all "real poetry" was "simply *honesty* of heart, soul and expression." He believed that "all children are poets . . . all pure, lovely women and good men are, and can't help being."[6]

Riley often claimed that most of his verse was "written from actual occurrences and careful and consistent observation," and that some of his most enduring juvenile poems, such as "The Bear Story" and "The Runaway Boy," were merely the narratives of real children: "They are not mine . . . I did not make them . . . I listened to a little boy tell the bear story, and set it down. . . . I heard the child tell of its runaway, I reported it." He also stated that most of his verse about children was autobiographical—written "more from memory than anything else"—for he had "a very distinct and vivid recollection" of his childhood. Riley sometimes assumed his boyhood persona to appear as a character or narrator in many of his poems. He often referred to himself as "Bud," "Jamesy," or "Jim" in his works about childhood—all names he was called in his youth.[7]

The most autobiographical of Riley's works was *A Child-World*, first published in 1896.[8] All of the characters that Riley described in *A Child-World* were "veracious and veritable." When the volume came out, some of these characters were still living. Riley did not even bother to change their names. He stated that the names given in it were "the real names by which they were then familiarly known." According to Riley, *A Child-World* depicted real people and real events.[9] The anthology emphasized his humble origins and enhanced his public persona as a simple, modest soul.

A contemporary critic portrayed *A Child-World* as "a continuous poem describing scenes and characters in a Western Village."[10] This village was Riley's hometown of Greenfield, Indiana, twenty-five miles east of Indianapolis in Hancock County. By 1896, Riley had come to idealize this small, rural Indiana town as he knew it in his youth. In one poem, he described the inhabitants as "good, old-fashioned people— / The hale and hard-working people— / [who] . . . worked without no selfishness . . . / An' sheered with all jist ever'thing." As he remembered it, "there were no invidious [social] distinctions" in the village: "All were on a level—the rich and poor alike. Neighbors found a warm welcome in our family—we were blood brothers as Kipling says— Ringworm Frank, Little Orphant Annie, the barefoot boy[,] . . . the hired hand, old John Henry, the blind girl, and the convict back from a two years sentence— all were welcome. A man was a man whether he was white or green or black. Men did not go round then underlining their personality with red ink."[11]

Much of Riley's appeal, especially in poems such as *A Child-World,* was due to his ability to capture his own memories of childish innocence. In a letter written to the widow of a good friend, Edgar Wilson ("Bill") Nye, Riley stated that this book was "entirely" of his own childhood.[12] In this poem and in many others, Riley described a world in which he felt he had been truly happy; but, at the same time, he also depicted "the childhood of that vanished west which lay between the Ohio and the Mississippi" as other people wished to remember it. As one reviewer put it, Riley described the "earlier conditions of our national life, before our craze for wealth began, and the millionaire had not yet become the American ideal."[13]

Especially at the turn of the century, Riley inspired a nostalgic longing for the past. Within Riley's portrayals of his own golden childhood memories, there seemed to lurk memories "of the childhood of a people. . . , as well." Although Henry Beers suggested that Riley's childhood was typically American, there were many disparities among what children experienced according to social class, ethnicity, gender, and region. William Dean Howells, who grew up in southern Ohio, saw Riley's "picture of the peaceful kindly life in one village family . . . [as] the portrait of all village family life then and there." For Howells, Riley had managed to capture the essence of life in "the happiest land that ever there was under the sun."[14] Much that the poet described in *A Child-World* was indeed characteristic of the rural, middle-class, midwestern family. Although he drew most of this long narrative poem "from real things, with only the vaguest invention," at the same time, his depiction of this time and place was not absolutely and completely true.[15] Many of the details were accurate. However, Greenfield was never as idyllic, or as free from social tension, as he would have liked his readers to believe. As he was growing up, the people of his hometown experienced all of the economic and political upheavals of the age.

Riley agreed with Howells that the times of his boyhood in the Midwest were "wondrous." His parents, Reuben Riley and Elizabeth (Marine) Riley, were married at Union Port in Randolph County, Indiana, on 20 February 1844. Elizabeth often recounted stories to her children about the wedding and the celebration dinner that her brothers threw for the young couple. Before coming to Greenfield, in April 1844, Reuben and Elizabeth lived a short time with Reuben's mother. In December of that same year, Elizabeth gave birth to her first child, John Andrew, in a log cabin Reuben had built in Greenfield along the National Road. A second child, Martha Celestia, was born in February 1847. Two years later, James Whitcomb came into the world.

Like other early rural settlers in the Midwest, Reuben enlarged the cabin as soon as he could to provide his family a more substantial home that would introduce some privacy. When James Whitcomb was five, he and his family moved into the green-shuttered, white frame house his father built as an addition to the cabin. Here, Elizabeth gave birth to the three youngest of the Riley children—Elva May, in 1856, Reuben Alexander Humboldt, in 1859, and Mary Elizabeth, in 1864. This frame house and its environs composed the "*Child-World*" that Riley described in the volume of that same name.[16]

At the time Reuben and Elizabeth Riley came to Greenfield, the town had a population of only three hundred. Rich marshland and forest surrounded this small settlement; it had been designated Hancock County's seat of government when the county was officially organized by an act of the Indiana State Legislature at the end of 1827. The legislature dictated that the seat of justice should be located near the National Road, midway between the county's east and west borders. In June 1828, the original commissioners who were assigned to lay out the town gave it the name Greenfield. The original plat consisted of only sixty acres.[17]

At the eastern border of town was Brandywine Creek, which Riley made famous in "The Old Swimmin'-Hole." Beyond the woods to the west lay the Black Swamp, a boggy region overgrown with brush and thicket. The land was flat and the soil was fertile, but many parts of the territory continued to be relatively unbroken when the Rileys arrived. In 1844, Hancock County was still heavily timbered with stands of walnut, poplar, oak, and cherry trees.[18]

The first structures built in Greenfield were primitive log buildings, like the Riley cabin. As saw mills became more prevalent, small frame commercial structures and dwellings appeared. The town's most imposing building, the two-story brick courthouse, which was built in 1829–1830, stood on the public square, as was customary.

Many of the town's residents, including the Rileys, built their homes and businesses along the National Road. In Greenfield, the National Road was "the main street, and the main highway."[19] The Riley home provided the young James Whitcomb with a unique vista on this historic byway. As he grew older, Riley loved to look "squarely down" from the second-story windows and dream of scenes of people making their way westward:

> Of snowy caravans, in long parade
> Of covered vehicles, of every grade
> From oxcart of most primitive design,
> To Conestoga wagons, with their fine
> Deep-chested six-horse teams, in heavy gear . . .[20]

For Riley, the highway represented opportunity and adventure. As a young boy, he loved to listen to the stories of Greenfield's first inhabitants about the roadside forests, where wolves, panthers, and highwaymen prowled.[21] But even more importantly, the National Road held much romance for Riley and embodied the vision of the possibilities and the hopes that the United States offered as a nation:

> A Nation's thoroughfare of hopes and fears,
> First blazed by heroic pioneers
> Who gave up old-home idols and set face
> Toward the unbroken West, to found a race
> And tame a wilderness no mightier than
> All peoples and all tracts American.[22]

When Riley was a child, the "Sounds of the town . . . and the great highway" penetrated the family home. One could hear "The Mover-wagons' rumble, and the neigh / Of over-traveled horses, and the bleat / Of sheep and low of cattle through the street."[23] Riley described his home as a "simple old frame house . . . [with] eight rooms in all." The site of the house "was portioned into three / Distinctive lots." The front yard faced the highway. During the spring and summer, this part of the yard bloomed with lilacs, dahlias, and roses. Behind the house were a woodshed and a workshop. Inside the workshop, where Reuben Riley fashioned furniture, tools, and gun-stocks, one found "shelved quilting frames," a "tool chest," and an old box filled with "refuse nails and screws."[24]

When he was a boy, Reuben's tools fascinated Riley. Riley remembered that along the wall of the workshop hung a "compass," drafting "square," "drawing-knife," and "smoothing-plane." Hung up out of the boy's reach was a cane fishing pole and tackle; yet, Reuben permitted his son to use "a little jack-plane . . . [to turn] out countless curls and loops of bright, / Fine satin [wood] shavings," which pleased young Riley immensely.[25] Like other fathers in rural and suburban areas, Reuben encouraged his son to handle his tools so that he would learn many practical carpentering skills.

The Riley family raised livestock and grew fruit and vegetables for their own consumption. An apple tree grew beside the woodshed, which Riley considered his "*own tree,* in many ways." Not only did he eagerly gather its sweet fruit, but its girth and height made it a perfect tree for a boy to climb. More apple trees stood in a row at the rear of the yard. In addition, some currant bushes, a quince tree, a cherry tree, and a grape arbor could be found in their garden. Near the apple trees, Reuben kept a hive of bees for their honey and to help pollinate his little orchard. A small, charming stable housed the family's horses and chickens, and a pig lived in the sty behind it.[26]

Inside the house, one heard "the household din . . . / the dull jar and thump / Of churning; and the 'glung-glung' of the [water] pump." In the kitchen, kettles clanged and the cook stove door banged "In sweetest tinny, coppery, pewtery tone / Of music hungry ear has ever known." Riley remembered the "dear old-fashioned dinners" that came from there: "Redolent savorings of home-cured meats, / Potatoes, beans and cabbage; turnips, beets / And parsnips." He loved the spicy smell of cinnamon, cloves, and nutmeg that wafted through the air when puddings, cakes, and pies baked in the oven.[27]

In the parlor, Riley remembered that a clock chatted on "confidingly" and in summer "a rose / . . . [often tapped] at the window." In "Spring-time through the open door," could be heard the "bee's dim hum, and the far shout and laughter of the children at their play." Sunlight seemed to throw "A brilliant, jostling checkerwork of shine / And shadow, like a Persian-loom design, / Across the home-made carpet." When he was a boy, Riley would read picture-books "prone on the floor . . . with a rapt, ecstatic look" while his mother worked nearby.[28]

Riley shared this "*Child-World*" most closely with those siblings who survived beyond early childhood. In 1851, Reuben and Elizabeth Riley's oldest daughter, Martha Celestia, died of scarlet fever at the age of four. The experiences of Riley's remaining brothers and sisters reflected the same childish perspective on the local scenes that he described in this volume of poetry. By the time that Riley and his brothers and sisters were growing up, most middle-class Americans believed that children were precious, valuable resources and recognized childhood as an important and unique life stage. Like other parents of their class, Reuben and Elizabeth believed that children were naturally innocent and loving. For this reason, they sheltered their offspring from dangerous outside influences. The poet felt safe and protected; he and his siblings were "five happy Hoosier chaps / Inhabiting this wee little world of their own." In describing himself and his family in "*A Child-World,*" Riley used names that were "only known to the family" and referred to himself in the third person "to accommodate the very modest writer."[29]

First, Riley described his older brother John, whom he called "Johnty" in this volume. As the eldest child, Johnty naturally served as the "leader," but Riley also felt that he was "the best, perhaps," of the group. John was the practical businessman among the Riley brothers. Johnty always set a good example, protected Riley when he was a child, and counseled him about his literary work early in his career.[30]

Next, Riley described himself, Johnty's "little towhead brother—Bud, by name," a child who was "apt in make believes" who very early possessed an ear and memory for language: he "would "hear / His Grandma talk or read with such an ear / And memory of both subject and big words, / That he would take a book up afterwards / And feign to 'read aloud,' with such success / As caused his truthful elders real distress."[31]

Elva May, the older of the two sisters, was affectionately called "Maymie." In *A Child-World,* her brother pictured her when she was a beautiful child, "with her hazy cloud of hair, / And the blue skies of eyes beneath it there." Riley said that she had "dignified and 'little lady' airs" and that she was so unselfish "That [she] 'gave up,' for the rest, the ripest pear / Or peach or apple in the garden." To prepare them for their roles as mothers and household managers, girls like Maymie were taught to be feminine and to put the needs of others first. Maymie thought the world of her brother Bud. He understood when he saw her weep for joy at their mother's return after being absent for many hours, and he always chose the right book or story to read to her and his other younger siblings.[32]

Riley introduced his younger brother, Alexander Humboldt, as "Alex" in *A Child-World,* although he was more commonly referred to by the nickname "Hum." Like Riley, Alex had freckles when he was a child, but he was not a blond. Elizabeth Riley described his hair as "*amber-colored.*" Although he sometimes exhibited "freaks of temper," "Alex was affectionate beyond / The average child." Intimates of the Riley family believed that Alexander Humboldt possessed many of the same talents as his poet brother. He was an excellent musician and had a beautiful singing voice. Appearing many times in local, amateur theater productions, he also displayed much ability as an actor.[33]

Mary Elizabeth, otherwise known as "Lizzie," was the baby of the family. She had dark expressive eyes, hair the color of burnished gold, and "elfin lips." Although Lizzie had a "velvet lisp" when she first began to talk, Riley loved to teach her to say large and often nonexistent words. He also taught her stories that she recited. Like Riley, she possessed a vivid imagination and enjoyed reading. As the youngest, "Lizzie" was everyone's favorite, especially her father's and her brothers'. Lizzie had a strong emotional bond with her poet brother, who protected her through adulthood.[34]

A Child-World describes a home that was seldom without guests. At one time or another, all of Riley's uncles lived in the family homestead; and his "Cousin Rufus," Will Hough, resided there while he read the law under the tutelage of Reuben. Neighbors and their children often visited, and groups sometimes gathered at the home for an evening of entertainment, including the telling of stories and the reciting of poems. Everyone was welcome to participate: even the hired hands and the children joined in the revelry. Riley gave an account of one of these parties in *A Child-World.* According to Riley, this party had actually taken place, and some of the stories he presented in the poem had really been told by children who attended the function.[35]

"SUCH was the Child-World of the long ago," as Riley remembered it.[36] Rigid cultural hierarchies and boundaries did not yet exist, and entertainment did not always involve passive spectatorship. By the 1850s and 1860s, some paid performers—professional musicians, touring theatrical companies, lecturers, and circuses—regularly traveled through the state;[37] however, in places such as Greenfield, people primarily entertained themselves. The populace freely played their own games, told their own stories, and sang their own songs, and they were themselves featured in their own amateur theater productions.

In *A Child-World,* Riley demonstrated this participatory spirit by becoming many different speakers throughout the work. As he did before an audience, he exhibited great flexibility by assuming different roles in quick succession. In a sense, Riley was always an actor, and poetry was his greatest stage. For Riley, *A Child-World* was more than a reflection on his childhood; it represented a true expression of the quintessential ideals of American republicanism and democracy.

Riley certainly painted an idyllic picture in *A Child-World.* Yet, as even he admitted in this volume, dedicated entirely to memorializing life as it had been in the past, the "Good Old" days were only "'good old times' because they're dead and gone!" During much of the nineteenth century, life in Greenfield meant enduring much hardship and physical privation. The low-lying wetlands that bordered the town on the east and west were unhealthy. An early history of Hancock County stated that many people fell victim to "malaria and miasmatic diseases" and that there was "a great deal of ague and fever, bilious fever, and considerable milk sickness" in the county.[38] Death visited Greenfield's settlers frequently; and, of course, the Riley family, having lost Martha Celestia, was no stranger to it. Riley wrote over sixty poems on the subject of bereavement, reflecting his familiarity with grief. Many of these poems, such as "Bereaved," "Our Little Girl," "When Our Baby Died," and "The Little White Hearse" were about the loss of children.[39] Children from all socioeconomic groups were highly susceptible to infectious diseases. Like Reuben and Elizabeth Riley, most parents faced the death of one or more offspring before they reached maturity.[40] While "richer and poorer children sometimes played apart, often were schooled differently, and usually looked forward to different economic opportunities, . . . death took them democratically."[41]

Life in Greenfield was also relatively primitive. Not long before Riley's birth, the townspeople of Greenfield considered watches, clocks, and carriages luxury items which only the rich could afford to own. Those who possessed timepieces were compelled to pay a 25-percent tax on them, "more than the tax on one hundred acres of the best land." Streets in the town were typically unpaved and ungraded. If they existed at all, sidewalks were constructed of wood planks.[42]

Just as in other towns and cities, most of the buildings were "cheap, rude structures" made of wood. This made Greenfield extremely susceptible to fire. Throughout the nineteenth century, fires repeatedly took lives and destroyed much property. In 1839, a fire destroyed all the businesses located on the north side of the National Road; and, in 1857, another bad fire raged through the town. Many other smaller blazes ruined private homes, mills, stables, and warehouses. Toward the end of the century, the author of the Hancock County history complained that Greenfield was still ill-prepared to combat fire. This author feared that any conflagration could quickly get out of control because the town lacked effective fire protection.[43]

Before railroads arrived in 1853, the people of Greenfield had to be largely self-sufficient. The Dayton and Indianapolis stagecoach was the only form of transportation that passed daily along the National Road. When the railroad was completed through town, it helped to ease the distribution of many commodities. During the 1850s, Indiana saw the greatest increase in railroad mileage in its history. As with other early lines in the state, the Indiana Central Railroad, which ran through Greenfield, radiated from Indianapolis. It connected the state capital to Richmond.[44] In a letter Reuben Riley wrote to his brother in 1856, he stated that six to eight train cars of the Indiana Central came through Greenfield each day. However, the train did not provide a solution to all of the early settlers' difficulties with the shipment of resources. Although Reuben told his brother that "grain . . . of all kinds" was abundant, "money [remained] close and scarce."[45]

Riley remembered the era of his childhood as a time that was relatively untroubled by inequalities in wealth; however, in reality, during the first half of the nineteenth century, class differences increased at an alarming rate in America. The dislocation of the populace that was created by the growth of the market economy widened the gap between the rich and the poor more rapidly between 1825 and 1860 than during the periods before or after. The cost of living increased astronomically throughout this time, peaking in the midst of an economic depression in 1855. This financial crisis, which followed the economic boom created by the 1848 gold rush, only deepened the misery of thousands.

The world of Riley's childhood, therefore, was marked by social and economic uncertainty. However, the Rileys lived in relative comfort during the

1850s. Reuben finished the house on the National Road, which he described to his brother as "a large two-story dwelling house," and managed to purchase, in partnership with another gentleman, a "fine farm," which was located one-half mile west of town and consisted of 194 acres.[46] Although Riley emphasized the modesty of his upbringing in *A Child-World,* his father actually belonged to a rather select group of middle-class landholders. Fewer than half of the free white males living in the United States at mid-century could afford to own any real estate. Reuben Riley's ability to employ domestic help also reflected middle-class status. Riley peppered his poetry with accounts of the "hired man" and the "hired girl," regular fixtures in his boyhood home who carried out a variety of tasks within the household.[47] The labor of these hired hands substantially reduced the number of chores that might otherwise have been done by the Riley children. Therefore, they had more opportunity for schooling and leisure than less privileged youngsters.[48]

Thus, before the Civil War, Reuben provided his family with a relatively stable and comfortable environment in which his children felt secure. As a child, Riley held his father in awe. Reuben was a "lawyer and a leading citizen" of Greenfield who loved nature and outdoor manual labor. Young James Whitcomb and his siblings admired Reuben's accomplishments and thought him "Superior of stature as of grace."[49]

Riley described Reuben as being "swarthy" in appearance—"black-eyed, / Black-haired, and high of forehead." He and his siblings believed that their father "was the most self-sufficient man possible under all circumstances." To them, Reuben exemplified the rugged individualism, dynamism, and self-reliance characteristic of the frontiersman: "Put him in a virgin wilderness, with no human being near him, or surround him with thousands, when action or advice was required, and he had himself equally in hand." John remembered Reuben's "force of body, and of mind, and that courageous light in his eyes when he was at his best."[50]

Riley believed that the main traits of his father's personality were "strongly Irish." He was convinced that Reuben's mental and physical "zest in life" came from his Irish roots. The poet clung to the idea that his father's family came from Ireland: "I'm Irish from the word go. I show it in my tastes, I show it in my face—my face, you know, is a map of Ireland in itself—and I show it in my name."[51]

In fact, Reuben Alexander Riley was probably primarily of English and German descent. Born on 7 June 1819 in the Pennsylvania Dutch country of Bedford County, Pennsylvania, he was the fifth child of Andrew and Margaret (Slick) Riley. Riley admitted that his father "was born a Pennsylvania Dutchman" and that he had spoken a German dialect before he spoke English. Although he had been told by his older relatives that the name Riley probably came from the more German-sounding "Ryland," he still held to the family tradition that claimed that one of Riley's great-grandfathers, James, originally came to this region of Pennsylvania from Cork County, Ireland.[52]

Although this theory of the Riley family origins has not been completely disproved, extensive genealogical research, conducted on behalf of Riley's nephew Edmund H. Eitel, revealed that Riley's great-grandfather's name was indeed "Reylandt," "Ryland," or "Riland," not "Riley." Records from Pennsylvania show no person by the name of "Riley" living in Bedford County at the end of the eighteenth or the beginning of the nineteenth centuries. A James Riley was a resident of Washington County, Pennsylvania, at the time of the 1790 census, but it is extremely unlikely that Riley was his descendant. Evidence points to the fact that no James Riley from Cork County ever existed in the family ancestry. Instead, Riley's great grandfather was James Ryland, born in Cumru Township, Berks County, Pennsylvania (near Reading) in 1765, the son of Germans, Paul and Louisa Reylandt.[53]

James Ryland married Rebecca Harvey. Harvey's family was English and probably Quaker. Alfred L. Holman, a genealogist at the Newberry Library in Chicago who conducted this research for Eitel, believed that Rebecca Harvey's family had already been on the American continent for two or three generations by the last half of the eighteenth century. Among James and Rebecca Ryland's children was Andrew, born around 1790. Land records from Bedford County demonstrate that James Ryland moved with his family to Bedford County by 1792. These same records reveal that an Andrew and John Ryland were also landholders in Bedford County at this time. Holman concluded that "the name Riley never came in until Andrew (Riley's grandfather) changed his name from Ryland to Riley."[54]

Andrew's wife, Margaret, born in 1793, was the daughter of John Slick and Elizabeth Wilson Slick. John Slick's family, of German heritage, came to Bedford County via New Jersey and Maryland. Margaret's mother, Elizabeth Wilson, was Scotch and English. Riley's paternal grandparents may have known each other since childhood as both the Slicks and the Rylands "lived .. . eight miles North of Bedford town, not far from Philadelphia." Here Andrew Riley owned a small wedge-shaped farm commonly called "Dutch Corner." James Whitcomb Riley's uncle, John S. Riley, remembered that his father "frequently talk[ed] of hauling oats to Philadelphia in wagons."[55]

Andrew and Margaret Riley left Pennsylvania with their five living children between 1821 and 1825. They first settled in Montgomery County, Ohio, near Dayton and then moved further west to Randolph County, Indiana, near the small town of Windsor, several years later.[56] In Ohio and Indiana, Margaret gave birth eight more times. Over the course of her marriage, she had fourteen children, nine of whom survived to adulthood.

Reuben Riley and his siblings received little formal schooling. Reuben did attend some classes at the Randolph County Seminary in Winchester, Indiana;

but, on the whole, schools were poor and, where they existed, were rarely open. But Margaret Riley valued education and devoted herself to teaching to make sure her children obtained the rudiments of a primary education. She was strict with her children and was a capable teacher. Four of her sons entered middle-class professions. Two were doctors. Riley's father Reuben became a lawyer, and his brother Frank served as treasurer of Marion County, Indiana.[57] Riley remembered that his grandmother Margaret was very interested in religion, history, and politics. She read everything she could get her hands on and did not hesitate to join in among groups of men on debates about politics and religion. Riley said that "she could argue with the best."[58]

Like most frontier women, Margaret Riley was active and industrious. At some point after her husband Andrew died, she came to live in Greenfield in a small house to be near her son and his family. Her grandson, John Riley, remembered the pleasures of her kitchen, believing as a child that she had invented fried apples. She also prepared crocks of sauerkraut, which did not please him as well. More than anything he recalled how devout she was—"how constant and faithful at preaching, and class and prayer meetings."[59]

Riley knew much less about his grandfather Andrew, and it seems that Margaret Riley was probably the stronger presence within the family. From the time he came to Indiana until he died, Andrew kept an inn in Windsor and was a shoemaker by trade. He also possessed a good-sized farm outside this Randolph County town. In 1913, Edmund Eitel commented that everyone he talked to was reticent about Andrew Riley and his ancestors. He surmised that Andrew perhaps "drank very hard" because most of his sons were serious drinkers—a fact about which the family was not proud. Another report tends to suggest that Andrew was not a good role model for his children. A man who knew the Rileys when they resided in Randolph County stated that Andrew, despite his landholdings, struggled to provide for his family and claimed that he had not taught his sons to work very hard.[60]

Andrew died at the end of November 1840, at age fifty. The medical records list typhoid fever as the probable cause of death. Reuben Riley served as executor of his father's will. However, for some unknown reason, Reuben "made a failure [of] settling his father's little estate." It remained unsettled for ten years until finally "another man was called in to assist."[61]

Reuben was the logical choice to become administrator of Andrew's property as he had begun to read law in the office of Andrew Kennedy in Muncie, Indiana, in the months before his father died. Before settling on the law as a career, Reuben taught school in Randolph, Rush, and Vigo counties during 1839 and part of 1840. He entered the Bar in 1841. During the fall of 1842, he moved to Marion, Iowa, where he practiced law until he returned to Indiana in December 1843.[62]

Back in Indiana, Reuben started to court Elizabeth Marine, whom he met while teaching in a village school at Union Port in Randolph County. Elizabeth was reportedly considered quite a prize, "the most charming young woman of the neighborhood." People in Union Port thought her "remarkably pretty, with a style and spirit all her own."[63]

At the time that Reuben courted her, Elizabeth Marine lived with her older brother William who owned a store in Union Port and two grist mills on nearby Cabin Creek, a tributary of the Mississinewa River. Another brother, John D. Marine, also lived in Union Port and operated the store in partnership with William until he decided to become a doctor. Elizabeth presumably had come to live with William some time after her mother died in 1835. Before her marriage, Elizabeth's father, John Marine, Sr., spent part of his time with his children in Union Port.[64]

Family tradition held that the Marines were originally Huguenots who fled France during the second half of the seventeenth century. This may be correct, but a search of genealogical records designed to trace the family back to France proved inconclusive. The records do demonstrate that some of the Marine ancestors were originally Quakers who first settled in Maryland.[65]

John Marine, Sr. married Elizabeth's mother, Frances Jones, the daughter of John Jones, a North Carolina plantation owner reportedly of Welsh origins, on 16 November 1803. Marine, a merchant, farmer, and Methodist preacher, set up housekeeping with his wife in the Marlborough District of South Carolina but later moved to adjacent Richmond County, North Carolina, where Elizabeth was born, the tenth of eleven children, on 16 October 1823.[66]

The Marine family came to Indiana from North Carolina some time after Elizabeth's birth during the 1820s. Marine supposedly moved north because he objected to the institution of slavery. He freed the slaves who worked his plantation in North Carolina, but many of them came with him to Wayne County, Indiana. Here he joined one of his older brothers, who was one of the county's first white settlers.[67]

James Whitcomb Riley remembered his grandfather Marine smoking in front of the fireplace of the Riley home in Greenfield. Marine would make smoke rings "that drifted straight from him and then dipped down gracefully before they went up the chimney. This he would do by the hour." Riley said that his grandfather continually attempted to tame his younger brother Humboldt, whom Riley described as an "impetuous, passionate boy." Marine tried to make the boy more calm and submissive by sitting him on his lap and telling him stories about the childhood of Christ from the Bible.[68] Because the democratic form of government was comparatively new, people thought that teaching children obedience and self-control was of prime importance to counteract the anarchic tendencies of democratic individualism.[69]

Another grandchild, Alice Thornburg, the daughter of Elizabeth Marine's sister, remembered how proud she was as a child to see Marine as he arrived at their home "wearing a silk hat and a long, back broadcloth cloak,—the kind [Alfred] Tennyson has on in many of his pictures."[70] Marine seemed to her a *"true born aristocrat"* who was a deep thinker and writer of poetry on religious topics. According to family legend, he had even written an autobiography in verse; but he lost it fording a stream when coming across the Blue Ridge Mountains.[71]

Although Reuben Riley wrote some poetry, Riley believed that much of his talent came from the Marines. When Hamlin Garland asked him where he got his "verse-writing from," Riley responded, "Mainly from my mother's side of the family. . . . A characteristic of the whole family is their ability to write rhymes, but all unambitiously. They write rhymed letters to each other, and joke and jim-crow with the Muses." Riley's cousin, William R. Hough, always said that Riley more closely resembled the Marines than the Rileys in physical appearance as well. He said that Riley not only looked like them but also had their temperament.[72]

Riley, who was very fair in complexion, did indeed resemble his mother more than he did his father. Elizabeth Riley was medium in stature and, like her son, had expressive blue eyes and fine light brown hair. In *A Child-World*, Riley described his mother's "fair hair's glimmering strands, / . . . [her] little rose-leaf cheeks and dewy lips." She had a "mild, plaintive face / [that] Was purely fair . . . / And . . . luminous when joy made glad / Her features with a smile." Among the children in the Riley household, she was "A being . . . exalted—even more" than was his father. He remembered her soft touch and the sympathetic way she handled his "childish grief."[73] As Americans increasingly recognized the importance of childhood, the role of mothers took on new significance. Middle-class mothers like Elizabeth acquired the primary responsibility for child rearing. It was their duty to teach their sons and daughters the values necessary for success, and they exercised the most influence on children in their formative years.[74]

Riley pictured his mother enthroned in her rocking chair with her sewing on her knee. Her small, slender hands were deft with a needle, making articles of clothing with "flounce or frill" or fashioning "in complicated design, / All rich embroideries of leaf and vine, . . . bud and bloom." Riley said that his mother was a dreamer. He remembered her as "she paused with a needle uplifted in her hand and the pupils of her eyes showing full, utterly oblivious to all about her."[75]

Although she usually had some hired help, with five children she still had to work hard at household tasks. Middle-class mothers typically had chores that kept them busy a good part of the day, but they also devoted considerable time to their children. Elizabeth was always there to soothe her children. She often entered into their games, told them stories, and made up rhymes. Her rapport with her youngsters was unusual. She was "never parental in her attitude" but treated them as if she were their elder sister: "She never ordered them about, but would ask them if they would do something for their mother—whereupon they always complied."[76]

The Riley home provided Elizabeth with sanctuary. By the mid-nineteenth century, the home had become the woman's separate sphere. Elizabeth's life centered around her marriage, her children, and her household. She seldom called on neighbors and never traveled far, but she always welcomed visitors—"the more the merrier." Most people described her as a refined, sensitive woman who was "delicate but of courageous as well as poetic temperament." Although her household chores left her little time to read, she did write some poetry. However, "she didn't write a very good hand." Therefore, most of her poems went unrecorded on paper.[77]

After Reuben and Elizabeth Riley moved to Hancock County as newly-weds, Reuben quickly built up his law practice and entered the political arena. These pursuits often took him away from Greenfield over the course of their marriage. Reuben's principal role as a middle-class father was "to work outside the home to maintain the status of the family."[78] William Hough thought that his aunt became accustomed to Reuben's frequent absences and after a while "didn't pay much attention to it." Instead, she busied herself with the work that needed to be done at home and focused her attention on her children. Hough, who lived with the Rileys during the 1850s, observed that "she was a good mother, the nicest kind of a mother." To him, she represented the "ideal" of womanhood.[79]

Though always strong in his convictions, Reuben Riley, late in his life, always claimed that he entered politics against his will. Soon after arriving in Greenfield in April 1844, Reuben was drawn into the presidential campaign between the incumbent Whig president, John Tyler, and the Democratic nominee, James K. Polk. At this time, Reuben was a staunch Jacksonian Democrat. He canvassed Hancock and other Indiana counties in favor of Polk, who won the election by a wide margin.[80]

Polk's victory was no surprise. Americans were generally discontented with the Tyler administration. Tyler, who served during the most serious economic depression that the country had suffered up to that point, had succeeded William Henry Harrison in the presidency after Harrison died of pneumonia in April 1841 and was therefore popularly known as "His Accidency." Through his indecision in office, Tyler even managed to alienate the Whigs. Despite Polk's easy victory, Reuben's work for the Democratic party earned him a nomination to the Indiana State General Assembly, to which he was elected for the 1845–1846 term.[81]

Sworn into office on 1 December 1845 at the age of twenty-six, Reuben was believed to have been the youngest person then in the legislature. He was elected to a second term in 1848. While in the General Assembly, he was most active as a member of its judiciary committee. Reuben served during the tenure of Governor James Whitcomb, whom he so greatly admired that he named his second son, the poet, after him. Like Reuben, Whitcomb had Hancock County ties, having been the first prosecuting attorney for its circuit court in 1828.[82]

When the legislature was not in session, Reuben built up his law practice. By the early 1850s, he had become a well-known, prominent attorney and represented clients in Hancock, Marion, Shelby, Johnson, Madison, and other counties. An able litigator, he served as prosecuting attorney for the Fifth Indiana Circuit from 1852 to 1854. In 1856, he complained to his brother that his professional business had grown so steadily that it was "more than one man ought to be encumbered with."[83]

Reuben's overriding generosity was in part responsible for this overload of clients. He gave free legal counsel to the poor, and a day seldom passed when he did not have a visitor at the house from the country—a client who came from the courtroom to dinner. Riley's older brother, John, remembered that as Reuben was coming home from Indianapolis by horse and buggy one evening before the railroad, he "took pity on an old German tramp[,] brought him home with him and gave him work for many months." This tramp undoubtedly was one of the models for Riley's "Raggedy Man."[84]

Reuben's nephew, William R. Hough, a respected Hancock County attorney and judge, criticized the way in which Reuben conducted his law practice and spent his money. He thought that Reuben sometimes waived his fees at the expense of his own family. For example, Hough knew of one instance in which Reuben, acting as justice of the peace, returned his remuneration to a man and woman whom he had just married, saying he knew what money meant to a young couple starting out in life. "At the same time," Hough contended, "his own children hadn't good shoe leather between their feet and the ground." He complained that Reuben rarely gave his aunt any money, "so . . . she rarely had anything attractive to wear. . . , [and] once . . . [he] bought her a very handsome silk cape. It was a beautiful present but she had nothing else in keeping with it and could have used the money to far better advantage."[85]

Hough thought that Reuben could have been a very "wealthy and distinguished man had he had as much steadfastness of purpose as he had power of concentration and enthusiasm." He felt that his uncle neglected his law practice in favor of politics, "spend[ing] days at a time in Indianapolis when he should have been at work" in his office.[86] What Hough said about Reuben was, in many ways, true; and often his family suffered as a result of the decisions he made.

However, Reuben Riley had high principles. He considered the concepts of fairness, justice, liberty, and freedom more important than his own political fortune or personal wealth. People who knew Reuben well stated that he "was too openhanded and bighearted to make a successful politician. He was no trickster and detested the little combines and secret backstabbings often necessary to gain one's political ends."[87]

Although James Whitcomb Riley looked back on the era of his childhood with much nostalgia and longing, the pre–Civil War period was actually rife with political uncertainty and dissension. The issue of slavery threatened to destroy the American experiment. During the late 1840s and early 1850s, Reuben felt that serving the Indiana Democratic Party was his patriotic duty as an American citizen. After serving in the legislature, he sat on the State Central Committee of the party; but everything changed with the introduction of the Kansas-Nebraska Act of 1854. In a letter to his brother written in the spring of 1856, Reuben described the disquieting political climate and predicted an ominous future:

> Here the seeming subsiding of political excitement is only the lulling of the storm, to be renewed with redoubled vigor. There was a verry [sic] strong inclination all through the Northern States among all parties, (these fanatical abolitionists excepted . . .) to cease all agitation on the vexed and perplexing question of slavery, to leave it where it was undisturbed, and to enforce to the letter the fugitive slave law—until the repeal of the Missouri Compromise, like a fire bell in the night, sounded the alarm. And the forays of the Missourians & others upon that Territory [sic], the election riots, pipe-laying, expulsion of the free state members, and the laws or pretended laws they enacted has vastly increased the excitement, and done more to destroy confidence in the South, and embitter the North against the South, than all pre-existing causes since the formation of the [United States] government."[88]

As Reuben suggested in this letter, the existence of slavery did not bother him as much as the apparent desire of the South and its sympathizers to put its own interests above those of the nation as a whole. With the repeal of the Missouri Compromise, he and many of the other leading Democrats in Indiana could not reconcile themselves to support a party that rejected the principle that the United States Congress held constitutional authority for prohibiting the extension of slavery in the territories. They were disturbed by the Democratic Party's endorsement of the Kansas-Nebraska Act, which expressly made slavery a matter of popular sovereignty in each territory.[89]

At the State Convention of the Democratic Party on 24 May 1854, "the opposition of the anti-Nebraska wing of the party developed into an insurgency."[90] Reuben, as a strong member of this "insurgency," broke away from the Democrats and with many like him joined other groups who denounced the 1854 Democratic Party platform to form the People's Party—a forerunner of the Republican Party in Indiana. During this time, Reuben made frequent trips to Indianapolis. James Whitcomb's older brother John remembered that Reuben often left for the train depot early in the morning, accompanied by his dog, and that the dog learned Reuben's routine so well that he knew when to go back to the station to greet his master upon his return.[91]

Between 1854 and 1860, Reuben would become a key organizer of this new political force in the state. In 1856, he was a favorite for the congressional seat in Indiana's sixth electoral district; but, in the end, the former Whig, Albert Gallatin Porter, won the new party's nomination. The Riley family was most proud of Reuben's participation as a delegate-at-large at the Chicago Republican Convention where he helped to nominate Abraham Lincoln for the first time in 1860. After attending the convention, Reuben returned to Greenfield in the middle of the night. The Riley children got up to hear their father tell about the "the thrilling incidents of the nomination, and how the West was victorious over the east in the defeat of [William Henry] Seward."[92]

Along with men such as Oliver P. Morton, Civil War governor of Indiana, the new Republican Party called on Reuben Riley to canvass the state. Riley's role in this campaign was important because the Republicans needed to carry Indiana to elect Lincoln. He and other former Democrats assumed a large share of the campaign work in the election of 1860. By this time, Reuben's speech-making talents were already well known. In 1857, the *Greenfield Sentinel* announced that Reuben had performed with a "blaze of glory" during an early party convention. With pride, the newspaper proclaimed that "Democracy fell and Republicanism rose" upon the power of Reuben's rhetoric. "Possessing a fine mind and a right sense of humor," he "set political audiences on fire with character stories dramatically told and always with a point at the end to clinch an argument or embarrass an opponent by setting the audience roaring." James Whitcomb Riley remembered that his father's speeches often made "crowds jump up and down and whoop. Something would touch the mainspring of his 'speechifying' genius, and eloquence would flow in a stream from his lips." Those who later recalled hearing him asserted "that he expounded the principles of the young party as no other orator in Indiana at the time."[93]

In America before the Civil War, Reuben's dramatic oratorical style was typical. His impassioned delivery appealed to an audience that feasted on sensation. Through descriptions of Reuben's speeches, one can sense how he enthralled people in attendance with his stories and his arguments. They responded enthusiastically, creating a raucous atmosphere as they jumped up and down and "whoop[ed]." Punctuated with humor, Reuben's lecture style was personal and allowed for such interjections. This unconstrained expression of ideas was distinctive of much antebellum oratory. At political rallies, a high level of interaction existed between audience and participants rarely seen today in a culture where election campaigns take place to a great extent through electronic media.[94]

Moreover, the rallies where Reuben gave many of his speeches were usually not just political. These events often included the expression of religious ideas, poetry readings, and musical performance. In America before the Civil War, much exchange occurred between different cultural idioms. The popular music of the day incorporated ideas that reflected social issues. Sermons from the pulpit as well as speeches from the political podium were very theatrical, and all forms of popular oratory drew much from acting.[95]

James Whitcomb Riley was exposed to all elements of this performance culture. His poetic talents came through the Marines, but he owed his natural ability to perform to his father's side of the family. Many people noted Riley's "magnetic touch" as they had with his father. Riley's teacher and mentor, Lee O. Harris, stated that Riley was always an actor—that through Reuben acting "was born in him."[96]

However, Riley did not believe that his oratorical gifts really matched his father's. Reuben almost always spoke extemporaneously. Reflecting the great emphasis on oratory in the nineteenth century, he was able to hold his audience's attention for a considerable time. Some of his speeches lasted as long as three hours.[97] Although Riley believed that by nature he should be as good as Reuben, he lacked his father's talents: "I'm forever and eternally trying to make a speech . . . but to save my life I can't do it. My father was a great speechmaker, and I know perfectly well that by nature I am. I think one reason I can't make a speech is because I've been accustomed so many years to commit to memory, and it has spoiled me for extemporaneous work." Moreover, Riley declared that his lack of memory kept him in a constant state of nervous anxiety when he was performing. He was continually haunted by the idea that he would forget his own poems and could be found off-stage "muttering over the familiar words," so that he had command over them when he faced an audience.[98]

At the outbreak of the Civil War, leaders of the Republican Party in Indiana knew that in Reuben A. Riley they had "a faithful, honest and earnest advocate; a Republican from principle and not policy." Indeed, Reuben felt so strongly about the Union cause that he abandoned his law practice in the spring of 1861 to organize the first company of Indiana Volunteers from Hancock County, although he was already forty-one years old. Elected captain of Company I of the Eighth Indiana Regiment, he and his men joined a three-month campaign in West Virginia during the summer of 1861. Reuben's company engaged in battle on Rich Mountain in July of that same year. During this engagement, an enemy shell burst near Reuben which nearly paralyzed his left side for a time and which destroyed his hearing in his left ear. He returned to Greenfield an invalid when his company was mustered out in August 1861.[99]

However, Reuben managed to recover enough to reenlist in August 1862 in response to the President's call for six hundred thousand men. This time his company joined the Fifth Cavalry (90th Regiment) of Indiana Volunteers, and he again was captain. He hoped because of his age and experience to be promoted to major, but was repeatedly passed over.

Lesser men might have been embittered by this, but not Reuben Riley. In a letter to his old friend Oliver P. Morton in the Statehouse, he declared: "I have no other desire than to serve my country in its terible [*sic*] extremity in that position where I can be most useful," and he did as he promised. Letters show that he was a good leader and an able advocate for his men when issues of rations, payment, and even personal problems interfered with duties and dampened morale. He also often came to the aid of injured men on the battlefield.[100]

In July 1863, Reuben's company participated in the attack on Morgan's Raiders, heading off Morgan's forces at Buffington Island, Ohio. Members of the company drove Morgan's men from the river and the adjacent hills, killing and capturing many. The Fifth Cavalry's capture of Morgan and his raiders was one of the most notable events in Reuben's army career.[101]

While Reuben served in the Civil War, Elizabeth and her children struggled at home. The government made few provisions for soldiers' dependents. The hardships suffered by wives and families left behind in the war and deprived of their normal income were second only to the sufferings of the men on the battlefield. Reuben could spare little money to send home to his wife. In March 1863, he told her that he was owed $300 in back pay. His son, John, recalled that the "larder would run very low" at home during this time.[102]

Although struggling economically, Elizabeth, who was always very compassionate, took in a young girl named Mary Alice Smith as a boarder in the winter of 1862. At the time her uncle brought her to the Riley home, Mary Alice was twelve years old. Her circumstances before her arrival at the Rileys remain largely unknown. Her parents apparently left her in her uncle's care following a marital separation when she was four years old. Riley recalled that she was at first mistrustful, but Elizabeth and her children soon made her feel at home. As was the custom for hired hands, Mary Alice worked alongside her employer to earn her board and keep, and lived and ate with the family. She enchanted Riley and his brothers and sisters with the weird and often frightening tales she told them at night before they retired to bed. She made such a deep impression on Riley that he never forgot her. He honored that memory by writing one of his most beloved poems, "Little Orphant Annie," about her.[103]

Soon after his regiment's confrontations with Morgan's Raiders, Reuben became too ill to accompany his men on expeditions in East Tennessee. By December 1863, his health had become so impaired that he reluctantly resigned from active service. Following combat, Reuben served a short time as army advocate general near Leavenworth, Kansas, where he prosecuted several cases against men suspected of treason to the Union cause.[104]

Here, Reuben caught "the Kansas fever," as Riley later put it. "He got it so badly," Riley said," that he bought . . . a farm near Leavenworth, and intended to move out there." The prospect of moving to Kansas excited Reuben because it reminded him of the relatively unbroken land of Indiana in the 1830s and 1840s. Although a lawyer, Reuben had been raised on a farm and few things pleased him more "than to hold onto the handles of a plow, with the lines about his shoulders, and have the team jerk him over the ground."[105] Reuben made several trips to his new property and tried to coax Elizabeth to move, espousing the benefits of a "pleasant and comfortable home" where crops would flourish. However, he was unable to convince her to move away from her family and friends in Indiana.[106]

Because of his poetry, many people had the impression that Reuben's son had also lived a great part of his life on a farm. The Riley family always lived in town, but Riley was certainly not totally lacking in farm experience. As one newspaper reporter said, Greenfield was one of those places where boys had "the advantage of being town boys and country boys at the same time." Reuben wanted his sons to know the meaning of laboring in the soil with one's hands. For that reason, he held on to his farm near Greenfield. He sent Riley out to work his land; but, as Riley said, "the results were meager, nothing but a few facts for a poem—flickers on the fence rails, blackbirds quarreling in the furrows, and a few shots from a shotgun before dinner."[107]

Although Riley did not acquire his father's love for farming, he did learn his hatred of affectation and his love of the common people from him. Riley's father liked nothing better than a talk with a blacksmith, carpenter, farm section-boss, or janitor. The young James Whitcomb was often present during these conversations at home and in his father's courtroom. There, he absorbed the dialect of the poor, rural Hoosiers that he would later use in his poems. In 1886 the *Chicago Morning News* reported Riley's own impressions of this process:

> In replying to questions as to himself, Mr. Riley said that his appreciation of dialect and his ability to represent it . . . must have been imbibed when a lad. . . . His father had him put on boy's clothes long before his mother thought it advisable, and used to take him down to the court-house. He was white-haired and freckled beyond redemption, and yet his father seemed to delight to keep him by him during the long legal trials in which he was engaged. That was the only period of his life when he lived for any length of time among those whose strongly characteristic dialect he has in late years tried to represent. He has visited, and still studies them, but believes the early impressions of his childhood more greatly influence and shape the conception he has, later in life, endeavored to portray.[108]

Reuben liked to show off his young son, who he hoped would some day grow up to be a fine lawyer, like his namesake, Governor James Whitcomb. Before the war, Reuben told his brother that his sons were growing "finely," "learning rapidly," and were "apt and intelligent." He was indeed a proud father; but Elizabeth thought that her husband expected too much of Riley too soon. Characteristically, middle-class parents raised boys and girls very similarly when they were young. Until they were about seven, they were even dressed alike: first in long gowns, then in short coats, and, between the ages of three and seven, in short petticoats and pants. When he took him to the courthouse, Reuben introduced Riley very early to the real competitive world of work. He always demanded that his second son perform up to his standards; and, when Riley was unable to meet them, his father's fiery temper exploded. As a boy, the poet feared his father's rage.[109]

James Whitcomb was a "a quiet boy, not talkative, . . . [who] would go about much with one eye shut, as he observed and speculated." While Reuben was strict and exacting, Elizabeth in his absence allowed her son "to grow up wild."[110] In the country, young boys were expected to spend much of the day roaming the fields and patches of woodland. Outdoor play permitted Riley considerable freedom of movement away from adult supervision. Such experiences developed his independence. When he was only five or six years old, he already wandered by himself as far away as Brandywine Creek, on the other side of town. Wading in the Brandywine was a favorite pastime for the children of Greenfield. Riley loved to roll "up his trousers as high as possible and with a hand holding up each leg of them he . . . kick[ed] the water and look[ed] for the deep places."[111] He described such exploits in "The Barefoot Boy":

> A barefoot boy! I mark him at his play—
> For May is here once more, and so is he,—
> His dusty trousers, rolled half to the knee,
> And his bare ankles grimy, too, as they;
> Cross-hatchings of the nettle, in array
> Of feverish stripes, hint vividly to me
> Of woody pathways winding endlessly
> Along the creek, where even yesterday
> He plunged his shrinking body—gasped and shook—
> Yet called the water "warm," with never lack
> Of joy. And so, half enviously I look
> Upon this graceless barefoot and his track.[112]

In later years, Riley, in many of his poems, expressed memories of his childhood delight exploring with his boyhood "chums" the creek bed, fields, and woods surrounding Greenfield. He learned much of his love and respect for nature from his father. Reuben was an enthusiastic naturalist. He often took his sons and some of their friends deep into the woods. On these hikes, he taught them many skills that had been crucial to their ancestors' survival on the frontier. He showed them where to find the wild birds and animals that were native to the area. He also demonstrated how to identify different trees and plants and explained their properties and uses. Riley claimed that Reuben always carried an ax with him on his excursions into the forest and collected specimens of wood from every kind of tree he could find.[113]

Imaginary creatures filled the woods Riley enjoyed exploring. From an early age, he delighted in the stories his mother told about "Giants, trolls, or fairies"—characters that later found their way into his poems. Elizabeth Riley put faith in the powers of mysticism and the supernatural. Well into the nineteenth century, especially in poorer rural areas, magical thinking and belief in the occult persisted. Elizabeth's son John described the "'Spirit rappings' on headboards of beds, bureaus, or tables" that occurred frequently in the Riley home when his mother was around. Riley, too, was deeply affected by this way of thinking. He insisted on the existence of an afterlife and imagined that the spirits of his deceased family and friends surrounded him. While he was preparing to write *A Child-World*, he wrote to his brother: "In that time [I have] been continually recalling our old home, our long-vanished youth, and the dear father and mother who so loved us, and who were so loved by us that we may not doubt but they are still with us, though we see them not—loving us ever the same—and being loved by us ever and ever the same."[114]

Elizabeth Riley's influence is evident in much of Riley's work. Some of Riley's poems, most notably "Flying Islands of the Night," are surreal—set in a magical netherworld filled with mythical characters. Other poems, such as "Away," more directly relate Riley's attitudes about death and an afterlife. When criticized for the mystical quality of some of his work, Riley replied, "If poetry has not to do with fairies, sorcery, empyrean realms, mysticism, etc., then I don't understand its province."[115]

As a boy, Riley used his vivid imagination to improvise performances and theatricals. Riley first performed his shows in the back of a grocery store. He recited jingles his mother had written, mimicked his friends, and played tunes "by singing through a coarse comb covered with paper." Later, he and his friend Ed Howard launched barn shows. Until the 1870s, boys and girls played together without the benefit of many toys. Few parents could afford the expensive manufactured toys, which came primarily from Germany. Children used handmade items, played games, and used their imaginations. They went fishing and hiking in summer, and sledded and had snowball fights in winter. Riley's ability to come up with ideas for these play activities made him popular with the other boys in Greenfield. The "early demonstration of [Riley's] ability as a delineator and his keen powers of observation[,] which enabled him to successfully imitate almost any character he chose[,] easily placed him, without dissension, as the head of a coterie of his own selection." This select group of friends often "regaled an eagerly waiting public with a Circus Minstrel Show" because of Riley's love and fascination for this kind of entertainment.[116]

Sometimes Riley's imitations of circus performers were impromptu and informal. A cousin remembered that "Riley would get up on a chair and pretend to be a barker for a circus. He would accuse her of being the Fat Lady, some one else of being the Living Skeleton." At other times, however, Riley and his friends planned rather elaborate neighborhood shows and charged "twenty pins [admission] / At the barn."[117]

Riley described these childish attempts to recreate the circus in "When We First Played 'Show.'" In this poem, Riley reconstructed the roles each of his boyhood friends played in their performances. One of them would be the ringmaster, another would be the clown, and someone else would be the "'Injarubber'-Man." Together, they put on acrobatic acts—"'Tumblin' on the sawdust." They also included bareback riding. Riley thinly disguised himself as the character "Jamesy," who in the poem pretended to be a daring high wire artist: "Jamesy on the slack-rope / In a wild retreat, / Grappling back, to start again—When he chalked his feet!"[118]

Noah Bixler, a friend and "hero" of both John and Jim Riley when they were children, captured and tamed wild raccoons, foxes, hawks, and owls, which were always available to be part of these expositions. Bixler once gave Riley a flying squirrel that Riley trained to become a special part of the boys' circus; but, before it could be included in the show, Riley accidentally suffocated the animal as it slept with him in bed. Someone else's pet fawn had to be substituted as the star attraction of the boy's animal act.[119]

Bixler also gave the young Riley a pair of stilts that he had made. Many people noted that Riley possessed great acrobatic ability that lent itself beautifully to the neighborhood circus. His brother John said that when Riley first learned to turn a handspring, a somersault, and walk on his hands he gave his "undivided attention to it." Envious of his younger brother's abilities, John remarked that he "nearly killed . . . [himself] a score of times trying to acquire the art." Riley's uncle, Joe, claimed that Riley, as a boy of five or six, could walk "along the fence on his hands for a distance of a hundred feet at a time."[120]

Although he could never read a musical note, Riley also had a natural talent for music. When John Riley brought home a guitar, Riley "quickly surpassed him in his ability to play it." Riley also learned to play the violin and during his teens joined the Greenfield Cornet Band as a snare drummer. He also sometimes played in the Adelphian Band, the Cornet Band's successor. In his youth, Riley often serenaded people in his company with renditions of such contemporary tunes as "Swanee River" and "The Arkansas Traveler." He became proficient enough on the violin that he appeared at the Greenfield Masonic Hall.[121]

Riley's poetry is filled with references to music and musical instruments. He wrote poems about the instruments he played and described "The voice of poetry" as "pure music." Riley saw the poet as a bard or singer, who could be found "softly crooning [words] over and over to himself" which repeated the "melody" and "purity of tone" found in nature. Although "examples of exquisite verse might be quoted from Elizabeth Barrett Browning, Tennyson, Whittier, Holmes, Lowell, and a host of others whose names are echoed round the world, . . . [Riley believed that] the tribute of true praise may oftentimes as justly rest upon the vagrant verses of the singer all unknown to fame." For Riley, the music of poetry was egalitarian and universal: "Poetry is about us everywhere. Its influence has a hold on every heart. . . . There are unconscious poets all about us: men and women, who, in their most common-place duties and avocations, are unconsciously sweetening their lives and our own with the poetic drippings of their melodious natures."[122]

When Riley and his friends were not outdoors playing in the woods or putting on amateur shows, they often gathered at the shoemaker shop of English immigrant Tom Snow. Snow had a great interest in books and was instrumental in establishing the first library in Greenfield. The boys would listen to Snow tell stories, and he often read to them from his favorite books, such as *Robinson Crusoe* and *The Swiss Family Robinson*. In Snow's shop, Riley also first became acquainted with the work of Charles Dickens.[123]

Dickens gave Riley and his friends another idea for their role playing—a secret boys' club in which each member took the identity of a character from *Oliver Twist*. Clint Hamilton, one of the club's members, later recalled: "We had also, under his [Riley's] inception[,] an organization suggested by Dickens, under guidance of Fagin (Riley) in which I proudly bore the name of "The Artful Dodger"—though no acts of real meanness could be charged to us." The club "met in a sort of cave or cellar under an old barn—and much weird mystery attended membership & meetings."[124]

Riley identified Dickens as an early literary influence in "St. Lirriper":

> When Dickens first dawned on us . . . Hey! to wake
> Brain-fast on such an appetizing spread . . .
> Writing like this must be, not from the wrist,
> But from the heart no reader may resist.[125]

Other poems, such as "Christmas Season" and "God Bless Us Every One," have direct Dickens references. Riley never lost his great admiration and respect for this author. He read many of Dickens's works over and over again with "change-less liking." In addition to *Oliver Twist*, he particularly loved one of the *Christ-*

mas Carols, "Mrs. Lirriper's Lodgings" (for which the poem mentioned earlier was named) and the novel *David Copperfield.* In Dickens, Riley found "a most engaging *exhibitor* of life's characters." Riley considered Dickens "a master of masters" because he presented "the cheeriest, tenderest, most novel yet most natural appearing scenes and types of character and situations set down by any . . . story teller." Not coincidentally, many critics described the scenes and characters Riley depicted in his poems in a similar way. Riley emulated Dickens because his short stories and novels seemed realistic and yet were still uplifting.[126]

Riley developed a love of literature and books very young. Others in addition to Tom Snow helped to expose him to the world of letters. As he stated in *A Child-World,* the picture books he perused at his mother's knee enthralled him. His mother, Elizabeth, and his father's youngest brother, Mart, taught Riley to read at home before he ever spent a day in school. During the nineteenth century, reading was a favorite pastime. Children and adults read together. They took pleasure in literature with strong narratives, romantic characters, and high adventure. Through his Uncle Mart, Riley heard the stories of the *Arabian Nights* and *Baron Munchausen;* and, when Nathaniel Hawthorne's *Tanglewood* appeared in 1853, Mart read the whole book aloud to his nephews, John and Jim. Riley's grandmother read "old historical reviews" that made him aware of the world beyond Greenfield: "My Gran'ma she's read *all* books—ever' kind / They is, 'at tells all 'bout the land an' sea / An' Nations of the Earth!" Another boyhood friend, Almon ("Buck") Keefer, had a "great love of books, and a skill as well / In reading them aloud." Riley gathered with other boys under their favorite apple tree to listen to Almon as he read some of the favorite adventure stories of the time, such as *Tales of the Ocean, Jack Sheppard,* or *Dick Turpin.*[127]

Despite his love for books, Riley was a poor student. According to a classmate, he never spent "much time studying his lessons but would put in a good deal of time drawing pictures . . . or writing rhymes." His old friend also said that, by the time he went to school, Riley was "a great big-hearted[,] sociable boy [who] was liked by everyone."[128] Riley acquired his distaste for school very early: "I was sent to school at an early age—and then sent back again. At the very beginning I conceived a dislike for its iron discipline, whose sole object seemed to be to harness every mental energy into brutelike subjection, and then drive it wherever old bat-eye tyranny might suggest."[129] Riley was the victim of the teaching practices of his time. His instructors taught most subjects by drill. In the classroom, children acquired basic skills, but most did not learn to think for themselves. For Riley, this type of education was stultifying because it did not stimulate his creativity. The rigid, unappealing environment common in schools probably drove many young people who, like Riley, were easily bored by exercises in rote memorization, to choose seeking employment over finishing their education.[130]

In the preceding quotation, Riley alluded to the inconsistency of his education. Although a school law was passed during the state legislative session of 1852, which laid the foundations for a system of public schools supported by state taxation, Hancock County lacked public school facilities when Riley was a young boy. This situation was not atypical; education in Indiana as a whole during this period was very poor. During the mid-1850s, the state did not possess the funds to build adequate schools or to pay teacher salaries; and, where schools were open, the average term lasted only two and one-half months. For many of Indiana's early settlers, free schools did not have much appeal because they believed that such institutions were for the poor only. Although those who supported free education tried to combat the idea that free schools were "pauper schools," many communities, such as Greenfield, resisted organizing a local, government-funded educational system.[131]

Instead, individuals often opened private schools in their own homes, charging the parents of pupils a modest tuition . The school Riley first attended was one such as this. A Mrs. Neill, "a fat old lady with kind spectacles, . . . taught twenty scholars in one room of her tiny dwelling and kept house and her blind husband in the other." Riley described the room that she used for her class as "cold and dim." The Neill house was located down the street from the Rileys' on the National Road in Greenfield.[132]

The young Riley was often in trouble. On many occasions, Mrs. Neill reluctantly whipped Riley "with the same slender switch she used for a 'pointer,' and cried every lick herself." He remembered that Mrs. Neill "invariably" took him to "a little Dame-trot kitchen . . . after a whipping and gave . . . [him] two great slabs of bread cemented together with . . . butter and jam."[133] Teachers often meted out physical punishments. Obedience to authority was considered of principal importance because it served to make students law-abiding adults. In rural areas, where children roamed relatively freely, parents and teachers thought that discipline and moral instruction were necessary to restrain any wild tendencies in their charges before they became uncontrollable.[134]

Riley had nothing kind to say about his next teacher, who apparently was not so sympathetic when he administered punishment: "When old enough to be lifted by the ears, that office was performed by a pedagogue whom I promised to whip sure if he'd wait till I got big enough; and he is still waiting!"[135] This "pedagogue" later may have provided Riley with a model for "The Educator"—"a character sketch of an eastern school teacher, whose brains had been developed at the expense of the rest of him, and who made a funny mess of an object lesson to the primary class at the exhibition of his western country school."[136]

Reading was always Riley's best subject. In one interview he remarked, "As for reading, I got along with it very well, I usually read the books through for the stories before the class had mastered one-third of them." While most other subjects did not interest him, Riley read everything he could get his hands on, including popular, sensational stories and novels. In contrast to Elizabeth, who nurtured Riley's interest in mystical and fantastic tales, Reuben Riley disapproved of his son's frivolous literary interests. He thought that his son should read books that were more substantial in content. Riley remembered that "it was a frightful task" to plow through one of the books his father told him he ought to read. The books that Reuben put out of his son's reach—the ones that he considered unsuitable—were always the ones that Riley sought most.[137]

However, when Riley tackled books that pleased his father, he read them "with an imaginative eye": "Why, when I read 'Pilgrim's Progress' . . . I could see the whiskers on Giant Despair as plain as day. But I could not have read it had I known it was an allegory." Like other middle-class parents, Reuben wanted his son's reading not only to entertain but also to teach him moral values. Much to his father's despair, Riley did not comprehend Bunyan's underlying messages when he read the book. He only saw a wonderful make-believe world unfold in its pages.[138]

Riley's relationship with his father deteriorated after he returned to Greenfield in September 1864 toward the end of the Civil War. Reuben was a changed man. The rigors of battle had taken their toll on him. His hair had turned gray from its deep jet black, and the injuries he suffered in August 1861 left him permanently disabled. His left side was partially paralyzed, and he could not hear well. He returned to his law practice, "but only in a desultory manner, never having the strength of the heart to put in his work that he had before his injuries in the war." One of Riley's legal colleagues noted that Reuben no longer seemed to have "a continuity of purpose": "He would start in brisk on a thing, and then sidetrack."[139]

But he never lost his gift for oratory. Reuben gave one of his most powerful addresses following the assassination of President Lincoln. He moved his audience to tears and, when he finished, "dropped into his chair sobbing." His emotional response showed how seriously Reuben had taken his service to his country. Because of his age, he had not been obliged to go to war. "He made the sacrifice open-eyed, mainly because it was his conviction that a *man* does not care to be indebted to someone else, for his own security or that of his country, in peril-time of war." In the end, this sacrifice was indeed great, because he came close to losing everything he cared for.[140]

If anything, Reuben became more absolute in his personal beliefs. He needed to feel that the setbacks he experienced after the war were not in vain. With his inability to rebuild his law practice and his purchase of the property in Kansas, Reuben soon found himself overextended financially. He was forced to sell his house on the National Road to settle his debts, and he lost much of the respect he had earned before the war as the early accomplishments of his career retreated further and further into the past. He became known as a "man of very marked peculiarities and eccentricities." He appeared to take up what some people considered political fads. He was successively a Greenbacker, a Prohibitionist, and a Populist. Like many others, Reuben left the Republican Party toward the end of the nineteenth century because he believed it charted a path that veered too far from its initial guiding principles and, in this process, sold itself out in the name of greed. Other people did not understand that Reuben repeatedly changed his affiliations in a vain attempt to find a political party that would remain true to his convictions.[141]

In an effort to retain his status as an important man in the community, Reuben usually "wore a military cape, which he had made himself[,] . . . lined with red flannel[,] . . . [and] a brocaded velvet vest." He spent much of his time in his last years building furniture. For this reason, some people unjustly accused him of being "more woodworker than lawyer."[142]

While Reuben was away in the army, Elizabeth had continued to allow Riley to indulge his boyhood interests. By the time Reuben returned, he was a dreamy, undisciplined teenager who was extremely close to his mother temperamentally and emotionally. Reuben felt it was high time that Riley put away his childish things and learn how to become a man.

In Reuben's mind, his own life stood as an example of how a man should conduct himself, even if that meant self-sacrifice; and he expected no less from his sons. In an 1895 interview, Riley related an incident about skipping school to avoid making a recitation that he thought might make him cry. When his father asked why he had not been in school, Riley told him the truth, saying, "Father, I didn't want the boys to laugh at me, and I knew it would make me cry." Reuben did not like this answer and responded, "Well, I'll see if I can't make you cry." He then picked up a switch and gave his son one of the best whippings he had ever had.[143] Expressions of emotion associated with feminine qualities were not acceptable from men. Boys were taught to suppress feelings of despair, grief, fear, or pain. To make them better family providers, parents encouraged their sons to be competitive and aggressive. In this instance, Reuben thought that his son's actions had been babyish and unmanly. Therefore, he gave him a thrashing because he wanted him to become tougher and more disciplined. According to Riley, his father could "be as awfully grim and pitiless . . . [as he could] be natively tender and compassionate." As a young boy, Riley felt that his father's actions were unjust in this situation; and it was a long time before he felt close to his father again.[144]

Later, Riley better understood Reuben's lack of sympathy and tried to

forgive him for his rigid ideas. He knew that his father could not fully under-
stand the situation: "He probably thought my answer was merely an excuse to
get out of school." Indeed, Reuben may have reacted to Riley's truancy in part
because it was not an isolated incident. One of his classmates reported that he
and Riley often skipped school together.[145]

Riley's habit of missing school was just one of the ways he did not meet his
father's expectations. Although he excelled in reading, he did not do well in
arithmetic or spelling. Riley said that he "never liked the blanked crooked
things called figures and . . . couldn't see the sense of working away at them."
Riley's failure in mathematics did not sit well with his father because Reuben
"thought that the boy who couldn't learn arithmetic wouldn't amount to any-
thing."[146] Middle-class parents hoped that their sons could learn the new job
skills necessary to succeed in an industrial economy. Reuben saw Riley's poor
performance as evidence that he would be unable to compete in the changing
nineteenth-century employment market.[147]

Riley always got along best with teachers who recognized his interests in
literature and art. The first of these was Rhoda Houghton Millikan, a widow
who moved to Greenfield with her two children from Vermont after her
husband died. She encouraged Riley's writing of verse and taught him to draw.
Her house became almost like a second home to Riley; and her children, Nellie
and Jesse, became his lifelong friends.[148] Although Millikan was a kind and
supportive teacher, Riley said that he owed the first gratitude of his heart and
soul to his last instructor, Lee O. Harris. He first met Harris when he was a
boarder in the home of his grandmother, Margaret Riley, and, during the Civil
War, Harris served as second lieutenant in the Fifth Indiana Cavalry under
Riley's father. Riley referred to Harris as "a man of many gifts, a profound lover
of literature and a modest producer in story and in song, in history, and even in
romance and drama, although his life-effort was given first of all to educa-
tion."[149]

Riley had much affection for Harris. However, their first encounters were
not positive. After a period of "brief warfare" between teacher and pupil, Harris
decided it was pointless to force Riley to study subjects for which he had no
affinity, especially arithmetic: "I did not press him to study the uncongenial
things. He never did any good at mathematics, and I did not give him any more
of it than I could help."[150]

Early on in this relationship, Harris also discovered Riley's habit of reading
sensational stories hidden between the covers of his textbooks and managed to
divert him "from the yellow-back novel to good literature . . . he [Harris]
informed me gently but firmly that since I was so persistent in secretly reading
novels during school hours he would insist upon his right to choose the novels
I should read, whereupon the 'Beadle' and 'Munro' dime novels were discarded

for such genuine masterpieces of fiction as those of Washington Irving, Cooper, Dickens, Thackeray, and Scott." Thus, Harris introduced Riley to his first serious study of literature.[151]

After pointing Riley in the right direction, Harris said he "just turned him loose where he could find grazing to suit him." Riley spent his last year in school with Harris in the study of rhetoric. He said that he did not study "figures of speech, style, [and] punctuation ... so much as he "was delving into the beauties of literature found in . . . quotations." Riley's studies spilled into the hours outside school. He used to go out to Harris's house in the country and spend days with him discussing the books he read and the poetry he wrote.

Harris became more than just a teacher to Riley. Riley identified him as the first of his "literary friends and inspirers"; and, after Riley had gained success, Harris was extremely proud of the influence he had on Riley's development as a poet. His eyes lit up when he spoke of "Jim," and his voice thrilled with pride as he said, "The pupil has long outgrown his teacher."[152]

Harris first taught Riley in a church located just south of the railroad track. In January 1870, a public school building finally opened in Greenfield. It was an elegant two-story brick building that could accommodate nine teachers and five hundred students. During the school's first term, Lee O. Harris was one of the teachers, and Riley was one of 236 students enrolled. Riley was already twenty, and this school term would be his last. In rural areas where the demands of farm labor often took older teenagers out of the classroom for lengthy periods, Riley's advanced age was not so unusual. However, many of the boys with whom he had grown up had already engaged themselves in various professions. For the week of 18 February, Riley ranked seventh in his class. He received good marks in reading and rhetoric, and his performance in mathematics was passable. The following week he bettered his scores in mathematics, winning himself a place on the school's honor roll.[153]

Although Riley seemed to apply himself during this last term, his education was sporadic and remained at best uneven and mediocre. In 1892, the *Indianapolis Journal* informed the public that Riley knew nothing at all of mathematics, geography, and science. He could not "formally know a nominative from an objective"; yet he moved in circles among America's foremost literary figures and belonged "to the intellectual classes."[154] Ironically, many critics later considered his lack of formal education a blessing. One newspaper reporter proclaimed that this was, in fact, "the true secret of . . . [his] fame":

> his poetic vision has fortunately not been obscured by any fog nor cloud from scholastic attainment, although he is truly a finished scholar. Perhaps it would have ruined Riley to be or become a college student. His mind is one of the most highly sensitive organs of this century, and its utility and beauty of action have depended upon its freedom from restraint, and the unobscured

use of his native facilities. The barrenness of the past has been largely attrib-
utable to the fact that therein men refused to apply their minds directly to the
problem itself, going rather by the way of some stupid book.[155]

People romanticized Riley as a pupil of nature and the great outdoors, whose
works were informed only by his own native intelligence and untainted by the
artificial influences of the urban intellectual. His poetry celebrated the essence
of the Jeffersonian, agrarian ideal; and, as a consequence, Riley himself became
a symbol of all its perceived virtues.

Henry Beers saw Riley's refusal to conform to conventional standards of
male, adult behavior as a primary reason for his success as a poet: "Riley fol-
lowed the bent of his genius and gave himself just the kind of training to do his
work. He never had any regular education, adopted no trade or profession,
never married and had children, but kept himself free from set tasks and from
those responsibilities which distract the poet's soul." Beers identified the "tru-
ant" as Riley's muse, and he described the poet as "a runaway boy who kept the
heart of a boy into manhood and old age."[156]

As Riley grew from adolescence into adulthood, it was this refusal to
mature that so alarmed his father. After the Civil War, Reuben could no longer
afford to hire domestic labor. Many of the outside chores around the house and
the farm now fell to his sons. During his teen years, Riley sometimes refused to
do the work that his father asked him to do. After one such incident, Reuben
remarked to his wife in despair, "I don't believe there is any hope for that boy!"
To which Elizabeth responded, "Oh, Jimmie will come out all right." Despite
Elizabeth's reassurances, Reuben often became so exasperated with Riley that
he told him over and over again that the rest of the family would probably have
to support him through adulthood.[157]

Riley spent most of his life trying to prove himself to his father, but never
felt that he succeeded. The poet believed that his father always lacked his own
finer sensibilities and perceptions about the nature of the human heart. In 1895,
he expressed his disappointment in his father's inability to recognize his accom-
plishments: "The people of Indianapolis made a good deal of me, and now and
then rumors of my reputation reached the little country town where my father
was living. He couldn't see what the people saw in those things of mine to be
worth so much money, and he finally gave up trying to understand it."[158]

As long as she was alive, Riley's mother defended and comforted Riley. She
always understood his character and his temperament. Unfortunately, Eliza-
beth died suddenly from chronic heart disease in August 1870, when Riley was
twenty. Her death only served to deepen the resentment Riley felt toward his
father. "Riley would repeat with heartbreaking pathos the story of his mother's
poverty[,] her decline and death."[159] Riley blamed his father for the deteriora-

tion of Elizabeth's health after he lost the homestead on the National Road. He related how the family moved from house to house, each one successively more squalid, until finally the entire family was forced to move in with Riley's grandmother. Margaret Riley did not welcome Reuben and his family into her home. She saw their presence as an "invasion." "Riley remembered with resentment how his mother died there[,] in that inhospitable place[,] and how she was buried in a [pauper's] shroud."[160]

Following his mother's death, Riley always looked back nostalgically on that time in his childhood when his family was all together under the roof of that eight-room, frame house on the National Road. For Riley, it was a time of "boundless happiness"—a time when his mother was always there to comfort and support him, a time when he felt proud of his father and felt he still had his approval, and a time when he was surrounded by his brothers and sisters in a "wee world all their own."[161]

Riley believed that he had been happiest in this *"Child-World,"* and he idealized it as an earthly paradise:

> The Child-World—long and long since lost to view—
> A Fairy Paradise!—
> How always fair it was and fresh and new—
> How every affluent hour heaped heart and eyes
> With treasures of surprise! [. . .]
>
> O Child-World: After this world—just as when
> I found you first sufficed
> My soulmost need—if I found you again,
> With all my childish dream so realized,
> I should not be surprised.[162]

Riley forever regretted that his *"Child-World"* had been snatched away from him so cruelly by the events of war, poverty, and death—events which were responsible for his loss of innocence. Such longings for the days of one's childhood are certainly not unusual; however, as Beers pointed out, Riley continued to be able to escape back into the childhood of his imagination. Unlike many adults, he managed to retain enough of "the heart of a boy" so that he always understood the "fancies of . . . childhood." He always knew how to talk to children, to write about the things they loved, and to portray them in his poems.[163]

In Search of a Voice

TWO

In the summer of 1893, Hamlin Garland, on assignment for *McClure's Maga-zine*, visited James Whitcomb Riley at his childhood home in Greenfield. Riley, who was "very much in vogue," had just bought back the house, long "in alien hands[,] . . . because of old-time associations." Garland found him sitting comfortably on the porch.[1]

By this time, Greenfield was a prosperous agricultural town. However, Garland saw it as "the most unpromising field for literature, especially for poetry": "It has no hills, and no river nor lake. Nothing but vast and radiant sky, and blue vistas of fields between noble trees." Greenfield, like other small towns, had its "customary main street with stores fronting upon it; the usual small shops, and also its bar-rooms, swarming with loungers." The old courthouse had been replaced by one of more recent construction. "A grim and bare building," it was nonetheless the most prominent structure in town.[2]

To Garland, life in Greenfield appeared "slow-moving, purposeless, and uninteresting"; yet he knew that it was this place, more than any other, that inspired Riley's poems. Garland compared Riley with Robert Burns: he made the unremarkable landscape of central Indiana seem lovely and wonderful in the same way that Burns had revealed the beauty of the gray moors and craggy hills of Scotland. "[T]o study both the poet and his material," Garland was glad to find Riley "in the midst of his native surroundings."[3] Seeing Riley in this setting, it was hard to imagine him anywhere else.

By this time in his career, Riley knew how to shape his public image. Garland had asked to see Riley in Greenfield, and Riley was happy to oblige. He knew that his hometown offered him the best environment in which to present himself as a simple, unassuming man. Riley actively molded his own public persona to conform to his ideal of a homespun philosopher who was comfortable with nature and ordinary people. By using dialect expressions common to his fictional characters in his everyday conversations, he blurred the distinctions between his life and his poetry. When Garland complimented Riley by saying that his lack of formal education had worked "out beautifully for the glory of Indiana and Western literature," Riley responded with a sly grin: "I don't take no credit for my ignorance. Jest born thataway." In a moment, he added, "My work did itself." In this instance, Riley not only used dialect but discounted his own efforts in creating his work. He wanted his poems to seem the product of artless and spontaneous expression inspired directly from God.[4]

Riley's true personality was much more complex. Far from a country bumpkin, he was a wealthy man who had grown in sophistication over the years. However, Riley promoted himself as a man of the people because he understood that this was much of the secret to his popularity.

By shaping his public image, Riley began to create myths about himself that eventually took on a life of their own. In effect, he became an accomplice in the distortion of facts about certain aspects of his own life history. While many admired his seemingly unpretentious manner and homely demeanor, some critics only saw an intellectual simpleton whom they could not take seriously.[5]

Even while he was still alive, writers already misconstrued some aspects of Riley's life and career. They especially misled the public about his activities during much of the 1870s, when Riley was still in his youth. So much misinformation appeared that one friend who knew him well at this time once commented: "I have read so many different stories of his early life and can say I never read but one that was any ways near right." Some journalists of the time had a tendency to sensationalize certain details of Riley's life through this period to make them seem even more romantic and picaresque than they really were. In his interview with Garland, Riley complained about these misconceptions and wanted the resulting article in *McClure's* to be a forum in which to dispel the misinformation that had arisen in other pieces in the press.[6]

Yet Riley remained rather reticent about his young adulthood and often bent the truth about his early career to fit his respectable image. Although he claimed to be setting the record straight in this interview, Riley was not entirely truthful about his past.[7] The poet who became known for his honesty, sincerity, and innocence, through much of the 1870s, was a huckster who used his many talents in a number of confidence games to sell goods and services. The years he spent engaged in this world of sideshow barkers and itinerant peddlers did not jibe with the reputation he later worked hard to develop. During this time in his youth he skirted the margins of lawlessness and, through his experiences on the road with charlatans and mountebanks, realized that there was great opportunity for self-transformation in a society that was becoming increasingly mobile and anonymous. He used what he learned to influence how people perceived him. As a consequence, the real Riley often got lost behind the guises he chose to project.

When he dropped out of school in the spring of 1870, Riley was far from choosing a lifelong career. Even worse, he had gained a reputation for capricious behavior and bad habits. The parents of some of his friends perceived him to be a dangerous influence and a neighborhood ne'er-do-well. One of his comrades, Milt Crowell, was even forbidden to correspond with him:

> Now, Milt, as friends, there can be nothing improper in corresponding, but when, for this pleasure, we outstep a father's law, is it not wrong? Your father forbid your associating with me. Well, with his understanding of my character, he did what was right, in fact, he wouldn't do a father's duty if he did not—well, as long as he thinks me a mean boy, just so long, you must abide his law ... —sometime, maybe, I can show him my real character—but—as it now is do you think yo[u] do right in writing to me? We shouldn't do it, I only wish this barrier *was* removed, for nothing would give me greater pleasure than a proper right to correspond with you.[8]

Riley understood why Crowell's father thought that he was not an appropriate friend and correspondent for his son, but also wanted the opportunity to prove him wrong.

Many Greenfield residents, including his father, believed that Riley would never possess the discipline necessary to be successful at anything. Indeed, they had reason to think he was shiftless, for he disliked manual labor and often tended toward laziness. His interest in poetry and art seemed frivolous. In addition, Riley admitted that he could be wild and dissipated. At times, he drank so much that even some of his friends who often imbibed with him feared that he would injure his health.[9]

As soon as he quit school, he went to work as a shoe clerk in the shop of his old friend Tom Snow. However, the job lasted only a few weeks because Snow contracted tetanus and died suddenly. Following Snow's death, Riley painted houses in and around Greenfield; but he did not work very hard at it. At the end of May 1870, one of his friends reported that he was not doing "an extensive business."[10]

Without any true purpose or direction, Riley had few places to turn for emotional support and consolation, especially after his mother died in August 1870. Elizabeth Riley had understood him as no one else could. She had also shown confidence in his ability to succeed when few other people did. Without her, Riley felt lost. He drank whiskey in an effort to escape from his own despair. In his youth, he developed a drinking problem which would remain with him for life. One of the poems he wrote shortly following her death, "I Am Sitting Now and Sighing," reflects his deep state of grief and depression:

> I am sitting now and sighing,
> For I know my eyes are lieing [*sic*]
> With the tears that they are crying.
>
> Horrid visions I am seeing,
> Ghastly phantoms that are freeing
> The connections of my being . . . .
>
> And within my brain is wheeling
> Tortures of a nameless feeling
> Past the art and power of healing.
>
> Oh the sorrow and the sadness
> That usurps the place of gladness,
> Driving all my thoughts to madness.
>
> Ruined mind and brainless passion—
> Wearied weapons that are clashin'
> 'Gainst the shield of modern Fashion.'[11]

None of Elizabeth Riley's children received much comfort in their grief from their father. All five of them had been very dependent on Elizabeth and were deeply affected by her sudden demise. Mary, the youngest, was only six years old at the time; and even the eldest, John, who at first had trouble expressing his sorrow, wept uncontrollably following the funeral. The mood within the household was grim, and the family's financial situation remained poor. Riley said that sometimes water and crackers were all they had for dinner.[12]

Although Reuben prepared the family's meals and Riley's brother, Hum, washed the dishes, Elva May, who had not yet reached the age of sixteen, took over most housekeeping duties. Despondent and grief-stricken, Riley's sister continued to "'gaze in vacancy' the greater part of the time" even months after Elizabeth died; but Reuben, who seemed preoccupied with his economic problems and generally overwhelmed by the overall responsibilities of running his household, refused to bring in anyone to help her. Riley complained to his brother John, who had managed to escape to Indianapolis where he found a job: "John, I tell you, our noble House [*sic*] is on the wane—everything is going—going—the same old carelessness marks our 'progress' 'Till I well could weep' That bread should be so dear And flesh and blood so *cheap*. Father, *I guess* don't want to get, or *keep* a girl to assist May—oh no!"

At this point in his letter to John, Riley quoted his father. Reuben's statements were hurtful, and it appeared to Riley that he resented performing his duties as a parent: "Economy, you know and you folks at home expecting me composed of money &c. . . . and I don't know what would have become of you folks, if it had been *me* instead of poor Ma, who died." Riley sarcastically told his brother that his father's attitude was "enough to make home" a "fairy land" that he longed to see. He tried to put on a brave face to improve his mood but failed to feel any better: "I've been laughing forced laughs and dancing forced jigs, till I'm about gone up—they don't appear to take—it will take a *deeper* trick—'simulating' happiness, to be a success."[13]

Finding the circumstances unbearable, Riley moved to Rushville, Indiana, when house painting season ended in November 1870. Here, Riley became a Bible salesman. When he arrived, he had to find living accommodations, becoming one of an increasing number of young single men who lived outside the boundaries of family life. As traditional paternal systems of labor disappeared during the nineteenth century, living and working arrangements changed; and increasingly the workplace and the home became separate realms. Employers no longer provided shelter to their apprentices and other workers. Even in small towns such as Rushville, boardinghouses were established to function as places of residence to a transitory population of people who left their family homes behind in search of employment.

While he was in Rushville, Riley lived in a boardinghouse above a dressmaker's shop. He described his new abode as being "very pleasant[,] . . . just a perfect Home almost."[14] As this statement suggests, such boarding establishments provided more than just shelter. The system of relationships developed among residents substituted for those they experienced within their families. Inhabitants of boardinghouses became integrated into a household by sharing maintenance responsibilities and meals.

At the same time, living in a boardinghouse was different from what Riley had been accustomed to in Greenfield. He had always been very close to Elizabeth Riley and had never before been away from home for an extended period. Reuben complained that his wife had made his second son too sensitive and too soft. In contrast, Riley's experiences in Rushville initiated him into a free-wheeling male culture that encouraged competitiveness and aggressive-ness. Asserting his independence, he had a "first-class time" without fear of the scrutiny of parental authority.[15] For the next several years, this rough kind of lifestyle kept him on the fringes of society and the law.

In the few letters that still exist from this time, it appears as if Riley paid much more attention to the eligible young ladies of Rushville than he did to selling Bibles door to door. Living above a dressmaker's shop gave him ample opportunity to observe most of the young women who lived in town. He stated that the shop attracted a "jolly crowd of girls" and that he and his friends patronized the store when they had nothing else to do. They often encountered these young women in situations that would have been considered too familiar for young bachelors by most of Victorian society:

> There are a great many good-looking girls here only they don't like to be looked at—you ought to see 'em get out of the front room whenever they see Harry or I come in at the gate, occasionally, however we find them with their hair ornamented with curl-papers or tins. . . . I've found out that girls look better *after* their hair is crooked than they do *before*.[16]

While Riley was in Rushville, he was uncommunicative with his father. In mid-December, Reuben wrote a letter to his son. He had become quite con-cerned about Riley and had heard nothing about his Christmas plans. This letter shows that Reuben had neither confidence in Riley's bookselling enter-prise nor in his choice of companions and business associates:

> My Dear Boy:
> I have been patiently waiting a letter from you and have received none. Scarcely an hour passes by without thinking of you and wondering how you are getting along? How you are doing? How you are managing? What kind of man you are with? and wishing I could have seen him. Thinking how much more experiences I have had in the world than you. How all important to you that you associate with none but those of good character, that you be self reliant and aim high, and suffer no stain to attach to your character. And how I would like to counsel and advise with you. Please write me fully and confidently, and all assistance reasonably in my power I will render. We are all well, and been anxiously looking and waiting for you home. Some how I don't think your book business a paying institution but may be mistaken. Hope I am, and would like to know more about it, and the man who is with you? Don't fail to write immediately.[17]

Reuben's estimation of Riley's abilities as a Bible salesman proved accurate. However, nothing is known about this mysterious "man" who was with him in Rushville. No correspondence remains to elucidate how or with whom Riley had become involved in the Bible-selling business, though Reuben's letter seems to indicate that a man had recruited Riley while he was visiting Greenfield. Despite this, Riley did not refer to this person or his work at all in the existing letters from this period. He did spend time with two male friends, Shorty and Harry, whom he only mentioned in passing. Both of these men may have been engaged in the Bible selling business with Riley, but this is not clear.[18]

Later, Riley rarely mentioned that he had ever participated in such an endeavor. In fact, he usually glossed over his time in Rushville entirely. In all fairness, his stay there was so short that Riley may have considered it not worth talking about. He left Greenfield in the fall of 1870 and returned back home during the first part of 1871. Later, referring to this part of his life, Riley said, with a touch of sarcasm: "It turned out that citizens of Rushville had all the Bibles they needed; they had not time to read those they had."[19]

As a poet, Riley preferred to focus instead on his first experiences as a writer: he had already begun "to write a little" as a boy in Greenfield. Although he "used to recite these efforts at little social gatherings," he was reluctant to take credit for his original poems until he saw how these small groups accepted them. He had "a vague idea that there was a prejudice against home talent in the poetic line." For this same reason, the first Riley poem to appear in print, "The Same Old Story," was published in the *Greenfield Commercial* under the pen name "Edryn." Riley borrowed "Edryn" from Alfred Tennyson, who had created a character with this name, a knight, in *Idylls of the King*. "The Same Old Story" came out in the *Commercial* in September 1870, only three weeks after Riley's mother died.[20]

During the early 1870s, Riley also tried his hand at acting. Between 1869 and 1876, he appeared in many of the plays and performed comic recitations in many of the programs of the Adelphian Dramatic Club in Greenfield.[21] Riley participated in these programs with pride and enthusiasm. In the spring of 1870, he wrote to his friend Milt Crowell about the relative high quality of one of the recent productions: "If you'll believe me, we met with splendid success. . . . The performance was received with *eclat*. . . . All the parts were well acted. . . . Our scenery was very passable."[22]

Riley's enthusiasm was understandable; the club gave him an outlet for his many artistic talents. He toyed with the idea of becoming a professional musician when he played his violin or the drums in the Adelphian's instrumental ensembles. He showed great versatility as a comedic actor and created scenery for theatrical productions:

> Riley could take any part with great adaptability, and when there was any scenery needed to fit the stage, he was called upon to exercise his ingenuity in that direction, which he would do in his free and easy way. He never lost his presence of mind while upon the stage, and if he forgot his lines, he would improvise with remarkable readiness what was infinitely better. The small boys also recognized his talent, for if he was not always billed for the play, they

would say, "Well I'm going home, I know there'll be nothing funny if Jim Riley ain't in it!"[23]

In April 1870, Riley portrayed "Troubled Tom" in a play called *The Child of Waterloo*, written by Riley's teacher, Lee O. Harris. Harris later claimed that he wrote the play "to give Riley an opportunity to display his talent as an actor." Riley's character was supposed to be the son of a blacksmith left on the battlefield of Waterloo. Riley "made the character so funny, made so much out of it, that he made it the star part of the play." Riley helped make *The Child of Waterloo* a great success for the Adelphians. It played five consecutive nights and cleared $500 in receipts.[24]

During his time as a member of the Adelphians, Riley was probably most remembered for his role in a play called *The Chimney Corner*. Although Riley was only in his early twenties, he was cast as a ninety-one-year-old named Solomon Probity. While studying for this part, Riley followed Greenfield's oldest resident, Johnny Rardin, around by the hour. He noted this man's every gesture and mannerism so that he would be convincing as an old man on stage. Riley reprised the role of old man Probity in 1878.[25]

Obviously, Riley was much more interested in acting than he ever had been in school or in the jobs he briefly held. During the summer of 1871, an acquaintance, Irvin Walker, tried to convince Riley to join him on the professional stage. Irvin had seen Riley perform, and he offered to get him a contract at a theater when he got a contract for himself. Walker advised Riley to send him programs from some of his best performances, along with newspaper clippings containing reviews of his work, if such materials existed. However, he also assured Riley that it made "no difference to the manager whether" he had ever seen a theater or not. The important thing, Walker claimed, was to "play the business . . . engage[d] for satisfactorily." Although Walker admitted that he did not know him as well as he might, he believed that Riley could probably pass as a professional comedian.[26]

Riley never took Walker up on his offer. From the text of a letter Irvin wrote to Riley, one can infer that Reuben did not approve:

> He [Walker's father] is just like *your father*, he will not be persuaded, and he knows about as much about the stage as I do about Hebrew. I attribute his dislike for the stage to his ignorance on the subject, and will not talk to him any more about it. He thinks neither male nor female ever appears on the stage without being dressed completely in *tights* with a hole cut in the *fork* to show their *asses*, and that they all dress together. Besides, he thinks a man can't be an actor without being a *whore-monger* and drunkard.[27]

This viewpoint was typical and pervasive for nineteenth-century Americans, who had inherited a prejudice against the theater from their Puritan ancestors. Although such attitudes were changing in Indiana as the population increased and religious intensity decreased, some forms of entertainment continued to be deemed "unclean." Theater "was believed to be corrupt for its origins, for the character of those attracted to its employ, for the people who regularly attended it as audience members, and for its very nature."[28]

The minister of the Methodist Church in Greenfield, where Riley served for a short time as temporary secretary and where he illustrated Bible lessons on a chalkboard for children, agreed wholeheartedly. In 1875, Riley dropped out of the church's membership class because he discovered that the minister disapproved of the Adelphians' plays. Although not irreligious, Riley grew intolerant of church orthodoxy and never fully joined any religious congregation following this experience: "I will say here, that there may be no misunderstanding, that I have my convictions and ideas of the gospel of our divine Teacher, and do not desire to intrude them upon others." When asked where he worshiped, he often replied, "In the woods."[29]

Following his return home from Rushville, Riley began his next career. His father apprenticed him, for $100, to John Keefer, a local sign painter who had a workshop near the railroad tracks. Keefer was the father of Riley's boyhood friend, Almon, whom Riley described in *A Child-World*. Riley received a thorough training in all aspects of ornamental painting from Keefer. He studied the finer points of house painting, graining, sign writing, and crayon work. He even took a brief course in landscape painting. Keefer gave his apprentices instruction and then he took them out into the field to put into practice what they had learned.[30]

In his conversations with Hamlin Garland, Riley described Keefer as "an old Dutchman . . . who was an artist in his way." Riley stated that he had a "natural faculty for drawing" and implied that he quickly surpassed his master: "It's rather curious, but I hadn't been with the old fellow [Keefer] more than a week before I went to him and asked him why he didn't make his own letters. I couldn't see why he copied from the same old forms all the time. I hated to copy anything." Riley, therefore, showed great promise in this trade. When he finished his apprenticeship, he set up his own painting workshop above a drugstore.[31]

Although he demonstrated a natural talent for sign painting, Riley later denied he had ever been that interested in it: "I had a trade, but it was hardly what I wanted to do always." He claimed that he "was not very much in love with it" because he wished to give the impression that he had always been willing to sacrifice everything to become a poet.[32] However, when he was starting out in the early 1870s, the choice between writing and sign painting was not so clear. Moreover, Riley applied his talent for rhyming in the signs he painted by incorporating his own ingenious advertising jingles into them.

At the same time, Riley did not abandon writing more serious poems. He worked on them continually at home and in his paint shop; and, during the winter months when the weather did not permit him to work outside painting signs, Riley had much time to perfect his writing skills. After being published in the local papers in Greenfield, Riley decided to try to his luck with his poems in Indianapolis. At the beginning of 1872, he started to send poems to his brother, John, who acted as his agent. Riley always wrote in pencil on scraps of paper. His spelling and grammar were terrible. John corrected Riley's poems and copied them over before he took them to the editors of the Indianapolis newspapers. The first of these poems, "Man's Devotion," appeared in the *Indianapolis Saturday Mirror* on 30 March 1872. Riley wrote under the pseudonym "Jay Whit," which the *Mirror* mistook for "Jay White."[33]

This poem was the first of many of Riley's works the *Mirror* published during spring 1872; and, as the paper continued to accept them, Riley's confidence grew. By May of that same year, he had written a poem he thought so good that he told John he would only agree to have it published if an editor were willing to put it on a newspaper's front page: "If you *can't* get this on the *front page*—don't put it in—for *I* consider it *the best thing* I have ever written and I want to see it occupy a *front seat*,—or we'll let it *stand* till one can be procured."[34]

Although the *Mirror* promptly took this poem, entitled "A Ballad," and printed it on the front page as he wished, Riley was deeply disappointed by the fact that it appeared with changes from the text of his original manuscript. These changes completely altered the poem's style: "John, all the little articles, pronouns, etc. that have become changed, *were chief characteristics of ballad style:* I refer you to *any ballad* of Longfellow's, or any good poet's—It makes it simple, plain and natural, and I wouldn't have had it changed for *anything*, in that particular, excepting those *ands*—you were right *there*—I do not know whether you or the printer changed the other—I regret *that* more than anything else. It hurts me more that the poem was my favorite, and I had 'built an airy castle for it!'"[35]

This letter, as well as the others that he wrote to his brother during this period, shows that Riley already took his poetry very seriously. He studied the style, tone, rhyme, and measure of poets such as Longfellow and attempted to apply what he learned to his own work. As his skill increased, his poetry included increasingly difficult rhyme and measure. At the same time, he stated that he "avoided everything overdrawn and tried to make . . . characters all natural—in language and everything."[36]

As summer approached, Riley again devoted more time to sign painting. The opportunity to create original advertising held great allure for him because of the money it brought him, giving him a chance to fill his coffers and satisfy his many creditors.[37] Riley managed his money badly. He usually spent it as fast as he earned it, and was constantly struggling to get out of debt. At the end of May, Riley wrote his brother that he had been working for three or four days creating advertising signs for the Farmer's Grocery in Greenfield. Although he was "pretty sore physically" as a result, he was feeling "quite the contrary *Mentaly* [*sic*]," because he could "remove a load of about 6$ from [my] mind."[38]

Riley was really writing his brother to tell him about a new job opportunity. He had received an offer from "a young advertiser," named Jim McClanahan, "to travel and do Medicine advertising and such." Riley stated that the job would be good for his health as he would be "in the open air all the time." Although the position would take him away from home, he would be able to come back to Greenfield often. At this time, Riley really did like advertising, especially where he had "a chance of making 5 and 6$ a day." He was so enthusiastic about his prospects that he exclaimed, "It won't be a great while before I show advertisers what advertising *is!*"[39]

McClanahan was an advance agent for Doctor Samuel B. McCrillus, a manufacturer of patent medicines from Anderson, Indiana. During the summers, McCrillus peddled a variety of nostrums, including a "Tonic Blood Purifier," "European Balsam," and "Oriental Liniment." McCrillus said that he compounded these "Standard Remedies" from "the best *Barks, Roots, and Gums.*" As a leaflet advertising his Blood Purifier demonstrates, McCrillus claimed that his elixirs were magical cure-alls:

> McCrillus' TONIC BLOOD PURIFIER . . . can be taken under all circumstances; and by the most delicate. . . . it has been used for *Bilious Complaints,* and *Impurities of the Blood,* it cures *Bilious* and *Intermittent Fevers, Chills* and *Fever, Scrofula, Sick Headache, Dizziness, Weakness, Loss of Appetite, Restlessness, Jaundice, Dyspepsia, Constipation, Mental Depression, Etc.* And to express in a few words, it is a *most Powerful Tonic, Alterative and Slight Purgative.* It removes the morbid secretions of the *Liver* and *Spleen,* and unlike any other *Blood Purifier* it acts directly upon the *Kidneys.* Thus giving tone and vigor to the system.[40]

According to McCrillus, Riley approached him. McCrillus thought that Riley showed talent and was interested in offering him a position, but he was concerned that Reuben Riley might not allow his son to leave home. Before leaving Greenfield in the middle of June, McCrillus went to Reuben's office to ask if Riley could accompany him on the road. Reuben supposedly responded, "Yes, take the boy, if you can do something with him."[41]

Conditions at home had apparently not improved much since Riley had written to his brother John about the sorry state of family affairs almost one year earlier. Reuben continued to be disappointed in Riley's irresponsible behavior and his inability to contribute to the household income. Yet, Reuben himself was still struggling financially and sometimes left his children at home for days by themselves without any money.[42]

In mid-June 1872, Riley wrote to his brother that he was leaving for Anderson within the next few days. Although he was concerned that he would not have as much time for his writing, he believed that an advertising career held a brighter economic future for him: "I go to Anderson this week and go to work. I expect it will knock my writing in the head—unless this last should wake the literary world to a sense of my merit. I think tho' I can make more money Advertising."

In this letter, he identified himself as a "Painter Poet" for the first time.[43] The appellation caught on quickly and gave Riley some local notoriety. Shortly after moving to Anderson, one of the town's newspapers published an article describing him in this fashion. Riley would characterize himself as a "Painter Poet" until the late 1870s.[44] "Painter" came first in this description because this was the principal way in which he earned his living. He continued to write and recite poems. He also continued to contribute his work to newspapers; but, at this point in his career, his more serious literary endeavors did not help to pay his bills.

Riley spent the first few weeks in McCrillus's employ getting acquainted with Anderson, which became his second home during the next several years. By mid-July 1872, Riley began his tour through the state peddling "Doc's" remedies. He played a number of roles in McCrillus's entourage. As advance man and all-round assistant, he designed trademarks for the medicines, painted ads for them on farmers' barns, wrote jingles to promote sales, and attracted potential customers by telling stories and singing while he played the guitar.[45]

Riley proved very successful as a minstrel and storyteller in the sideshow acts he helped to create. In essence, his childhood dreams came alive as he became part of this subculture of itinerants that included real circus performers, puppeteers, carnival managers, and peddlers. Riley's travels away from Greenfield meant a chance for adventure, an escape from the disapproving eye of his father and his hometown neighbors, and even opportunities to transform his own identity.

Entrepreneurs like McCrillus understood how useful entertainers were to help lure in purchasers of the products they wished to sell; and, in his employ, Riley learned "that there were no sharp boundaries between salesmanship and other forms of performance." McCrillus, who forwarded himself as a doctor, was a charlatan; and, in his association with him, Riley became a huckster and mountebank who was willing to use chicanery to attract notice and make money.[46] The knowledge he gained as he worked in patent medicine shows later influenced his work as poet and performer and helped him become a master of self-promotion.

McCrillus's trips away from Anderson usually lasted two weeks and covered a distance of about two hundred miles. During July and August 1872, the company visited Middletown, Hagerstown, and Cambridge City along the White River. Later, the troupe traveled northwest through Alexandria, Elwood, Kokomo, Peru, and Wabash. By November, Riley had grown accustomed to "rambling '*North and South and West and East.*'" He had traveled so much that he told his brother that he had almost forgotten what Greenfield was like; and, when he did go there, he treated it just as he did any other place: "I'm forgetting home almost, but when I do go there it seems like a strange town, and I catch myself making mental calculations of the probable amount of *work* we'll do there—and they're always *small.*"[47] The experiences he accumulated as he visited towns and small hamlets throughout the state inspired such poems as "Regardin' Terry Hut":

> Sence I tuk holt o' Gibbses' Churn
> And be'n a-handlin' the concern,
> I've traveled round the grand old State
> Of Indiany, lots, o' late!—
> I've canvassed Crawferdsville and sweat
> Around the town o' Lafayette;
> I've saw a many a County-seat
> I *ust* to think was hard to beat:
> At constant dreenage and expense
> I've worked Greencastle and Vincennes—
> Drapped out o' Putnam into Clay,
> Owen, and on down thataway
> Plum into Knox, on the back-trac
> Fer home ag'in—and I'm glad I'm back!"[48]

This poem reflected the unprecedented mobility of nineteenth-century society. With improved roads and modes of transportation, the market spread beyond local boundaries. Peddlers and salesmen of all kinds of wares, such as the one who handled "Gibbses' Churn" in Riley's poem, even brought the market to the margins of the settled countryside. As the market expanded, relationships between buyers and sellers grew increasingly distant and were characterized by anonymity and mistrust. In this new environment, merchants of goods and services had to rely more and more on the manipulation of appearances to be successful.[49]

Although peddlers sold a wide variety of goods in rural America during the mid-nineteenth century, elixirs and patent medicines brought in larger profits than anything else. The public bought huge amounts of these products, manufactured by men such as McCrillus. Some patent medicine companies were exceedingly prosperous, becoming "the earliest and most successful national advertisers, the biggest spenders, [and] the best clients for the advertising agencies that began to form in the 1860s and 1870s." Their enormous success can be explained by constant demand, low capital investment, and a largely incompetent medical profession. However, the populace's persisting beliefs in magic also played an important role in the popularity of these products.[50]

These beliefs in magic were not confined to any one class, ethnic background, or region in the United States. The example of Riley's own family demonstrates that even Protestant, middle-class households were not immune to these ideas. Riley and his siblings acquired beliefs about magic, mysticism, and the supernatural from their mother in childhood. Riley had also been fascinated by the mysticism of the orient depicted in such stories as *The Arabian Nights*. He understood that applying images associated with mysteries of the exotic and the unknown in his advertising for patent medicines created illusions that promoted sales. Riley created an exotic and sensual image for McCrillus's elixirs and made them appear to have magical properties.[51]

For example, one sign Riley painted advertising the doctor's "Tonic Blood Purifier" depicted a young woman wearing a loosely fitting robe that exposed one bare breast. With her arms folded over her head, part of her hair and her face are obstructed from view. The young woman is enigmatic. Her origins and her social position are ambiguous. She looks as if she could have been lifted out of a classical, history genre painting set in an exotic, oriental environment. Such oriental influences evoked prurient Victorian fantasies about the mysterious East. Surrounded by rich folds of red drapery that form a proscenium arch in the painting, this woman could also be an actress on the stage; yet she is dressed for her boudoir. Actresses were often associated with the demimonde of courtesans and prostitutes. Riley's painting suggested that McCrillus's tonic held the promise of entrance into a world of forbidden pleasures and the possibility of a magical and dramatic metamorphosis of the self. He portrayed McCrillus's elixirs as magical potions that would enable his audiences to transcend their own physical and emotional problems, a tactic common among advertisers at that time. McCrillus used Riley's illustration for bottle labels and in his printed advertising circulars.[52]

Besides advertising for McCrillus, Riley and McClanahan found extra jobs painting signs for local stores and other small enterprises. In fact, the two men worked together as sign painters in and out of McCrillus's employ for much of 1872 and 1873. One of the tricks that Riley and McClanahan used once to get clients became almost legendary. While visiting Peru, Indiana, the two men came up with a new idea to attract business. In the tradition of hucksters both in America and Europe, Riley and McClanahan "mingled entertainment and moneymaking, provoking an ambiguous response of titillation, laughter and suspicion."[53] On this occasion, Riley decided to pose as a blind sign painter. In his interview with Garland, Riley described how the scenario worked:

> One day we were in a small town. . . , and a great crowd [was] watching us in breathless wonder and curiosity; and one of our party [McClanahan] said: "Riley, let me introduce you as a blind sign-painter." So just for mischief I put on a crazy look in the eyes and pretended to be blind. They led me carefully to the ladder, and handed me my brush and paints. It was great fun. I'd hear them saying as I worked, "That feller ain't blind." "Yes, he is, see his eyes." "No, he ain't, I tell you, he's playin' off." "I tell you he *is* blind. Didn't you see him fall over a box there and spill all his paints?"[54]

Rumors about the blind painter spread quickly through the little town, and local entrepreneurs were eager to hire him. While Riley hid nearby on a secluded riverbank, McClanahan procured work contracts. As the story goes, the whole scenario had been performed so skillfully and ingeniously that the town's residents were not even upset when they discovered the ruse. Besides, Riley claimed that their actions were really quite harmless. As he pointed out, "It was like the tricks boys play at college. . . . We were . . . boys, and jokers, naturally enough, but not lawless." No matter how harmless the blind sign painter scheme might seem, Riley and McClanahan had discovered how successful such trickery could be. They continued to use deceptive tactics to con people out of their money.[55]

Many accounts later claimed that Riley had traveled all over the state as a blind sign painter, but as Riley put it: "I was a blind sign-painter one day, and forgot it the next."[56] However, people of the time latched onto this story and exaggerated it. The story was not only comical, it also fascinated people because it held the allure of disguise and subterfuge.

This one episode in Riley's life not only revealed possibilities for adventure but also reflected the potential for self transformation. As society became more anonymous and more mobile, ideas about personal identity became more fluid. In this story, Riley was a carefree rogue who could enter a town and fabricate an entirely new identity for himself. Riley demonstrated an exciting prospect. He showed people that they could reinvent themselves over and over again.[57]

Through their sign painting partnership, Riley and McClanahan made a fair amount of money as they toured through the state. However, Riley always ran through his earnings quickly and spent them foolishly. For example, on a trip to Wabash, he spent forty dollars on an overcoat, which represented a large proportion of the money he had earned painting signs there. After paying for the coat, he had only seven dollars left—"the latter . . . departed some two or three days" hence.[58]

Riley also continued in his lazy habits. At the end of August 1872, he extended a visit to his home in Greenfield. Although McClanahan wrote Riley almost daily urging him to come join him in some projects he was undertaking, Riley remained in Greenfield, working only sporadically. He believed he deserved a break having "worked hard all summer." He therefore put McClanahan off by telling him that he had obtained some sign painting jobs at home. This was indeed true; however, Riley admitted to his brother John that he was not working very hard.[59]

When he returned to Anderson at the end of October 1872, Riley had no money left. During the winter, McCrillus remained in Anderson manufacturing his medicines to replenish the supply that had been sold during the previous months, and Riley and McClanahan were left to shift for themselves. They, too, made Anderson the base for their operations. Having saved no money for the off-season, Riley told his brother he resembled a "'dead beat' [with] plenty of clothes but no money."[60]

He certainly made that kind of impression on his landlady and her family in Anderson. Riley lived in a boardinghouse owned by a Mrs. H. E. Whitmore. Mrs. Whitmore's daughter later described Riley as a "lazy young man who gave considerable attention to dress, provided some one would furnish him with clothing." Indeed, Riley sometimes wrote asking his brother John to send him a particular kind of shirt, coat, or tie from Indianapolis. Later, John Riley recalled: "Years ago, when Jim first began to write verses, he had an up-hill climb of it, and I was doing better financially tha[n] he. At that time, Jim would have been mighty glad to have had some of my pants to wear; now, I'd like some of Jim's."[61] As his interest in clothing would suggest, Riley was very concerned about his appearance. In his twenties, he did not yet wear glasses, and he grew a very large red mustache "that was the pride of his life." He spent a great deal of time curling it.[62]

By November 1872, Riley and McClanahan had accumulated thirty-five to forty dollars in debt. To escape their creditors, they went to Marion, Indiana, in search of work. They left Anderson without paying for their board, and Riley said that they "even had to borrow money to get out of there." He did not even have enough blankets to keep him warm at night during the time he and McClanahan spent in Marion at the beginning of that winter: "I didn't have enough covers on my bed, only a counterpane. I laid newspapers in between that and the sheet to keep out the cold." Bad weather was fast approaching, and the sign painting partners had little hope of earning more than what they needed to repay the money they owed their creditors in Anderson.[63]

This situation was certainly not unusual for Riley. Sometimes he had so little money he practically starved. Riley never paid some of the bills he incurred during this time. While they were in Marion, he and McClanahan stayed in "an old rat-trap"; and sometimes Riley was not sure how he would pay his next board bill. Luckily, when he returned to Anderson early in 1873, his landlady, Mrs. Whitmore, forgave Riley his delinquency in paying his rent because she liked his manner and desired his presence in her house.[64]

Riley was a jovial and well-behaved boarder. He got along well with the other guests. He was entertaining—always ready to pick up his guitar, if some one were willing to sing along with him. He composed amusing rhymes at the table. Although he was pleasant to have around, Mrs. Whitmore sometimes sternly scolded him for his indolence, hoping that he would go out and get more work so that he could pay her what he owed.[65]

Many people assume that Riley drank heavily during his sign painting days. At least for the time in which he was a resident in her mother's home, Whitmore's daughter claimed that stories about Riley's alcohol consumption were grossly exaggerated. She said that she rarely if ever saw him under the influence. This may very well have been true. He could indeed go for months at a time without consuming any alcohol.[66]

By 1873, Riley had become well acquainted with Anderson. In the spring, he wrote his impressions of the town in a letter to the editor of the *Mooresville Enterprise:*

> Anderson is a very hansome [*sic*] little city of about 5000 inhabitants,—good people, speaking generally, though, of course, "it takes all kinds of people," etc. Yet vice is not as rampant here as in days of whilom. It grows weaker every day; and religion and law, hand in hand, are fast driving it from the land. The Methodist Church is strong in power here; and noble, and energetic ministers and members are doing great and good work. The leading business men are principally workers in the church—as I believe they are in every thriving place.... If the city here has one flaw it is its Court House;—that looks really lost and out of place and uncomfortable, surrounded as it is with beautiful business blocks; and I sometimes think it is a pity it couldn't attend the "Old Settlers' meetings" that it might go farther back in reminiscences than the oldest inhabitant, and tell of the youthful prowess of the Indian Chief Anderson, for whom the town was named. I can almost fancy there are old-time war whoop echoes lurking in its musty, time-dimmed architecture.[67]

This description reflected many of the changes that were occurring throughout the state as a whole. In the 1870s, Indiana was in a period of transition. It was still primarily rural and agricultural; but it could no longer be considered part of the western frontier. Between 1850 and 1880, the number of people living in Indiana doubled. It also reached its peak in population relative to other states during this period.[68]

At the same time, the population of the state was shifting. When Riley was a young boy, Indiana's chief population centers were located in the south along the Ohio River. With the advent of the railroad, access to river transportation was no longer as critical for distributing finished goods and raw materials. People were moving northward toward the areas in and surrounding Indianapolis. The state capital was becoming the most important city in Indiana, not only politically but economically. By the time Riley wrote this letter, the central region of the state, including Madison County, was experiencing great population growth and had gained significantly in importance.

Urbanization accompanied these increases in population throughout the state. In the early 1870s, Anderson could not be described as a sparsely inhabited, frontier village. Instead, it had already become a "little city of about 5,000" residents. When Riley was born in 1849, the number of people living in towns with populations of over twenty-five hundred totaled less than 5 percent in Indiana. Although much of Indiana remained rural, its urban population had increased to almost 20 percent by 1880.[69]

The commercial development of Anderson also reflected the pressures of urbanization. The "time-dimmed architecture" of the Madison County courthouse contrasted sharply with the new and "beautiful business blocks" that had sprung up around it. Anderson was a civilized little city where the influences of religion and the law had reduced the amount of vice. Most of its citizens were God-fearing people who did "great and good" works.[70]

As he gave his impressions, Riley spoke with a certain wistfulness. With the rule of law and religion, some of the freedom of the frontier was lost. No one was old enough to remember Anderson's early days when Indians roamed the surrounding forests. Only the courthouse, now considered a blight on the landscape, reminded people of the past. The stories his father had told him when he was a child made him a true believer in the myth of the frontier. He already feared that the frontier spirit, which had instilled in Americans such bravery and resourcefulness, was in danger of disappearing.[71]

During January and February of 1873, Riley accumulated enough sign painting business in Anderson to last him until spring. Riley did much of this work in cooperation with McClanahan; and they continued to do some sign work for McCrillus as well. However, Riley and McClanahan did not plan to travel again with the old "doctor." Instead, they wanted to travel on their own through the state as general advertisers when the winter weather broke.[72]

Having enough contracts to get by for a while financially, Riley and McClanahan had time "to perfect . . . arrangements for a scathing summer season." They had their own business cards printed for "Riley & McClanahan Advertising Company," which contained the slogan, "Advertise with Paint on Barns and Fences—That's the Way." Riley believed that the future looked bright: "things are looking propitious, and I can't but feel that my wildest dreams will be realized."[73]

Riley had high hopes for his partnership with McClanahan, but this did not mean that he had given up on his writing. Riley wrote whenever inspired and whenever time allowed. One friend from his sign painting days remembered watching Riley compose his poems and recalled that "he always wrote on what he called tea paper with a pencil." In the middle of February 1873, Riley sent several verses to John in Indianapolis, who continued to act as his informal literary agent. He told his brother to use his judgment "in regard to their publication," but he directed him to send one poem, "Flirtation," to the New York *Graphic*.[74]

The *Graphic* was popular with designers at this time. Because they wanted people to associate them with this fashionable periodical, Riley and McClanahan changed the name of their business to "The Graphic Advertisers" when two other men, Will J. Ethell and Turner A. Wickersham, joined them in their advertising scheme. Riley never divulged how he and McClanahan met Ethell and Wickersham. However, he did say that they were "good fellows. All had nice homes and good people." Apparently he especially enjoyed the company of Ethell, whom he gave the nickname "The Smiler." Riley described Ethell as "a young erratic law student" who hailed from South Bend, Indiana. Riley and McClanahan probably met Wickersham in Anderson. Following his association with Riley, Wickersham continued in the sign painting business and moved for a short time to the Southeast. The original four members of the Graphic Advertisers were also joined briefly by other young men, most of whom were probably from Anderson, but not much else is known about them.[75]

Riley told Garland that all members of this "band of roving, roystering [*sic*] fellows" were "musicians as well as handy painters." They used to "capture" the towns they visited with their music: "One fellow could whistle like a nightingale, another sang like an angel, and another played the banjo. . . . [Riley] scuffled along with the violin and guitar." The Graphics also "dressed loud" to attract attention: "You could hear our clothes an incalculable distance. We had an idea it helped business." Riley "wore a tall, white hat and a pair of speckled pants and carried a small cane."[76]

Riley's dress went against post–Civil War fashion trends. At midcentury, men had chosen to wear flamboyant clothing; but, by the 1870s, with the rise of large corporations, the expansion of the middle classes, and the growth of government power, standard dress became more conservative: the forerunner to the modern business suit, which included a dark coat and plain white linen shirt. Therefore, in dress as in all else, Riley and his friends were expressing their rebellion against the conventions of society. Everything in the Graphics' presentation lent itself to a carnivalesque atmosphere.[77]

The company's "plan" involved painting advertising on every fence post and barn along every road leading into a town for "one firm of each kind of business in the town." In his conversations with Garland, Riley stated that he and his comrades "made a good thing at it." The Graphics, in essence, "sold" their signs by convincing the enterprises they approached that this type of advertising would set them apart from all other businesses providing the same kinds of goods or services in that particular commercial district. Later, an article in the *Indianapolis Journal* claimed that it had been the Graphics "who had introduced the system of large signs" to Indiana. As they traveled through the state, they plastered "advertisements over the entire side of buildings and in out-of-the-way places, or on impossible heights."[78]

Whether or not they had pioneered this practice, Riley and the other Graphics invaded the countryside with a new brand of commercialism by creating these large, outdoor signs. However, not everyone approved of their work. The Graphics sometimes angered farmers by painting on their property without their permission. Moreover, many people frowned on the transformation of barns and fence posts into public billboards. They believed that such signs desecrated the purity of the pastoral landscape. Although the crusade against billboards persists today, outdoor advertising was considered a normal part of modern business practice by the turn of the twentieth century.[79] While the Graphics roamed through Indiana, Riley said that they "had more fun than anybody." However, Riley suffered from bouts of homesickness. In a letter to his brother in August 1873, he said: "I tell you, sir, there are times when the cock-eyed monster 'Homesickness' knocks the tail-piece out o' my feelins'." Riley missed his father and his brothers and sisters; but he hesitated to go home because his father had remarried. Reuben Riley had taken Martha Lukens, a Quaker from Pendleton, Indiana, as his new bride in March 1873. Martha had been married before and had a daughter, Hannah, who also came to live in Reuben's Greenfield home. At the time Riley wrote this letter to John, he still had not gone home to meet his new relatives. However, he was doing his best to accustom himself to the idea of having a stepmother; and he wanted very much to like her: "Mother. It's going to be hard work for that to sound natural—I'm learning though—I talk about her considerable to Ethell—so much in fact that I am nearly enthusiastic—WELL I only hope she is what I fancy her."[80]

Although Riley did his best to prepare himself for his first meeting with his father's new wife, sign painting kept him far away from Greenfield for the rest of the summer and much of the fall. During this time, he and his friends concentrated their work in the northern part of the state, taking assignments in Warsaw, Plymouth, Mishawaka, and South Bend.[81]

In the towns they visited, Riley apparently could make quite an impression: "I've been having a mighty fine time at South Bend for five weeks—a continued round of social enjoyment.…I've been ranking high among the South Benders quite a celebrity for being smart and *eccentric.*" By this time, he had become a cunning trickster who subverted established authority and mocked its pretensions. His bohemian appearance and behavior probably both fascinated and disturbed. In a developing market society, where identities could be shifted and fraudulent representations abounded, itinerant mountebanks like Riley provoked anxiety but also held the allure of a life of excitement and adventure removed from ordinary, everyday small-town existence. Moreover, through their advertisements, the Graphics professed an almost magical ability to transform people's lives.[82]

Despite their success finding business, Riley and his friends spent as much time concentrating on having fun as they did on their work. After paying for his room and board and amusements, he saved little more from the proceeds of their sign-painting assignments than what he needed to get by: "I fag along, am as wealthy as usual—can indulge in cent letters."[83] Riley was not making the profits he had hoped for when he and McClanahan had set out from Anderson at the beginning of the summer. Although the poet never referred to the severe economic depression of 1873 in any of the letters he wrote at this time, this financial crisis assuredly affected the Graphic Advertisers' business prospects. Of course, part of the problem was also due to the personalities of Riley and his friends. People later remembered the Graphics as "happy-go-lucky fellows, who let to-morrow take care of itself." They were not necessarily interested in building their partnership into a stable business concern. Although the Graphics were innovators in some ways, they had more in common temperamentally with early modern, itinerant peddlers than with entrepreneurs who developed the corporate advertising agencies emerging in the 1860s and 1870s.[84]

Toward the end of the summer, Riley lost his enthusiasm for his involvement in the Graphic Advertisers; and the partnership itself began to disintegrate. McClanahan, who worked as the advance man and business agent, was not always terribly reliable. In August, Riley found himself in Mishawaka alone with Ethell. While the two of them were finishing their work there, McClanahan had gone ahead to drum up some more business. Riley became a bit aggravated when, after two weeks, he had not heard from McClanahan. He fretted that "the Advertising 'bis' . . . [had] gone down—like the wreck of the Lady Elgin." McClanahan meant well, but he was "a rattle-brained[,] reckless[,] lovable boy, with a good heart and extravagant ideas."[85]

Riley too had extravagant ideas, and was just as reckless as McClanahan. However, he knew he could neither depend on McClanahan nor on other members of the Graphics to help find him work. Because of his talent, Riley started to receive independent sign-painting assignments. In late summer, Stockford & Blowney, the best sign painter in South Bend, approached him to paint a gigantic sign contrasting how the town had looked as a pioneer settlement in 1833 with the prosperous city it had become by 1873. The figures in this sign were "life-sized." Riley particularly interested himself in painting scenes of the earlier era—"surrounded with all the circumstances of frontier obstacles." He had gained such confidence in his abilities that he boasted he was doing the best sign work west of New York.[86]

By October, Riley had been on his own for over two months. He returned to South Bend where he began to work exclusively for Stockford & Blowney. Riley had impressed the two partners in this company. With his previous assignment from them, he had demonstrated how much he already knew about sign painting and ornamental work and showed an interest and enthusiasm for learning more. Riley had some awareness of national trends in publishing, advertising, and design. He was aware not only of publications such as the New York *Graphic,* but also of the leading innovators in printing and lithography. Riley said that Blowney could copy the work of Louis Prang "to make the original tame almost." (Prang was a successful Boston chromolithographer who pioneered the mass production of high-toned color advertisements for the national market.)[87]

Riley liked his employers. Stockford, whom Riley characterized as "a good sign painter[,] . . . a thorough gentleman, and good warm friend," was about thirty-five. Blowney and Riley took a particular fancy to each other. Blowney, twenty or more years Riley's senior, had been a sign painter for nearly forty years. According to Riley, he was the best colorist he ever encountered. However, Blowney had no talent as a designer. He therefore viewed Riley's originality and creativity as a great asset to his firm. Riley was amazed that Stockford & Blowney were willing to entrust him with important accounts: "They can get signs, you know, that no one would trust *me* to write, and when they want a 'hot' design—something original—they say, 'Here, Riley—I guess you'd better do this!' and when an old sign-painter of 50, and a good one too!—talks like that, I sometimes think, 'well I guess I ain't so slow after all.'" Riley believed that he might even become a full partner in the business: "if I'm not very careful my name will get stuck to the tail end of the biggest and best sign-writing depot in the state." Riley claimed that the signs Stockford & Blowney produced were not only the best that Indiana had to offer but also second to none in Chicago.[88]

Although his assignments with Stockford & Blowney kept him busy, Riley had not completely laid his literary aspirations aside. At the end of October, Riley wrote to his brother quite excited about the prospect of hearing Bret Harte lecture in South Bend. Riley admired Harte because he had managed to sell one of his short stories to *Scribner's Monthly Magazine* for $1,000. Riley knew that he probably would not have a chance to "get a shake of the hand that built . . . [this] MS," but he was eager enough to try if the opportunity presented itself.[89] Harte demonstrated to Riley that it was indeed possible to make a living as a writer.

Despite his enthusiasm for Stockford & Blowney, Riley did not stay in South Bend long. When he visited the town before, his friend and partner in the Graphics, Ethell, a South Bend native, had still been with him. This time, Riley found the social habits of the inhabitants "peculiar." Now that it seemed as if he might settle among them more permanently, their fascination turned to distrust. In communities like South Bend, people judged individuals, especially newcomers, by the way they looked and behaved: "They handle a stranger very carefully for a few months weighing his merits [*sic*], and feeling his clothes— and snuffing critically his brand of perfume—and if his raiment be strictly all wool &c & etc. . . . they, at once proceed to swallow him whole." Riley resisted being scrutinized in this fashion, preferring to remain a mysterious figure and an outsider. As a consequence of his rebellion against their social intrusion, South Bend's inhabitants did not know what to make of him: "there are some say 'He's smart,' some shake their heads and say, 'I dunno. He's a little too quiet for that'—others—'I don't think he *drinks*,' and others that he does, but anyway I don't like 'em as a class and so I leave 'em alone."[90] At this point, Riley did not care what others thought about his character.

Much about his behavior and appearance precluded his acceptance in respectable society. His drinking was most problematic. Riley admitted that rumors were circulating about his thirst for alcohol.[91] His itinerant lifestyle throughout this period lent itself easily to giving in to a desire to drink. He probably drank a lot when he and his friends had money to spend; but he also drank when he was feeling depressed, homesick, or lonely. Moreover, with or without his friends, saloons offered an attractive place to socialize. In pre-Prohibition America, men went to saloons "to exchange ideas, to laugh and boast and dare, to relax, to forget the dull toil of tiresome nights and days."[92] Although he did not admit it in the letters he wrote to family members, Riley probably spent much of what he earned on whiskey as well as on clothing.

For whatever reason, Riley ended his relationship with Blowney & Stock-ford and returned to Anderson in November 1873. The "scathing summer season" had not ended as Riley had expected. He had not seen another member of the Graphic Advertisers for months. Being back where they had spent so much time together, Riley especially missed his friend and partner Jim McClan-ahan. Of the Graphics, McClanahan was his oldest friend, and the only one Riley mentioned by name in the letters he wrote at this time.[93]

Although he did occasionally produce signs for other business concerns in Anderson, Riley again worked primarily for McCrillus. In a letter to his brother dated 16 November 1873, Riley claimed that he was "doing some red-hot" work for the old doctor and that he was designing an advertising card that would be his "masterpiece."[94] Riley gave John the impression that he planned to reestab-lish himself in Anderson for the whole winter; however, he never stayed anywhere very long. Soon after writing this letter, he went back to Greenfield. He apparently had not received enough advertising assignments in Anderson to sustain him and after such a lengthy absence was lonesome for home.

When Riley arrived in Greenfield, he met his stepmother for the first time. Up to this point, his father's new marriage had really had very little impact on him. Riley was an adult away from home even before his father had started to court Martha (Mattie) Lukens. Upon meeting her, Riley hoped that he could learn to love his new stepmother and be able to say: "She's purt' nigh good as Mother was!" However, more than anything else, the idea that a stepmother could relieve his sister, Elva May, of some household duties pleased him. Although he had long anticipated this meeting and had spent hours musing about what his new stepmother was like, no records exist to reveal his first impressions of her.[95] In fact, Riley mentioned his stepmother relatively rarely in the many volumes of correspondence that still exist. As long as she was a part of the family, Mattie always lived in Elizabeth Riley's shadow.

Indeed, Elizabeth left difficult shoes to fill. Her memory loomed large in the minds of all her children. They remembered her as a "gentle[,] loving[,] self-sacrificing mother." To them, she was nearly a saint. After her death, Riley held her up as a model for the poem, "The Mother Sainted": ". . . God sees in her a worth / Too great for this dull earth, / And, beckoning, stands / At Heaven's open gate / Where all His angels wait / With welcoming hands."[96]

In all fairness, therefore, any woman would probably have had problems taking Elizabeth's place. Although Mattie wanted to be accepted by Reuben's children, she never completely succeeded. In a letter she wrote in 1875, she seemed to be on the defensive, attempting to prove to Riley that she really loved him and his siblings: "My dear boy thou knowest not what an interest I feel in the welfare of you all[,] especially the Eternal . . . I love our dear children very much, and have a great deal of confidence in you."[97] However, her confidence in them was often shaken because they did not seem to listen to her and frequently went against her wishes, and Mattie felt her efforts went unappreciated.

In the next sentence of the preceding letter, Mattie disclosed that she was upset by the unwillingness of Riley's youngest brother and sister, Humboldt and Mary, to attend church Sunday school with her. Unfortunately, as a Quaker, Mattie was much more rigid and dogmatic than Elizabeth had ever been. Although they may well have needed her discipline, the Riley children probably did not react well to Mattie's sanctions because their real mother had never been parental in her attitude. She had behaved more like an older sister. Mattie's behavior reflected an older, Protestant style of child rearing. She emphasized harsh discipline and religious training in a desire to save her stepchildren's souls. She probably held onto the old belief that children by nature were sinful and depraved rather than innocent and loving. Mattie undoubtedly meant well, but she was too interested in the "Eternal" well-being of the Riley children. She might have been more readily accepted by them if she had done as much to fulfill their immediate emotional needs as she did attempting to make them follow religious conventions.[98]

Almost twenty years later, the tone of Mattie's letters to Riley had not changed much: "It seems so long since thee was at home father & I want thee to come home so much will do all we can to make thy visit pleasant—if thee will come to see us." However, Mattie's motives may have seemed less sincere because she also often asked Riley for money. Although she claimed it worried her that she was compelled to ask favors of him, she implored him in this letter to lend her what she needed to replace the carpets and window blinds in his father's house. Whereas Elizabeth had been "self-sacrificing," Mattie was miserly and, at times, even appeared greedy. One of Riley's relatives complained that she thought "more of the mity [*sic*] dollar than anything else." According to his youngest sister Mary, Riley often said: "if one gives Ma [Mattie] a 'nickel' she saves *eight cents* out of it."[99]

Back in Greenfield, Riley found himself at loose ends. Luckily, Lee O. Harris, his old teacher and friend, was still in town. Together, the two men revived the Adelphian Dramatic Club. During the winter of 1873–1874, Riley appeared in many of the club's productions, including a historical drama about the king of Sweden and a comedy called *Uncle Robert,* in which Riley played the lead.[100] Harris also encouraged Riley to spend more time on his writing. Having reached an audience in the *Indianapolis Saturday Mirror* during the previous year, Riley decided to submit some of his poems to the *Danbury News* in Connecticut. This paper had a wide circulation and catered to amateur contributors. In February 1874, "At Last" was the first of Riley's poems to appear in the *News;* others followed. The paper's editor, C. E. McGeachy, encouraged Riley. He told him that he was a good writer "and a promising one": "If you keep on improving as you have you will acquire what is everything for a scribe, namely, *fame,* and this secured your writings will command remuneration of your own figuring."[101]

McGeachy's words now seem prophetic, but there were times when Riley despaired. Like most authors of his day, he first broke into print in the newspapers. Newspaper poetry flourished during the second half of the nineteenth century; but, as Riley found out, few newspaper publishers paid poets for their work.[102] Despite some recognition of his writing talent, Riley earned most of his money through his sign painting throughout most of the 1870s.

Riley sometimes locked himself away for hours writing. Many residents of Greenfield continued to consider his interest in poetry frivolous. Small periodicals paid writers little or nothing, and a lot of people still held onto the idea that writing should be an avocation rather than a professional activity.[103] In the eyes of such people, Riley continued to lack discipline and purpose. Too poor to afford new clothes, Riley realized that his personal appearance at this time also did much to complete the picture of a neighborhood ne'er-do-well: "I am not looked upon as I was in the days of yore. I used to run about the town in very dilapidated garments. My trousers bagged at the knee then worse than now, and my coat was not free from evidence of rents. The truth is my vesture was by no means conventional."[104]

On the surface, Riley seemed to lead "a happy, careless life with but few thorns hidden among the rose leaves." However, Riley was often in ill health for weeks at a time. During the winter months, he suffered from repeated respiratory illnesses and a bad cough. In his interview with Garland, he said, "My health was bad—very bad—bad as I was." His health was not improved by his frenzied periods of writing activity or his drinking. His friends were sometimes alarmed by his appearance when he emerged from hours of writing alone in a poorly lighted room. Depression and sickness sometimes followed. Despite his ill health, he continued to drink and often slept most of the day away. Riley also sometimes got into fights. One of his friends, John Skinner, with whom he shared a room in the mid-1870s, later recalled that "Riley in his younger days was somewhat of a pugilist." He particularly remembered one fight Riley had in Greenfield which ended in his arrest.[105]

When Riley remembered this period in his life, he sometimes commented that he "engaged in almost everything but work and so became quite prominent." As a result of his fighting and carousing, his reputation in Greenfield and beyond certainly did not improve. In late February 1874, Riley's old acquaintance, Irvin Walker, became concerned and wrote from Pendleton, Indiana. Walker hoped he had heard wrong, but news had reached him about Riley's drinking. In an effort to save his friend, Walker suggested that the two of them should go into partnership together. He thought that they should try to buy out Pendleton's local newspaper. Walker told Riley that he was a good writer and that taking over the paper would give him "something to do." He eventually wanted to save enough to establish a dramatic company with Riley. However, Walker warned him that he would only enter into partnership with him if Riley were willing to mend his ways: "If you are willing to be *steady,* and to work and save, and try to be a good or better man, come over and see me."[106]

Riley was no stranger to the newspaper business. His Uncle Mart was a printer, and Riley had set some type for him from the time he could read. However, he did not have the money to take Irvin up on his offer. Instead, Riley continued to work on his poetry and take sign painting jobs. During the early spring, Riley moved to Mooresville to stay with his Uncle Jim and Aunt Ann

Marine and set up a painting workshop, hoping that he could get more business there than in Greenfield. He later remembered painting a sign for a dentist in this town; and, in return the old doctor put him "into his operating chair ... and socked 7 teeth full of hammered agony and cheap gold." While in Mooresville, he wrote some pieces for the Morgan County newspapers and informally entertained, playing his guitar and giving recitations in addition to doing sign work.[107]

These impromptu performances in private homes served as trials for his first public, one-man show. This form of entertainment was a natural extension of the nineteenth-century practice of reciting literature and reading books out loud in the family circle. Following the Civil War, the one-man show reached the height of its popularity in the United States. In part, that popularity stemmed from a widespread interest in reading, literature, and speech. During the second half of the nineteenth century, improving the literacy rate was coupled with an interest in elocution. In the American classroom, children were taught to read by reciting aloud from their textbooks. Therefore, in many instances, reading was not a silent, solitary activity. As when Riley performed for his aunt and uncle and their friends, reading often became a social event.[108]

Riley's desire to do a one-man show also grew out of his experiences as an actor in the Adelphian Dramatic Club and as an entertainer in patent medicine shows. While these pursuits were not considered respectable, readings and speeches from the lecture platform were upheld "as an edifying force in American culture." Prejudice against the theater created a need for other types of entertainment. Because lectures and recitations ordinarily did not involve the use of costuming, makeup, and scenery—devices thought to seduce an unwary audience away from reality into a false, fantasy world—the lecture rostrum provided a legitimate outlet for Riley's many talents.[109]

In contrast to theater productions, public lectures and readings were considered genteel and dignified. They appealed to large numbers of people because a distinctive mass culture had not yet fully emerged in the United States. During the second half of the nineteenth century, much of the literature now classified as part of the canon of great books enjoyed a popular audience. Reading became a national pastime, and many writers attained celebrity status. Although authors' readings today typically only attract small groups of artists and intellectuals, authors and performers in postbellum America could assume that their programs of recitations would draw a general audience.[110]

In performing on the lecture stage, Riley followed in the footsteps of such literary greats as William Makepeace Thackeray and Charles Dickens. Dickens's reading tour through the United States in 1867–1868 was especially popular, creating a sensation that "was unparalleled until the arrival of the Beatles in the early 1960s." Tom Snow had wanted to take the young Riley to hear Dickens read while he was on this tour and was very disappointed when the author did not travel further west than Buffalo.[111]

Because of his great admiration for Dickens, as a lecturer and recitationist, Riley attempted to model himself after the famous British novelist as well as after other successful authors such as Bret Harte, whom he saw perform in South Bend in 1873. From the time he had traveled with Doc McCrillus and the Graphics, Riley designed much of his writing for performance. Explaining the reason for this, Riley said, "I couldn't find printed poetry that was natural enough to speak."[112]

During the first months of 1874, Riley turned his attention increasingly to developing his own character sketches and recitations. In January and February, he appeared as a solo act in variety shows at Greenfield's Masonic hall; by spring, he was looking for an opportunity to perform in public alone.[113]

This opportunity came while he was still in Mooresville with his aunt and uncle. After he had been particularly successful performing at a party, Riley wrote excitedly to his brother John that some residents of nearby Monrovia, Indiana, had invited him "to give a public entertainment" the following weekend. He mustered up enough material to give two original programs: one for Saturday night, another for Monday. Riley said that he could "get some pecuniary assistance" for publicity and other expenses, but he asked John to send him five dollars. He did not want to ask Monrovia's inhabitants for money "on an experiment." However, at the same time, Riley felt "confident of success." "[B]ut then," he added, "I *always* do."[114]

Unfortunately, this "experiment" failed. His audience in Monrovia was hostile. But Riley did not give up. He returned to Greenfield and established himself again there as a sign painter, but he also continued to try out his original material on audiences wherever he could. He gave programs in Charlottesville, Indiana, and entertained children at Roberts Park Methodist Church in Indianapolis. By the fall of 1874, he was beginning to feel more confident on stage. His friend Will Otwell often traveled on these excursions with him. Otwell contributed to these performances and lent Riley his moral support.[115]

In June 1875, a younger man named Oliver P. Moore joined Riley on a tour of some central Indiana towns near Greenfield, including Eden, Fortville, and Pendleton. During his performances, Riley recited from his own work but also read some poems by Longfellow and other poets. He interspersed these readings with playing the guitar. Everywhere they went they distributed handbills in which Riley advertised himself as a "Delineator and Caricaturist." Moore said that these handbills "had a big red border around them that would surprise the natives." He remembered that Riley "made so mutch [*sic*] fun of them."[116]

This lecture tour abruptly came to an end after Riley and Moore appeared in Anderson. They lost money on their show, and Riley's old Anderson friends got him drunk after it was over. Moore and Riley were supposed to continue their tour in Crawfordsville, but they quarreled and broke off their partnership. Riley returned to Greenfield demoralized. However, the Anderson papers gave him some good notices, which stated that Riley needed polish but showed promise.[117]

Writing and performing original material for these programs was arduous but provided Riley with invaluable experience. The more he tried out his material the better he understood the tastes of his audiences. In an interview with a magazine reporter, Riley commented on these early tests of his talents on stage: "It is just as difficult for me to write to-day as it was in the old days, when I was experimenting before country audiences, trying to make money, and, at the same time, striving to learn what the people wanted; and it was many many weary years before I began to really find out."[118]

When he was not away from home, Riley worked without pay for Will Hartpence, editor of the *Greenfield News*. He became a regular contributor of poems, prose pieces, and news items to this paper during the latter part of 1874. The *News* published such early Riley poems as "Tradin' Joe."[119] Riley also continued to "have plenty to do in sign work." In April 1875, he wrote to John that he had completed so much work that he had "old Grainfield spangled off like a circus clown."[120]

That same spring, Riley received his first payment for publication of his work. After receiving encouragement from the editor of the *Danbury News*, Riley believed that he should submit a poem to a magazine, since magazines offered more opportunity for remuneration. Therefore, he contributed a poem, which he then entitled "A Destiny," to *Hearth and Home*, a weekly, family-oriented magazine in which Edward Eggleston's novel *The Hoosier School-Master* first appeared. When the poem was published in the magazine's 10 April 1875 issue, Riley received a check for eight dollars. He later renamed the poem, calling it "Mr. Hammond's Parable" or "The Dreamer," and included it in *A Child-World*. Like the other poems in this anthology, "Mr. Hammond's Parable" was autobiographical.[121] It presented the story of a dreamer who encountered a farmer who thought the young man should get to work and earn a living:

> He was a Dreamer of the Days:
> Indolent as a lazy breeze
> Of midsummer, in idlest ways
> Lolling about in the shade of trees,
> The farmer turned—as he passed him by
> Under the hillside where he kneeled
> Plucking a flower—with scornful eye

> And rode ahead in the harvest-field
> Muttering—"Lawz! ef that-air shirk
> Of a boy wuz mine fer a week er so,
> He'd quit *dreamin'* and git to work
> And *airn* his livin'—er—Well! *I* know!"
> And even kindlier rumor said,
> Tapping with his finger a shaking head,—
> Got such a curious kind o' way—
> Wouldn't surprise me much, I say!"[122]

Riley was so enthused about being paid for a poem that he already believed that he was on the way to making his fortune as a writer. However, his eight dollars did not go very far. The country had not yet recovered from the economic depression that began in 1873. As the financial crisis continued, many businesses could not withstand the strain and fell into bankruptcy. The next poem Riley submitted to *Hearth and Home* was sent back to him; the publication was going out of business. At the same time, Will Hartpence was forced to sell the *Greenfield News*. Riley claimed that Hartpence had offered him a paying job "doing local work" and that he "was just about to take it when the paper went to smash."[123]

Reuben Riley was becoming increasingly concerned about his son's future. Riley was twenty-five years old and seemed no more ready to take on adult responsibilities than he had been when he was twenty. Over the course of the past five years, Riley had flitted from job to job and from location to location; and, at this point, Reuben was unconvinced that any of his ventures would ever lead him anywhere. He now insisted that Riley come to study the law in his office.

Reuben had wanted Riley to take over his practice from the time he was a boy. He had named Riley after Governor James Whitcomb with the hope that he would some day become as great an attorney as his namesake. During the early summer of 1875, Riley succumbed to his father's wishes and made an attempt to study for the bar. Reuben probably thought that this was his last chance to straighten out this feckless, self-indulgent son of his. He hoped beyond hope that Riley would finally prove capable of fulfilling the ambitions he had for him.

However, Reuben's plan to make a lawyer out of his son was doomed to fail. When he agreed to study in his father's office, Riley was doing his best to please Reuben but had no real interest in the law. The profession certainly did not fit his temperament. In 1898, Riley explained this situation to a newspaper reporter in Columbus, Ohio: "I have never taken to the serious side of life. . . . In my youth it was destined by my father that I should become a lawyer, but I expect that I forgot the precepts of Blackstone with a greater facility than I was ever able to learn them."[124]

Riley later compared being compelled to study law by his father to being trapped into serving a prison term: "My father is a lawyer, and lured me into his office for a three months sentence." For much of the summer of 1875, Reuben left Riley in "a dingy little office at the top of a rickety stairway," where he was supposed to learn how to practice law. According to one of his friends, the room was sparsely furnished: "The office furniture consisted of an ancient roll-top desk, two . . . chairs, and a window-shade that served admirably as a sieve for the sunshine." "[A] few musty law books reposed at various angles on top of the desk[,]" and Riley had plenty of "'scratch paper' and a sharp pointed pencil" within easy reach. Although Reuben intended them for use in his law studies, Riley often used his "'scratch paper' and . . . pencil" to compose poems instead. For example, during this time Riley wrote "An Old Sweetheart of Mine," which became a popular favorite when it was later published.[125]

Although he was now working for his father to become a respectable lawyer, his sartorial style had not improved: "the young lawyer's personal appearance would not have satisfied the requirements of a haberdasher in search of a model. His trousers were frayed at the extremities, and his coat had the shine that should have been on his shoes." Alone in this dreary office, Riley did not care how he looked. Besides, with the continuing economic crisis, many people could not afford to buy new clothing. Instead of focusing on such superficialities, Riley and his friends "plunged" into their favorite subjects of language and literature "[w]ith the rosy enthusiasm and abounding hopefulness of youth." In these discussions, Riley did "most of the talking."[126]

Toward the end of summer, Riley "made good . . . [his] escape" from his dingy prison. In August 1875, a patent medicine concert wagon came to Greenfield. Riley was automatically drawn to "its gilt and spangles" and the "open air entertainment" provided by its several musicians who performed to attract customers. Seeing this medicine show, which was run by Dr. C. M. "Doxy" Townsend of Lima, Ohio, made Riley, who felt trapped in Greenfield, nostalgic for his days on the open road with Doc McCrillus and Jim McClanahan. Riley found out that one of Townsend's musicians had left the show, inquired about taking his place, and was hired by Townsend. Riley was to be a "general utility man[,] and [he] was to fill in the program [of entertainment] with . . . recitations." Riley described the period he spent with Townsend and his troupe of musicians as one of the happiest times of his life.[127]

Riley later often conflated his two associations with patent medicine manufacturers to form one cohesive narrative, and rarely divulged that they had been two separate and distinct episodes. He did this to hide his age; still living with the memories of his father's admonitions about his irresponsibility, Riley really did not want to admit how very immature he had been. Also, patent medicine peddlers had always existed on the margins of society, along with circus performers and carnival impresarios. Participation in this world was becoming even less respectable as the American consumer became more sophisticated and as medicine became more professionalized. Being lured away from Greenfield by charlatans who professed to be medical doctors before he was old enough to know better could be forgiven by society. In reality, he was almost twenty-three when he started to work for McCrillus, and nearly twenty-six when he left Greenfield with Townsend.[128]

In his stories, Riley always preferred to describe Townsend rather than McCrillus. However, he usually placed his experience with Townsend back in the time when he had actually been employed by McCrillus, before his apprenticeship in his father's office and before he and his friends had come together as the Graphic Advertisers. Although neither man was a diplomaed physician, Riley had greater respect for Townsend. He thought that Townsend "was a mighty fine man," observing that he "was kind to his horses" and that "[h]e was a man of good habits." More importantly, his son presumed that, if Riley were frank, he would have to admit that Townsend "was kinder and more tender to him in those days than was his own father."[129]

When Riley spoke of traveling with patent medicine shows, he admitted that he had some experiences that he "wouldn't part with for a great deal." However, even at the time he was working for Townsend, Riley set himself apart from this class of social marginals that made a career of being confidence men. Riley was very well aware of social distinctions: "I am having a first-rate time considering the boys I am with—they, you know, are hardly my kind, but they are pleasant and agreeable." Since he came from a solid middle-class background, he knew that he was lowering himself by working as a strolling actor and artist. Yet, he balanced this fact with the freedom that this life offered him. Away from the restrictions of Greenfield society, to a great extent Riley could be an autonomous, self-willed individual, doing what he wanted when he wanted. He was really happy as he traveled between towns with his companions in Townsend's entourage: "We sing along the road when we tire of talking, and when we tire of *that* and the *scenery,* we lay ourselves along the seats and 'dream the happy hours away,' as blissfully as the time-honored 'baby in the sugar trough.'"[130]

During the late summer and fall of 1875, Riley attended county fairs in the Indiana towns of Fortville, Anderson, Muncie, Winchester, and Union City with Townsend's party. The troupe also visited fairs in western Ohio. When the medicine wagon arrived in town for a fair, the entertainers would wait until evening to light their torches and begin their show. Riley said, "The music was sure to attract a crowd." On his first stop in Fortville, Riley played the bass drum; and Townsend soon realized that "he had finally got a man, who . . . beat them all." He was very impressed with Riley's "talent for street work."[131]

Riley told his friend John Skinner that he was "thoroughly solid with 'Doxy'" Townsend. The doctor employed no one else who possessed Riley's range of skills. Riley could be musician, artist, and actor during the course of one evening's entertainment. During performances, he played his violin and sang songs; and he often acted, portraying different characters in various skits. When Riley acted, he most often turned up his collar, put a bandanna around his neck, and parodied an old man. Riley was making good use of his close observations of old Johnny Rardin of Greenfield.[132]

According to Riley, Townsend most appreciated his artistic skills. When Townsend climbed down on the footboard of his patent medicine wagon to address the "howling mob," Riley accompanied his speeches by drawing illustrations on blackboards. In a letter to Skinner, Riley described his "blackboard system of advertising": "I have two boards about 3ft by *four*, which—during the street concert—I fasten on the sides of the wagon and *letter* and *illustrate* during the performance and throughout the lecture. There are dozens in the crowd that stay to watch the work going on that otherwise would drift from the fold during the dryer portions of the Doctor's harangue."[133]

Riley followed certain formulas for his blackboard advertisements, which progressed over the course of Townsend's speeches. At the beginning of the doctor's lecture on his "blood purifier," Riley drew a picture of an emaciated woman lying in bed. By the time Townsend reached his climax, Riley had transformed her into a "healthy[,] handsome woman" who was sitting up looking into a mirror. Riley personified "Townsend's Cholera Balm." He drew a bottle of the remedy "*on legs*" and put a "bland smile" on its cork. Riley gave the bottle gestures that scared away skeletons and made the Grim Reaper drop his scythe and hourglass and turn to flee.[134] "Riley's approach typified much advertising practice throughout the nineteenth century and into the twentieth."[135]

When advertising another product, "Townsend's Magic Oil," Riley said that he created a sensation by playing on the words of Shakespeare: "Why let pain your pleasures spoil, / For want of Townsend's Magic Oil?" He accompanied this couplet with a drawing of a life-sized bust of the bard.[136] Riley could toy with this language because most people had some knowledge of Shakespeare's works even if they had little or no formal education.

When Alexis de Tocqueville traveled through the United States in the early 1830s, he noted, "There is hardly a pioneer's hut that does not contain a few odd volumes of Shakespeare."[137] The English bard's works were even more popular on the stage. His plays dominated the theater; and, where theaters did not exist, makeshift productions took place in churches, halls, saloons, and even by the campfire. Most of these performances involved the recitation of short scenes or soliloquies, and many of them were very informal and spontaneous.

For example, Walt Whitman remembered "declaiming some stormy passages from Julius Caesar or Richard" as he rode in Broadway omnibuses as a young man.[138]

People were so familiar with Shakespeare that parodies and burlesques of his work were commonplace. Numerous productions openly lampooned Shakespeare's plays; and parodies often appeared as short skits, brief references, or satiric songs inserted in other kinds of entertainment. Therefore, when he used Shakespeare in his advertisement for "Townsend's Magic Oil," Riley merely took advantage of one of the most popular forms of humor available to him.[139]

Since Townsend's troupe characteristically performed only at night, Riley often had very little to do during the day. Sometimes he and some of the musicians played a little music in the mornings to entice a crowd to return for a regular show, but Riley usually had so much time on his hands that he "drift[ed] away from the wagon for hours." According to Riley, this situation left him and his colleagues with nothing to do "but to plunge into the vortex of Dissipation [*sic*]." The atmosphere of the county fairs where they worked lent itself to intemperance. During these fairs, the inhabitants of the small towns where they took place and the farmers who came from rural surrounding areas to participate in them "indulge[d] themselves." Under these circumstances, Riley was always "in for a good time."[140]

Held at harvest time, these festivals celebrated abundance and had much in common with the European Carnival or Mardi Gras holiday. The primary object of both "was pleasure and consumption." People came to the fair to eat, drink, and enjoy themselves. Carnival was also associated with sexual abandon. In a letter to Skinner, Riley indicated that the whole milieu of the county fair similarly tended toward a temporary loosening of sexual mores: "I was here, you know[,] two or three years since [with McCrillus] . . . [.] I expect to find a girl or two who will still remember me, but it really doesn't matter whether they do or not, for a smile or two seldom fails to 'bring them down'—especially *fair times.*"[141]

These local festivals also had much in common with early modern European market fairs. Nineteenth-century American county fairs offered a temporary escape from daily burdens and routines and promoted new tastes and desires. They not only displayed the many commodities yielded from the harvest but also linked rural consumers to outside urban markets and exposed them to new products. Like European fairs, they brought denizens of the farm and the small town into contact with the exotic and the bizarre. When they strolled through the fairgrounds, people encountered quacks such as Townsend and transient musicians and actors such as Riley. "There were side-shows of performing Chinese, fire-eaters and the like; wheels of fortune, and barkers selling razors, can-openers, and glass-cutters."[142]

However, the fair's performers were not the only ones to provide spectacle. For Riley, the carnival atmosphere could transform an entire town into a theater. In these circumstances, Riley the actor also became a spectator. The county fair served as a perfect environment for Riley to observe local townsfolk and farmers and fed his flair for "idiomatic turns of speech, odd sayings and pictorial episode." As Edgar Lee Masters, author of *Spoon River Anthology*, pointed out, county fairs had a way of quickly revealing the "flavor and character" of a community by bringing the majority of its inhabitants together in one place.[143]

For Masters, the allegory of a county fair held the key to understanding the importance of Riley's life and work. Masters saw the whole state of Indiana come alive as a county fair through Riley's eyes: "Indiana was a happy County Fair to him, which he saw under unusual advantages, and with eyes peculiarly gifted for gathering in what was quaint and joyous and innocent in country and village life." Masters understood the county fair as a microcosm of rural society as it existed at the turn of the century, and he thought that Riley likewise brought together in his work everything that was culturally distinctive about small, hometown America, especially in Indiana. However, what Masters found so extraordinary was that, while the experience of the county fair was ephemeral, Riley managed to capture the essence of life as it was then for everyone to remember.[144] Moreover, just like the county fair, Riley and his poetry became a vehicle for the intersection of the provincial and the cosmopolitan. As a bestselling author, he demonstrated that poetry was not just for the social and cultural elite. He exposed the character of the young and the old, of those who "held county office and waged the wars," and of "[q]ueer characters . . . [and] rural wits" to a wide audience that included members of sophisticated, urban society.[145] Riley's fame brought attention to the region he called home and, in turn, made people living there, and in similar areas, more aware of the opportunities beyond its boundaries. Riley's own personality also mixed the provincial and the cosmopolitan. In a sense, he belonged to both worlds; and he was beloved by many in each. Finally, celebrations of Riley's life sometimes really did physically bring the provincial and cosmopolitan together in one place.

Following the fair season of 1875, Riley returned with Townsend to his home in Lima, Ohio. While there, he spent most of his time designing advertising and "making wrappers and cartons" for the doctor's "Magic Oil" bottles. He was impressed with Townsend's establishment. Shortly after he started working there, he wrote to his friend Will Hammel of Greenfield, giving him a "glowing account of Dr. Townsend's laboratory."[146]

Although he moved to a boardinghouse shortly thereafter his arrival in Lima, Riley spent much time in the Townsend home. The doctor treated Riley "same as one of his own lovely family." He became an especially good friend of

Townsend's son, who was also named Jim. Jim Townsend later recalled that Riley "was so gentle and kind that he soon won everybodys [*sic*] . . . warm affections." Townsend also remembered how easily Riley blushed "until his face, hair, and mustache made him all a red glow." However, he noted that Riley suffered from mood swings: "He was so natural and sunshiny, then again a little somber and sad." On some days, Riley's face was "wreathed in smiles"; and you could hear him "breaking out into the most intoxicating and joyous laughter." Then, following these joyous days, "he would have long spells of silence."[147]

Riley still suffered periods of depression; but evidence suggests that he drank little during his stay in Lima. Riley remarked to Skinner about his "estrangement from the saloon," and he asked God to help him on his "good way." Riley probably managed to stay away from liquor because he was more content than he had been at other times. He was living in better conditions; and, as he said, Doc Townsend helped him "amazingly." For once, he felt understood and appreciated.[148]

Despite this, Riley had not completely reformed his behavior. In Lima, Riley continued "sort of living from day to day, weaving into each . . . natural and simple pleasures and incidents." As did so many others, Jim Townsend noticed that Riley was "decidedly opposed to manual labor." For example, Riley refused to help him and his father reshingle their house. When pressed to join them in this task, Riley simply said: "Well, Doc, you tried to make a good many things out of me, but you can't make a carpenter." Jim Townsend explained Riley's carefree and lazy habits by rationalizing that while "his talents and genius . . . [were] all there, [they were] yet not awake."[149]

Riley often entertained the Townsends in the parlor of their family home. Jim Townsend enjoyed watching Riley play his violin: "He had a loving way of leaning over onto it, when at such times the mustache seemed to spread out and mingle with the strings. . . . He produced very sweet tones on this instrument and when he played such tunes as 'Down on the Swaunee [*sic*] River' they easily awakened my deeper feelings." Doc Townsend's eldest daughter sometimes accompanied him on the organ, and Riley wrote verses for her "which he would tell her could be sung . . . to certain pieces of music."[150]

Wherever he went, Riley wanted to create the impression that he was a ladies' man. His trunk from his sign painting days was reportedly full of love letters. At one time during his travels with McCrillus, Riley boasted to a young woman named Kate that he received "from 30 to 35 letters from enamored females" daily. Considering that Riley saved nearly all of the letters sent to him, evidence suggests that he got nowhere near that number. A desire to make Kate jealous proably motivated Riley's statement, but he assured her that hers was the first he ever took the trouble to answer.[151]

Although he exaggerated, Riley did have other love interests and actively sought out romantic relationships with the opposite sex. Besides Kate, Riley corresponded with at least two other young women who had a romantic interest in him during the first part of the 1870s, Mellie Ryan and Angie Williams. As a young man, Riley "[o]ccasionally . . . went a-wooing two girls at a time, hoping to win one; but that . . . was love and labor in vain. Following the two hares he was sure to catch neither."[152]

With no strong attachment to any one particular woman, Riley said that he "had no one in mind" when he wrote "An Old Sweetheart of Mine" in Greenfield during the summer of 1875. He was certainly not ready for a serious, long-standing, romantic involvement. In a letter to John Skinner in September of that same year, Riley insinuated that he had a girl in every county seat in Indiana. When he wrote Skinner again in October, only a few days after his arrival in Lima, he was already thinking about chasing after the most attractive young women in town. He had noticed that there were "a slashin' lot of girls" there. Riley had only made the acquaintance of two or three of them, the ones he "didn't care to know"; but he informed Skinner that he would "make it Hot for 'em shortly!"[153]

Riley's quest for love in Lima went unfulfilled. He was usually most successful courting women with his pen. Although he was vain about his large, dashing, red mustache in his twenties, he was always very sensitive about his physical appearance. He thought that he was ugly and usually used deprecatory terms in describing himself to others. Because his hair was very thin and light in color, he claimed he looked bald. He said that his complexion was "blotchy"; and, although he was of medium height at five feet seven inches tall, he thought of himself as a "little weenty-teenty man."[154] In an attempt to compensate for these perceived inadequacies, he always dressed as well as he could. Even then, Riley could appear "peculiar and awkward."[155]

In letters, he did not have to worry about his looks or keeping his composure; and he knew he was quite capable of charming women with his words. He admitted as much to Kate: "Believe me, my heart comes bumping into my throat so that, were I *talking*, it would be as hard for you to understand what I was saying as it is now! (There! I've sharpened my pencil, and taken a fresh chew of tobacco let us proceed!)." Proceed he did. He abandoned his clumsy, boyish stance and inserted a verse that promised love and intimacy: "Come closer darling closer—let me see / Deep down into your eyes, and happy be / With your dear arms put out caressingly / About my neck, and listening to me." He signed this letter "J. W. Romeo."[156]

Although he enchanted many women by showing them his sensitive, romantic side, Riley believed that he was unlucky in love: "The Poet commonly remarked, referring to his young manhood days, that when he fell in love with a girl a rival would promptly court her and marry her. Courtship was a losing game." In many ways, Riley did not feel worthy of love. For example, after he left Greenfield to travel with Townsend, Riley seemed surprised to learn that Angie Williams was deeply affected: "I'm sorry to learn that Angie seems disappointed at my abrupt departure.... I am flattered to think . . . she *has* that regard for me. . . . I am glad and sorry too, glad that *some* one can see something of worth among so much rubbish and sorry that there is not less of the latter." Riley assumed that when a young woman such as Angie did have feelings for him she would eventually see the error of her ways and marry someone else, or, else she would soon be dissuaded by her parents from continuing in a relationship with him. In the case of Angie Williams, Riley was well aware that her father disapproved of him: "I think her father eminently correct in fancying that I shall never amount to much."[157]

Although Doc Townsend showed him kindness and understanding, Riley still had little faith in himself. At every turn, his ambitions seemed foiled by fate. Through the years, he came to believe that he really would never find happiness. Riley did not condemn himself for the decisions he made; but, at the same time, it seemed he always made the wrong ones: "I have no censure for my course—'Beggars[,]' you know, 'can't be choosers,' and even tho' they could *my* choice would doubtless be unwise." Riley was also troubled by the idea that so many people doubted his intentions. Perversely, he thought that people tended to believe him only when he lied: "Why is it everybody doubts me? When I *lie* I can find believers plenty—but when I tell the *truth* and *am* sincere [*sic*] in heart and soul, the Devil winks and says, 'There's one after my own heart.' I guess he's the best friend I've got after all."[158]

As this passage suggests, Riley, in his bitter moods, believed that his life was somehow cursed, or "hoodooed," as he preferred to put it. This feeling never changed. He always thought that he should have accomplished more before he did; and, despite the fame and fortune he finally achieved, he was haunted by the idea that somehow he personally remained a failure and a pawn of misfortune. In a letter to a young friend, Riley used his boyhood nickname, "Bud," to describe how he felt about himself: "As usual, Bud is behind-time with *everything*—till it just seems he can't never catch up again no more! And he's a confirmed *hoodoo*, everything he *wants* and *tries* to a-complish he just *can't.*"[159]

Riley was always trying to free himself from these personal demons. From the early 1870s on, he did this increasingly through his writing. When he wrote, Riley escaped into his own ideal world—a Rousseauesque world that was close to nature, where people lived simply and honestly and treated their fellow men with kindness and respect.

By the end of 1875, Riley grew less interested in his work for the patent medicine show. With Doc Townsend's son, Jim, he discussed "getting ahead in the world." Riley was turning his attention to his poetry, and he began to see more possibilities for himself as a writer. He told his friend Skinner that he was "rapidly growing in public favor" and that his poems would "be out in book form yet."[160] At Christmas time, Greenfield beckoned; and Riley left Lima and Doc Townsend behind. Townsend gave him the following recommendation upon his departure: "I take grate [sic] plesure [sic] in saying that James W. Riley is the most efficient Advertiser I have ever had in my employ. Throughout an engagement of four months duration I have found him ever prompt, industrious and reliable."[161] However, Riley never made as much use of this recommendation as he might have. Although he would continue to do some sign painting, he would never go out on the road with a paintbrush again.

When he arrived in Greenfield in mid-December, Riley moved back in with his father, stepmother, stepsister, and younger siblings, who were now living in the town's old academy building. After Christmas, Riley's father urged him to come back to his office to study the law. Riley obliged him, but now definitely had other ambitions. During the previous year, Riley had made the acquaintance of Benjamin S. Parker, a newspaper editor and poet from Newcastle, Indiana, through his old friend and teacher Lee O. Harris. Parker, along with Harris, became one of Riley's mentors; and both men urged Riley to pursue a writing career. In 1875 and again in 1876, Parker asked Riley to join him in putting together an anthology of Indiana poets to be published for the Christmas holidays.[162]

By July 1876, Riley had completely abandoned the idea of becoming a lawyer. He began to write constantly and gained in recognition reciting his work in public. For example, he wrote a poem called "Silent Victors," which he read in a local celebration of Decoration Day in New Castle, Indiana, to which he had been invited by Parker, and composed another poem and recited it for the United States Centennial. Following these events, one of Riley's romantic interests, Eda L. Brown, reported to a friend that Riley was "doing wonders in the Poetry [sic] line": "He wrote the poem on the occasion of the decoration of the soldiers graves and people went wild over it. . . . Then he wrote the Centennial poem[,] and[,] Oh[,] . . . it was grand."[163]

When she wrote this letter, Riley and Eda Brown had already been corresponding for a few months. They started writing to one another because of Riley's old partner, Jim McClanahan. Brown was McClanahan's fiancée. McClanahan encouraged Riley to correspond with Brown because she deserved "literary friends." She liked to write stories and gave music lessons on the piano, harp, guitar, and violin. Brown quickly became enamored with Riley through his letters: "I love you and am so proud of you. How can you know just what kind of letters to write me at different times? No two letters are alike, and yet I'd know they were all yours, for no one else could ever write like you." As he often did when he carried on a relationship with a woman through the mail,

Riley idealized Brown and believed that he, too, had fallen in love. Despite his friendship with McClanahan, this relationship continued through 1877.[164]

Although Riley still identified himself as a "Painter Poet," between the summer of 1875 and the end of 1876, his entire outlook and attitude changed as his life began to take a new direction. Whereas previously "Painter" preceded "Poet" in his definition of himself, Riley started to reverse their importance in his mind. Although he still needed to take sign painting work to survive economically, Riley began to transform himself into a professional writer. As a result, he became increasingly interested in obtaining a newspaper job, so that he could at least support himself entirely by his pen. Riley knew that taking such a job could have important consequences as newspapers were the first medium in which many aspiring writers managed to start to establish a name for themselves. In October 1876, Riley asked Parker for a position as his assistant at the *New Castle Mercury:* "I had once a few weeks experience as the local Editor of our little paper. I liked it better than anything I ever tried to do, and I write to say that I would like to be with you in that capacity."[165]

Throughout most of 1876, Riley's friends from the Graphic Advertisers tried to cajole him to come back to work with them. McClanahan and Wickersham wrote repeatedly attempting to seduce him into traveling through the country painting signs and putting on shows. Unable to secure a position with Parker at the *Mercury,* Riley was in debt and considered going with them.[166]

Riley's relationship with Eda Brown complicated his decision. By involving himself in a romantic triangle with Brown and McClanahan, Riley endangered his friendship with his old partner. Brown described the complexity of the situation: "I am so proud in the possession of you for you belong to us (Mack & me) don't you? I love you next to Mack. He loves you next to me, and you love me after him, & we all love each other. Bless me what a cobweb." The next time she wrote, Brown felt guilty that she had professed her love for Riley and asked him to destroy their latest correspondence so that they could "begin all over again."[167]

However, the tone of their letters did not change. As early as July 1876, Brown claimed that she no longer felt anything for McClanahan: "I am sure I could meet him and feel no throb of old love; could hear the old familiar voice, pleading as it used to do—and only smile, remembering that my heart is filled with *SOMEONE ELSE.*" At this time, McClanahan was wandering the countryside as a roving actor and advertiser. He rarely wrote to his fiancée and had not seen her for months. As long as McClanahan stayed out of the picture, Riley felt free to continue the romance.[168]

Brown realized that if Riley were to travel with McClanahan their correspondence would become more difficult. At one point, she discouraged Riley from going with "Mack" and Wickersham and told him that, if he did, the two of them would have to be clever so that "Mack" would not discover the true nature of their relationship. When McClanahan later told her that Riley was going to become a member of an acting troupe with which he was traveling, she begged Riley to permit her to come along.[169]

However, Riley neither again traveled with the Graphics nor joined any acting company. Although Riley was tempted, the advertising business and the open road no longer held the allure for him that they had once had. In fact, by the end of 1876, he had different aspirations. He had instigated many of the schemes the Graphics used to trick their audiences, but he felt ashamed that he had ever allowed himself to become involved in such confidence games: "I someway feel as tho' I was doing something to be ashamed of . . . as tho' I were being made a tool of to advance the interests of those who would smile to think 'what a fool he is!'" He understood that he would always be outside the mainstream playing the part of the fool if he continued his life traveling as an advertiser. He now decided to apply the skills that he had acquired as an intinerant sign painter and patent medicine show performer to more legitimate pursuits in the literary world. Riley had begun to reinvent his identity.[170]

Riley had undergone a "reformation." He decided that he would no longer engage in occupations that he found disagreeable unless fate dictated that he do otherwise: "Since my reformation[,] I begin to feel an unusual sense of my importance, and if I *do* lower myself to some uncongenial pursuit, it will be because an adverse fate drives me to it." With this "reformation," Riley resolved to dedicate himself to pursuing his literary career. Encouraged by Parker, he placed his hopes on seeking the endorsement of Longfellow and some other distinguished men of letters to see if any of them believed that he had talent. After all the turns his life had already taken, Riley hoped that he had finally found what he was meant to do.[171]

Rising Ambition

"A great many persons . . . seem to think indorsement far more important than either hard work or special aptitude," Riley once commented to a reporter for the *Chicago Daily News*. By 1897, when he made this statement, Riley was beginning to feel overwhelmed by the consequences of his fame; and some of the methods he had used to help him achieve his notoriety had come back to haunt him. In this interview, the reporter asked Riley what advice he would give to struggling young authors. In response, Riley complained, "Why, I am . . . in receipt of a never-ending stream of letters inclosing verse and asking for my indorsement. . . . If I were to give attention to every one of them I should have little time to attend to my own affairs. . . . And what makes it worse, . . . " he added, "is that nearly every one of the writers reminds me that I once sent some verses of mine to Mr. Longfellow and that he very kindly answered my letter."[1]

When such letters flooded in to the office of his publisher, Bowen-Merrill, Riley sometimes wished that he had never told reporters that he had sent some of his poems to Longfellow. In an attempt to discourage people from requesting endorsements from him, Riley, in this particular interview, did not want to admit just how much importance he had once placed on receiving a reply from this much beloved American poet late in 1876. However, he admitted at other times that he had almost staked his entire career upon learning Longfellow's estimation of his talent: "I took a lot of my poems and sent them to Longfellow, asking him if he thought from them I could ever amount to anything. I made up my mind that if he said no, I would quit all that kind of thing forever."[2]

Longfellow's opinion meant much to Riley, because he loved "him above all other poets." He considered Longfellow's works a "poetical bible." They provided him with a source of endless inspiration: "His songs are ever fresh. I turn to them again and again, ever with the delight of the first reading."[3] Riley deemphasized the role that Longfellow's response to his letter ultimately played in the making of his career. However, he purposely and repeatedly called attention to his connections to this great American literary figure. These associations were key components of the Riley myth.

In the *Chicago Daily News* article, Riley consciously placed himself as inheritor of Longfellow's role as the most recognized living American poet. Although he complained about it, Riley made it clear that people wrote to him for the very same reasons that he had written to Longfellow so long ago. Riley pointed out that he was in a position to give aspiring young writers the same kinds of advice that Longfellow had given him while he was still alive. When they appealed to him seeking approval and encouragement, Riley responded by emphasizing that success depended most on diligence and perseverance: "Impress upon all . . . the message that, no matter how great the gift, all the indorsement in the world will not help them half so much as constant, persistent study of the use of words, close observation of humanity[,] and plenty of hard work." Riley then placed himself on an equal footing with Longfellow in experience and wisdom: "When Mr. Longfellow wrote the letter I am so often reminded of nowadays he sought to impress upon me the truth of what I have just been saying."[4]

Riley had not always followed this advice, and his manipulation of the press and public opinion had not always been this subtle and sophisticated. Especially when he was fresh from his experiences huckstering for patent medicine shows, he was not above using tricks and deception in an attempt to further his reputation. He looked for shortcuts to the fame and fortune he so much desired. He knew how effective some of the methods he had used as an advertiser had been for the sale of commercial products and services, and saw no difference between the methods appropriate for selling patent medicines and those appropriate for selling himself and his poems to the literary market. Riley was still very insecure. There were many dark days when he doubted he could ever succeed, but he wanted to prove to himself and the world that he could amount to something, and would use every means available to make that possible.

As a poet living in the West, Riley believed the odds were against him. Working in a place where writing as a profession was not taken seriously, he often felt very much alone and very much misunderstood. In 1888, he expressed what it was like to establish a career as a poet in this environment:

> It is difficult for poets to write with real ambition in the West, because they have so few associates of their own ambition to encourage them. It is a barren task, and transcendent genius, I dare say, would starve to death if it depended on poetry to keep alive. The result is any one who writes poetry has to do it at odd times, because his business requires especial attention. Very few of these singers have the hardihood to ask for money for their productions. In fact, money for poems with them is a secondary consideration. They have the delight of seeing their thoughts in cold type, and that is recompense enough.[5]

For Riley, seeing his thoughts "in cold type" had not been enough. In his late twenties, he not only wanted to be paid for his work but also sought recognition as a poet from the literary establishment in the East. The editors of America's most prestigious magazines, such as the *Atlantic Monthly,* rejected Riley's early submissions. He came to realize how especially hard writers who were outside New England and New York's literary circles had to struggle to attain any respect from the nation's best-known critics. Becoming resentful of what he perceived as literary prejudice, Riley's first attempts to thwart it in the late 1870s were bittersweet.

When he wrote to Eda L. Brown about his personal "reformation" late in November 1876, Riley had already sent his letter to Longfellow. In it, he told Longfellow that he would like to enter the "literary field in earnest" but wanted to be assured that he possessed "real talent." He enclosed several poems, including one entitled "In the Dark," which Riley had written in imitation of Longfellow's "The Day Is Done." Riley knew that he could not count on receiving an answer from such a celebrated figure. He therefore also sent letters enclosing poems to John Townsend Trowbridge "and two or three lesser literary lights." Although he did not have anywhere near the prestige of Longfellow, Trowbridge was a well-respected reformer and author of the time. He wrote plays, poetry, and novels and was a friend of Whitman, Longfellow, and Oliver Wendell Holmes.[6]

Although he told Brown that he had every reason to expect "gratifying comments" from Longfellow, Trowbridge, and the others, Riley knew that, if fate again treated him badly, he could still go back into business with one of his partners in the Graphic advertising company as a last resort. Throughout the winter and on into the next spring, McClanahan and Wickersham continued to press him about accompanying them. They were unconvinced that Riley was really ready to give up the life of a roving advertiser once and for all.[7]

In his letter to Brown, Riley said that he was relieved that he had not heard from any of the Graphics for several days. Some of his old friends did not fully understand that he was in the process of redefining himself and his world. Although he continued to socialize with people he had known then, the relationships that he had formed when he was a sign painter and advertiser would become less and less important to him. Some people later criticized Riley for denying his past affiliations: "It is now said of him that it is with great difficulty that he is able to recognize his former friends and associates." Many people with whom he fraternized during his sign painting days believed that he betrayed their friendship and unfortunately grew jealous of his success.[8]

During 1876 and 1877, Riley tried to continue his older friendships; but he was also nurturing other relationships. Eda Brown's letters enthralled him. He said that she wrote "like a practical angel" and described her letters "as prose poems throughout." He had also begun writing to authors such as Mary Hannah Krout, a Crawfordsville poet who had contributed her verses to such journals as the *Boston Transcript* and the *New York Tribune*. He believed that his new correspondents were really "worthy of his steel."[9]

While he awaited responses from his "literary lights," Riley busily occupied himself with his writing and was happy with what his efforts were yielding: "I've had a perfect hemmorage [*sic*] of inspiration—producing quite a number of poems *and* of better quality than ever." As he wrote this, Riley did not know that he only had a couple more days to wait before receiving the coveted answer from Longfellow.[10]

Longfellow's response was brief. He did not "enter into any minute discussions of the merits of the poems" Riley had enclosed. Instead, he discussed them only "in general terms": "I have read them with great pleasure, and think they show the true poetic faculty and insight." This statement sent Riley into "a perfect hurricane of delight." Longfellow did take the time to make one criticism. He found that Riley had misused a word in "Destiny," which had appeared in *Hearth and Home*: "The only criticism I shall make is on your use of the word *prone* in the thirteenth line of 'Destiny.' Prone means face downward. You meant to say *supine,* as the context shows." Riley later claimed that Longfellow's criticism meant more to him than his encouragement: "I fancy I was prouder of the fact that he thought my work really worth criticizing than the words of praise."[11]

Unable to restrain his excitement, Riley carried Longfellow's letter with him everywhere and showed it to everyone he possibly could. He also copied the letter and sent it to Benjamin Parker in New Castle. Parker wrote back to tell him that he had "taken the liberty to have it put in type" for that week's edition of the *Mercury*. Longfellow's letter to Riley also soon appeared in the *Hancock Democrat,* with the following introduction: "*The Democrat* has frequently commented upon the poetic merits of our young fellow townsman, James W. Riley, and on this occasion we take great pleasure in announcing, and we feel assured that the readers of *The Democrat* will be gratified to learn, that his poetic talent has not only been appreciated by his friends at home, but has received the recognition of America's most eminent poet, Henry W. Longfellow."[12]

For the moment, Riley could hold his head up high in his hometown. The article printed in the *Democrat* even went so far as to remark that Riley's "brilliant futurity . . . [was] almost assured." Word spread about Riley's good news. Will Ethell wrote from Anderson to tell him that almost everyone in town knew of his letter from Longfellow, and Albert W. Macy wrote from Richmond wanting permission to reprint it in an upcoming issue of the *Earlhamite,* a publication produced by Earlham College in Richmond, Indiana. However, Longfellow's endorsement did little to improve Riley's immediate financial situation. He was far from his dream of being able to "drive into Greenfield—headed by a brass band" with a thousand dollars in his pocket.[13]

Parker warned Riley not to feel "to[o] much flattered by Mr. Longfellow's letter." He did not blame Riley for "being elated" and admitted that he himself would be "wild with delight" if Longfellow had flattered his verses as he had Riley's. Nevertheless, Parker cautioned Riley that he could ill afford to rest on these laurels. He advised him to take further steps to develop his reputation as a writer: "proceed, discreetly, to cultivate the acquaintance of other distinguished and influential men of letters." "The most valuable kind of recognition," Parker said, " . . . will be that which secures a position among the contributors to some one or more of our best American magazines . . . and papers." For this reason, Parker suggested that Riley send some of his best poems to men such as Howells, who at this time was still editor of the *Atlantic Monthly.* Publication in such journals as the *Atlantic Monthly, Harper's Monthly,* or *Scribner's* would build Riley's reputation and bring him prestige because they set literary and intellectual standards for the nation.[14]

Despite Parker's cautions, Longfellow's letter gave Riley a new sense of confidence. By this time, he had also received a complimentary letter from Trowbridge; but it was Longfellow's he valued most. If Longfellow saw "the true poetic faculty and insight" in his work, then he felt that he really did have a future as a writer. Charles Philips, the editor of the *Kokomo Tribune,* recalled that Riley carried this letter around with him until it was worn and tattered: "I remember with what pride you showed me a little, old yellow letter from Longfellow, which you had carried about in your pocket, & looked at so often that the edges of the paper looked ragged & the envelope scarcely hung together."[15]

Riley thanked Parker for his advice and told him that he always followed it to the best of his ability. Armed with Longfellow's letter, he sent a poem called

"A Funny Little Fellow" to *Scribner's,* which the magazine's editor promptly rejected. Riley also decided to try for publication in the metropolitan press. Early in 1877, he submitted several poems and a prose sketch to the *Indianapolis Journal.* The *Journal* was a major metropolitan daily and the leading Republican party organ in the state.[16] This newspaper looked more favorably on Riley's work than *Scribner's* did. During January and early February, the *Journal* published two of Riley's poems, "Song of the New Year" and "An Empty Nest," and accepted the first of his prose sketches, "A Remarkable Man."[17]

This short prose sketch has much in common with Herman Melville's short story "Lightning-Rod Man" and his novel covering the same themes, *The Confidence-Man,* published just prior to the Civil War. In "A Remarkable Man," Riley entered the domain of the mountebank, delving into a subject with which he had become personally familiar working for patent medicine shows. Like Melville's "Lightning-Rod Man" and the succession of confidence men who appear in his novel, Riley's character is a shadowy figure who exists on the margins of society and manipulates perceptions of reality.[18]

At the beginning of Riley's story, the narrator happens upon a "remarkable man," dressed like a tramp, who seems to take dictation directly from authors of the classics, long since departed from this world. The narrator is "at first completely mystified" as he witnesses this performance. The "remarkable man" holds a pencil in his hand high over his head and then suddenly pounces on paper to write in a frenzy. Each line the man writes seems to "appear as if by magic." However, when the exercise is repeated, the narrator "determine[s] to conquer the superstition that had almost overpowered" him and catches on to the old man's confidence game. This "remarkable man" has written clever imitations of old authors and poets, committed them to memory, and then passed himself off as a psychic medium for their supposed transmission from the grave.[19]

As did Melville in "The Lightning-Rod Man" and *The Confidence-Man,* Riley revealed the possibilities of deception within this prose sketch and demonstrated that reality is not always transparent. Riley captured the growing anxiety of people in mid-nineteenth-century America about what Walt Whitman called the "terrible doubt of appearances."[20] In a society that was increasingly mobile and anonymous, confidence men, such as the "remarkable man" whom Riley described, could exist in larger numbers than ever before. People feared that everything and everyone they encountered might not be what they seemed. Riley demystified the "remarkable man" and thus exposed this truth. In this story, Riley's character represented destabilizing influences within society that led people to suspect that reality could change from one minute to the next. Nevertheless, Riley's readers could take pleasure in the fact that the "remarkable man" did not get away with his deceit.[21]

Riley described "A Remarkable Man" as a literary "bonanza." The *India-*

napolis Journal paid him $10 to publish it; and, after it appeared in its columns, he received "no less than 20 letters from literary people thr[ough]out the state, all containing the most flattering comments." Even more importantly, it caught the attention of E. B. Martindale, the paper's owner and publisher, who was to play a considerable role in helping Riley develop his career.[22]

A few days after "A Remarkable Man" appeared in the *Journal*, Riley found out from a friend that Martindale "regard[ed] it as a decided hit—a literary success" and that he had even spoken of Riley "as a genius." Martindale was so enthusiastic about Riley that he pledged to help him in any way he could: "I want to thank you for the article and poem sent the Journal. I am sure 'You have a future' and will help with the Journal to make it whatever your application & industry deserves. I hope you will call on me when you are in the City. I may be able to make some suggestions and afford you encouragement. I like to help young men who help themselves."[23]

With each contribution to the *Journal,* Riley rose in Martindale's estimation. In early March, Riley decided to send the paper "An Old Sweetheart of Mine," which he had composed while studying law during the summer of 1875. When he read it, Martindale judged that this poem was equal to anything he had read in years and was so eager to publish more of Riley's work that he offered to pay him for anything else he submitted: "I will take in the future any prose or poetry you may write and will compensate you in future for what you furnish."[24]

Because newspapers rarely paid for poetry, Riley could not believe his good fortune. He thanked Martindale for his generous offer and assured him that he was ready to do everything in his power to be worthy of his patronage: "Since you avow the belief you do of my future promise, and are so ready to 'help me make it whatever my application and industry deserves,'—I am ready and willing to exercise every faculty I may possess to that end. I have been working for years, as best I could with this purpose in view; but never until now have I felt so assured of attaining it." Characteristically, Riley pointed out to Martindale that he was not the only gentleman who recognized "whatever germ of talent" he possessed, citing the "letters of compliment" he had received from Longfellow and Trowbridge.[25]

After mentioning these two nationally known literary figures, Riley did not wish to give the impression that help from Martindale was unneeded: "I am still painfully conscious of the many deficiencies under which I labor, and the formidable obstacles I have yet to encounter." Still unable to make a living as a writer, Riley continued to do sign painting work in Greenfield. He was grateful for Martindale's attention but also wanted more than just to be paid for his contributions. Riley hoped that this letter would further enhance Martindale's opinion of him so that he might be willing to give him a regular job. He promised Martindale that he would be very careful "to bestow every care and attention" to whatever he might contribute to the *Indianapolis Journal* in the future.[26]

Riley enlisted his uncle Frank Riley to approach Martindale on his behalf to help him secure a position with the *Journal*. His uncle had a certain amount of influence in Indianapolis because he served as the treasurer of Marion County and, as such, was an active member of the Republican Party. Frank Riley had a long talk with Martindale; and, although they did not agree on a salary, Martindale told him to tell his nephew that he would give him a position and make arrangements that would be satisfactory to him.[27]

Apparently Riley did not agree with whatever Martindale had in mind. In early April, he wrote to his brother John that he was leaving Greenfield to go back to Anderson. Despite his lack of success in being hired by the *Journal*, Riley had not lost hope in his writing career. Following publication of "A Remarkable Man," Riley found himself "in the best possible spirits." Having seen Riley's poems and articles in the *Indianapolis Journal*, editors of papers in other parts of Indiana solicited contributions from him. Other newspapers started to copy his poems from the *Journal*'s columns. Soon after he arrived in Anderson, Riley boasted to his brother that "In the Dark," one of the poems he had sent to Longfellow, was being copied in papers throughout the country. By the end of the month, Will M. Croan hired Riley to be city editor of the *Anderson Democrat*, although he had little experience working as a journalist. Riley had first met Croan in the days when he worked for Doc McCrillus. He stated that Croan took it for granted that he would be "a valuable man in the local and advertising departments."[28]

As one of the owners of the *Democrat*, Croan employed Riley at $40 a month. Soon after he started working as a reporter, a rival newspaper, the *Anderson Herald*, lampooned the owners of the *Democrat* for hiring Riley. It questioned the wisdom of putting Riley on staff at a newspaper full-time as he had earned a reputation as a shiftless dreamer during his previous residence in the town: "The talented young poet, J. W. Riley, has taken a position on the *Anderson Democrat*, and will devote his attention to local affairs. Riley is a dreamer and without practical newspaper knowledge, but he has more brains by two or three bucketfuls than the proprietors of the paper."[29]

During the nineteenth century, such needling of rivals in the press was very common. Most newspapers had political party affiliations so they naturally debated over their differing points of view. Moreover, in a face-to-face society, the public rarely distinguished between people and their businesses. Therefore, editors from opposing newspapers often became engaged in feuds that involved personal insults and attacks as they competed for political loyalty and readership within a community.[30]

During the next few months, Riley would prove that the proprietors of the *Democrat* were, in fact, wise to have foreseen his value to their weekly journal. For the first time, Riley was earning a regular salary; and he took it seriously. Riley quickly became known around town as the "Perspiring Poet."[31] As the *Democrat's* editor, Riley gathered the local news and did "a multitude of other things that must be done on a country paper."[32] He once commented that the *Democrat* gave him the opportunity to write on a broad range of topics. His investigation of such subjects as the treatment of the indigent on the county poor farm also took him places where he otherwise would never have gone.[33]

This local weekly was not unlike the newspapers "on which Whitman had worked around New York, on which Howells had worked in rural Ohio, or on which Twain had been employed in the West."[34] The newspaper world, especially at this level, was still very artisanal. Twain and Howells had risen through the ranks of journalism to become professional writers by first learning the printing trade. Characteristically, printers became editors and then often used this position to enter politics.[35] Although he had little formal experience, Riley was certainly not unfamiliar with the newspaper business. He had learned much from working at the *Greenfield News* and was also no stranger to the printing room.[36]

Printing had not changed much over the course of the past few centuries. Type was still set by hand. Compositors selected individual pieces of type from a special compartmentalized case. They placed these pieces of type in a holder or stick. As each stick was filled with type, they transferred the composed type to shallow trays called galleys. After checking the galleys for errors, compositors arranged the type into pages and locked them into a metal frame. A pressman then locked the form onto a press and prepared to print the page. Typically, country newspapers owned "flatbed" presses. With this type of press, "paper traveled around a cylinder that pressed it against a type form locked into a flat bed."[37] The press was operated by turning a crank or by a water system. When printing was complete, the type was cleaned and re-sorted.[38]

This technology limited the length of most small-town newspapers to three or four pages.[39] Moreover, the dearth of material available to print restricted the paper's size. There was little to report except the local news. At the *Anderson Democrat*, Riley filled any extra space with information and clippings he lifted from other journals or with creations from his own pen. During the nineteenth century, newspapers customarily exchanged stories. They traded subscriptions and borrowed material from one another to create an informal syndicate. Although it offered no payment, this system of newspaper exchanges gave Riley the opportunity to gain a wider audience and become better known as a journalist outside the confines of the small town in which he worked.[40]

Like other country newspaper editors, Riley served not only as the paper's editor but also as its reporter and printer's helper.[41] Therefore, Riley's job at the *Democrat* kept him very occupied. Toward the end of May, he stated to a friend: "I've been too busy this week to avoid creditors even, and I'm chuffin' away here in the night like a steam man with . . . heart trouble." His hard work paid off. Within a month after he started work at the *Democrat,* the circulation of the paper doubled. To reward him for his part in the publication's growing success, Croan raised his salary to $60 per month.[42]

As long as he kept busy and things were going well, Riley was less vulnerable to giving in to his vice, alcohol. When he moved back to Anderson, Riley had heeded the advice of his old friend Will Hammel that the only thing that stood in the way of success was his weakness. While employed at the *Democrat,* he did not allow drinking to interfere with his work. A letter from Riley to the Indiana temperance lecturer Luther Benson during 1877 shows that it was a constant struggle: "I would escape from a curse which has enshrouded in starless midnight all the days of my life. I would gain the strength that will enable me to stand forth in the future before the world a man; to finish the remainder of my life in something of repose though it be like that which follows the wreck-strewn coast of the sea when its waves have subsided after the tempest has become stilled; I would escape the last of the fiend, the fell spirit alcohol."[43]

By this time, Riley's relationship with Eda Brown was on the wane. Now that he was living in Anderson, his loyalty to his old friend began again to outweigh this romantic attachment. Riley lived with McClanahan while he worked at the *Democrat,* which made his involvement with Brown increasingly untenable. In the months before he returned to Anderson, Brown had admitted her feelings for Riley to McClanahan. As a result, McClanahan had asked her to stop writing to him. Instead of heeding this request, however, Brown continued to correspond with both men and attempted to make each jealous of the other. Finally in May 1877, Brown visited Anderson and met Riley. This meeting did not diminish her feelings for him. Professing to be more in love with him than ever, Brown went to the home of her sister in Minnesota and vowed to wait for Riley to come for her there. However, in the end, it was McClanahan rather than Riley who pursued and wed her.[44]

Riley had lost interest in Brown. Another woman had caught his eye: Will Croan's sister-in-law, Eudora Kate (Kit) Myers. They became seriously involved, and he even asked her to marry him. Riley had probably met Kit when he was in Anderson before. She very likely was the same woman to whom he had boasted back in 1872 that he daily received "from 30 to 35 letters from enamored females." Riley and Myers remained engaged until sometime after he left Anderson in late August 1877.[45]

Despite Riley's engagement to Kit Myers, Dickey has identified Brown as Riley's "golden girl," who had "an uncommon measure of . . . [his] ideal" of womanhood in her character. This argument is unconvincing; Riley's letters to Myers and other women were just as ardent as those he wrote to Brown throughout his youth and most of his adulthood. For instance, he often addressed the Wisconsin poet Ella Wheeler Wilcox, with whom he later started a correspondence, as the woman of his dreams and once called her "Dearest—best—only—'One Woman in the World for Me.'"[46]

Besides, by the time they met, Riley realized that Brown was far from ideal. During the course of their correspondence, Brown revealed to him that she had already possessed many lovers: "LOVERS I had yes . . . One person was not enough—I wanted a crowd." Such a confession must have shocked and probably in some ways titillated his Victorian sensibilities. In addition, Brown had demonstrated that she could lie and be deceitful.[47]

Riley was looking for a woman to replace his mother. He sometimes thought of himself as "a little helpless child" and, even as an adult, longed for someone to comfort him as his mother had.[48] He always described Elizabeth Riley as an ethereal, saintly woman who presided over the private space of the home with grace and a gentle, understanding authority. In essence, Riley had internalized a vision of womanhood that encompassed what was normalized as the feminine ideal in America in the mid-nineteenth century—a woman who was closed away from the physical world to the extent that she seemed opposed to all tangible bodily life and force.[49] Although he did not lack for female admirers, as he stated in a letter to Ella Wheeler Wilcox, no woman could ever meet his expectations:

> The city has been thronged with peerless maidens from all quarters of the globe—and they all love me; madly—passionately—devotedly; and even as I write, a clamorous semicircle of them lies at my feet—"Like a rainbow fallen on the grass"—all wanting me to fly with them and be their own. But I'm an ambitious sort o' prince, you know, and shall not fly just yet—having "register'd a fatal vow" to wed only *an angel* without fleck or flaw or earthly imperfection, and with a pair of snowy wings 'leven feet from tip to tip.[50]

In addition to renewing old acquaintances on his return to Anderson in spring 1877, Riley made many new friends. One of the most important of these was Samuel Richards, a local artist whom he met soon after his arrival there. In a letter to his brother, Riley described Richards as "a young artist . . . on the high road to fame." Richards started out as a photographer but gave "more attention to the brush than the camera." He would eventually become a member of the Hoosier Group of painters along with such men as T. C. Steele and William

Forsyth. Although legend has it that Steele and Riley painted signs together in 1873, no evidence exists to verify the story. Selma and Theodore L. Steele, the painter's widow and son, admitted that this version of events is probably apocryphal. Because Riley never mentioned Steele in the correspondence dating from this earlier period, the pair more likely met through Richards sometime after Riley moved to Anderson to work at the *Democrat*.[51]

Riley and Richards quickly became artistic collaborators and remained friends for life. Richards illustrated many of the poems that Riley contributed to each issue of the *Democrat* with woodblock engravings. According to Riley, these woodblocks "were pretty crude because he [Richards] did not know much about engravings[;] but the poems were goody-goody affairs and nothing to boast of themselves."[52]

Riley, therefore, admitted that much of what he wrote for the *Democrat* was not his best work; and he also revealed that many of his verses actually appeared as advertising for local businesses. Croan immediately put him in charge of this department of the paper because of his past experience. Riley "inaugurated at once a feature of free doggerel advertising." He wrote some serious verse for inclusion on the *Democrat's* editorial page but also wrote "reams and miles" of advertising jingles. Lee O. Harris thought that even some of these had merit: "I did not think that I would ever offer anyone congratulations on an advertising poem but yours is simply immense—The best thing of the kind I ever saw."[53]

Considering his success as an editor, Harris believed that Riley had finally found his professional niche: "I must most sincerely congratulate you on your success as an editor. It is certainly your 'mission[.]' [Y]our paper is already widely known and copied from[,] and some of its contributions are considered worth stealing." As Harris said, the newspaper's reputation was growing quickly; and editors throughout Indiana copied Riley's work.[54]

Riley's contributions made the *Democrat* so popular in Anderson that the owners of its competitor, the *Herald,* felt threatened. The *Democrat's* readers believed that Riley's column of serious poetry "was extremely meritorious, while his comic verse, found on every page of the paper, created no end of amusement." Less than one month after making fun of the *Democrat's* owners, the *Herald's* proprietors were forced to hire a poet of their own: "No first class newspaper should be without a poet. Aware of this requirement, *The Herald* has secured the services of one who with this issue strides down the flowery realms of fancy and throws the shining dance of poesy full and fair at the brazen form of song. Stand back Riley."[55]

The heightened rivalry between these two newspapers, in part, led to one of the most infamous episodes of Riley's career. Over the course of the first few months he spent in Anderson, Riley and some other young men formed a circle to regularly meet to discuss art and literature. Included in this group were

William Kinnard, editor of the *Herald,* as well as the artist Samuel Richards and Riley's old friends Will Ethell and Jim McClanahan. Despite the competition between them, Riley and Kinnard had become friends. However, Kinnard was always laughing at his "pretensions as a poet." During a meeting of this small, informal club in July, part of the group, led by Kinnard, provoked Riley by telling him that the continued rejection of his work by magazines in the East showed that his poems had no real merit.[56]

Kinnard and the other members of the party present knew that this was a sensitive issue for him. Since his appointment to the staff of the *Democrat,* Riley had grown increasingly ambitious. He believed that he had an excellent chance of being accepted by the national magazines when many different newspapers started to pick up and print his poems. Unfortunately, these magazines rejected every poem he sent to them.

Riley became very defensive in response to Kinnard's gibes that these rejections demonstrated that he should "[q]uit pushing . . . [his] pencil and go to painting signs." The magazines had not published his poems because his name was not known to their editors: "the only trouble was . . . I was not known. If a popular writer sent those verses in, I argued, they would at once be accepted." It was therefore for Kinnard's benefit that he concocted the scheme that became known as the "Poe hoax."[57]

Following his July meeting with his local literary friends, Riley became haunted by the idea of preparing a poem "carefully immitating [*sic*] the style of some popular American poet, deceased." He then wanted to introduce it to the public as a newly discovered manuscript written by this same writer. However, Riley knew that he could not publish this poem himself without attracting suspicion that he was its author. Therefore, he wrote to the editor of the *Kokomo Dispatch,* J. O. Henderson, outlining his plan for this hoax and entreating his assistance. Having seen Riley's poems in the *Indianapolis Journal,* Henderson had invited Riley to contribute to the *Dispatch* through a mutual acquaintance just before Riley moved to Anderson in April. Since Henderson had solicited him for "favors" from his pen, Riley believed that he might be amenable to going along with his scheme of deception. In his letter to Henderson, Riley did not reveal the truth about his disagreement with Kinnard. He merely said that he was bored and "yearn[ed] for something to stir things from their comatose condition." He expressed the hope that Henderson shared a "like inclination."[58]

As the preceding citation suggests, Riley tempted Henderson to participate in perpetrating this hoax by making it sound as enticing as possible. Riley put his skills as a salesman to work. He sold his plan to Henderson as an opportunity for attention and publicity that was too exciting and intriguing to pass up:

You may "*give it* [the poem] *to the world for the first time*" thro' the columns of your paper.—Prefacing it, in some ingenious manner, with the assertion that the *original M.S.* was found in the album of an old lady living in your town— and in the hand-writing of the poet unimitated—together with signature, etc—etc.—You can fix the story—only be sure to clinch it so as to defy the scrutiny of the most critical lens. If we succeed, and I think sheer audacity sufficient capital to assure that end,—after "working up" . . . the folks, and smiling over the encomiums of the Press, don't you know; we will then "rise up William Riley," and bust our literary bladder before a bewildered and enlightened world!!!

Riley further built up the allure of the project by telling Henderson that he needed a speedy response and emphasizing the need for confidentiality.[59]

Henderson "tumbled to it [Riley's idea] with eagerness," because it was so "cunningly conceived." He admitted "that newspaper men, as a rule would rather sacrifice honor, liberty, or life itself, than to deviate from the paths of truth—but the idea of getting in a juicy 'scoop' upon the rural exchanges" proved irresistible. Henderson sent his affirmative response to Riley by return mail. So that it could be included in the *Dispatch* the following week, he asked Riley to send him copy for the poem and the article introducing it.[60]

Despite Henderson's homage to "the paths of truth," small-town nineteenth-century newspapermen did not necessarily follow today's norms of objective journalism.[61] These journalists endeavored to establish a vision of community that mirrored the values and goals of its owners and financial backers.[62] The idea of proving Riley's premise true attracted Henderson because he agreed that western writers suffered a great deal of prejudice in the eastern press. Moreover, Riley's scheme gave him a unique opportunity to bring attention to his newspaper and to Kokomo. He could boost his hometown as an enlightened community and, at the same time, demonstrate that the West could produce writers of the same merit as the East.

For this hoax, Riley chose the poem "Leonainie," which he had written in imitation of Edgar Allan Poe's "Annabel Lee." Riley later said that he selected Poe because he "thought that he would enjoy the joke . . . and would not care if . . . [he] took some liberty with his name." Riley liked Poe's insistent use of "an even, metrical flow in versification" and could identify with Poe's "hopeless despair."[63]

Henderson asked Riley to develop a story to explain how a poem penned by this author might fall into the hands of someone living in rural Indiana and then remain undiscovered for many years. However, as "Leonainie" was to be unearthed in Kokomo, Riley thought it would be better for Henderson to manufacture a scenario "to suit the surroundings." Riley gave Henderson some suggestions for this story; but he feared that, if he wrote the introduction to the poem himself, he might betray his own authorship through "some peculiarity of composition." He emphasized that the entire article would receive the "most rigid scrutiny" and that Riley and Henderson had to plan this ruse carefully and be very clever to succeed.[64]

"Leonainie" appeared in the *Kokomo Dispatch* on 2 August 1877 under the following headline: "Posthumous Poetry, A Hitherto Unpublished Poem of the Lamented Edgar Allan Poe—Written on the Fly-Leaf of an Old Book Now in Possession of a Gentleman in this City." Henderson had taken Riley's suggestions and altered them "materially" so that the story behind the poem seemed plausible. He had located an old gentleman by the name of Hurd living in Kokomo, whom he believed would be perfect to identify as the person who held the poem in his possession. Henderson could weave a tale including Hurd that sounded authentic because this man and his family were former residents of Virginia, where Poe had spent much of his time as a young man. Henderson fabricated a story in which he claimed that he had been visiting Hurd "on a business errand" when this man drew his attention "to a poem written on the fly-leaf of an old book." Henderson then stated that he noticed the initials "E. A. P." at the bottom of the page and, with growing excitement, asked Hurd if he knew who had written the poem.[65]

Sure that members of the press and the public would interrogate him about the origins of "Leonainie," Henderson "primed" Hurd about the details of the case as he wanted them to be presented. He carefully shaped the narrative so that Hurd would have to have as little knowledge as possible about this literary manuscript without ruining the story's believability. For example, Hurd would not have to claim direct knowledge of the author of the poem. In his text, Henderson wrote that it had been Hurd's grandfather, the proprietor of a country inn outside Richmond, Virginia, who had encountered the young man who had inscribed "Leonainie" in a book and left it behind in his lodgings. In addition, Henderson observed that it would be "quite natural that . . . [Hurd] should allow the great literary treasure to go for so many years unpublished" as he was uneducated and illiterate.[66]

At the same time, Henderson added details to his story to make it more plausible. Since anyone familiar with Poe would have known his reputation for drinking, Henderson stated that the young man who came to the door of Hurd's grandfather's inn "showed plainly the marks of dissipation." He also described how the poem appeared on the page as if this old book in which it had supposedly been found really existed: "The poem is written in Roman characters, and is almost as legible as print itself, although somewhat faded through lapse of time."[67]

The townspeople of Kokomo fully accepted this story. Henderson related to Riley that they thought "it the finest poem" Poe ever wrote. "Those best aquainted [*sic*] with him declare[d] 'Leoanie' [*sic*] to be Poe-tical in every detail." However, success in Kokomo obviously did not go far enough to prove Riley's hypothesis. Henderson therefore sent marked copies of the "Posthumous Poetry" article to "the Cincinnati, Indianapolis, Boston, New York, Chicago, and Louisville papers." He also sent this issue of the *Dispatch* "to the Monthlies—Atlantic, Harpers, Scribner's[,] etc." Henderson was sure that their voices would "soon be re-verberating throughout the length and breadth of the Commonwealth."[68]

Riley wrote Henderson he was "well pleased . . . and especially grateful for the evident interest" that he had bestowed upon their plan to foist "Leonainie" onto the public. Riley thought Henderson's introduction to "Leonainie" was "superb." He believed that "a neater, sweeter lie was never uttered." Although he perceived that some weak points existed in the narrative which Henderson had pieced together, Riley said that they would actually serve him well by escalating discussions about the poem's authenticity: "There may be a feature or two open to attack, but that's as it should be, for once the excitement of controversy [is] started, a thousand hydra-headed critics will rise up in its behalf—if only to be *contrary.*"[69] These statements show that Riley understood that the more heightened and widespread the controversy became, the greater effect the poem would have on his reputation when he finally revealed that he was its author.

Besides Henderson and himself, only two other people knew the truth about "Leonainie." Riley called them the "'ring' around the literary torpedo." He assigned each a different role in his stratagem and swore both to secrecy. One of these individuals was none other than William Kinnard of the *Anderson Herald.* Riley made Kinnard privy to the conspiracy to prove him wrong about his contentions concerning his lack of talent as a poet. As part of his elaborate plan to throw people off guard, Riley determined that he himself would express doubts about the authorship of "Leonainie" in the *Democrat* to deflect any suspicion that he might have written the poem; and he convinced Kinnard to pretend to believe the poem was really Poe's. The day after Henderson released "Leonainie" to the press, Kinnard copied the poem and predicted "a rhapsody of jealous censure from the jingling editor . . . of *The Democrat.*" He prophesied that Riley would attack it with "exhausting and damning criticism."[70] Although Riley planned to fulfill Kinnard's predictions, he did not want to appear to be provoked into responding one way or another.[71]

Riley planned the appearance of his article respecting the publication of "Leonainie" carefully. He waited to see how newspapers outside Anderson and Kokomo would react to Henderson's notices. Some papers, such as the *Indianapolis News,* waited a few days and then published stories that doubted the poem had such venerable origins. Riley told Henderson that they could not "expect the public to gulp it [their story] whole." He explained that people were "bound to suspect the 'worm' contained a hook." Despite receiving some negative comment, Riley determined it was too early to be discouraged, especially because no real literary authority had yet made any argument respecting the poem: "The singular reticence of the . . . dailies may auger good—or—bad—Time only will disclose; and bear in mind no *critic* has as yet pronounced upon it. We will give them 'a long pull—a strong pull, and a pull all together,' and in the meantime let me assure you that my ardor is not in the least dampened."[72]

The "long[,] . . . strong pull" to which Riley referred involved a gentle prodding of literary critics through the press. Because he did not want newspapers to drop the story, he deemed that the timing was now perfect for the appearance of his critical review. Before printing his editorial in the next issue of the *Democrat,* Riley warned Henderson that he would have to state that he was perhaps the victim of a "clever deception." However, Riley tempered his negative comments in this article with compliments about the poem's overall quality:

> To sum the poem as a whole we are at some loss. It most certainly contains rare attributes of grace and beauty; and although we have not the temerity to accuse the gifted Poe of its authorship, for equal strength of reason we can not deny it is his production; but as for the enthusiastic editor of *The Dispatch,* we are not inclined, as yet, to the belief that he is wholly impervious to the wiles of deception.

Riley explained that, although he ostensibly set out to condemn the poem, he ultimately "furnished more praise than blame." He wanted his words to manifest "a covert jealousy of the 'Dispatch'" and would "do anything to throw unfavorable comment out o' gear."[73]

In case his review "caus[ed] any public comment to its detriment," Riley furnished Henderson with a private letter in which he expressed the belief that the poem was genuine so that he could answer the *Democrat's* article by reproducing it. Riley also encouraged Henderson to respond to his editorial by openly disparaging him: "It would be well, perhaps for you to give me a slur of some kind this week—in response to our notice in [the] last issue. Make it hot—call us jealous etc. &c."[74]

To further balance his own negative review, he enlisted the help of Dulcina Mason Jordan of the *Richmond Independent.* Jordan, a poet as well as an editor whom Riley greatly admired at the time, was the final member of his "'ring' around the literary torpedo." Riley directed her to write an article supporting the view that Poe was indeed the poem's author: "I don't want you to *really* admire it—but I do want you to *pretend* to, and *eulogize* over [it] at rapturous length, and as though you were assured it was in reality the work of Poe himself.

... Our object is to work up the 'Press' broadcast if possible, and then to unsack the feline." Riley understood that if his plot were to succeed he needed to keep the story before the public eye in the newspapers until "time ... ripened the deception."[75]

Although the newspapers had not yet reacted as he wished, Riley noticed that the claims Henderson had forwarded about "Leonainie" worried many editors. Some critics even called "Leonainie" a "fine" and "grand thing." Such pronouncements convinced Riley that they wanted to trust in its authenticity: "*Everybody would like to believe*—they *want to* the worst way." He told Henderson that he thought the critics' reluctance to reject the poem as a fraud was "a good sign" and that patience and a steadfast dedication to their original plan would result in success. Riley even concluded that he would be rewarded for the ingeniousness of his deception, as he had been for pulling off more minor shams in the past: "... the 'euchred' public will be forced not only to forgive, but render homage."[76]

Within a couple of days, Henderson and Riley began to learn that major newspapers were beginning to pick up the "Leonainie" story. Henderson reported to Riley that the plot they had manufactured to introduce the poem "seem[ed] to somewhat disarm criticism." The *New York Herald* republished the *Dispatch*'s article in its entirety on 5 August, and publication of the poem soon followed in the *New York Sun,* the *Indianapolis Journal,* and the *Cincinnati Gazette.* By the middle of August, "Leonainie" had appeared in the *New York World Tribune,* the *New York Post,* the *Chicago Tribune,* the *Chicago Inter-Ocean,* the *Boston Globe,* and the *Louisville Courier-Journal.* Among those who were fully taken in by the fraud was Edmund Clarence Stedman, a highly regarded poet and editor who was considered one of the deans of American letters.[77]

Both men were overwhelmed with the sudden success of their hoax, but Henderson was ebullient: "Think of the N.Y. *Herald*! the grandest journal in christendom, gulping it down!" He proclaimed that no article ever published in a "country," Indiana newspaper had ever been so widely reprinted, and believed that Riley's fame was assured and that "Leonainie" had enough merit to "place it in the front ranks of poetry in America."[78]

However, Henderson and Riley were just about to lose control of the situation. William F. Gill, a Poe biographer and owner of a publishing company in Boston, contacted Henderson requesting the original manuscript of "Leonainie." Gill owned the original autograph copy of Poe's poem "The Bells" and, therefore, told Henderson that he could positively identify the handwriting. Henderson wrote to Riley asking him how he should respond.[79]

With this new complication, Riley brought his friend Samuel Richards into the inner circle. To produce a manuscript they hoped would satisfy Gill, Richards imitated Poe's handwriting and copied "Leonainie" into an old dictionary. Riley delivered it to Henderson by train. His trip to Kokomo raised some suspicions.[80]

At about this same time, the secret leaked out to Steve Metcalf, an employee of the *Anderson Herald.* Riley later admitted to Henderson that he planned the disclosure that led to Metcalf's knowledge of the hoax without realizing all the ramifications. Metcalf threatened to expose the fraud in the next edition of his newspaper. However, Kinnard, who owned controlling interest in the *Herald,* prevented this from occurring.[81]

Rebuffed by his own newspaper, Metcalf sent the story to the *Kokomo Tribune,* the *Dispatch's* rival. The owners of the *Tribune* printed an exposé of the Poe hoax on 25 August, a couple of days after they received Mecalf's letter. The *Tribune's* article would force Henderson and Riley to admit that they had instigated the entire scenario. Henderson thought that they should try to "'scoop' the *Tribune* again [by] turn[ing] the joke on them." He suggested that they claim that they "had arranged with a friend in Anderson to write to the *Tribune* under cover of secrecy and 'expose' the *ruse,* knowing that they [the owners] would do it heartily and with all their soul, hoping thereby to 'get even' with *The Dispatch.*" Henderson did not wish to reveal the whole truth. Instead, he wanted to deflect attention from his own misdeeds by making it look as if he and Riley had duped the *Tribune* into printing the exposé.[82]

Riley later admitted to Henderson that much of what he said about how the *Tribune* had gotten the story was actually true. Without Henderson's knowledge, Riley had allowed the *Tribune* to discover the Poe hoax. He apologized for not conferring with Henderson on his "ruse for throwing the expose in the *Tribune's* hands." Riley said that he had badly misjudged the situation: "for instead . . . of my *'pretended'* enemy [who] was the medium of its disclosure—it was a *pretended* friend into whose hands I threw it. I did not think of the result, and did it more for a private test than anything else."[83]

Despite the article in the *Tribune,* Riley had no desire to put an end to his experiment or confirm that he was responsible. Although he and Henderson had been successful in getting "Leonainie" a wide audience, many of the newspapers that republished the poem remained unwilling to pronounce any firm opinion as to whether or not Poe was its author. For this reason, Riley resisted conceding to the facts: "I do not like the idea of being *compelled* to confess the fraud before real critical tests have been applied." Although Henderson had acknowledged the truth verbally, Riley contended that they did not yet need to admit the ruse. The *Tribune's* exposé could still be refuted. Henderson could say that Riley had manufactured this story for the newspaper because he wanted to claim a poem whose excellence he envied. Riley advised Henderson to then "express regret that one so full of promise could stoop to such a depth." Refusing to recognize that he had lost control of circumstances,

Riley insisted that he would confess only when he was ready. He still believed that he could select his "own good time."[84]

Henderson replied that the *Dispatch* could no longer keep silent because the *Tribune* was "fairly ranting." In his next issue, he revealed that Riley was the author of "Leonainie" and portrayed the whole thing as a "harmless ruse" that he had used "to play a clever joke on the *Tribune* . . . and to assist a rising poet to receive criticism all over the land at the hands of the ablest critics free from sectional feeling or local jealousy." In the meantime, Riley sent a parody of "Leonainie" to the *Tribune* in an effort to further confound the public about his role in the hoax.[85]

Five days after the first exposé had appeared in the *Tribune,* Riley finally admitted that he was the author of "Leonainie" and explained the entire scheme in a letter to the editor of the *Indianapolis Journal.* Riley said that he and his other friends involved had not come forward earlier because the plot had advanced farther than they ever anticipated and that, as a result, they feared the consequences of their actions: "for when we found our literary bombshell bounding throughout the length and breadth of the Union, we were so bewildered and involved we knew not how to act. Our only intercourse had been by post, and we could not advise together fairly in that way; in consequence a fibrous growth of circumstances had chained us in a manner, and a fear of unjust censure combined to hold us silent for so long."[86]

At this point, people were even suspicious of Riley's confession because of all he had done to obscure the truth. Riley was still scheming to confuse the issue of "Leonainie's" authorship on the same day that his letter appeared in the *Indianapolis Journal.* He wrote an anonymous letter to the editor of the *Indianapolis Sentinel* to cast doubt on the idea that he had written the poem:

> I notice in this mornings [*sic*] Indianapolis Journal . . . a covert attempt to claim for their pet poet J. W. Riley . . . the authorship of the lately discovered poem of Poe's, the beautiful and mysterious "Leonainie," which has for some weeks been bewildering the literary world. The article refered [*sic*] [to] apparantly [*sic*] sides with an article taken from the Kokomo Tribune—jealous of the good fortune of . . . the rival paper whose good fortune it was to . . . find the original Ms. and first publish it. Whether the poem is indeed Poe's I do not undertake to say, but this much I am assured of[,] that the well laid plan of Riley, . . . the Kokomo Tribune and the Journal is altogether too thin a proposition to go down in this community. Riley . . . may and doubtless does possess some Genious [*sic*] for verse-making but he can juggle with truth gracefully, and his recent visit to Kokomo points directly to his complicity with the Tribune's story of the poem's paternity.[87]

This letter demonstrates how unwilling Riley was to give up his desire to prove that his poetry was just as worthy of admiration as that written by authors whom the literary establishment recognized as being great. He was so obsessed by the idea that he thought nothing about ruining his own personal reputation for integrity in the process.

Some people wanted to see Riley punished for using the press in an attempt to fool the public with the intent of furthering his own purposes. The staff of the *Kokomo Tribune* not only published a severe rebuke but also talked against him in the streets. Will Croan dismissed Riley from the *Anderson Democrat,* and even J. O. Henderson questioned his judgment and his loyalty after he submitted his parody, "Leoloony," to the *Tribune.* Many of his friends abandoned him, and no other newspaper would hire him. Finding himself again without steady employment, Riley was forced to return to Greenfield. Although his fiancée, Kit Myers, stood by him, their relationship was doomed. He now had no means with which to support her and, soon after the incident was over, fell into depression and started drinking.[88]

Riley described this period as one of the darkest in his life. "The whole matter started as a thoughtless joke," Riley later said, "and ended in being one of the most unpleasant experiences of my life."[89] Obviously, many people did not accept that Riley had been "blameless of all dishonorable motives ... [when he] feigned ignorance of the real authorship of the poem." The editors of the *Cincinnati Commercial* made fun of what they perceived as self-aggrandizement. They criticized Riley for overstating the hoax's success:

> It is probable the world is entirely ignorant, or was until the letter of "My DEAR RILEY" was put to print, of the prodigious effect that had been produced by his imposition. The crushed editors and journalists of the land, including those of the New York Evening *Post,* appear to have gone about their daily business of collecting, disseminating and commenting upon the current news, unconscious of the enjoyment "My Dear RILEY" derived from their self-inflicted writhings, bitings, and stingings.... If it were not that this extraordinary genius is of consequence to the world, and what he does, says and thinks of matters of great public concern, it might be safely assumed that the publishers and editors who gave currency to his verses have not been as sadly afflicted as he imagines them to be. As a rule they do not make large pretensions to literary attainments, nor do they sit in the high seat of judgment upon purely literary performances. Their chief business in life is to collect and distribute the news of the day, and they have ordinarily very little space in their newspapers to devote to literature.[90]

Ironically, by remarking at length on this letter, the editors of the *Commercial,* in effect, gave Riley the importance they wanted so much to deny him.

In the following months, Riley did not remain silent about the affair in the hope that people would soon forget about it. Instead, he continued to justify his actions publicly to win sympathy and to keep his name in the newspapers.[91] For example, in October 1877, Riley wrote a letter to John M. Anderson of the *Cincinnati Gazette,* in which he painted himself as the victim of rebukes of unjustified severity because "Leonainie" had fooled so many people. He complained that he received the most serious reproaches from newspapers that had accepted his false claims:

> it is but a segment of the abuse that has been heaped upon it by an irate press throughout the entire country, and only condemned in that it was the means of duping that owl-wise institution almost from A to izzard. . . . Well, it went, and "Everybody took it." . . . Not only was it gobbled by the State press, but by the ablest literary journals of the country, not to except William Cullen Bryant's *New York Post.* This latter named oracle, no sooner aquainted [*sic*] with our expose, wheeled about, as did a hundred others, and heaped upon the poor, puny baby verses every species of malignity and venom they could coax out of their bills. So mad, in fact, so duped and thistle-whipped, they could but writhe and bite to sting themselves. . . . When the poem has been attacked, the assault has come direct from some poor victim of the fraud.[92]

Some of his friends, such as Benjamin Parker, though sympathetic toward him, were quick to suspect Riley of "tricks and subterfuges" to promote himself in the years immediately following the publication of "Leonainie." Throughout his life, Riley continued to describe the Poe hoax as a "boy's fool trick" and contended that he never supposed that "Leonainie" would go beyond the newspaper exchanges within the state. Riley was nearly twenty-eight, so this can hardly be classified as a youthful indiscretion, and his correspondence from the time disproves this characterization of the events. Although the scheme was foolish and immature, Riley took it very seriously once he had undertaken it. He knew that Henderson meant to send clippings of their article to all of the most important metropolitan newspapers and most prestigious monthly magazines. He certainly did nothing to discourage him and hoped that these publications would pick up the story. Even after "Leonainie" had been reprinted in a great many of these journals, Riley did not want to abandon the scheme because he did not feel that his theory about works by famous authors had been adequately tested.[93]

In some ways, Riley was naive. He fully believed that he would be able to control the evolution of the plot and see that his drama had a happy ending. Because the smaller schemes he had designed as a sign painter and advertiser had almost all ended positively without any real recrimination against him, Riley also thought that his audience would easily forgive his deceit and reward him for his cleverness and talent. He had not allowed himself to think about all the ways that his plan could backfire.[94]

Furthermore, when things went wrong, Riley was disinclined to take responsibility for his actions. Instead, he believed that choosing Poe as the author to imitate for the scheme brought him bad luck and continued to do so until the end of his days. "Dangers," Riley remarked, "and harpies, bad tidings. . ., disappointments, distressful conditions—I draw them like a lightning rod." He said that these disasters dated from the night he wrote the Poe poem. By writing "Leonainie," he believed that he brought the bad luck that had been Poe's upon himself. Riley already felt that he was tied mystically to Poe, as he had been born on the day that Poe died; and he convinced himself that "Leonainie" only served to cement the supernatural connections between them. Because of the hoax, other writers sometimes noted similarities between the lives of two men and even suggested that Riley was Poe reincarnated.[95]

From time to time, the "Leonainie" controversy resurfaced, forcing Riley to explain what had happened over and over. Some people did not accept what he told them and could not be persuaded that he, not Poe, was the poem's author. When he recounted the story, he claimed that newspapers would not print his explanation of the hoax "for weeks," when in fact the *Indianapolis Journal* published his confession as soon as it was received. Riley liked to exaggerate such details, including the success of the hoax and the misfortune it brought him. He painted as dark a picture as possible of his loneliness and despair following the incident: " . . . I stood outside, alone, and walked around the courthouse square at night, and through the drizzle and the rain peered longingly at the dim light in the office where I used to sleep, with a heart as hard and obdurate as the towel in the composing room."[96]

In the short run, the Poe hoax did indeed bring Riley nothing but grief. At the end of 1877, as he sat without a job in Greenfield, his future looked bleak. Because of the attacks he received, he probably believed he would never be welcome again in the literary world. However, "Leonainie" brought Riley notoriety. For the first time, people outside Indiana had an opportunity to become familiar with his name. Moreover, Riley was never entirely without defenders. Some people sympathized with him and understood why he had undertaken such a foolish experiment, for it was true that writers in the West had trouble gaining recognition.[97]

In the end, "Leonainie" did Riley more good than harm. As D. M. Jordan cleverly suggested through a play on words in a letter she wrote soon after its climax, the scandal made Riley an interesting personality who drew public attention: "It ["Leonainie"] has made a commotion hasn't it? The question is, has Leonainie made you 'lion' any? I think it has." The poem and the intrigue surrounding it indirectly launched him on the road to fame and became an important facet of the Riley legend.[98]

Exploring Literary Possibilities

After he had attained wealth and fame, Riley liked to remind his readers that his success had not come easily. He told about how a writer friend once came to him heartbroken at his lack of success in getting published. Riley asked him how long this had been going on, and the young man answered three years. "'My dear man . . . [, Riley replied,] keep on trying till you have spent as many years at it as I did.' 'As many years as you did!' he exclaimed. 'Yes, sir, through years, through sleepless nights, through almost helpless days. For twenty years I tried to get into one magazine; back came my manuscripts eternally. I kept on. In the twentieth year, that magazine accepted one of my articles.'"[1]

Riley was referring to the *Atlantic Monthly,* to which he had sent poem after poem starting in the late 1870s. He persisted until this grand old monthly finally agreed to publish "The Sermon of the Rose" in 1898.[2] Riley did not believe that he was truly successful as a writer until the *Atlantic* accepted his work. He had already been published in other quality magazines, but Riley considered the *Atlantic Monthly* the ultimate literary journal. As the oldest publication in this category, it had been the chief supporter of high-literary professional writers and upheld a cultural ethos that permitted them to pursue their vision as creators of fine literature. When the *Atlantic* published his verse, Riley could feel that he finally had attained his goal. He had never given up on this dream, which had led him to foist the Poe hoax upon the public.[3]

Believing him responsible for trying to deceive journalists and critics to gain recognition, some publications were anything but eager to print Riley's work for a time. Indeed, Riley maintained that the Poe hoax kept his verse out of magazines for at least three or four years because their editors were not convinced that the poems he submitted were his own.[4] Despite his discouragement, he was determined to overcome their prejudices.

Although he ultimately wanted to be considered an artist, single-mindedly devoted to mastering his craft, Riley never felt a need to separate his writing from commercial interests. At the time that his career as a poet was emerging in the decades following the Civil War, writing itself was in the process of being redefined as a social activity in America. In the postbellum period, the new institutions created by the great expansion of publishing, a high literacy rate, and increased leisure time brought more opportunities to writers and stabilized the support they received from the public. However, with these new developments, the field of writing became increasingly stratified. Writers began to engage in different types of literary production to appeal to separate segments of the population.[5]

When these new literary cultures were just emerging, authors of Riley's generation had a variety of options. Even as a poet, Riley could write for the masses as well as for an educated elite. The writing of poetry was not yet necessarily considered an esoteric pursuit, best left to intellectuals and artists outside the cultural mainstream. Riley saved his best and most ambitious work for the literary magazines but also took advantage of opportunities offered by local newspapers that were "seemingly eager to advance and lend assistance to the poor bedrabbled strugglers in the ever-standing army of poets, jingle-ringers, and verse-carpenters."[6]

By the turn of the century, Riley's homely Hoosier verses, "once satisfied with a place in an Indiana newspaper, are now made into Christmas books, superbly bound, with fine colored illustrations, as though the author ranked with Tennyson or Browning. And, in fact, he does."[7] Printed in book format, Riley's poems had become a sign of taste to be displayed in the parlor.

During the late 1870s, having his poetry bound in leather with gilt edges and high-quality illustrations was a distant prospect for Riley. Although at first he believed the Poe hoax represented a setback, he did not abandon his ambition. He began to mature as an artist and started to separate himself from the poets he considered masters to develop a style of his own. Following the example of Dickens and Poe, he also bolstered his reputation as a poet by performing his original work on the lecture platform. In a continual search for a means to succeed, Riley evolved as a writer who was willing to embrace the different work experiences that the literary cultures of the late nineteenth century offered.[8]

"I have been damned up hill and down dale till I enjoy it," Riley said sarcastically to J. O. Henderson in September 1877, shortly after the *Kokomo Tribune* revealed that he had written "Leonainie." He told Henderson that he had "been quite ill in consequence" and that he could "do no head-work for a while." Following a quick escape to Greenfield, Riley summoned the courage to return to Anderson a few days later and, when he wrote to Henderson, had only recently learned that he had lost his job at the *Democrat.* Although he found that he had just as many friends as enemies in the town that had become his second home, he opted to go back to Greenfield to salvage what he could of his life and career. He promised to send Henderson "his earliest efforts" once he started to write again.[9]

When melancholy, Riley turned to alcohol. For nearly two weeks after his role in the Poe hoax was exposed, Riley drank incessantly. In his letter to Henderson, Riley tried to cover up his drinking by referring to it as an "illness." Drinking only served to multiply his problems and made the ones he already had seem worse. Alcohol fed his depression, and the more he drank the more difficult he found it to stop. Riley felt cursed by his drinking problem. At one time, he remarked to George Ade that once he took a drink he wanted "a churn full."[10]

Although he attempted to hide the true nature of his shortcomings from his fiancée, Kit Myers, Riley ended up admitting to her how low he had fallen. He compared this drinking bout to a descent into hell:

> O Kit you do me wrong—indeed you do! My love for you is so great that I have tried to hold from you, only that which would give you extra pain and God knows I give you misery enough. . . . I have walked down . . . in Hell so far that your dear voice had almost failed to reach me, but thank God I can *hear* you, though I may not touch your hand till I have washed my own in tears of true repentance. . . . I *have* been sick, dear Kit, but of the *soul,* for had so fierce a malady attacked the *body,* I would have died with all hell hugged in my arms. I can speak of this *now* because I can tell you *I am saved.*[11]

Beginning in the 1830s, many people in America equated drinking with sin and damnation and abstinence with salvation.[12] Despite the infiltration of medical language into the area of social reform, the chronic abuse of alcohol was considered a vice rather than a disease. During the late 1800s, even the medical profession did not understand this problem well. In fact, the term "alcoholism" itself was very new.[13] Many people persisted in using the now archaic "dipsomania" to describe this addiction on into the twentieth century.[14]

Especially in America, drinking was defined as a religious and moral problem. Drunkards were perceived as "weak, self-indulgent, profoundly flawed individuals."[15] As the nineteenth century progressed, the view of alcoholics became more unforgiving. They were increasingly portrayed as morally reprehensible and personally disgusting.[16] Like much of the rest of society, doctors and social reformers held drinkers responsible for their actions and thought that they threatened the social order. Alcoholics were commonly isolated against their will to break their dependence. On the occasions when they were admitted to hospitals, the institutions' personnel stigmatized them. Preventive programs involved "the promotion of moral awareness and civic responsibility."[17] As classification and treatment were put in moral and religious terms, it was natural for Riley to make an analogy about his habit which included hell, repentance, and spiritual redemption.

Because she stood by him despite the disgrace of the "Leonainie" affair, Riley felt he could reveal his vulnerabilities to Myers. Nevertheless, he reassured her that he had emerged from his sorry state and had undergone what he likened to a religious conversion to suggest to her that he had given up drinking for good.[18] Regardless of the circumstances, because she loved him, Myers was sympathetic. She professed that she could not love him more. However, she made it clear that she expected him to stay sober for her sake as well as his own: "All I ask is that you remain just as pure and noble as you now are."[19] Riley wished to continue his relationship with Myers. Furthermore, he knew that he could not write as long as he was under the influence of alcohol. Although he meant to keep away from liquor, he was incapable of doing what Myers asked of him. Riley always said that "Drink is a very insistent and cushion-footed enemy." Sometime during October 1877, Riley's engagement to Myers ended.[20]

As he emerged from his drunken depression, Riley started to write again. He submitted his work to newspapers that backed him strongly in the past. The *Indianapolis Journal*, the *Indianapolis Herald*, the *Kokomo Dispatch*, and the *New Castle Mercury* did not hesitate to print Riley's poems in their columns.[21]

Support also came from unexpected places. Ironically, Riley started corresponding with Charles Philips, who was an owner of the *Kokomo Tribune*, the paper that had exposed the Poe hoax. Until he died in 1881, this Kokomo publisher turned out to be one of Riley's most important professional connections.[22]

During the last months of 1877, Riley immersed himself in his literary pursuits but found little else to interest him at home in Greenfield. The small town bored him, and he missed the stimulus of the company of many of his old friends:

I've been home for *years,* this last time. Altho' Greenfield is in better *health* than I ever knew her to enjoy before, she has detioriated [*sic*] *mentally* till, I grieve to say, I find her anything but companionable; not that I've grown so uncommon wise, for I have not (as you perceive)—but that all my friends are gone and their places mushroomed o'er with milk-and-water intellects. . . . Jess [Millikan] is away you know, and John S[kinner] as well; and to draw on Jim Walsh or George Hauck for *literary* sympathy would be like drawing for—well, the boss prize in a cock and bull lottery.[23]

Riley would soon find the "*literary* sympathy" he so desired from Clara Louise Bottsford, a young schoolmistress who was boarding at his father's home. Riley, who always preferred brunettes, not only found her intelligent but also was attracted to her "black, black hair and dark mysterious eyes."[24] He wrote about Clara in a letter to his old friend Nellie (Millikan) Cooley and thanked her for putting in a good word for him with this new object of his affections: "By the bye, Miss Bottsford now boards at the Riley Hostlery [*sic*], and as I'm there occasionally myself I've gotten almost acquainted with her at last. Sometimes I walk with her to school, like Mary's little lamb; in fact Miss B. is quite companionable. She often speaks of you, and told me only yesterday that you had given her the first view of my real character—for which me thanks!"[25]

Difficult circumstances had brought this young woman to Greenfield. Clara's parents had died a few years earlier, leaving her and five younger children behind to fend for themselves. Clara became the head of household. She and her brother Beaumont (Bona) assumed responsibility for overseeing the operation of the family farm, which her father Elijah purchased in 1860. During the depression years of the 1870s, this 160-acre parcel of land, located in Sugar Creek Township near New Philadelphia, Indiana, decreased in worth. In the face of deteriorating land values and declining farm commodity prices, Clara was forced to take a position as a teacher in Greenfield to give herself and her brothers and sisters another source of income. Bottsford's employers in the Greenfield school district admired her industry and her will to rise above the adverse situation in which she found herself.[26]

In Clara, Riley found a sympathetic soul. Although the opportunities offered by the Hancock County public schools limited her formal education, Clara, like Riley, acquired an interest in writing. In addition to all of her other duties, she found time to write poems and submitted them under a pseudonym for publication in local newspapers. Moreover, she hoped someday to be able to devote herself full-time to her literary work. Therefore, Clara fully understood the obstacles that Riley faced as an author; and she helped fill the void left by his old friends with whom he had discussed mythology and literature. Sharing similar interests and aspirations, Riley and Bottsford started to fall in love.[27]

Despite the prospect of a new relationship and the support of his friends, Riley remained discouraged by the professional setback that followed the Poe hoax. With many acquaintants, he struggled to be cheerful and denied that the negative criticisms he had received in the press in past months bothered him, declaring that he was "not so sensitive." Nevertheless, Riley bemoaned the fact that he was "difficult . . . and about as much at home in practical life as a man in a milliner shop."[28] Although outwardly optimistic, he had no money and often thought his prospects held no hope of change. A poem called "We are Not Always Glad When We Smile," which he submitted to the *Indianapolis Journal* in early December 1877, revealed much about his outlook:

> We are not always glad when we smile:
> Though we wear a fair face and are gay,
> And the world we deceive
> May not ever believe
> We could laugh in a happier way.—
>
> Yet, down in the deeps of the soul,
> Ofttimes, without faces aglow,
> There's an ache and a moan
> That we know of alone,
> And as only the hopeless may know.[29]

In his continuing despair over his drinking problem, Riley reached out to the temperance lecturer Luther Benson for help. He read Benson's autobiography, *Fifteen Years in Hell,* and took heart. Benson had once been an uncontrolled drinker. He was one of many reformed alcoholics who preached temperance during the mid-nineteenth century and made a success by recounting how alcohol had almost destroyed their lives.

This phenomenon grew out of the Washingtonian movement, which began in 1840. In Baltimore, a small group of men drinking in a bar sent representatives to a temperance lecture. They repented and became the core of the Washingtonian movement. This temperance movement expanded rapidly. By 1841, the Washingtonians had one hundred thousand members; and, within two years, half a million men belonged. These reformed alcoholics spread their message by acting out the miseries associated with drunkenness. Their leader, John Bartholomew Gough, was one of the most popular lecturers in America. Benson's speeches resembled those given by Gough. He terrified his audiences by telling sensational stories about the horrors of delirium tremens and alcohol-induced crime.[30]

In his autobiography, Benson told about the physical and spiritual destruction his alcohol consumption caused. This was a common narrative formula of nineteenth-century temperance tracts and works of fiction. Social reform literature, including novels and short stories, followed characters from their first misguided sip to destitution and even death.[31] Benson's autobiography so deeply affected Riley that he wrote a poem dedicated to its author in which he depicted the popular lecturer's victimization and ultimate deliverance from drink. Riley could have been describing himself in much of the poem, for he was also a "Poor victim of that vulture curse / That hovers o'er the universe, / With ready talons quick to strike."[32] Although Riley often parodied the popular lecturer, he knew that the two of them were very similar.[33] If Benson could quit drinking, the poet thought that he perhaps could do the same.

By the beginning of 1878, Benson had been corresponding with Riley for quite some time. He visited Riley in Greenfield, and they became good friends. Because of his past, Benson could identify with Riley's troubles. He took a strong interest in Riley and admired his talents. Benson not only tried to help Riley in his battle against drinking but also bought him a new suit of clothes as he saw that Riley was ill-clad and possessed little money. At this time, Riley was preparing for a public lecture. Benson recognized Riley's potential as an entertainer and knew that he needed to look respectable to succeed.[34]

Although sympathetic, many of Riley's closest friends understood that he brought much of the misery he experienced upon himself. They thought he expected too much for himself too soon and hoped that he had learned that there were few shortcuts to fame and fortune. For example, Samuel Richards told Riley that "true, lasting success comes only by honest, faithful, persistent industry . . . and lastly but not least by the enduring patience of years." He encouraged Riley to persevere and pointed out that he needed the experience that only long periods of careful study and writing could bring.[35]

Despite this advice, ambition drove Riley to try his luck with the monthly magazines once more. In mid-January, he sent the first of many poems to Josiah Gilbert Holland, the editor of *Scribner's Monthly*. Although Holland found that Riley's writings showed "good poetic feeling" and were "much above the average," he feared that they fell "short of literature." Holland was not totally discouraging. He was convinced that Riley only needed to mature as an author. However, receiving such an assessment probably only frustrated Riley more, for yet another party was telling him he could "afford to wait" to gain a national hearing.[36]

At least in one regard, Riley could not afford to wait. Most immediately, he needed the income that publication in a magazine would bring. With no steady employment, Riley explored every possible avenue to find a way to make a living. When he was most disconsolate about his condition, he reminded himself that he had another trade if writing did not work out for him; and, during this time, he was willing to take some assignments as a sign painter so that he would have a little money in his pockets.[37]

Riley's experience was far from uncommon for writers who were not independently wealthy. Walt Whitman flailed around trying to find an audience for his poetry; and to support himself he worked as carpenter, newspaper editor, and government clerk.[38] In addition to taking different kinds of jobs, many young artists and authors were willing to submit their work to a variety of different literary vehicles. For example, Louisa May Alcott wrote sensational stories for the emerging pulp fiction market at the same time that she contributed her more ambitious writings to *Atlantic Monthly*. Still other literary figures, such as Theodore Dreiser, at intervals gave up some of their autonomy to work for the tabloid press for the security of a regular paycheck.[39]

A regular paycheck was exactly what Riley hoped for when he wrote his old patron E. B. Martindale of the *Indianapolis Journal* in January 1878. Remembering that the newspaperman had once offered him a job, Riley was determined to demonstrate that he was worthy of the many former kindnesses Martindale had shown him:

> I am more than eager to please you and to be of service; and wherein I fail may be due only to my not comprehending fully the exact character of the work you asked me to do.
>
> It may be an erroneous idea—certainly not an egotistical one—to feel the assurance I do of pleasing the public with quaint paragraphs—at any rate I certainly desire that the test be made, and if I fail, I will meet the disappointment like a man . . . .
>
> Will you do me the honor to write to me a line or two, when leisure affords, and tell me frankly where my failings are![40]

Apparently Riley was aware that he had lost credibility with Martindale because of the Poe hoax. Therefore, he reassured Martindale that from now on he would test his poetry in the market in a legitimate way, and would take any disappointments "like a man."[41] He obviously hoped to get back in Martindale's good graces.

But Martindale remained cool over the course of the next few months. He even gave Riley the impression that he might stop publishing his poems and prose sketches.[42] He certainly was not ready to offer him a job. Thankfully, employment at the *Journal* was not Riley's only option. He was assured by Luther Benson and others that lecturing was a viable means to earn some money. By the time Riley was getting ready to enter this arena on a regular basis in the late 1870s, lectures were "a national and pervading institution." In fact, John Gentile calls the last quarter of the nineteenth century the "golden age" of platform performances.[43]

Because many towns possessed few theaters or concert halls, traveling lecturers enjoyed great popularity. Most of these lecturers were provided by the lyceum, an institution first organized by Josiah Holbrook in Connecticut in

1826. In communities across the country, lyceums coordinated lectures in the arts, sciences, religion, and literature, which helped fulfill the highly literate American public's demand for information. Because lectures covered many different topics, the platform attracted a wide range of well-known novelists, poets, preachers, and politicians, as well as famous actors and actresses.[44]

Throughout 1876 and most of 1877, Riley did recitations in churches and schoolhouses; but, by the end of 1877, he was ready to enter more seriously into the lecture circuit. Always interested in marketing himself effectively, Riley studied the talent the lyceum bureaus listed in their schedules. Noting that many of the performers under contract were humorists, Riley thought he had a good chance of succeeding if he created funny characters for his readings. By presenting predominantly humorous material, he followed the lead of Samuel L. Clemens ("Mark Twain"), David Ross Locke ("Petroleum V. Nasby"), James M. Bailey ("The Danbury Newsman"), and Henry Wheeler Shaw ("Josh Billings"), who were some of the best nineteenth-century American humorists and among the most popular platform performers.[45]

Riley was also following in the footsteps of Will Carleton, another popular midwestern poet and performer. Born on a farm in Michigan in 1845, Carleton was the first poet who gained a national audience largely through his readings of the poems he wrote depicting midwestern rural life. Although Henry Wadsworth Longfellow, James Russell Lowell, Oliver Wendell Holmes, and John Greenleaf Whittier sometimes did public readings, because of their lack of ability on the platform none of them earned much of a reputation for their performances. Edgar Allan Poe intended much of his work for recitation, but he lacked the organizational skills needed to make arrangements for successful public appearances and achieved his widespread popularity too late to capitalize on a lecture career. In contrast, Carleton began by lecturing and writing for a local newspaper. By 1871, he was performing his poetry five nights a week, earning between $75 and $100 each time he went out on the rostrum. Between Longfellow's death in 1882 and 1888, when Riley eclipsed him, he was the most popular poet in the United States. As poet-performers, Carleton and Riley set precedents for the economics of poetry in the twentieth century. Performance played a prominent role in the careers of such American poets as Carl Sandburg and Robert Frost, and "today's poets frequently earn more from their public readings than from royalties."[46]

In late January 1878, Riley was ready to go out on the rostrum; but he did not have the money or the reputation to join a lyceum bureau. As a professional booking organization, the lyceum bureau "served as agent between the lecturer [or reader] and the contracting party, usually for a ten per cent commission."[47] In addition to taking a percentage of the receipts, these organizations also sometimes asked the performer to pay for part of the advertising costs, which

Riley could ill afford. Therefore, for his initial appearances, Riley's friends helped to arrange his bookings and publicity.[48]

With this objective in mind, Riley wrote to his friend J. O. Henderson requesting his help to organize a reading for him in Kokomo: "Noticing the paragraph in to-day's Dispatch that 'anything from Julius Ceaser [sic] to a second-class can-can would catch you show-going people just now,' I write to ask what chances I would have there with Original and select Readings."[49] Already well known as the author of "Leonainie," Riley thought that he would have a good chance of drawing an audience in a town of "show-going people," where everything from a Shakespearean history drama to the burlesque would "catch."[50]

Such statements implied a hunger for all types of performance. Following the Civil War, people wanted to forget about the past years of political and military upheaval, and after the excitement of the battlefield, war veterans sought relief from the mundane routines of everyday life. As one of Riley's later stage managers, James B. Pond, once commented, "when over a million men had returned from military strife to civil pursuits . . . there came an unprecedented demand for entertainment and amusements."[51]

Riley indicates his awareness that a cultural hierarchy had begun to emerge with his reference to "anything from Julius Ceaser [sic] to a second-class can-can." However, a shared public culture still existed in nineteenth-century America. Eventually Shakespeare would be categorized at the high end of the cultural spectrum; but when Riley began performing regularly in the late 1870s, boundaries between high, popular, and middlebrow culture had not yet solidified. Riley thought his readings were not that different from those of an actor performing Shakespearean soliloquies alone on the stage.[52]

Riley must have been disappointed when Henderson replied that although almost any kind of show would interest Kokomo residents, turnouts for the programs scheduled during the early part of the lyceum's winter season had been lower than expected. Therefore, Henderson told Riley to "not anticipate too largely." Because of economic hard times, he could not promise a large crowd. They were still eager to be entertained, but for many, prolonged economic depression made attendance at lectures and other programs a luxury.[53]

The deterioration of the financial position of the farmer had great impact on rural communities like Kokomo. Throughout the depression years of the 1870s, the agricultural sector of the economy declined. Following the Homestead Act of 1862, more land than ever before was under cultivation. High production lowered commodity prices. As a result, the cash value of the corn crop in Indiana dropped drastically to only slightly more than what it had been near the end of the Civil War. This situation was exacerbated by the high costs of transporting crops to market and adherence to the Gold Standard. Farmers fell victim to railroad interests and had to pay their bills with inflated gold. At a time when farmers and small town merchants who depended on their trade sorely needed distraction from the problems caused by a shrinking market for their products and mounting debts, they could not afford many of the amusements they craved.[54]

Although he could not guarantee a large audience, Henderson promised to do everything in his power to help ensure that Riley's appearance in Kokomo would be a success. Charles Philips of the *Tribune* also pledged his support. In fact, Philips was so sure that Riley's lecture would "be first rate" that he assumed financial liability for the production's costs. With the publishers of both newspapers behind him, Riley was engaged to perform in mid-February. Unsure of himself, he agreed to come to Kokomo for the nominal sum of fifteen dollars. Both Henderson and Philips advertised Riley's lecture in their papers; and Philips set about printing other forms of publicity, including handbills and show cards for shop windows.[55]

Indeed, Henderson and Philips gave Riley all of the positive publicity they could to win him an audience. They asked the town's residents to "give the author of 'Leonainie' a rousing reception" and made it clear that they held no grudge for the Poe hoax.[56] Describing Riley as a man of great intellect who was "a complete master of the humorous and pathetic," Philips promised that "the lecture will be one of the most entertaining ever given here, and will be brim full of humor and mimicry."[57]

Apparently Riley's skills as a performer had greatly improved since 1874, for his readings lived up to expectations. Riley learned how to validate this type of audience by making fun of the big-city sophisticates who threatened their means of existence and by praising denizens of the countryside for their common sense and native wisdom. His idyllic vision of the simpler past also appealed to rural audiences who resisted the social and economic changes being imposed by corporate America.

Like his literary idol Charles Dickens, Riley performed his poetry "with an actor's inclination for strong characterization."[58] In Anderson, this approach was such a success that Philips made it clear to Riley that a return appearance would be welcome and that, next time, he would have no trouble attracting a large audience: "You set the people wild here. They're all talking of Riley now. Think we can give a big house when you come again."[59]

By performing publicly, Riley provided his own best advertising. His lecture in Kokomo served to promote him in surrounding communities. At the beginning of March, he was invited to lecture at Tipton. A week later, he appeared in Noblesville. Riley made a strong impression wherever he went, and people started to call him "the coming Poet of Indiana."[60] Having received such positive responses from his lecture appearances, Riley gained some confidence in his abilities. His experiences confirmed that giving readings was a good way to publicize himself and his literary work.

Because of his growing prominence as a poet-entertainer and as a regular contributor to several weekly newspapers, in May 1878, local dignitaries in Indianapolis invited Riley to read an original poem for the city's official commemoration of Decoration Day (now called Memorial Day) at Crown Hill Cemetery.[61] From this time until he suffered a stroke in 1910, Riley regularly performed his poetry during civic celebrations. In the nineteenth century, such occasions for public oratory and elocution abounded. Beyond traditional forums of the courts, the legislature, and the church, speechmaking took place in many different situations and sought to maintain a public consensus about democratic values and beliefs.[62]

In August, Riley recited "A Child Home of Long Ago" at an Old Settlers' Meeting in Oakland, a small community just outside Indianapolis. As was characteristic during this era, such public meetings combined political speeches with the reading of poetry and religious passages. Large numbers of people from Marion County and from the surrounding counties of Hancock and Hamilton gathered in a grove of trees for this Old Settlers' Meeting to hear speeches, recitations, and music which celebrated the simpler and more primitive ways of life that existed in the state when it was first settled.[63]

Riley's presentation followed remarks made by Indiana's governor, James D. Williams. The *Indianapolis Journal* recorded the reaction to Riley's reading: "Mr. J. W. Riley was then introduced and read a poem composed expressly for the occasion. The production made a happy hit, being highly appreciated by the people who were fortunate enough to hear it. The reading of the poem, which was in a loud and clear voice, was frequently interrupted by cheers, some of the pictures presented of cabin life in the old times arousing the greatest enthusiasms of the audience."[64]

Until the end of the nineteenth century, many audiences did not participate only as passive spectators. At the theater, political rallies, and other civic events, the atmosphere was loud and raucous. Those present did not hesitate to interrupt speakers or performers to show their approval or disapproval. Therefore, Riley's experience at the Old Settlers' Meeting was typical and shows a degree of audience engagement and interaction rarely seen today.[65]

In addition to the growing demand for Riley to read his poems at public events, an increasing number of newspaper editors actively sought to print his poems. After the success of Riley's lecture in Kokomo, Charles Philips could not get enough of his poems for the *Tribune*. They also appeared weekly in the *Indianapolis Herald*. The *Herald's* editor, George C. Harding, was an important influence in Indianapolis literary circles. During this period, he greatly encouraged Riley and assisted him with his career.[66] In addition, Riley continued to send poetry to the *Indianapolis Journal, Kokomo Dispatch,* and *New Castle Mercury.* Sometimes the *Indianapolis News* accepted a poem or prose sketch for publication, and occasionally out-of-state newspapers printed his work, including the *Peoria Call* and the *Cincinnati Commercial.* Supplying copy to all of these various sources, Riley entered the most prolific period of his career. In a letter to Harris, he stated that he was so busy with writing that he was "as prolific as an over 'physicked' publishing house."[67]

Although he was becoming better known across the state, Riley still suffered financially. His economic woes led him to give in to the temptation of alcohol. Hearing that his brother was indulging again, John Riley wrote pleading with him to find the strength to stop:

> I am pained to learn from several sources that you have been drinking— perhaps not deeply—but steadily. Jim, as you know, I have never spoken very much to you on this subject unless it was when I found you under its influence. I have trusted to your own good sense and manliness to correct the habit. . . . You have a strong will if you would only exert it fully. You have grand prospects with your talent if you will forever step aside from this one fault. I regret so deeply to hear of it again and again. . . . I do beseech you as in the sight of our dearest mother that you will no longer suffer yourself to be the victim of this death in life. Show yourself character that your talents so fully fit you for.[68]

During this period, drinking gave Riley a means of escape from the torments of his personal privations. The weekly newspapers, where most of his writings were printed, could not afford to pay him for his work, and his platform performances did not bring in enough money to support him adequately.

Attempting to remedy this situation, Riley went under contract to the Western Lyceum Bureau. A letter to Riley's booking agent, Charles E. Gard, shows that lyceum bureaus operated quite haphazardly at this time. Riley received several applications from the lecture committees of small communities wanting him to come give readings, which he referred to Gard. However, after forwarding these invitations, Riley heard nothing further from him. Disorganization permeated the lyceum system as each local lecture committee, composed of community leaders, organized its own schedule of events. While they provided speakers, the bureaus had no formal control over coordinating local lectures. They had neither an official role in determining scheduling according to content and dates nor a stake in the success or failure of a local lecture series.[69]

Lecture committees competed for the same pool of talent. Smaller communities had problems bringing in quality lecturers because they could not make their lyceums profitable enough to afford these performers' fees. As he stated in his letter to Gard, Riley feared that some of the committees that attempted to engage him took it for granted that the "'Bureau' terms . . . [were] beyond their pecuniary grasp." Riley asked Gard if he could possibly make engagements independent of the lyceum, admitting that he was "sadly needful": "[I] can ill afford to lose any opportunity that may benefit me financially."[70]

Therefore, even with the help of a lyceum bureau Riley failed to get the attention he thought he deserved. He felt that he continued to be the victim of harsh and unjust criticism. Although he gained many supporters, Riley also accumulated enemies. Some people were very slow to forget the Poe hoax and distrusted Riley for years. Foremost among these was Steve Metcalf of the *Anderson Herald,* who never tired of attacking Riley in his newspaper. According to Benjamin S. Parker, Metcalf had never gotten over "Leonainie." Parker defended Riley in the face of Metcalf's "pure enmity, malice and hatred." Although he was more sensitive to Metcalf's criticisms than he cared to admit, Riley thanked Parker for his support and denied that Metcalf's negative comments bothered him: "they only nettle me like stinging gnats."[71]

In some ways, Riley brought this criticism upon himself. Riley appeared not to hold himself to the same standards to which he held others. In December 1877, Riley attacked a rival poet named Frank Mayfield, claiming that he plagiarized Maurice Thompson: "I have just sent Harding [editor of the *Indianapolis Herald*] a whack at Mayfield's 'Summer Isles' . . . —which by the way is as pure a case of plagiarism as I ever saw. It is a cheeky transposition of Maurice Thompson's 'Looking Southward.'" Although Riley had been involved in the propagation of fraud himself, he thought that Mayfield deserved to be punished severely: "I'd like to see him wiped out like a chalk-work—he deserves to be buried alive and his tomb stone tarred and feathered before his 'verry [*sic*] eyes.'"[72] Apparently, Riley either considered his crime not as serious as Mayfield's or he thought that his fellow poet deserved the same treatment the press had given him following the Poe hoax.

A full year after "Leonainie" first appeared in the *Kokomo Tribune,* another Riley poem would again draw much attention from journalists. Starting in June 1878, Riley anonymously contributed a number of poems interspersed with prose to the *Indianapolis Herald* under the heading "The Respectfully Declined Papers of the Buzz Club." These were inspired by Charles Dickens's *Pickwick Papers,* and, like them, were published in a series of numbered installments. For the purposes of this column, Riley created a fictitious literary club which he filled with characters as eccentric as the "Pickwickians." Of the members of the group who regularly made an appearance in the column, "Mr. Clickwad" and "Mr. Bryce" most clearly reflected elements of Riley's own personality.[73] Clickwad represented Riley as the bright and rebellious maverick: he was "the fantastic figure of the group, an enduring surprise, an eternal enigma—erratic, abrupt, eruptive, and interruptive; a combatant of known rules and modes, a grotesque defier of all critical opinion, whose startling imagination was seemingly at times beyond his control even had he cared to bridle it."[74] Mr. Bryce revealed Riley's self-conscious and melancholy side. Riley described him as "a sad-faced, seedy gentleman, of a slender architecture, and a restless air indicative of a highly sensitive temperament.... His dress, although much worn and sadly lacking in length of leg and sleeve, still held a certain elegance that retained respect."[75]

Making fun of the social pretensions of local literary clubs, Riley envisioned a circle of people "whose only ambition is to please itself—fully conscious that the public is too engrossed with matters of importance to listen to its jargon." Neither *The Pickwick Papers* nor "The Respectfully Declined Papers of the Buzz Club" set out to present any deep philosophical principles. Instead, both works are irreverent and were ostensibly intended to entertain.[76]

Riley remained evasive about his authorship of the column; but, by the time the fourth installment of the "Buzz Club" papers was printed, it was "pretty generally known" that he had written them. This fourth installment included "The Flying Islands of the Night," "a fantastic drama in verse." Over the course of the next several months, this poem brought Riley almost as much publicity as had the Poe hoax.[77]

"Flying Islands of the Night" is Riley's only play. Its title and its fantastic nature suggest that he may have used *A Midsummer Night's Dream* as a model. The American poet Richard Hovey, who wrote multi-part plays in verse on Arthurian themes, even classified "Flying Islands" as "a modern 'Midsummer Night's Dream[,]' full of poetry, pathos, and fun." It is written in iambic pentameter, and readers and critics have often noted its general similarities with Shakespearean drama.[78]

Written in three acts, "Flying Islands" marks an instance in which Riley attempted to introduce himself as a serious poet who could compose works that were larger in scale than his usual short dialect and lyric poems. However, by putting this creation in the mouth of Mr. Clickwad, Riley did so very tentatively. Readers could assume that Riley was ridiculing his character's literary pretensions. The juxtaposition of embedding an Elizabethan-style play in a prose sketch that was reminiscent of Dickens may seem absurd today; but, in the process, Riley was doing more than just hiding his own insecurities. As Dickens was the most popular novelist and Shakespeare was the most popular playwright in nineteenth-century America, Riley's literary references in the "Buzz Club" papers were familiar to his audience; and, because a cultural hierarchy had not yet fully developed, it would not have seemed strange for them to appear alongside each other.[79]

Like *A Midsummer Night's Dream*, "Flying Islands of the Night" takes place in a remote, dreamlike world. For this play, Riley created two imaginary floating kingdoms called Spirkland and Wunkland, each inhabited by a king, queen, prince, princess, dwarf, and "Tune-Fool."[80] Whereas Shakespeare drew his characters from Greek mythology, English folklore, and the Elizabethan peasantry of the English countryside, Riley's were inspired by the folktales and fairy stories his mother told him as a child.[81]

Riley described his play as a "capricious" composition: "[it] is nothing more than my good-nature—for "Flying Islands" is but, at best, a smile."[82] Riley's self-appraisal is similar to much nineteenth-century criticism of *A Midsummer Night's Dream* which characterized Shakespeare's archetypal comedy as an insubstantial fantasy. An 1817 essay written by the English writer William Hazlitt exemplified this school of thought. Hazlitt regarded *A Midsummer Night's Dream* as "merely an airy shape, a dream, a passing thought." By calling it "but . . . a smile," Riley, in a similar way, relegated "Flying Islands of the Night" to "'the regions of fancy.'"[83] He further emphasized its remoteness from everyday realities by refusing either to reveal what drove him to write the play or to explain its meaning. When his childhood friend Minnie Belle Mitchell told him that she did not "understand a word of it," Riley replied, "Well, Minnie Belle, I have to confess—I don't know what that poem is all about myself. It was given to me, you know."[84]

As with *A Midsummer Night's Dream*, "Flying Islands" suggests "weird & beautiful fancies" with its "winning witchery."[85] Many people have been struck by the delightful vision of "Flying Islands"—by its "exuberant beauty—its gorgeous imagery & blossoming of unknown worlds."[86] However, like the Shakespearean play, it also has a dark side. In fact, "Flying Islands" may be read as a symbolic portrayal of the struggle between Riley's better self and his inner demons which made him prone to drink.[87]

Drugs and alcohol play a large role in driving the action of "Flying Islands of the Night" and reveal Riley's fears about his own addiction. However, Riley disguised these fears by placing the action of the play in imaginary lands and by creating his own mythical characters. The entire play is like a dream, giving voice to thoughts ordinarily repressed by the conscious mind by veiling their true meaning.

Much of "Flying Islands of the Night" could have been inspired by alcohol-induced dreams and hallucinations or nightmares. The play begins in Spirkland, a kingdom tormented by evil. In the opening scene, there are "[s]warming forms and features seen in the air coming and going, blending and intermingling in domed ceiling-spaces." Spirkland's queen, Crestillomeem, is "discovered languidly reclining at foot of empty throne, an overturned goblet lying near, as though just drained." A chorus of "[m]ystic, luminous, beautiful faces" identifies her as "Sin's Empress."[88] Crestillomeem, who has "angel in her face and devil in her heart," symbolizes the temptations of alcohol. To prevent a marriage alliance, she has already transformed Spraivoll, the daughter of her husband, King Krung, into a Tune-Fool, "a vague mystic bird" who sings a constant nonsense verse.[89] Griefstricken because he thinks his daughter is dead, Krung falls an easy prey to his wife's powers. Through "her craft and wanton flatteries," Crestillomeem holds her husband under her spell with her drugs:

> At present doth the King lie in a sleep
> Drug-wrought and deep as death—the after-phase
> Of an unconscious state, in which each act
> Of his throughout his waking hours is so
> Rehearsed, in manner, motion, deed and word,
> Her spies (the Queen's) that watch him, serving there
> As guardians o'er his royal slumbers, may
> Inform her of her lord's most secret thought.[90]

While Krung is drugged, Crestillomeem schemes to take control of the throne with her son, a misshapen dwarf named Jucklet.[91]

The only remaining legitimate heir to Spirkland's throne, Amphine, Crestillomeem's stepson, has fallen in love with Dwainie, the good princess of Wunkland. As she expresses her love for Amphine, Dwainie dreams of a time when she can take Amphine away from Spirkland, where "[a]*ll havoc hath been wrangled with the drugs*," to her own kingdom, where happiness and goodness rules:

> That I but blend them all with dreams of when,
> With thy warm hand clasped close in this of mine
> We cross the floating bridge that soon again
> Will span the all-unfathomable gulfs
> Of nether air betwixt this isle of strife
> And my most glorious realm of changeless peace,
> Where summer night reigns ever and the moon
> Hangs ever ripe and lush with radiance
> Above a land where roses float on wings
> And fan their fragrance out so lavishly . . . .[92]

Dwainie learns of Crestillomeem's plans to take control of Spirkland and to deprive Amphine of his legitimate rights as a prince of the realm. Realizing that Jucklet is Crestillomeem's "accessory," Dwainie decides to "vex him" with her sorcery when the dwarf grows "drunken" after a large meal. She haunts Jucklet with nightmares as he falls into an alcohol-induced stupor. These nightmares are personified in characters to whom Riley gave the names Creech and Gritchfang.[93]

Through her magic, Wunkland's princess coaxes the evil out of Jucklet. Frightened by the nightmares she created, the dwarf begs forgiveness for his past sins and exposes his mother's plan to seize the king's crown. At that moment, Crestillomeem's spell is broken. Krung realizes that beneath Crestillomeem's alluring beauty lies depravity: "O woman! while / Your face was fair, and heart was pure, and lips / Were true, and hope as golden as your hair, / I should have strangled you!"[94] Dwainie has enabled Spirkland's "complete deliverance." Krung's potency is restored to him; his daughter Spraivoll changes back to a princess and takes the place left vacant by the queen. With the return of Spraivoll, Amphine is free to marry Dwainie. Released from Crestillomeem's wickedness, Spirkland is a kingdom where peace and tranquility can reign and where an alliance with Wunkland can be established.[95]

Drugs wrought "havoc" in all of Spirkland as alcohol did all too often in Riley's life. In the end, "Flying Islands of the Night" is a morality play in which the benevolent princess Dwainie struggles to deliver Spirkland from the malevolent influences of Crestillomeem. In other instances, Riley personified "the fell spirit alcohol" as an evil "fiend" like Crestillomeem; and, in his personal life, he was always looking for an ideal woman like Dwainie—an angel who would bring him the strength to overcome his weaknesses and find tranquility.[96]

Several characters represent aspects of Riley.[97] In one way or another, the king, the dwarf, the prince, and the Tune-Fool all have fallen victim to the queen. It is no accident that Riley depicts Crestillomeem as an evil seductress. With the aid of drugs she has manufactured through her "craft," she has Krung, Jucklet, and Spraivoll under her spell.[98] They are unable to follow their own wills. In the same way, because of some of alcohol's attractions, Riley sometimes felt powerless to escape from the grip of his desire for drink.

In "Flying Islands of the Night," Crestillomeem even prevents the virtuous prince Amphine, who represents the sober Riley, from marrying the good princess Dwainie and thus from carrying out his destiny of uniting the kingdoms of Spirkland and Wunkland. In his own life, Riley's alcohol problem had already ended his engagement to Kit Myers and was hindering his relationship with Clara Bottsford.[99] Riley feared that he was failing Bottsford, as he had Myers, and believed himself to be a lost soul in need of deliverance: "I know I have not always been to you what I ought—for you were ever good and kind and all that's worshipful—for I was strangely built of crooked stuff and full of knots and flaws and such defects as made me nameless and a floating danger even to myself."[100] His use of the words "floating danger" in this description is significant, as it reflects the same vision of his universe that he presents in "Flying Islands of the Night," "where swarming forms and features [are] seen in the air coming and going."[101]

In his play, Riley's wishes are fulfilled. Dwainie succeeds in driving the evils of Crestillomeem from her lover's life; but Myers's attempts to get Riley to stop drinking failed. At the time he was writing the play, Riley pledged his love to Bottsford and dreamed of finding the security he needed in her arms. However, he feared that he would bring her nothing but unhappiness: "I come to you now as I would creep away and nestle in the warmest hope the world has ever given me. I want to do whatever my good Dream would have me; but wherein I fail don't blame me, for unless God pities me and lifts me out at last I am lost forever."[102] Riley wanted to find life as he envisioned it in Dwainie's Wunkland. He dreamed of a world full of "bud and bloom, and sunshine," but he feared he would forever be unable to "cross the floating bridge . . . [from his] isle of strife . . . [to the] most glorious realm of changeless peace."[103]

When it first appeared, Riley's only play evoked strong contradictory reactions. It was received with both adulation and ridicule. Shortly after it appeared in the *Herald,* the *Indianapolis News* declared, "[Riley's] 'Flying Islands of the Night' shows an exuberance of fancy, a command of language and control of circumstances that promise future greatness."[104] However, many people were puzzled by the poem. Even Riley's friend and supporter Benjamin S. Parker found little merit in it:

> The last of these intrusions, if not the last the lengthiest, is a piece of night-mare "thing-um-me-jig" rhyme called "The Flying Islands of the Night" which occupies a whole page of the Saturday Herald of August 24th. What is it? Well we don't know. It is a waif of nothing on a warp of nought. It is a drama in which beings appear that never existed any where except in Riley's brain, and they inhabit countries the very names of which are foreign to anything else in Earth except Riley's fancy. They are not faries [*sic*], nor eldrich [*sic*] things, such as used to inhabit the Earth and hold high carnival in the corollas of wood Flowers, but they are new creations. WE can't describe the poem and shan't try. It is full of pretty pictures, delicate creations of the most sensitive genius, but no practical soul can ever guess what they mean.[105]

Riley was hurt by his friend's criticisms; but it was the response of Enos B. Reed, editor of an Indianapolis newspaper called *The People,* which escalated into a "War of the Poets."[106] Reed established this Sunday weekly "devoted to local news, literature, and politics" in 1870. The quality of the paper deterio-rated, and it became known primarily for its sensational stories of crime and scandal.[107] Many of Reed's contemporaries, including George Harding of the *Herald,* greatly disliked him. They thought that he was a pompous and arrogant individual "who imagined he could write poetry and grind out pure litera-ture."[108] Although Harding had edited a column for Reed, he regularly attacked him when he began publishing the *Indianapolis Herald* in 1873.[109] Riley got caught in the ongoing feud between the two editors. With publication of

"Flying Islands of the Night," this feud escalated into an old-fashioned newspaper war.[110]

After it appeared in the *Herald,* Reed classified "Flying Islands of the Night" as an "immoderate flow of nonsense" and denigrated Riley's literary capabilities:

> Riley possesses mediocre talent, and exuberant fancy, and they are "running away with him." His poems are entirely unlimited by any of the rhetorical methods which abound in the poet's fancies. There is an excess of exaggeration and confusion of hyperbole that become ridiculous. Riley attained his summit in the "Flying Islands," where one quality, for which we give him ample credit, is ingenuity. This he certainly merits. But the composition of words, the conglomeration of odd and dissimilar fancies, the jingling of rhymes is not the gift of poesy; whilst ingenuity and originality are natural attributes of genius, they do not constitute genius in itself.[111]

Riley's friends rallied to his defense in the columns of the *Indianapolis Herald,* and a derisive exchange of words about Riley and the worth of his work ensued. As the preceding citation testifies, those involved in this newspaper war were not above name-calling and vituperation, both classic rhetorical tactics of partisan journalism.[112]

For people who knew the details of the Poe hoax, many of the tactics Riley used to arouse attention with the "Buzz Club" papers, where "Flying Islands" first appeared, seemed all too familiar. At first, he evaded admitting that he was author of the column; and then he helped to heighten the debate that emerged surrounding it. Some have concluded that Riley wrote his own criticism of "Flying Islands of the Night" for the *Herald* early on in this "Poetic War."[113] If Riley did not write this critical editorial himself, he certainly coached his good friend W. C. Cooper, who signed it, about its wording and its content. This review tempered negative comments with compliments about the beauty of the poem's language and its overall originality. Although it seemed to criticize Riley for the "insubstantiality" and the "baselessness" of this poetic drama, the article also reminded readers that "[i]t is the function and glory of genius to *create;* it is the practice of mere talent to copy."[114] Although it evidently set out to condemn "Flying Islands of the Night," this review actually praised the ingenuity of the poem more than it cast aspersions upon its "mellifluous weirdness." In spirit, the editorial was very similar to Riley's critical review of "Leonainie" which appeared in the *Anderson Democrat* right after the *Kokomo Dispatch* published its first story about the "Poe" poem.[115]

With this review, Riley and his friends hoped to escalate discussions about "Flying Islands of the Night" even further. Riley also wrote a poem attacking Reed, entitled "To the Bard," and Reed answered with his own negative verse:

"The 'Bard' Responds to the Son of 'Wunkland.'" At this point, the nature of the attacks became personal. Riley goaded Reed by remarking, "What a pity the Bard's fine poetic mind should be distorted by jealousy of a brother poet." Reed vehemently protested this accusation: "'The Bard's fine poetic mind' is distorted by nothing. Because one cannot stomach Riley, how ridiculous to charge one with jealousy."[116]

By mid-October 1878, the *Herald* declared that the "Poetic War" was "assuming formidable proportions." To undermine Reed's position, Riley and his friends, who were writing for the *Herald,* put him on the defensive by stating that Riley had full advantage in the battle between them: "If the Bard had confined himself to the line of criticism in which he first started out, and had shown, as he attempted, that it did not require genius to spin a flimsy gossamer web equal to "Flying Islands,' which was published in the PEOPLE, he lost his only advantage, and made it a personal 'war of poets,' in which the Bard has not the ghost of a chance to succeed."[117] The article in which this argument appeared claimed that while Reed was "not only wasting his wind but doing himself harm," Riley should be "much gratified at the vigorous slang of the other 'poick,'" as it only served "to extend the fame of the 'Flying Islands.'"[118]

In this case, Riley and his supporters fully understood the principle that all publicity was good publicity. Nevertheless, many who were sympathetic toward Riley contended that his behavior was not altogether above reproach. Even the *Indianapolis Herald* questioned the means by which Riley aroused public attention: "Riley deserves criticism for his uncalled for attack on Mayfield last winter, and for his doubtful efforts to catch the public ear prior to the publication of the 'Flying Islands,' and I would not be surprised to find that the 'war of the poets' is another of his devices for the same purpose. Riley has made a gigantic stride up the hill of fame, and if he will confine himself to legitimate effort his genius will soon place him at the very top; but he must leave off 'monkeying.'" Parker echoed these sentiments in the *New Castle Mercury.* He warned Riley that he had used "subterfuges" to build his reputation too many times. All "of this talk of Riley" was wearing thin. From here on, even Riley's friends thought it best that he depend solely upon the merits of his productions to perpetuate and advance his fame.[119]

Respecting the substance of Riley's latest composition, Parker advised Riley that "no man can write many successful poems of the intangible class to which 'The Flying Islands' belongs." "Flying Islands of the Night" does have many "intangible" qualities. The play tends to the melodramatic and romantic, and its setting and its characters are far removed from reality, so much so that Parker classified it as "nonsense rhyme."[120] Although Riley drew his ideas for his play and for his characters from folklore and fairy tales, they were uniquely his own; and their exact sources are not immediately clear: Riley "originated not only ideas but language and characters and attributes and in fact . . . scenery, time, place and all accessories of . . . [the] play."[121]

When referring to "Flying Islands of the Night," Parker told Riley that he "should call a halt in that kind of poetry"[122] and warned him that the "public is patient but practical." If he wrote much more poetry like it, Riley was in danger of losing his audience; and it would be difficult "to woo back."[123] Parker suggested that Riley would do better applying what he had mastered in writing the play to poetry more firmly planted in reality: "The brilliance of illustration and delicacy of imagery shown in that production you can now use to good advantage in works that rest upon a solid basis." These statements reflect changes in language, style, and taste that were beginning to occur in the United States during the last decades of the nineteenth century. Such changes affected the way people viewed poetry as a literary genre, the way Riley approached his work, and the way his poems have been viewed throughout time.

For much of the nineteenth century, Americans were more comfortable with listening than reading. Generations of people were accustomed to reciting and hearing the language of the King James Version of the Bible and Shakespeare. Poetry, in general, was also very popular in a culture that emphasized the importance of public speaking and rhetoric. Most people learned by reading out loud, and rhymed verse lent itself well to recitation. It was a commonly held nineteenth-century belief that dramatic performance of written works benefited both the reader and the audience intellectually and morally. Such readings supposedly sharpened the mind of the reader and helped him or her to increase elocutionary skills while the audience was "similarly improved by being exposed to the subject and the rhetorical qualities of the work."[124]

With increased literacy, the importance of this oral culture diminished. As the emphasis on elocution declined and great masterpieces began to be taught more as literature than as oratory, interest in poetry as a literary genre also decreased. No longer exposed to readings of Shakespeare as they had been in the past, Americans became especially uncomfortable with poetic drama written in the language and style of "Flying Islands of the Night," which seemed less and less relevant to their everyday experience. When the play was finally published in book form, the American author and politician Ignatius Donnely classified Riley's play as an "anachronism."[125]

In such an atmosphere, Riley had to make his poetry more immediately accessible and understandable to keep the interest of the general public. With "Flying Islands of the Night," Riley was testing his limits as a poet. Thereafter, Riley restricted himself to subjects he believed would have more appeal to a general audience, and never again strayed far from familiar scenes from his everyday existence. Dialect poems became a focus of his work because of the positive response they received. When asked how dialect poetry became his "peculiar forte," Riley responded, "Not from choice, but because I found that the public wanted it. My first choice was a different sort of writing, but I found that the more serious and earnest I became, the less my writings were liked; so I went to work and gave the public something that it wanted."[126]

However, Riley did not abandon his play. He revised it continually until he felt secure enough to permit its release as a book in 1891. At that point, Riley had published six poetry anthologies and was firmly established in national literary circles. Nevertheless, some reviewers of the book readily recognized it as "one of his very early experimental attempts" because it was "so full of the poet's early weaknesses and faults" and so different from everything else he had published.[127] Many found it "bizarre" and "inartistic."[128] Even in publications where Riley was acknowledged for his overall talent, "Flying Islands" received harsh reviews:

> Mr. Riley is a poet of no common sort. He has won his way to the hearts of the English-reading people all over the world. We have a natural desire to praise everything he writes; but we cannot praise this book for its verse. It is a beautiful little volume; the publishers have done their part with taste and with judgment. *The Flying Islands of the Night,* however, as a poem, is certainly not creditable to Mr. Riley's genius. What does it mean? "What is he driving at?" Is it nonsense verse he is giving us? Whatever his aim has been the work strikes us as amazingly jumbled and meaningless. It begins nowhere and ends in the same place.[129]

On the other hand, many of Riley's literary friends congratulated him on the high quality of "Flying Islands." For example, the statesman and author John Hay thought it was "striking" and "original." He "read it with the greatest pleasure" and reveled in the "strange, exotic color, the play of fancy, the rich reckless, spend thrift imagination . . . through the poem from beginning to end."[130] An eminent British editor, biographer, and critic of the day, Joseph Knight, stated that "[i]ts lyrical and imaginative gifts are of a high order" and labeled it a "*tour de force.*"[131]

Riley admitted to William Dean Howells that his play received much the same response as it had when it was printed in the *Indianapolis Herald* thirteen years earlier: "Of my last book venture I want to keep still but I can't.—*The Flying Islands of the Night.* Some first literary people write me in strong praise of it and full indorsement—others cry aloud and spare not."[132] Madison Cawein attempted to explain the reasons for this extreme difference of opinion by claiming that only those with "poetical temperaments" could fully appreciate "Flying Islands": "The book is a book for poets & people with poetical temperaments, and may not appeal so strongly to the masses as your previous delicious works. Nevertheless you have the assurance . . . of the very best literary authorities—What do you fear? not an ephemeral notice in a daily newspaper, which is only read in order to be forgotten."[133]

Between the time that "Flying Islands" was first published and when it appeared in print again in 1891, a change in attitudes had occurred. Far from ignoring reviews of the poem he received in the local newspapers in 1878, Riley took them seriously; and his rebuttal evolved into a literary debate that lasted several weeks. In this "War of the Poets," newspapers provided Riley, his friends, and his literary combatants a forum in which to debate literary issues. People participated in this "war" without any particular literary accomplishments or educational credentials, and they believed the opinions they voiced were no less valid than those of anyone else.

By the 1890s, writers such as Cawein no longer thought newspapers were a legitimate arena for the discussion of literature. He told Riley that he should only heed what experts—"the best literary authorities"—had to say about his work. The world of poetry was turning into an exclusive realm reserved only for "poets & people with poetical temperaments." As writing in the United States became professionalized following the Civil War, authors who considered themselves to be crafting serious literature increasingly set themselves apart from the cultural mainstream represented by the daily press and other popular journals.[134]

Despite all of the negative criticism it received, "Flying Islands of the Night" was clearly was one of Riley's favorite compositions. He said that it became "his most particularly 'strong weakness.'"[135] It may, in fact, more closely represent the real Riley than many of his other works. As Anthony and Dorothy Russo pointed out in their 1944 Riley bibliography, an article written for the *Pittsburgh Commercial Gazette* sums up the prevailing attitudes toward the poem: "You can hardly realize that it emanated from the same brain that gave birth to 'Raggedy Man,' 'When the Frost Is on the Punkin,' and 'Goodbye Jim.' . . . This work will not be as satisfactory to the general readers as his others, although some admire it most of all."[136]

At the beginning of October 1878, when the "War of the Poets" was still raging, E. B. Martindale's attitude toward Riley began to soften. He asked Riley to send the *Indianapolis Journal* everything he could produce for the paper's Sunday literary supplements. This time the publicity attached to Riley's name contained no stigma. His growing notoriety made him an attractive asset, and Martindale was eager to negotiate an exclusive deal. He told Riley he would make it "profitable" for him to give the *Journal* all of his work and attempted to convince him that his reputation would benefit from such an arrangement.[137]

Martindale's desire for an exclusive arrangement was understandable. With Riley, Martindale saw an opportunity to give his newspaper a greater national reputation. In addition to feature stories, reviews, and serialized fiction, nearly every newspaper in the country offered a column of popular verse. Although the popularity of the genre as a whole had begun to decline, newspaper poetry still flourished, and some of these poets became famous.[138] Riley had begun to attract many followers and admirers. Martindale wanted exclusive rights to his work before other newspaper editors realized his potential and competed to make him a part of their staffs. Not only was Riley's popularity growing within Indiana but also an increasing number of his poems were being copied in newspapers across the nation. A shrewd businessman, Martindale foresaw that associating Riley's name with that of the *Journal* would be good for the *Journal's* circulation.

With the vast expansion of the American market for literary goods during the second half of the nineteenth century, Martindale understood that writers had the potential to become star-quality celebrities. Books such as Harriet Beecher Stowe's *Uncle Tom's Cabin* sold hundreds of thousands of copies. Because of these staggering sales, writers acquired a broad name recognition which they had never possessed before. Mass journalism played a large role in stimulating this phenomenon through literary publicity campaigns.[139] In the case of Riley, Martindale and other members of the press would be vital in molding the poet's reputation and increasing his popularity. Although he agreed to contribute weekly to the *Journal,* Riley did not become the paper's resident poet; he decided to keep his professional options open.[140] Only a few months earlier, he would have jumped at the chance; but now Riley did not want to be pinned down to a newspaper job as he had just as great an interest in pursuing a career as a lecturer as he did as a writer: "My time is most delightfully diversified . . . by occasional calls to lecture, and since I've made this confession, I must admit that I've as strong an ambition in that peculiar field as in literature."[141]

In nineteenth-century culture, where literature was still largely taught as oratory, the two fields were not necessarily mutually exclusive. In his article "Poet as Entertainer," Paul H. Gray claims that "Riley wanted to be a performer, not a writer" and that "he wound up writing poetry because it turned out to be what he performed best."[142] While it is true that as a young man Riley loved performing, he wrote poems for different purposes and audiences. Many of them were not necessarily intended for his public readings. As already pointed out, many authors did readings in the nineteenth century. In a culture where recitation, oratory, and the lyceum stage were so popular, Riley was only following an example that other authors set for him. He knew that lecturing could be lucrative, and his overriding ambition led him to take advantage of every avenue open to him to promote himself and make a living.

By the beginning months of 1879, Riley's ambitiousness began to pay off;

and he had to adjust to the new impositions on his time. "Not long ago my time was wholly mine," Riley wrote to his friend the writer and historian George S. Cottman, "now it . . . [is] vanishing like the generallity [*sic*] of 'blessed priveledges [*sic*].'"[143] He was in Indianapolis, on average, once a week to meet the demands of the *Indianapolis Journal;* and his success as a lecturer was exceeding even his "vainest expectations."[144]

Despite this new success, Riley was still often short of funds. He made little if anything from his newspaper contributions and often agreed to lecture on behalf of charity. For a short time, he thought he might try to find a government position to support himself, as Walt Whitman and Herman Melville had done. To get by, he still occasionally took sign painting assignments.[145] His clothes were shabby, and he looked decidedly bohemian. "When Riley came first to the Journal Office," the son of E. B. Martindale once said, "he was the most striking piece of agricultural verdancy I ever saw—long coat, mustache and broad brimmed hat and cane."[146]

Because of his economic situation, Riley still felt his future as a writer was "dubious": "I know what I'd like to be, but am in great doubt at times as to my cramped condition financially ever allowing me to attain that ambition."[147] Riley did not have enough money to live on his own. Although he found spending time with his stepmother unpleasant, he had no choice but to continue to live under his father's roof in Greenfield. To escape from these surroundings, Riley did manage to keep a small office in downtown Greenfield where he could more easily do his work when he was not in Indianapolis or away lecturing.[148]

As his fame as a lecturer grew, Riley found that he was away from Greenfield an increasing amount of the time. Not lacking in ego, by March 1879, he was already advertising himself as "Indiana's Poet." Other poets who made Indiana their home, such as Benjamin Parker, objected to his use of this label. Riley responded by saying that he was actually being modest by only identifying himself as "Indiana's Poet" rather than as "Indiana's Favorite Poet," as he claimed many people were calling him. Riley refused to admit his arrogance and defensively defied Parker to prove what he was saying was not true.[149]

By this time, Riley's confidence had grown to the point that he no longer used many selections by other authors in his programs. He increasingly included only a few short pieces from Longfellow and a couple of other authors along with his own character sketches and dialect poems. As he made his way around the state, Riley was developing a reputation for possessing "a fund of anecdote" and for making "a funny story out of anything."[150] He also became known for his imitations. In addition to presenting poems and sketches of colorful Hoosier characters, Riley also satirized the programs of other lecturers. Demonstrating how popular this form of entertainment was in nineteenth-century America, people were so familiar with the lecture platform's most famous performers that Riley's impersonations of them delighted his audiences. His "condensed Lectures after . . . [Robert] Ingersoll" made an especially big impression.[151] Riley had heard this famous orator speak when he visited Greenfield in October 1876. Riley admired his eloquence and absorbed how he spoke and constructed his arguments. Ingersoll was a radical Republican and an agnostic. Although he drew large audiences, his views of religion and immortality were controversial.[152] When he gave his "condensed" Ingersoll lectures, Riley copied this other speaker's manner and rhetoric and effectively satirized his treatment of such sacred topics:

> He never heard Ingersoll but once, he says and yet in those two hours he caught the salient points of his style. The tone of voice, the happy jesture [*sic*], and the full round sentences flushed with the language of poetry are copied with an exactness that must delight even the famous orator himself. Without accusing the Colonel of the indulgence of such insincerity Mr. Riley believes it within the power of Ingersoll's peculiar quality of oratory to take any topic, no matter how inviolate in sacred worth or how fixed in its relation with the law as of fact and assault it with apparent success. In illustration, he [Riley] selects "Friendship" "Virtue" or some similar topic and imitating Ingersoll's style proves them myths and shams. The effect upon an audience is wonderful.[153]

In these performances, Riley proved himself versatile but not terribly original. Samuel Clemens and other humorists regularly used satire as part of their humor, and Bret Harte experimented with dialect. Moreover, the dialect poems and character sketches that Riley presented in his readings were much like those of Will Carleton. Just as Riley did, Carleton captured the "typical characters and attitudes" of the Midwest when he read his poems. In his *Farm Ballads*, Carleton established "rural authenticity" by using humor and dialect and by making farmers and other country denizens the narrators of his poems. Still others who appeared on the lecture circuit also created humorous regional characters.[154] Many of these men used these characters in their writings as well as on the stage. Often the fictional personas they created were better known than they themselves. Today, Clemens's "Mark Twain" remains the most familiar.

Through the mid-1880s, Riley experimented with creating such a fictional persona for himself. Early in his career, Riley had employed a number of pen names. In the early 1870s, he signed his first poems to make it into print "Edryn" (the name of Tennyson's character from *Idylls of the King*) and then "Jay Whit" because he feared rejection. With a pen name, he could stand by and wait to see how readers received his compositions without being publicly humiliated if he failed artistically. From another standpoint, Riley also thought that if they were signed with his own name his efforts would not be rewarded. As Riley said, he had "a vague idea that there was a prejudice against home talent in the poetic line."[155] Of course, with "Leonainie," he set out to prove that very thing as he attempted to expose the literary prejudices of the East.

In 1879, Riley created a rustic, rural character to pose as author of a fictional "Home Department" for Charles Philips at the *Kokomo Tribune*. At first, Riley and Philips were going to call this fictional contributor to the paper "Lige Rockey," but Riley later decided that this was not a plausible name. Therefore, he changed it to "John C. Walker" because it "sound[ed] more like a Real one." He did not want his character to be too obviously a caricature.[156]

As "Walker," Riley was to provide irreverent commentary, poems, stories and reports. Riley later described Walker as "a 'corduroy poet' of Greenfield, who wrote a rough sort of doggerel, though occasionally rising to an excellent plane of humor."[157] Behind the mask of such a character, Riley could allow parts of his personality to emerge which, in ordinary circumstances, would be inappropriate for him to project. When he was introduced to readers in late March, the *Tribune* said that "Walker" was "fearless and free." In other words, as this innocent rustic, Riley could be free of inhibitions and say whatever he pleased, even to the point of making fun of what the *Tribune*'s readers held most dear: "We don't approve of some of his ideas, but can't help but admire his pluck in walking right into our Home and attacking the very foundation of the institution."[158] In the poem to which this statement referred, "Make Home Attractive," Riley made fun of Victorian housekeeping and child-rearing practices:

> O make home attractive! be cheerful and free,
>   And encourage the children at play;
> Let them roll down the stairs in their unrestrained glee,
>   And break an arm three times a day.
> Let them tear up the floor, and slam the front door
>   Till the panels are shivered and split;
> Be cheerful and free, as I mentioned before
>   And your homes will be brighter for it.[159]

At the time that Philips initiated "Walker's" "Home Department," Riley also continued to contribute to the *Indianapolis Journal* and the *Indianapolis Herald*. In October of 1878, Riley had promised his work to the *Journal*. As "Walker," Riley could submit writings to the *Tribune* without Martindale being aware of it. During this period, Riley also left unsigned many of the poems he wrote for the *Indianapolis Herald*.[160] At one point in 1879, Riley bragged that he was publishing under three *noms de plume* aside from his own.[161]

By using pseudonyms, Riley experimented with employing various voices in his work. In the same way that other authors used pen names to submit cheap, sensational fiction to emerging story papers, such as *Frank Leslie's Illustrated Newspapers,* Riley started to use pen names for his less serious dialect poetry and reserved using his own name for more lofty compositions which he thought might have a chance to be published in the quality magazines.[162] With "John C. Walker," Philips told Riley this scheme would be very "fruitful": "By this plan, you are winning *two* reputations. While J. W. Riley is steadily gaining all the while in his own field, John C. Walker will be winning additional laurels through the press of the country, in an entirely different channel."[163]

Having secured Riley for a department in the *Tribune,* Philips was very concerned about the growing competition for Riley's work. He decided to make what Riley wrote for his paper "outshine all other among [newspaper] exchanges." "I am determined," he told Riley, "that the 'Kokomo Tribune' shall be the trademark."[164]

Philips followed through on this promise. He tirelessly promoted Riley's "Walker" poems by sending clippings of them to newspapers across the country. In May 1879, he was rewarded for his efforts. Newspapers as far east as Baltimore and as far west as Quincy, Illinois, picked up "Tom Johnson's Quit," a "Walker" dialect poem. This poem marks an instance in which Riley directly addressed the subject of drinking and temperance, albeit in a humorous way.[165]

After a lull during the Civil War, Prohibition reemerged as a major political issue in the United States. Although it did little to change voting patterns, the Prohibition Party was created in 1869 and was active in some twenty states. During the early 1870s, Elizabeth Thompson, of Hillsboro, Ohio, led nonviolent protests that targeted saloons and liquor dealers. As far away as California, women followed Thompson's example, picketing alcohol-selling establishments. Mother Thompson's Women's Crusade, as this movement came to be called, received a lot of attention in newspapers and for a time reduced liquor sales significantly in Ohio and Indiana. However, the effects of its activities were much more fleeting than those of the Women's Christian Temperance Union, founded in 1874. This organization's effective lobbying efforts, along with those of the Anti-Saloon League, established after Riley wrote "Tom Johnson's Quit," eventually made Prohibition inevitable.[166]

Before they gathered the momentum necessary for national legislation to be passed, prohibitionists were easily depicted as religious fanatics or cranks; and many of the cause's most visible activists, such as the hatchet-wielding Carry Nation, were indeed eccentrics.[167] Moreover, like other American authors, Riley perceived that there was a wide gap between the profession and practice of people who embraced temperance. Some reformed alcoholics who preached this cause, including Riley's friend Luther Benson, were known backsliders and were a favorite butt of ridicule.[168]

"Tom Johnson" represents a common character type in nineteenth-century

American literature. In some ways he resembles the Dauphin in *Huckleberry Finn*. In Twain's book, this con artist boasted that he had "'ben a-runnin' a little temperance revival' in order to raise funds to buy whisky."[169] Like the Dauphin, Johnson is an "intemperate temperance advocate." Many nineteenth-century authors employed this character type to reveal the hypocrisy of this social reform movement.[170]

"Tom Johnson's Quit" ironically commented on the inefficacies, ambiguities, and contradictions that undermined the temperance cause. The poem's narrator was surprised and doubtful about the title character's promise to stop drinking, for he had "spiled more whisky, boy an' man, / And seed more trouble, high an' low, / Than any chap but Tom could stand.... *He's* too nigh dead / Fer Tempr'nce to benefit!"[171] Nevertheless, Johnson signed a pledge of abstinence and wore the blue ribbon that symbolized the cause.[172] In this poem, Riley revealed the irony of holding up such a figure as an individual who deserved admiration.[173]

Riley recognized that he was prone to the same kind of lapses. Although he swore over and over again that he would stop, Riley never completely weaned himself from the bottle. He knew how difficult it was to abstain from imbibing.[174] Therefore, "Tom Johnson's Quit" also reflected the poet's inability to control his own drinking habits.

After "Tom Johnson's Quit" received widespread acclaim in the press, Philips decided to seek endorsements for "Walker" from respected authors. He considered sending "Tom Johnson's Quit" and another "Walker" poem "Romancin'," to John Hay, Bret Harte, and Will Carleton, but finally settled on Robert Burdette, a well-known humorist and editor for the *Burlington Hawkeye*. Despite the fact that he knew larger newspapers considered the *Tribune* "a 'country joke,'" Philips hoped that Burdette would find that "Walker's" poems had so much merit that he would print them in the *Hawkeye* along with words of praise. If he received an endorsement from Burdette, Philips thought he could promote "Walker" even further and attract other Indiana writers as contributors to the *Tribune* because of the prominence he had given him.[175] For a short time, the *Tribune* attained a national reputation as a literary journal, publishing works not only by Riley but also by Maurice Thompson, Benjamin S. Parker, and Sarah T. Bolton.[176]

Burdette responded positively to the packet of materials Philips sent to him and dubbed "Walker" the "Bret Harte of Indiana."[177] By making this contact with Burdette, Philips helped Riley even more than he realized; Burdette would later be instrumental in launching Riley's first lecture tour to the East. In the short run, Philips used Burdette's article in the *Burlington Hawkeye* to start a discussion about "Walker's" true identity. Philip's strategy worked. He heightened "Walker's" visibility without revealing who he really was. When he called "Walker" the "Bret Harte of Indiana," people became curious about this poet whom no one had ever seen.[178]

It did not take long for writers and newspaper editors who were familiar with Riley's work to guess who "John C. Walker" might be. "*Kokomo Tribune*, we'll wager a year's subscription to the Enterprise that your 'John C. Walker,' whose charming little poems have been such a brilliant feature of your paper, is none other than J. W. Riley, Indiana's rising young poet, in disguise. We can't just prove it, but if Riley didn't write 'Tom Johnson's Quit' and 'Romancin', he ought to have done so."[179] Indiana author Maurice Thompson, who had already made his reputation as a poet and nature writer, commented to a *Cincinnati Gazette* reporter that "poets who can write 'Tom Johnson's Quit' don't spring up full-fledged in a day" and that he saw "Riley in every line of it."[180] Although Riley continued to use this pen name into the early 1880s, he and Philips could no longer fool anyone about the true identity of "Walker" with this kind of publicity.[181]

"The 'John C. Walker' boom has been a big one for me," Riley wrote to his friend John Anderson of the *Cincinnati Gazette*.[182] Indeed, the pieces he wrote using this pseudonym proved positive for his career. With "Walker," Riley established his reputation as a dialectician. As a result, people clamored to schedule him to lecture; and, by the end of summer 1879, Riley regularly furnished four newspapers with poetry and prose sketches. He was also making plans to write a book in partnership with Mary Hartwell Catherwood, with whom he had been corresponding since April 1878.[183]

Catherwood was originally from Ohio but when she married in 1877 settled in the small Indiana town of Fairfield, located in Howard County north of Indianapolis. She earned a reputation as a writer of local color fiction for which she gained attention because of its critical realism. Her most effective stories revealed the "ugliness and narrowness of mind found in rural life and in small towns."[184] Presumably, Riley and Catherwood wanted to compile a book of short prose sketches and poems. Although they never completed this book, they remained good friends, and Catherwood developed a strong relationship with Riley's sisters, especially Mary. Catherwood urged Riley to help her improve her work. Therefore, he had an immense influence on her literary leanings. In large part because of her friendship with Riley, she abandoned her stance as a realist and became an outspoken advocate of romanticism in literature. He managed to convince Catherwood that all literature should be uplifting and devoid of life's grim social realities and later used his influence to help get her popular novel *The Romance of Dollard* published by the Century Company.[185]

In 1879–1880, Riley was just too busy to collaborate successfully on a book with Catherwood. Although he was unable to follow through on his work with her, Catherwood was always ready to offer him her emotional support. She never hesitated to give him praise and tried to keep him from being depressed. When Enos B. Reed of the *People* renewed attacks on Riley in June 1879, Catherwood understood that Riley had "been excited terribly" by Reed's criticism and that "it had been a . . . shock" to his nerves. She urged Riley not to allow these negative comments to "tear" him all up.[186]

Catherwood was also one of the few people with whom Riley felt comfortable enough to share his family's troubles. The summer and fall of 1879 were hard on the Riley family. Riley's older brother John became ill and nearly died, and his younger brother Humboldt developed a drinking problem that was getting further and further out of control. Humboldt did many of the things Riley had in his twenties. When he was not unemployed, Humboldt traveled around the country doing advertising and unfortunately picked up some of the same bad habits as had his older brother.[187] While Riley eventually learned to control his alcoholism most of the time, his younger brother never could. In September 1879, Riley reported to Catherwood about John's recovery and expressed his concerns about Humboldt's worsening situation: "I'm all right myself, but my younger brother has been scandalously drunk for a square week, and I've been following him about the country for four days. He's anchored at last, thank God!—with a black eye variegated with green cherry-color, and purple shades, and a face on him like a spoiled sponge. My other brother is growing well, I think, but is yet quite feeble and oftentimes discouraged over his slow recovery."[188]

The events of Humboldt's life show what could have happened to Riley if he had continued to live a transient life on the margins of lawlessness. In contrast, John remained a model for Riley. He admired his older brother's innate goodness and appreciated his unyielding support.[189] Although he eventually recovered from this illness, John's health was fragile for the rest of his life.

In such times of trouble, Catherwood was not the only woman from whom Riley received emotional support. Although he was still romantically involved with Bottsford, he also confided in a young woman named Elizabeth Kahle, who lived in Pennsylvania. At the beginning of 1879, Kahle saw some of Riley's work in a newspaper and sent him a poem she wrote in admiration. As with Bottsford, her "poetic temperament" attracted him. Because she lived at a distance, Riley could engage in a friendship with her without endangering his relationship with Bottsford. Nevertheless, in Kahle, Riley thought he had found a kindred spirit. When he first wrote to her, Riley said that it seemed as if they had known each other all of their lives.[190] As they corresponded, the sense that they were soul mates only intensified. In August 1879, one of the poems she sent was "so passionately hopeless" that Riley told her it could have been his: "It is like the sound of my own voice—or yours—ours!"[191]

At a distance, it was easy for Riley to envision Kahle as his ideal woman. She was so very sympathetic that Riley could allow himself to be vulnerable in his letters to her. At every opportunity, Riley revealed many of his inadequacies. Despite this, Kahle continued to write to him and let him know how important he was to her: "I liked you better than anyone else from the very first, and could'nt [*sic*] do anything else now if I tried to. . . . I am happier since I have known you, and would be very miserable if I lost you."[192]

Such letters helped to boost his ego; and, because she seemed to accept him just as he was, Riley shared his dark moods with Kahle. He told her that he grew tired of ever yearning for "some indefinable good" that was forever being kept from him. Kahle's response showed great concern for Riley. She tried to lift him out of his despair and to find ways to soothe his frazzled nerves. Her words were very comforting. When she sent him a photograph of herself, Riley thought her image better than anything that he had imagined: "You are not exactly like the picture I have been holding up before my fancy's eye—You are even more *womanly* than my ideal—and O so womanly was she. That is the best word of all—WOMAN. It is so regal, high and pure and white! God bless you, WOMAN!"[193]

However, as he put her on such a pedestal, Riley still feared what Kahle would think if she met him. He believed himself physically unattractive and procrastinated about sending Kahle a picture of himself. He thought he was so unphotogenic that she would think him uglier than he really was; "and," as Riley told her, "that's bad enough."[194]

For many reasons, therefore, Riley continued to be most comfortable courting women with his pen. He did not have to worry about his looks, and writing was a safe way for him to reveal his feelings. By expressing himself in letters, he could avoid the humiliation of being rejected in person. Riley never got over thinking himself unworthy of a woman's esteem or love. In a letter to Kahle, he warned her not to get too involved with him. He described himself as a "paradox" and told her that all the affection he could offer her in return was as "vain" as it was "wild and fervid." Although on the road to fame, Riley was convinced that his life would continue to be "made up of disappointments and despair." Riley said he did not want to pull Kahle into this dark world.[195]

Riley repeatedly made plans to go see Kahle while on lecture tours, but he avoided a face-to-face encounter, in part because of his many personal insecurities. Kahle was just as nervous about meeting him. She feared that their relationship might be ruined if they confronted each other in person: "sometime in the future when you're even more famous, and come this way to lecture, of course you'll stop and see me, and like the traditional 'ancient maiden lady,' I'll meet you in a rusty silk gown, and you'll forever regret that we spoilt the romance by meeting at all, and wonder how you ever could have thought me the least bit nice."[196]

This evaluation of the situation was probably true. As long as he did not meet her, Kahle could remain an embodiment of Riley's feminine ideal—a "regal, high and pure and white" being unsullied by connections with the material world.[197] Meeting her would only serve to bring her down to earth. For Riley, Kahle became a replacement for his mother, for whom he still had unresolved feelings. With Kahle, Riley could revert to being a child. He yearned for the comfort and care that Kahle offered the little boy that still existed within him, but he also stated that he resisted completely submitting to her: "Surely if you feel like that, then indeed you comprehend me *just as I am.*—a little, helpless child—who would thank God with all his boyish heart if you just *could*—now, this minute—'put your hands over my eyes and say, Now you must sleep.'—only—only—I want to be strong enough to bear my burden, and your dear words make me weak."[198]

These statements reflect Riley's ambivalent feelings about his mother and, by extension, women in general. Although he openly worshiped his mother's memory, Riley, on some level, was probably always angered by her sudden abandonment of him when she died. He was constantly searching for someone to take her place, but he also expressed the notion that the women with whom he became involved had the potential to destroy as well as to nurture him. He had not totally integrated the picture he had of Elizabeth Riley into a realistic whole. Riley could not accept his mother as a sexual being who was neither the purest nor the most defiled of women. For this reason, he had a tendency to see women either as angels or as whores; and he always feared that the latter disguised themselves as the former.

New pressures on the perception of men and women's roles in society that arose in the nineteenth century intensified such anxieties. In earlier centuries, women had participated in a large number of activities that were gradually denied them. They had been involved in running family workshops, had helped operate the enterprises of skilled craftsmen, and had played the highly visible role of midwives. With the rise of modern professions and large-scale manufacturing, women no longer could hold such positions of power. In households that attained a certain amount of wealth, women left the public workplace. It gradually became unrespectable for women to work outside this domestic sphere. Women's lives were supposed to center around marriage, children, and household. Ideally, they were to become specialists in emotional and spiritual life, protect family tradition, and provide a stable refuge from the outside world.[199]

During the 1840s and 1850s, women started to try to reassert themselves in an attempt to recover some of the ground that they had lost. As this movement for women's rights gained strength during the second half of the nineteenth century, there was a growing sense that manhood itself was in danger.[200] Consequently, "no century depicted woman as vampire, as castrator, as killer so consistently, so programmatically, so nakedly as the nineteenth."[201] While nineteenth-century men viewed women as the incarnation of purity, they also perceived them to be full of contradictions and mysteries. Although they were far from new, these theories defined women as inconsistent and changeable. They had the potential for extreme good or extreme evil. In other words, a woman could be either like the Madonna or Medusa or Delilah.[202]

In letters to Kahle, Riley expressed these conflicting ideas. Although he often characterized her as his feminine ideal, at the same time Riley was afraid that Kahle in her letters tantalized him with her compassion and sensitivity only to ravish his powers. As he said, her words alone made him "weak."[203] These attitudes surfaced repeatedly in his relationships with women and are certainly not absent from his literary work. The characters Riley created for "Flying Islands of the Night" reflect this same duality in ideas about women. He depicted devouring females, such as Crestillomeem, just as often as he portrayed women as saints.

In reality, it was Riley's own self-destructive behavior that posed a threat to his strength and vitality. Riley had a tendency to exhaust himself in his drive to succeed and admitted to Kahle that his worries and the overwhelming demands for his work endangered his health: "So you will see I am indeed overwhelmed. And I must throw in, too, by way of good measure, the fact that I'm in rather ill health. I don't like to acknowledge this, but I feel that I will be better for the confession. I am very nervous and worry a great deal more than is good for me. And the doctor says if I don't give up night-work (my time of all times for work) I'll just naturally 'go out' like a candle. "[204]

But Riley did not acknowledge all his weaknesses to Kahle. He did not reveal to her that working long hours late at night without sleep was just one of his bad habits. As always, when anxious, Riley was particularly tempted to drink. At this time, he complained in a letter to another friend that he lacked congenial companionship in Greenfield, which only compounded this situation. Many of his childhood comrades had left town; and Bottsford was no longer living at the home of his parents. She had taken a position in Edinburg, a small town south of Indianapolis; and, when she was in Hancock County, she stayed at her family farm outside Greenfield.[205] Therefore, Riley could not spend as much time with her as he liked. Moreover, in his hometown, Riley was still perceived as a misfit and ne'er-do-well. He claimed that people all stopped talking as he passed along the street.[206]

However, Riley did his best not to succumb to temptation. Coming face to face with Humboldt's alcohol problem affected him deeply. Riley was embarrassed by his younger brother's behavior and probably realized that, in the past, he had acted similarly when drunk. Although alcohol offered him temporary escape from his loneliness and worries, he knew that if he allowed himself to fall victim to its charms it ultimately could ruin any chances he had for success. Constantly attempting to prove that he could amount to something, Riley wanted neither to humiliate his family nor to bring himself harm. In the letter in which he reported to Catherwood about Humboldt being "scandalously drunk for a square week," Riley told her that he was battling to remain sober: "It's big work I'm doing now just staying straight, but you can bet your bottom dollar I'll do that though all things else go to pieces."[207]

Not all of Riley's friends were as sympathetic as Kahle and Catherwood. "You ought to be *happy*—if you ain't *rich,*" Charles Philips wrote to Riley in late August 1879. He pointed out that Riley really had no reason to be depressed: "You are getting your reward in *praise* now & dollars and cents are *sure* to follow. But, honestly, dear boy, I do not see why you should get so blue and melancholy at times. I know it's hard to go about like a pauper & all that, but remember, no writer in history—not *one*—has ever had the rapid success that has come to you."[208]

Despite their impatience with his dark moods, many of Riley's friends and acquaintances were genuinely concerned about the amount of writing he was trying to do. Philips told Riley not to work too hard and attempted to convince him that he already had established his reputation and need not exhaust himself trying to prove his talent and versatility.[209] Aware of Riley's nervousness, his delicate health, and probably also of his tendency to drink, Maurice Thompson predicted that Riley did not possess the physical stamina to maintain a long and successful literary career: "I've a notion . . . that Riley hasn't enough of the physical to sustain the mental into the years of a ripened manhood. There are exceptions, of course, but as a rule the writer who sustains himself, growing stronger and better as the years multiply, must have a strong, healthy vigorous body. Otherwise there come sickly sentiments in the place of ripe thoughts."[210]

Although he heard these warnings, Riley thought he had no choice but to continue to work at a tiring pace. As Philips said, he was still living like a pauper; and he could not afford to relax until he made the money he would have if he had entered a conventional profession. In his father's shadow, he had to prove that he was not a failure. Nevertheless, Riley continued to submit his writings to newspapers without any hope of compensation. Dan Paine, editor of the *Indianapolis News,* not only told Riley to stop working so hard but also to stop contributing to publications that did not pay him: "Do you know there is much imagery and poetry in the work you have turned out this week as would suffice many a man who breaks into the magazines at a round price, for half a year? And you are doing it for nothing! You mustn't do it. Save yourself, or work at something more prosaic."[211]

When he wrote this, Paine was not aware that several newspapers were pursuing Riley to come to work for them. Because of the reputation Riley had built for his newspaper as "Walker," Philips wanted to give him a job on the *Kokomo Tribune*. Riley also had offers from the Terre Haute *Saturday Courier*, the *Peoria Saturday Evening Call*, and the Quincy (Illinois) *Modern Argo*.[212] At the same time, the Common-Sense Literary Bureau inquired about the possibility of putting Riley under contract for its fall lecture season.[213] In response to the variety of possibilities available to him, Riley said to Catherwood: "The old promises for my brilliant future are still promising—they never let up on that, and I'm still believing as of old that I'm goin' to make it.—Though just now I'm considerably muddled with a complication of prospects."[214]

Going on staff at a newspaper was not Riley's first choice. He preferred the idea of doing readings. Working on the lecture circuit was potentially more lucrative. One of Riley's friends, Henry William Taylor, a physician and amateur poet, made this fact very clear to him: "The lecture field is the place for *you*—don't you forget it. Mere *writing* is a d——n starvation process. A fellow is like to die of inanition. . . . And it makes no difference how *good* the writing may be. A fellow must run the gauntlet of carping criticism."[215] Riley was not the only writer enticed to the lyceum stage because of the lure of financial gain. For many nineteenth-century authors, the possible monetary rewards from doing readings were their primary motivation for appearing on the lecture platform.[216]

Lecturing had other attractions for Riley. Traveling from place to place on a lecture tour would give him more visibility than working on a local newspaper. As the social organization of entertainment underwent a revolution during the second half of the nineteenth century, performers gained an increasing amount of public visibility in American society. Prior to 1850, people tended to engage in forms of amusement in which the private was not necessarily split from the communal, pleasure was not necessarily removed from productive labor, and members of audiences were also active participants. After midcentury, entertainment increasingly became mass spectacle and began to be understood as an article of consumption, where those who attended passively watched what happened on the stage. As part of this process, artistic performance was more broadly publicized than ever before. This publicity drew large audiences and created a growing amount of notoriety for the performers involved.[217] Riley was well aware of this phenomenon. Lecturing also offered Riley some freedom and flexibility. The lyceum circuit was seasonal. As a performer, Riley would be contracted for programs only during the winter months. In other words, it offered Riley a way to perfect his talents as a reader while making enough money to permit him to dedicate himself to writing for the rest of the year. Nevertheless, Riley kept his options open in case performing did not work out for him.[218]

Favorably enough impressed by the press notices and recommendations

Riley sent by mail, the Common-Sense Bureau wanted to represent him but required him to provide the circulars and postage necessary to publicize his lectures. He had to turn down this opportunity because he did not possess the capital to pay for them. Unhappy with the way another lyceum bureau had represented him, Riley, without help, could not get past this "kink" in his affairs.[219]

Knowing Riley was frustrated that financial success did not readily follow from his growing acclaim, his many friends decided to help solve this problem by organizing a benefit for him at the Park Theater, the only large performance hall then standing in Indianapolis.[220] Set for mid-October, the Indianapolis newspapers launched a publicity campaign to ensure the success of Riley's program. An article in the *Indianapolis Herald* announced: "Numerous as the benefits have been in this city, there has seldom been one where the beneficiary has so well earned the tribute. In all countries and ages mankind has delighted to honor its geniuses. Mr. Riley has received plenty of praise, but as yet little money."[221] Other publicity for Riley's benefit reading was just as exuberant. "Let there be no mistake in regard to the reception," an article in the *Indianapolis Journal* advised on the day of the performance. "Let it be warm, enthusiastic and generous. The city cannot afford to allow it to be otherwise."[222]

Thus, newspapers broadcast that it would be embarrassing if the citizens of Indianapolis did not turn out to hear Riley. Between fifteen hundred and two thousand people "ought to attend and demonstrate their admiration" because he was an individual "who brought honor to the city and to the state by his happy efforts in the world of literature."[223] The *Journal* was not alone in establishing Riley not only as a local personality who should be in popular demand but also as an important literary figure on the verge of national fame. The *Herald* proclaimed confidently that Riley's reputation would go well beyond the borders of Indiana and the Midwest: "Everybody should feel a common pride in attesting his admiration of Mr. Riley's literary work. Some day he will have a national fame, and it will be worth something . . . to know that we appreciated him and attested our appreciation before everybody else did."[224]

As these editorials demonstrate, newspapers continued to play an invaluable role in helping to mold Riley's image. From observing his father's political work behind the scenes, he understood that much of what was accomplished in business and politics came through the informal ties of personal friendship. Starting with "Leonainie," Riley had learned how to use his journalistic connections to his best advantage; and, at this point, they were paying off. The publicity he received for this benefit made his voluntary contributions to the Indianapolis press worthwhile. Because his work appeared regularly in their newspapers, it was in the interest of the editors of the *Journal* and the *Herald* to give Riley positive advance notices.

Although he was only on the brink of lecturing outside of Indiana, some of the themes that appeared in these notices, especially those in the *Herald,* followed Riley throughout his career. Alluding to his talents as an actor and entertainer, George Harding of the *Herald* remarked that as he portrayed eight to ten characters during the course of his readings Riley did not come before the public "solely as a poet and writer."[225] Over the years, many reviews of Riley's stage work stated that his abilities as a reader and actor equaled those he possessed as a poet.[226]

According to Harding, Riley's dialect was "perfectly natural"; and he praised him for not sullying it with "a coarse or profane word." He found that Riley's depictions of rustic, rural characters did not seem to be caricatures but instead "perfectly portrayed the poetical and gentler side of common life." Harding's estimation of Riley's use of language and realism sounds similar to that of Howells, who twenty years later said, "No poet has shown such a passion for the humble things of life, or has dared to portray them with such unshrinking fidelity, such fond and unpatronizing tenderness."[227] Moreover, Harding already identified Riley as a poetic genius who expressed the sentiments of Americans as a people: "His readings are a pleasing change from the hackneyed stage readings most professional readers select. They are his own creations, and represent people of the times, and the thought and feeling of the age."[228] Riley circulated such statements to publicize his later appearances. They helped to establish him as a figure of consequence and then became cornerstones of his image.

The night of the benefit, it poured down rain. In addition, Riley had to compete with a circus for spectators. He believed that fate had again dealt him a heavy blow. A friend to whom Riley sent complimentary tickets remembered his pessimistic mood right before the performance. While they were dining at a cafe, Riley reportedly said to him, "Just my d———d luck when I attempt to do *anything* something conspires to thwart my attempt."[229]

In fact, Riley had a fair-sized audience for his show that responded positively to the selections he presented. He described his readings as a lecture on "poetry and character" and stated that his program was "less profound than entertaining but . . . [had] quite a tang of the former element."[230] For the more educational or "profound" segment of his lecture, Riley spoke about the refining nature of poetry and of dialect poetry in particular.[231] Responding to residual objections to the theater and acting that still persisted, Riley included this didactic monologue because lectures were intended primarily to teach. Both the lyceum and Chautaqua were founded to improve American audiences morally and intellectually.[232]

However, with his lack of formal training, Riley did not excel at educating.

In fact, one reviewer of Riley's Indianapolis benefit stated that "[t]he didactic part of his lecture was objectionable" because he did not connect it adequately to the rest of his readings, which made it "in some degree irrelevant."[233] With lecturers such as Riley, programs presented in a more theatrical style became increasingly accepted as the century came to a close. As evidence of this trend, Riley later said, "I find as a rule that people would rather be entertained than instructed in something profound enough to require mental effort."[234] Riley always sought first to please his audiences. To bring characters alive, he used what he had learned as an actor in the Adelphian Dramatic Club's productions. Meredith Nicholson identified Riley's "unerring dramatic instinct" as a distinctive part of his style and appeal: "Many of his poems—those indeed that we know best, are in effect little dramas, perfect in setting and atmosphere, wherein the characters he has so abundantly discovered or created are endowed with life and rare as veritable as though we met and talked with them."[235] In this way, the distinctions between acting and lecturing became blurred, helping to bring about a change in attitudes toward theater throughout the country.[236]

According to one newspaper account, Riley's benefit performance lasted for "more than an hour, yet the time seemed so short that the audience lingered and insisted upon an encore."[237] This tolerance for such a long one-man show reflects more than just Riley's talent. Nineteenth-century audiences were intensely interested in rhetoric and oratory and often sat mesmerized by political speeches and debates that lasted for hours.[238] The press carefully scrutinized Riley's elocutionary skills in reviews of his program, further revealing this popular interest in speechmaking.

More than one newspaper critic commented that Riley's voice was not loud enough to reach all parts of a large hall.[239] The *Indianapolis Herald* also remarked that some of the subtleties of Riley's program were lost:

> But he must cultivate his voice for larger spaces than the parlors and small halls which have hitherto been his field. He could with difficulty be heard at all on the back seats at the Park, and his finest points were wholly lost, partly in inadequate volume of sound, and partly in indistinctness. This is a more serious matter with him than with ordinary actors or elocutionists, because his delineations are so finely drawn, with such delicate shades of tone and language, that the loss of the least is the failure of the whole. He must look to this, for the best performance possible is worth nothing to a deaf man, and when it can't be properly heard, the audience might as well be deaf.[240]

Such reviews demonstrate that the literate public had more than just a surface knowledge of rhetorical skills. These people were "well aware of the importance of standard elocutionary techniques such as the modulated voice, timing and emphasis in reading, and control over gesture."[241]

Despite the criticisms, Riley had reason to be proud of his reception. Over the course of his performance, he introduced seven or eight poems and sketches which demonstrated his versatility and the breadth of emotion he could evoke from his audience. The comic poem "The Tree Toad" "brought down the house, and "Leetle Poy of Mine" [in German dialect] moistened many eyes."[242] The *Indianapolis News* declared that Riley had "a fertility and exuberance of imagination, a felicity of expression, and a power of delineation that should make him one of the first readers of America."[243]

The Park Theater benefit marked a turning point for Riley. With the reviews he received, he was able to launch his first truly successful lecture season. During fall and winter 1879–1880, communities throughout Indiana clamored to engage Riley to come speak; and he appeared in some towns more than once. Moreover, he gave readings for the first time out of state in Illinois.[244]

In a conscious effort to look more conventional and successful, Riley also made a significant change in his physical appearance. At the end of September 1879, Riley explained to Elizabeth Kahle that he felt he had to shave off his large "amber-colored" mustache and that once it was gone he would never grow another: "I've concluded to sacrifice the mustache in the interest of my character readings, and once off it must remain so,—'cause it would argue to the dear public, seeing me first with and then without beard, that I had no stabillity [*sic*] of character and all that—So really it is a very serious change to contemplate. Beside, I've worn a moustache [*sic*] now for years and years. In fact this is my first as it must be my last."[245]

Starting with the mustache, Riley was beginning to abandon his bohemian appearance. Throughout his youth he had worn his mustache, a long Prince Albert coat that was not free from rents, trousers that bagged at the knee, and a broad-brimmed felt hat, and had carried a cane. As he later recalled, his "vesture was by no means conventional."[246] The flamboyant mustache and nonconformist clothes were emblems of his rebellion against his father and the middle-class culture he represented.[247] In a world that was still based primarily on face-to-face relationships, how one looked and behaved in public defined much about one's individual self image. By his earlier dress and modes of behavior, Riley had identified himself as an outsider. With the backing of many of the more notable citizens of Indianapolis, Riley's attitude toward himself and society was changing. From this time forward, he made more and more concessions to middle-class propriety in his desire to be accepted. He relinquished his idiosyncratic dress and adopted more standardized male attire. Clean-shaven and wearing a dark coat and white shirt, he looked more like a thriving businessman than a struggling poet. If he appeared prosperous, he surmised that editors would not dare to offer him a small price for his poems or at least be ashamed of the paltry sums they gave him. In other words, he concluded that to be successful he must look successful. Riley so internalized this idea that he later told the famous *New York World* journalist Nellie Bly that "the secret of success is a good personal appearance."[248]

In November 1879, E. B. Martindale finally convinced Riley to come work for him at the *Indianapolis Journal.* Of all the newspapers that approached him, the *Journal* was the only large metropolitan daily. Martindale offered him regular employment while allowing him to carry out a full lecture schedule. In this way, Martindale was more than just his employer. He also acted as his patron. Although he wanted Riley to supply him weekly with as much of his poetry and prose as possible, Martindale encouraged him not to give up on being published by *Atlantic Monthly* and other prestigious magazines. He reportedly advised Riley to send them his very best work—those poems that had "the stamps of genius on them."[249]

Therefore, in addition to providing Riley a certain amount of security, Martindale enabled Riley to explore every avenue open to him as an author in late-nineteenth-century America. Nevertheless, at the end of 1879, Riley was already most recognized as a writer and reader in dialect. His "John C. Walker" poems brought him more widespread attention than others, and overall, the reception of his serious work, "Flying Islands of the Night," was disappointing. With the applause and praise he received for his comely portrayals of rural life, Riley realized that he needed to stick to humble and familiar scenes to further endear himself to the public. He found that audiences loved the way he was able to capture the simple quaintness and the speech of country people in his poems. Working for the *Journal* and lecturing around the country, Riley would continue to develop his concepts of "poetry and character" to make his mark on the national literary scene.

Newspaper Poet

FIVE

"I am sick and tired of talking about myself. It savors too much of egotism," Riley told a *Detroit Free Press* reporter in March 1893.[1] "However, the newspaper boys are not content to leave me alone, but must stick in something about my whims and peculiarities and my thinklets until I am quite thoroughly devoured, and only the core of an apple remains."[2] Ironically, he made these comments to a journalist no different from those about whom he complained, one who had followed Riley from the moment he arrived in Detroit for a lecture engagement, hoping to get a few words with him.

Protective of his privacy at first, Riley avoided the newspaperman, going immediately to his hotel from the train station and secluding himself in his room, where he entertained no visitors and gave the reporter little material for a story. However, the reporter did not give up. He remained at the hotel, determined to get an interview. At last Riley emerged from his quarters to dine, and the young man cornered him as he left the hotel's restaurant. At this point, Riley relented and permitted the interviewer to question him.[3] He disliked this kind of intrusion, but understood that it was part of being a celebrity: "Of course, this is the enterprise of American newspapers, and thousands of others have to put up with the same thing."[4]

Like other famous people, Riley was ambivalent about journalists. Reporters could not always be avoided, because one's celebrity status could not be maintained without a certain amount of publicity. Nevertheless, Riley was tired of finding even the most minute details about himself exposed in print. He compared this process to being "devoured" to the core, like an apple. With increased circulation and the advent of syndication, the national press forced Riley's private world to become public; as a celebrity, his image became a salable commodity in the emerging modern consumer culture.[5]

But as much as he disliked this aspect of journalism, as Riley told this same reporter, for the most part he "admir[ed] American newspaper men as a class." Despite some negative experiences, Riley owed journalists too much to think ill of them as a group. He respected them for being "up with the times, wide-awake, energetic, enterprising, [and] clever in many ways," and recognized that most of the brightest writers and critics were "graduates of the reporter's desk."[6]

Riley had risen through the literary ranks in the same manner. Like many other prominent nineteenth-century authors, he realized that his newspaper experience had had great impact on his writing: "It brought me into contact with all phases of human life and gave me an insight into human nature that I could have acquired in no other way. My journalistic work also gave me a good idea of what the public wants, and this knowledge has stood me well in all my work."[7] His time at the *Indianapolis Journal* was especially valuable. It was while he was employed at this paper that Riley really began to come into his own as a writer. The *Journal* first printed many of his most memorable poems, and his job there gave him the security, stability, and connections he needed to reach national prominence.

Shortly after he moved to Indianapolis to become a regular employee for the *Journal* in November 1879, Riley wrote to his friend John Taylor, who lived in Crawfordsville: "I am having more bother about getting settled in this infernal city! I ain't used to it, and don't believe I ever will be. Lots o' features about it are loveable [*sic*]—but the rack and rattle of it all is positively awful—no monotony on God's earth like it!"[8] Although for the last few years he had often traveled back and forth between Greenfield and Indianapolis, Riley was unused to the constant noise and confusion he encountered in the larger city. By the end of the 1870s, the railroads had made Indianapolis a hustling and bustling transportation and manufacturing center. Since it was a transportation hub, retail and wholesale merchandising was also an important aspect of the city's economy.[9]

When Riley came to Indianapolis, railroad lines entered the city from every direction. Its two largest industries were slaughtering and meat packing and metalworking. The city ranked third in pork packing not only in the United States but also in the world. Foundries and machine shops produced railroad rails and farming implements. Other important industries included printing and publishing, carriages and wagons, and liquor and malt products.[10]

As Riley told Taylor, much about the city seemed hellish to newcomers from rural areas. Indianapolis, like most other cities at the time, lacked adequate municipal facilities. The sewage system was rudimentary; sewage went into the White River, along with industrial byproducts and wastes from slaughterhouses. Manufacturers released much soot and grime into the air. The noise, sights, and smells were overwhelming.[11]

Although many streets were illuminated by gas lights by 1870, their condition otherwise was deplorable. Major thoroughfares were paved with cobblestones while less important streets were only graveled. In wet weather, these graveled streets turned into mud; and, in dry weather, they covered everything with dust. When he first moved to Indianapolis, Riley either walked or took mule-powered streetcars everywhere he needed to go within its environs. These streetcars were the principal means of public transportation until the first electric cars replaced them in the 1890s.[12]

During the last part of the nineteenth century, Indianapolis became known as a "city of homes." Apartment houses were not plentiful in this state capital as they were in larger urban areas. Like most other single men who came to the city following the Civil War in search of work, Riley first lived in older buildings that had been converted into boardinghouses near the center of Indianapolis, inside its original mile-square boundaries. Living close to the Circle that formed the city's center, for Riley, work and recreation took place in the same few city blocks. The boardinghouse gave him more than just a roof over his head. It also provided friendship and community. When he first moved to the state capital, Riley roomed with his childhood friend Frank Hays, who was just starting out as a medical doctor.

Away from where Riley lived and worked, Indianapolis was expanding rapidly to accommodate its increasing population. Between 1870 and 1880, the number of Indianapolis residents rose from 48,200 to 75,000; and new subdivisions expanded its geographical area. By 1876, the city encompassed additions that doubled the land that had been platted around the Mile Square. As more affluent people migrated to the developing suburbs, the Mile Square's population became increasingly working class. The rich and poor were no longer as likely to live next to each other as they did in the city's early history. Many of the wealthier inhabitants built beautiful new homes in these outlying areas; and city and state leaders constructed several impressive and imposing buildings that reflected the growing stature of Indianapolis as an economic and political center.[13]

Upon his arrival, Riley plunged into his work at the *Indianapolis Journal* "like a house afire."[14] He could easily walk from his boardinghouse to the newspaper's offices, located in the southwest sector of the Circle. Because of the *Journal,* the Circle became strongly associated with newspaper life. When the *Journal* building was first built, at five stories tall, it was twice the height of any other structure in town.[15] It overlooked Circle Park. The Governor's Mansion that once stood on the site had long ago been razed. By the time Riley started work at the newspaper, the park was a well-kept area surrounded by an iron fence.[16]

At first, Riley was a bit homesick for Greenfield. "I miss my old ways o' doing things," he said to Clara Bottsford, "miss the old room—the old table— the old times—the old discomforts, but most of all I miss *You.*"[17] His writing and his lectures kept him so busy that he had to work Sundays, leaving him no time to travel to see her. They found this situation frustrating; but Riley explained that he had trouble keeping up with all of his responsibilities: "I have so many irons in the fire, it keeps me hoppin' to look after the half of them."[18] But on the whole, Riley thought that his life was going very well.[19] As always when he started new ventures, he was optimistic.

Riley projected this same optimism in regard to Clara Bottsford's aspirations for a literary career. He showed an avid interest in her writing and was eager for her to succeed. During 1879 and 1880, much of Riley's correspondence with Bottsford dealt with professional matters. After she asked him to write her a letter of introduction to Charles Philips of the *Kokomo Tribune* in July 1879, Riley edited her poems and counseled her about her submissions to newspapers and magazines.[20] Some of this advice was very practical. He sent her linen stationery for her correspondence with editors, told her what to write in the cover letters she included with her submissions to journals, and even explained how she should fold each sheet of paper.[21] The tone of these letters was almost paternal. Nineteenth-century society often characterized women as child-like beings who needed men's practical wisdom and protection. Rules and social habits tended to infantilize women, and laws reinforced their inferiority to men.[22]

However, Bottsford was neither innocent nor was she always submissive. Riley voiced a violent passion for her and alluded to the fact that she had some sexual experience: "Can't tell you how I yearn to grab you up, and crush and strangle you! You—with all former experience to direct your fancy—can't guess how I could swoop, and swirl, and storm you to death this day! I have been dying for ages to be knotted in the arms of you and tangled up and mixed and smothered out."[23]

As the preceding statements suggest, Riley often associated sex with violence and death. Many nineteenth-century physicians, clergymen, and teachers encouraged these associations by inventing and exaggerating the mental and physical threats posed by sexual indulgence.[24] Moreover, in an age in which the movement for women's rights was gaining strength, Riley was one of many men who manifested a latent fear of "the vengeful female, . . . the immortal vampire."[25] Riley depicted Bottsford in this way when she appeared to taunt or disobey him. His poem "The Werewife" (first entitled "My Ghoul") presents a most potent example of this. In January 1880, Riley wrote this poem in a fit of anger after Bottsford had not kept a promise to come see him in Indianapolis.[26] In a letter he wrote the day before the poem appeared in the *Indianapolis Journal,* Riley let Bottsford know she had inspired it.[27] It depicted Bottsford as a perfect and enchanting woman who could suddenly transform herself into a demonic, destructive beast:

> She came to me in dazzling guise
> Of gleaming tresses and glimmering eyes,
> With long, limp lashes that drooped and made
> For their baleful glances bowers of shade;
> And a face so white—so white and sleek
> That the roses blooming in either cheek
> Flamed and burned with a crimson glow
> Redder than the ruddiest roses blow—
> Redder than blood of the roses know
> That Autumn spills in the drifted snow.
> And what could my fluttering, moth-winged soul
> Do but hover in her control?—
> With its little, bewildered bead-eyes fixed
> Where the gold and white and the crimson mixed?
> And when the tune of her low laugh went
> Up from that ivory instrument
> That you would have called her throat, I swear
> The notes built nests in her gilded hair,
> And nestled and whistled and twittered there,
> And wooed me and won me to my despair.
> And thus it was that she lured me on,
> Till the latest gasp of my love was gone,
> And my soul lay dead, with a loathing face
> Turned in vain from her dread embrace,—
> For even its poor dead eyes could see
> Her sharp teeth sheathed in the flesh of me,
> And her dripping lips, as she turned to shake
> The red froth of that her greed did make,
> As my heart gripped hold of a deathless ache,
> And the kiss of her stung like the fang of a snake.[28]

In this same letter, Riley told Bottsford that he disapproved of much of what she wrote. He insinuated that her work was too masculine in subject and

157

style and asked that she write something that would be more appropriate for a female author: "[W]rite something tender, low and sweet—not those muscled things of passion you delight in—but just pure tenderness and warmpth [*sic*]."[29] Here, Riley expressed a sexual double standard. He had just written one of his most violent and passionate poems, but he admonished her for doing the same. Because she was a women, Riley found Bottsford's "muscled things of passion" threatening.

Decent women were supposed to be innocent, modest, and lacking in sexual appetites. This denial of female sensuality served to "safeguard man's sexual adequacy."[30] Involved with a woman who was aware of her own passions, Riley was presumably under greater pressure to perform sexually than if he were engaged in a relationship with someone ignorant of such matters. Riley thought that Bottsford should certainly not be alluding to this subject on paper and that expressions of eroticism were somehow unnatural to women. These attitudes, which minimized and denigrated female sexuality, reflected ideas that were prevalent at the time.[31]

During the 1879–1880 season, Riley's readings took him to all corners of Indiana. In his absence, Clara grew impatient. As his career seemed to be progressing well, Riley urged her not to be "blue" and reassured her that fate would bring them together.[32] By January, he lectured on average four times a week, and he was pleased with the reception he received in the many different towns to which he traveled.[33] That same month, the *Indianapolis Journal* announced that interest in Riley "seem[ed] to double with each public appearance."[34] In Crawfordsville, Maurice Thompson introduced him as "the greatest dialectician in the State, if not in the United States."[35]

Riley's lecture tour not only boosted his reputation but also gave him the opportunity to make invaluable professional connections, such as Robert Burdette of the *Burlington Hawkeye.* Since Philips had secured his endorsement for the "Walker" poems in the *Kokomo Tribune,* Riley had been eager to meet this writer and humorist. When he made Burdette's acquaintance following a lecture in Shelbyville, Indiana, Riley found that he was "just as true and pure and good" as he was funny.[36] The two men took an instant liking to one another and remained friends for life. He was already responsible for first calling Riley the Bret Harte of Indiana; and, after he met the poet and saw him perform, Burdette was willing personally to help him advance his career as a lecturer.

With endorsements from important figures such as Burdette and Thompson, demand for Riley's lectures increased, leaving him even less time to himself. Although in many ways he enjoyed being "so wonderfully busy," at the end of February, he grew tired of "speaking almost every night" for weeks at a time.[37] Despite his growing acclaim, he still was not meeting with the economic success he anticipated. He worried about the "old problem of existence"; but, no matter how hard he worked, he progressed little financially.[38] Throughout this lecture season, he complained that he remained just as poor as ever.[39] On the theory that a good physical appearance was the secret to success, he invested much of what he earned in creating an illusion of prosperity, characteristically spending his money before he had it; for this reason, his economic security continued to lag behind other aspects of his professional advancement.[40]

Demand for Riley's writings also rose. In April 1880, acclaimed editor and publisher Charles A. Dana printed a Riley poem called "Silence" in his newspaper, the *New York Sun*.[41] Riley declared this his "newest victory." For the first time, he had the opportunity to acquire a following outside the Midwest. However, he planned to make regular submissions to the *Sun* not only because it was a major East Coast publication but also because he understood that the *Sun* paid higher prices for its contributions than any magazine.[42]

Along with Longfellow, Riley later identified Dana as one of the people who most encouraged him in his early literary career.[43] During the next several months, Riley endeavored "with all of his might" to become one of this famous publisher's "lasting favorites."[44] However, Dana did not immediately accept all of the submissions that followed. He agreed with many members of the literary establishment, including Howells, that literature should be uplifting and wholesome. "Why add to the morbid poetry of the world," Dana remarked in one letter to Riley.[45] Although he found that the young poet's versification had much merit, Dana returned poems that were dark and melancholy in motif because he thought they were not healthful for the reader.[46]

Surprised by Dana's comments, Riley stated that he now realized that, in some instances, he chose topics unwisely: "[I]t is not improbable that oftentimes in selection of themes, I am unfortunate—though my effort, I assure you— however unpleasant my subject, is always directed against any unhealthful tone or touch of morbidness."[47] "Tom Johnson's Quit," which made light of one man's pledge to stop drinking, is an example of a questionable subject. Because it had earned him so much acclaim under the "Walker" pseudonym, Riley thought the poem had enough merit to be published in the *Sun*. However, Dana did not like it at all: "It has the radical defect of attempting to joke with a shocking subject."[48]

Riley respected Dana's opinion and promised he would be more guarded to ensure that his poems were healthful in tone and spirit.[49] As Henry Beers pointed out in his essay about Riley, one of the things that endeared him to his contemporaries was his cheerfulness. Beers called him "Sunny Jim" and commended him for leaving tragedy and bitterness out of his poems. At the same time, this eminent critic and Yale professor loved the "tender pathos, kindred to his humor, . . . everywhere present" in his work. According to Beers, Riley never failed "to hearten and console" audiences with his sentimentality.[50]

Riley was also often praised for his wholesomeness. In October 1915, former Vice President Charles W. Fairbanks claimed that Riley never wrote a poem that was even a little bit salacious: "It is one of the fine things to the credit of Mr. Riley that his pen is as clean as his purpose. He has written for the home, for girlhood, for boyhood and has never brought a blush to the cheek of either."[51] Ironically, these same qualities are some of the ones for which his poems are today most criticized.

Fairbanks would have been surprised if he had been reminded that Riley at one time wrote poems about subjects that could be considered sordid and disreputable. In the depths of depression, Riley also wrote poems filled with despair.[52] He composed most of these works during the early part of his career. Many of them never made it into print, but others appeared in Indiana newspapers. Riley left most of those that were published unsigned, or he allowed them to be printed under one of his pseudonyms. Some of the subjects included in this group of poems were the unsafe practices of the railroads, the hypocrisy of organized religion, and begging.[53]

At the time Dana criticized him for the morbid nature of the poems he sent to the *Sun*, Riley explained that the midwestern newspapers to which he was then making regular submissions asked for these "odd studies" and that he could ill afford not giving them what they wanted.[54] Throughout the nineteenth century, the working classes feasted on the sensational crime stories and ribald humor printed in newspapers. Riley fulfilled the demand for pieces of low humor. The poetry and character studies he wrote for this purpose generally depicted poor people. By printing sketches and poems that portrayed the underprivileged humorously, newspapers reinforced social hierarchies. While prominent citizens were lauded in society pages, the lower classes became the subjects of comic relief and were otherwise usually slighted or treated in a deprecatory manner.[55]

Several of Riley's "odd studies" made references to the problem of alcoholism. In poems such as "On Quitting California," "John Golliher's Third Womern," and "The Dismal Fate of Tit," he made overt references to the debilitating and destructive effects of excessive drinking, including delirium tremens. By the time Riley wrote, the horror of delirium tremens was an almost universal aspect of all dark temperance literature. The public had an almost grotesque fascination with it.[56] However, several of Riley's poems suggest that he probably had personal experience with this dreaded alcoholic symptom. Some of his poems, including "The Flying Islands of the Night," more than likely paralleled Riley's efforts to regulate his own behavior.[57]

In the "The Dismal Fate of Tit," which appeared in the *Indianapolis Journal* in January 1880, Riley described delirium tremens as the "jim-jams" and alluded to the fact that alcohol poisoning could be fatal: "O, there was a young fellow who had / The jim-jams so awfully bad, / That he fancied he tried / To commit suicide— / As he found that he had."[58] This poem warned where the profligacy of the lower classes could lead. Its other stanzas described a young man who dissipated himself by staying up all night and another who became a thief.[59] Because "The Dismal Fate of Tit" and many of the other poems Dana criticized were meant to be humorous overall and depicted the poor in familiar ways, they would not necessarily have shocked late nineteenth century readers.

Riley's poems reinforced attitudes about drinking. Poverty was thought to be the primary cause of alcoholism. Therefore, members of the lower classes were those who were usually characterized as drunks. However, drinking problems did not affect only the poor. A saloon existed for every three hundred Americans; and, in many circles, drinking was an accepted part of everyday life.[60] It was even more rampant in frontier America. For many settlers, liquor "was food, medicine, and the indispensable lubricant for civilized, enjoyable social intercourse."[61]

During Indiana's colonial period and its early statehood, "whiskey was the prevailing drink. . . . All churches tolerated its use. . . . [A] birth or a death, a wedding or a funeral, a log-rolling or a shucking, or a raising or a quilting, was incomplete and unsatisfactory without it."[62] This ardent spirit was also prescribed as a panacea for every possible ailment. Indiana's early inhabitants used whiskey to treat snake bites, milk sickness, rheumatism, and fevers. Riley's sister Elva May recalled that when she and her siblings were children their mother often dosed them with "strong medicine," undoubtedly composed primarily of alcohol.[63] In poems such as "In Smithses Settlement" and "John Golliher's Third Womern," Riley only accurately reflected the struggle of temperance activists to dispel the theory that liquor was the "good stuff of life."[64]

As the temperance movement spread and gained force during the last decades of the nineteenth century, alcohol came to be regarded as "society's most devastating scourge."[65] Attitudes toward the alcoholic became increasingly unforgiving.[66] As a result, Riley writings which referred to drinking became less and less acceptable. Moreover, his depictions of small-town rural life in frontier America which included drunkards as characters did not fit the picture that members of the still-dominant white Anglo-Saxon establishment had of their pioneer ancestors, whom they assumed always had behaved according to their own current standards of moral virtue. In general, following his contact with Dana, Riley took more care in choosing his topics so that his writings would be palatable to respectable audiences, including women and children. Just as with his own physical appearance, when he wrote, he became increasingly concerned with middle-class standards of propriety. Fewer and fewer of his poems were either irreverent or satirical; and, when his work was later published in anthologies, Riley customarily did not include poems that alluded to questionable subjects. Before they were published in book form, for the same reasons, Riley also cut some stanzas that originally appeared in some of his poems. For example, the poem "Afterwhiles" at one time incorporated the following lines:

> Afterwhile,—and you've inferred
> Doubtless, I will keep my word,
> And send to you this, my best,
> And least book of interest.
> Therefore, take it, as one takes
> Something bitter for "the shakes"—
> Palatable only when
> Down, and you're yourself again,
> Musing haply: "Well the pill,
> It is hard to swallow—still
> *He's* relieved, and I can smile
> And forgive him—afterwhile.[67]

By the time Riley and his nephew Ed Eitel compiled the comprehensive biographical edition of his work in 1913, people had forgotten he had ever written anything but the most decent and wholesome of poems. When Eitel consulted his uncle about early manuscripts and clippings that he found which included explicit references to sexuality, alcoholism, and other topics he considered unsavory, Riley asked him to suppress them.[68] However, there were exceptions to this rule. For example, "Tom Johnson's Quit" remained in collections of his poetry because of its popularity and because it could be interpreted to support the temperance cause.[69] Nevertheless, during his last years, Riley's editors and publishers ensured that his overall reputation as a writer of chaste, optimistic poems remained intact.

In May 1880, E. B. Martindale sold the *Indianapolis Journal* to John C. New, a banker and an attorney who was a well-known figure in the Republican party. As controlling owner of the *Journal,* New played a prominent role in shaping Republican policies. Because he was an astute businessman and politician, the paper flourished with him at its helm.[70] For a short time after this change in ownership, Riley feared that his job with the newspaper was in jeopardy. However, New never questioned Riley's employment because of his growing reputation.

Besides, Riley was incredibly prolific. At this time, the poet was writing one, two, and sometimes three poems per day, enough for the *Journal* and for contributions to other publications. Although some of his acquaintances thought that the quality of his writing would suffer under the pressure, Riley at first believed that he could produce many poems quickly that were of "really first-class" quality.[71] Even when composing at this rapid rate, he was not entirely pleased with himself and raised his expectations to an unrealistic level: "I want to get in the way of writing whether I feel like it or not, and if ever I should acquire the faculty of producing *365* poems *every year*, I shall be content—and not till then."[72]

Although he grew in favor with Dana, Riley was also dissatisfied because he had not yet conquered the eastern magazines. During the spring and summer of 1880, he made several submissions to *Scribner's, Atlantic Monthly,* and *Harper's Monthly,* only to receive rejection letters in return.[73] But Riley persevered. At this point, his dream of being published in the nation's most elite literary journals overcame all of his other interests: "Tell you what I'm doing I'm putting my best licks in now, for the magazines. I'm goin' to tackle every rebellious devil of 'em, and *make* 'em give my verse a chance! I wont [*sic*] have it any longer. They shall recognize me and my tremendous worth before I let 'em rest—the whole thick-headed, brain-deserted mob of 'em."[74] With this powerful drive to succeed, Riley worked night and day for weeks on end and often had little time for anything or anyone else.

Soon the pressures of this frenzied agenda caught up with him. By the middle of the summer of 1880, he recognized that he was "making little less than an automaton" of himself.[75] For financial reasons, the poet had no choice but to write poem after poem as quickly as possible. Even then, his pay from the *Journal* was anything but munificent; and, during the summer months, he did not have the luxury of supplementing his salary with lecture fees. Attempting to find other income, he committed himself to making regular contributions to several different newspapers and continued remitting applications to the magazines.[76]

When Charles Dana returned a poem because it did not "seem quite up to the mark," Riley realized that some of the things that he wrote at this frantic pace were not very good.[77] He toiled so hard that he thought he was losing a sense of who he really was: "It seems so strange! I have such brief interludes in which to be my real self—or selves."[78] As a writer and entertainer, Riley became entangled in a web of market relations that eventually reached far beyond his home. In the different situations he encountered, he sensed that he was changing certain parts of his identity to meet the needs and demands of others. The Hoosier poet was not alone. Many of Riley's contemporaries also grasped that the concept of selfhood was becoming increasingly mutable.[79]

With bureaucratization and industrialization, a decreasing percentage of the population was directly involved in economic production. Specialization of labor caused people to be increasingly dependent on others for products and services. In addition, fewer and fewer decisions about ordinary people's livelihoods were made locally. As the corporate and government elite centralized in cities took over decision-making processes, individuals had less control over their life circumstances; and personal autonomy was undermined. At the same time that the developing modern industrial capitalist system promoted social interdependence, it made society more impersonal. In an era in which there was increased anonymity and geographic mobility, people learned to adjust their attitudes and behavior according to the different social settings and locales in which they found themselves. In this mobile, fluid market society, the idea of selfhood no longer seemed as permanent or unified as it had when communities were perceived to be relatively stable and values instilled by parents and religious leaders provided a more solid grounding for the construction of personal identity.[80]

As a poet and lecturer, Riley was sensitive to the feelings and impressions of others and skillful at shifting his psychological stance to meet needs presented by diverse situations. This trait was especially useful to him when he was on the road lecturing. To be successful, it was imperative that he quickly ascertain the nature of the audiences in front of which he performed. However, Riley manipulated his various "selves" in all facets of his life as a means toward professional advancement.[81]

Riley was not entirely comfortable with this idea of unstable individual identity. In effect, the various fragments of self that he constructed became commodified.[82] Although he consciously assembled and manipulated these social masks for private gain, he sometimes longed for the past, when he had not defined the different parts of his personality so much to meet the demands of others. In his youth, he had been more inner-directed. As a bohemian artist and drifter, he had been concerned primarily with pleasing himself.

As the pressures of his professional career increased, Riley had less time to relax and to carouse and enjoy himself with friends. His lifestyle altered a great deal. To achieve fame and fortune, Riley came to understand that he had to become an industrious young man who spent most of his time tirelessly writing. He came to define this part of his personality as the "day" Riley.[83] However, he did not spend all of his time at his desk. He often took a break in the afternoon to saunter up and down Washington Street, Indianapolis' primary business thoroughfare. To come up with material for his poems, he peered into shop windows and observed people.[84]

When he had the opportunity, Riley also took time out to socialize. He met several of his friends in a back room of the *Indianapolis Journal*'s business office. With men such as Frank Hays and George Hitt, business manager of the *Journal,* he could temporarily revert back to being the old, fun-loving Riley who did his best to escape from worldly cares.[85] He sometimes attended all-night parties where he drank, sang songs, gave speeches, and told humorous stories.[86]

Despite his busy schedule, Riley tried to see Clara Bottsford about once a month. Because of his long visits to her at her family's farm, gossip began to circulate in Greenfield about their relationship; and Bottsford became quite upset that her reputation was being sullied. Although they were intimately involved, Riley reassured her that there were no grounds upon which their behavior could be called into question. As he lived miles away from her, he said that it was only natural for him to prolong his visits as much as possible. Even the propriety of his extended meetings with her was not really suspect because other family members were always on the premises when he saw her. If her family treated him cordially and believed that he had honorable intentions, Riley argued, the rest of the community had no reason to think anything untoward was going on. Therefore, he repeatedly encouraged Bottsford to disregard any malicious rumors.[87] Riley adopted a characteristic stance of lovers among the nineteenth-century middle classes. He did not deny his powerful erotic feelings for Bottsford. However, these emotions and the character of their relationship were no one else's affair.[88]

Bottsford apparently complained that Riley did not take the situation seriously enough: "You [Bottsford] say I look upon the matter lightly—being a man; and therefore less beholden in the eyes of the world as regards my good name[,] etc &c."[89] Indeed, during the nineteenth century, the acceptable boundaries of propriety were different for men and women. For men, almost anything was permitted during their bachelor years. It was a time for them to gain sexual experience and to enjoy fleeting love affairs. In contrast, women needed to appear modest and innocent to maintain their reputations and, even after they were engaged, had to carry their sexual reserve further than men; but, as Peter Gay points out, "how much further was not always clear."[90] No matter how far premarital experimentation progressed, women were at least technically supposed to be virgins at the time of matrimony.[91]

In his letters to Bottsford, Riley protested against vicious rumors about her. He said that she was "blameless" and maintained that any malicious attacks against her were "self-evidently false." Her only fault was being unable to immediately recognize "duplicity and malignant cunning."[92] However, other letters reveal that a high level of intimacy existed between them: "I want you though, and, in fancy, sometimes hold [you] till I wonder I can't hear you shriek aloud. Do you ever feel the arms o' me like that? God! How I do thrill just thinking of us. When will I see you—hold you—drink the kiss—the lips of you again?"[93]

Rumors about their affair were accompanied by reports about Riley's involvement with other women. Bottsford was so upset by all of the stories that swirled around her that she suggested that it would have been better for her if they had long ago parted company.[94] In the nineteenth century, marriage was a near necessity for women. Therefore, Bottsford was looking for a firm commitment from Riley. This was not the first time that she complained that he came to her with other women's kisses on his lips.[95] It looked to her as if he would never marry her; and she also feared that gossip about her might ruin her chances with any other man.

Although he claimed it hurt him to do it, Riley had to admit the truth of much of what Bottsford said. At thirty, he knew that he was expected to settle down soon and start a family. However, instead of pursuing a single relationship with the intention of marrying, he flirted with a number of different women. He continued to correspond with Elizabeth Kahle and had also recently started to write to the Wisconsin poet Ella Wheeler (later Wilcox).[96] In addition, his behavior toward his roommate's girlfriend, Louella White, was not altogether honorable. Apparently Frank Hays was unaware that Riley kissed his girl and wrote her love letters.[97] To make matters worse, Bottsford and White had become friends.[98]

Riley attempted to convince Bottsford that his relationships with other women had very little meaning and that he was not to blame for the attention they paid him: "The fact is, my position seems to be one of such peculiar character that the moment my attention is for one minute directed upon some particular woman, every other woman begins howling.—Not that *I* consider *myself* a 'catch' at all—but I suppose everybody thinks, from the infernal sentiment I sometimes write, and taking, too, my age into consideration—that I must either mean marriage or pure villainy."[99]

Part of Riley's "peculiar" position stemmed from his growing celebrity. Known as a "rising young poet," he received an increasing amount of attention from the opposite sex.[100] He took pleasure in his newfound allure and loved to encourage his female fans by writing them romantic letters and verses. Riley wanted Bottsford to believe that he was doing nothing to attract other women's attention; but, in truth, he pursued and enticed some of them with his "infernal sentiment."[101] His reassurances notwithstanding, telling her that he made other women "howl" indicates that he was trying to make Bottsford jealous and to appear more desirable to her.[102]

Riley hesitated to give up his bachelorhood just as his popularity was beginning to develop. He enjoyed boasting about how many females he was able to enthrall with his passionate words. In his letters to Wheeler, he admitted to seeing a number of different young ladies and described the summer of 1880 as "one long carnival of enjoyment." He told her that Indianapolis was "thronged with peerless maidens from all quarters of the globe." "They all love me; madly—passionately—devotedly," Riley bragged, "and even as I write, a clamorous semicircle of them lies at my feet."[103] While he used these letters to boost his ego, Riley did not take seriously into account what each of these young women might demand from him in return.

Although unwilling to give up these casual flirtations, he cared enough for Bottsford that he did not want to risk losing her. He proposed and, at the end of July, told her that he was arranging for an "early marriage," at which his good friend Myron Reed, a prominent Presbyterian minister in Indianapolis, would officiate.[104] Despite his stated intentions, Riley found a number of reasons to avoid carrying out this promise.

Few people in Indianapolis knew much about Bottsford. Many of Riley's friends and acquaintances had never seen her. In fact, Charles Dennis, who established the Indianapolis *Saturday Review* with George Harding in October 1880, asked Riley if Clara L. Bottsford were not a myth.[105] Because Riley had so often masqueraded under different pseudonyms, this journalist hypothesized that Riley and Bottsford "were simply one and the same individual."[106] Although his business partner moved in with Hays and Riley and was more familiar than most other people with the details of the poet's life, it still took quite a lot of convincing before Dennis would believe that Bottsford really existed.[107]

When she came in to the city to see him, she would leave Riley a note in the *Indianapolis Journal* counting room, at the corner of Market and Pennsylvania Streets, telling him where he could find her.[108] In this manner, they carried on their affair almost in secret. While this arrangement helped to preserve Bottsford's reputation, it gave Riley the opportunity to behave as if he were not engaged when she was not in town.

Riley continued to split his affections and even embarked on new relationships. Sometime during late summer 1880, he met a variety show singer and dancer named Grace Monk Morland, whom he called "his little Monk."[109] As he did with several of the women with whom he became involved, Riley made her believe that he was truly in love with her: "You [Riley] say you want me to want you. Oh God I cant [*sic*] any more than I do, only God knows how I want you, as I told you last night sometimes I am tempted to throw up everything and come to you. I must see you, my only darling. O I could not think of you any more than I do. You say be brave and have patience, how can I, when I am longing all the time for you, and you so far away from me. Must I tell you again how earnestly sincerely and devotedly I love you."[110]

Because she was a single working girl in the theater, and not of his class, Riley treated Monk with less respect than he did his other romantic interests. In general, women of the theater were considered sexually available—one step away from being prostitutes. As variety shows were particularly disreputable, female performers who appeared in them would have been seen as easy prey for men who thronged about stage and dressing room doors.[111] With the success and notoriety of actresses such as Sarah Bernhardt, some women hoped to use the stage as a way to rise in society either through their talent or through their liaisons with men.[112] Monk may have seen Riley as her passport to a better life; but he treated her as just another conquest. He had little sympathy for her feelings and abandoned her as soon as he lost interest.

Riley's relationship with Ella Wheeler was very different. He began corresponding with Wheeler because he admired her writing. From the time that he discovered her work, Riley considered her his equal: "I remember an odd sketch or two of yours, first read over and over all alone, till all their *hominess* and wholesome worth had soaxed [*sic*] in, and warmed me through and through with enthusiastic delight—then read aloud to my choicest friends, and mooned over and applauded, till we all in fancy gathered you in, and made you one of us, and still know you, on and on forever as one of *our kind.*"[113]

While Riley was on a hunting trip with Myron Reed in June 1880, the two poets met; and "a high-pressure love affair by mail" ensued.[114] Addressing her as his "own one woman in the world," Riley thought that he had finally found the woman of his dreams: "Since first I looked upon your pictured face it has seemed to me 'This woman is to be yours utterly. God made her for you.'"[115] As an author of poetry and prose he respected, he considered Wheeler the one woman capable of fully understanding him.

Most of the women with whom Riley had extended liaisons were writers. However, unlike the others, Wheeler had a successful literary career. In many ways, Riley was correct in identifying her as his female counterpart. Her poetry became very popular, and for several years she wrote poems daily for newspaper syndication. By the time she and Riley began corresponding, a number of magazines had already printed her work. She also had three published poetry anthologies.[116]

Although he felt that he and Wheeler were kindred spirits, Riley was jealous of her position in literary circles. He wanted her all to himself. He cursed fate for keeping her so far away from him and disliked the attention she received from other men. In fact, Wheeler admitted to Riley that she flew "around with more different 'fellows' than anybody."[117] However, Riley determined that her prominence as a writer posed the biggest threat to the future of their relationship: "And when, O when am I to have you here shut in my arms, and locked and barred and bottled safe away from all the jealous world?—My one great rival, and the only one that in reallity [*sic*] I fear."[118]

Wheeler's success as an author gave her more freedom than most other women. In fact, during the time she wrote regularly to Riley, she appeared to function almost as a man, choosing and discarding potential lovers at will.[119] Riley became one of those whom she threw aside. While he was in Milwaukee during the fall of 1880, Riley and Wheeler apparently spent a night together.

Upon leaving the city, Riley wrote: "It *was* so. All the long, long, night; but it has left me hungrier, hungrier!"[120] Their intimate encounter only deepened Riley's passion, and he begged Wheeler to permit him to be alone with her once more. "[L]et me see you soon, and alone," Riley entreated. "I never want to see you again if not so."[121]

But Wheeler no longer shared his desire. She did not agree to see him before his departure from Milwaukee; and the ardency of their correspondence quickly waned.[122] One week after their meeting, Riley already knew that he was not as "dear" to her as he had been before. The tone of their letters became more professional. For a few more weeks, they discussed their editors and critiqued each others' work; then they stopped corresponding altogether.[123]

Intrigued as he was by Wheeler, she also always represented a professional threat because she was in direct competition with him.[124] Riley knew that he and Wheeler submitted poems to many of the same publications; and she, thus far, had been more successful in being accepted.[125] As a consequence, after she rebuffed him, Riley did not always have kind words to say about her. Riley had a certain idea about what female writers should write and the way they should act; and, in his perception, Wheeler sometimes behaved in ways that were unbecoming.[126]

Riley was not alone in questioning Wheeler's propriety. The first publishers she approached with her most popular anthology, *Poems of Passion*, rejected it because it contained sexually suggestive material.[127] After it finally appeared in print, a reporter for the *Kansas City Star* asked Riley what he thought of it. In his response, Riley did not question the merit of *Poems of Passion;* but, because she was a woman, he criticized Wheeler for making such an erotic volume public: "She has written some beautiful things. As far as their alleged immorality is concerned, I think that every theme is the poet's—great passion, great love, great hate, and the only question is whether it is good taste for a girl, a miss, to publish them in a book."[128] Although he had been enchanted by her when he saw her three years earlier, Riley now attacked Wheeler's appearance. By disapproving the subjects of her poetry and saying that she dressed "pretty loud" and "seemed to be proud of her makeup," he suggested that she was not respectable.[129]

Wheeler denied that she presented herself to Riley in the way he described.[130] Her former lover's derogatory comments disguised his bitterness at her rejection as well as his envy of her rise to prominence in the literary field. Years later, Wheeler found a letter of Riley's which she had neglected to return to him after one of their "periodical squabbles."[131] She had no doubt that he would smile when he reread it. Both poets had mellowed since the time when they exchanged caustic words in the press, and Wheeler looked back on their relationship with some fondness: "[Y]ou could no more help writing love letters in those days than I could help receiving them! It was all material for our genius."[132]

Throughout the period that he was corresponding with Wheeler, Riley continued to write regularly to Elizabeth Kahle. His relationship with her was not nearly so turbulent as those he carried on with Wheeler, Bottsford, or Monk. Over the years, his correspondence with this shy young woman became increasingly brotherly and protective. He also was able to be candid with her about his opinions.

During the same summer that he proposed to Bottsford, Riley wrote a letter to Kahle in which he revealed his doubts about love and the institution of marriage: "I'm not quite sure that all of this life's happiness depends upon just love.—Not that I'm a cynic, but I have seen so many—oh so very many dear friends that had been happier had they remained just friends and never wed each other. But its [sic] a solemn thing to think of never having one's own home."[133] These statements reveal that Riley's desire for a comfortable home life conflicted with his fear of matrimony.

By the last decades of the nineteenth century, the romantic ideal of marriage had fully taken root among most classes in the United States. Riley never expected to marry for any reason but love. However, this emphasis on romantic love as the primary basis for union between men and women increased expectations for marital happiness—expectations that Riley was unsure he could fulfill.[134] The inverse was also true. No woman could ever meet his high standards. Once, when discussing the prospects of matrimony, Riley said that he thought of himself as "a very disagreeable young man ... [for whom] nothing in earth, or heaven" would satisfy.[135]

On the other hand, he greatly desired the acceptance, convenience, and respectability that a spouse would bring. At this point, Riley was growing tired of living in a dreary boardinghouse without amenities: ". . . my home is in no wise even worthy of the name. Its [sic] a place I never go . . . but when absolutely forced to by the fear that if I don't the outside world will know how really miserable a place it is."[136] A wife would at least cook, clean, and provide him with more creature comforts. Moreover, few people, especially men, remained single for life. Those who did not marry were viewed in some ways as failures. People who lived outside families were looked on with suspicion and existed without full acceptance from the rest of society. Riley was admired by many, but because he never married the rumor spread that he was "queer." According to those who held this opinion, bachelors were always "queer"; and, as a poet, Riley's lifestyle was even more suspect.[137]

In part because so many of Riley's poems were about children, a genre usually left to women, they were often described as having fine feminine qualities. Critics said they were filled with sentimentality, pathos, and tenderness. One reviewer stated that Riley's understanding of and appeal to children entitled him to be called, "without the least weakness of effeminacy, . . . a mother-man."[138] People did not even consider Riley's humor to possess masculine traits: "Riley's humor is of no such palpable thing. Elusive as a fairy, and as fragile as thistle-down, it is as impossible to catch, by any arrangement of words, . . . as it is to paint a perfume."[139]

Although he later made openly disapproving statements to the press about Wheeler's personal comportment, he said that writers, at least male writers such as Oscar Wilde, should be judged solely by the quality of their work. Again, Riley's attitudes revealed a sexual double standard. Perhaps because Riley was sensitive and often showed his emotions, Riley told Bottsford in 1881 that critics had no right to speak of Wilde's personal appearance and carriage.[140] Moreover, Riley did not deny that he thought he possessed some attributes ordinarily associated with the fairer sex. He even worked to enhance them. In a letter to the poet Louise Chandler Moulton, he stated that he believed that he was almost as perceptive and intuitive about human nature as any woman: "In the books—I feel you will find *some* assurance of the justice of your *divinings*— the *mainest* thing I'm envious of in a woman,—her divinings. Man's are far less accurate—though my own, I'm vain enough to think, are very nearly feminine, in subtlety and exactness—so that I humor them—have learned to—and let them have their way, at times, with no restraint whatever."[141]

Throughout his life, Riley had many strong same-sex relationships. In the early 1880s, while he carried on affairs with women, Riley was very close to Frank Hays, Charles Philips, George Hitt, and others. Sometimes he expressed himself to men in intense emotional terms. For example, in 1887, he wrote to his friend the physician and amateur poet James Newton Matthews: "It is a natural law that men shall love *women,* but I love *you,* and 'no knife shall cut our love in two!'"[142]

Despite his passion for Matthews, it would be dangerous to classify Riley as a homosexual. During the nineteenth century, overt displays of affection between people in this type of relationship were common. Gender roles had not yet solidified; and it was not necessarily scandalous for men to hug, kiss, sleep with, and proclaim their love for one another.[143] Riley's statements suggest that he understood that there was a limit to what was socially acceptable between people of the same gender; and no letters comparable to those he wrote to Bottsford or Wheeler, in which he expressed his sexual desire in relatively unveiled terms, exist for any of his male correspondents.

Furthermore, Riley told Matthews that he would like to have a home and children and asked him whether he advised marriage.[144] He wanted Matthews's opinion because much in his experience discouraged him from entering into wedlock. In addition to what he observed among his friends, he had watched his beloved mother suffer in his father's frequent absences and still blamed him for her early death. When he remarried, Reuben's new wife had certainly not brought happiness back to the family's home.

Riley's career as a writer and lecturer presented more obstacles to wedlock than anything else. In the early 1880s, he did not yet earn enough money to support a spouse and family well; and his readings often took him away from home for days at a time. His ambition also stood in the way. Riley was too interested in his own personal advancement to put the necessary energy into a relationship. His hunger for success made him selfish. "Its [*sic*] almost wrong, I think . . . sometimes, to work with the ambition that I do," Riley said to Kahle in July 1880 after not having written her in over a month. "But I am so eager to succeed," he continued, "so feverish in my desire to be something or some-body—that my effort never flags or falters for a minute, but, self-impelled, moves on and are [*sic*] gathering newer force and power with each succeeding hint of final victory."[145] Riley made a choice between marriage and his poetry. Above all, he had to make a name for himself; and, much of the time, he could think of little else.[146]

Fall 1880 held the prospect of being one of those periods in which Riley would have little time for his personal life. For months he continued to feel "crowded to the raw edge of distraction" just with his writing; and then he had to add making arrangements for the upcoming lyceum season to his already hectic schedule.[147] Because he was insecure about his public appearances, preparing for a new lecture was a painstaking business: "[I]f you can just imagine a little weenty-teenty man, with as little dignity as I possess, trying to appear serious before 'applausive [*sic*] thousands,' you can, perhaps, arrive at some conclusion of the ammount [*sic*] of preparation in the production of such a programme."[148]

As always, Riley's lecture planning included strategies for self promotion. During the winter lyceum season, he had little time to devote to poetry. Moreover, doing readings called on different parts of his personality than did writing. He said that "the business Riley" went out on the road to perform. In this mode, he concerned himself with advertising and finding the best ways to please each audience everywhere he went.[149]

In mid-September, Riley was scheduled to open the 1880–1881 season at the Grand Opera House in downtown Indianapolis. A week before this event, he told Wheeler that he was "scheming for a big house."[150] Riley always used his connections in the press to draw attention to his lectures and, as an employee of the *Journal*, probably had some control over the publicity this newspaper printed to advertise his upcoming performance. Whatever he did, his strategizing worked, for he had a fine audience. He received good reviews, and the lyceum bureau received many requests for future bookings.[151]

But Riley remained dissatisfied: "I have so much to make me happy—but so much more to make me miserable."[152] Overrun with requests for poems and lecture engagements, he did not know how he would be able to fulfill all of his commitments. His discontent intensified when he realized that he might have little money to show for all of his effort, even if he finished the work for which he was contracted. He found this process "absolutely damnable in the extreme."[153] As always, he never seemed quite able to meet the high expectations he had for himself.

To make matters worse, because he did not possess enough money yet to marry her, Bottsford put further pressure on him and threatened to go away some place where she might be able to make a more "brilliant match."[154] Riley assured Bottsford that he was doing his best to advance himself: "I've been writing a thousand things—scheming a thousand schemes—and withal have more redhot irons in the fire than a salamander could manipulate."[155] To appease her, he did not reveal to her how much stress he was under and boasted that he might be able to complete ten poems in one day.[156]

The demands placed on him by the *Indianapolis Journal* and other publications were sometimes almost unbearable: "if you only knew how they exasperate me,—these people I work for, and who pay so little—and how exacting they all are—and how everybody wants *theirs* to be better than all the others—and how little time they have to wait—and how I have to jump from dirges and dead marches to jingles and jim-cracks etc&—world without end.—You'd begin to think 'where on earth, in that little old hick'ry nut head of his' does he find enough extra room safely to stow away my name and address!"[157] The holiday season was particularly frantic. To his regular lecture schedule, Riley added performing at church festivals and concerts; and, on top of his regular newspaper contributions, he wrote Christmas sketches and poems. If he survived at all, Riley thought he might end up "a stark, staring, raving maniac."[158]

The pressures of the holidays indeed took their toll on Riley. During the first weeks of 1881, his alcohol problem got so out of control that he had to discontinue his public readings. Rejections from the nation's leading literary journals added to his despondency. In a letter to his friend the poet Rosaline E. Jones of Geneva, New York, he sarcastically referred to himself in the third person and remarked on his many failures to get his work published: "Why there is hardly a day passes that I don't receive a rejected poem of Riley's—'poor devil' . . . has gotten so used to such treatment he can no longer appreciate the dear old pain it used to give him in the past."[159] Although two juvenile magazines, *Wide Awake* and *St. Nicholas,* accepted a couple of his poems, he continued to have little luck with publications such as *Scribner's* and the *Atlantic*

Monthly.[160] Increasingly hardened to criticism and rejection, Riley tried to make light of this situation. Nevertheless, he tired of receiving letters which stated his poems were not suitable for publication in these journals. Alcohol helped him escape from the reality of these many disappointments.

By the middle of February, Riley was recovering and promised Bottsford that he would "soon be well and clean quit of the drinking business."[161] As much as he wanted this to be true, staying away from the bottle was an ongoing battle: "Havn't [*sic*] touched a taste today, and its [*sic*] now evening and I'll pull through till morning without—and so on to pure safety."[162] Knowing that his weakness for liquor was just another of many marks against him, he pleaded with Bottsford to be patient. Although the detoxification process proved difficult, Riley won this particular battle. In March, he was well enough to resume lecturing and, for several months, managed to give up all of his vices except tobacco.[163]

While his health improved, Riley's economic situation did not. He lost income when he was unable to work; and, with his growing acclaim, his creditors thought him more prosperous than he really was. At the beginning of 1881, some of them started vociferously demanding payment. His public visibility also made it easy for past financial indiscretions to catch up with him. For example, a South Bend restaurateur wrote asking for payment for an outstanding account incurred during two months in 1873 and promised that he would make it unpleasant for Riley if he did not make an effort to settle his bill.[164] In early April, as a result of his accumulated debt, he had so little money to cover his living expenses that he ran out of coal to heat his rooms.[165]

Soon thereafter, a visit from Robert Burdette gave Riley new hope. While he was in Indianapolis, Burdette assured Riley that he had a brilliant future ahead of him and pledged that he would help the poet in any way he could.[166] By this time, Riley's readings almost always drew large crowds. Because of his popularity and connections with local dignitaries, Burdette was convinced that the Redpath Lyceum Bureau, the most prestigious lecture agency in the country, might be willing to represent Riley during the following lecture season.[167]

Established by the journalist, reformer, and promoter James Redpath in 1868, this company, first known as the Boston Lyceum Bureau, managed the nation's most prominent lecturers—such eminent speakers as Henry Ward Beecher and Ralph Waldo Emerson. Along with his partner, George L. Fall, Redpath brought organization and a skill for marketing to the American lyceum system.[168]

These two men almost single-handedly made lecturing in the United States a successful business. Fall and Redpath devised contracts which guaranteed the fees that lyceum committees in various communities paid for each program. With these fees in place, towns and cities followed through on publicity to insure that each lecture was at least successful enough to cover their costs. The Redpath Bureau also instituted new scheduling arrangements. Instead of negotiating engagements performer by performer, Fall and Redpath offered lyceum committees a whole season of talent. They thereby were able to coordinate booking dates for an entire lecture calendar. Because Redpath and Fall were so successful, other lyceum bureaus soon followed their example. By the time Redpath became bored and sold the Bureau in 1875, this institution had become the most successful organization of its kind, with branches in all major cities.[169]

Another reason for the Redpath Bureau's success was its reputation for identifying and promoting artists and performers who could satisfy popular tastes.[170] Following Burdette's visit, Riley wanted desperately to have a chance to lecture on the East Coast under this agency's management.[171] Burdette recommended Riley to Redpath "as the rising star on the humorous platform."[172] Widely known as the "Burlington Hawkeye Man," Burdette had already established himself with Redpath as one of the best humorists in its stable of talent. Therefore, a reference from him went far in getting Riley the Bureau's representation. To further his chances, Burdette told Riley to follow up his endorsement with a letter which included recommendations and positive press notices.[173]

While he waited to receive an answer from the Redpath Lyceum Bureau about his application, Riley took on new responsibilities at the *Indianapolis Journal*. At the end of June 1881, New put him on the newspaper's editorial staff.[174] In this position, Riley primarily wrote humorous features but also commented on literature and popular personalities.[175] Although his "regular editorial work" kept him very busy, he enjoyed the change from writing poetry. With these articles, he pleased the newspaper's readers more than he ever dared to anticipate. Because he earned a larger salary writing these columns than he did as the *Journal*'s resident poet, Riley put much effort into this work. During the next several months, he wrote more humorous editorials than poems. These articles became popular, and other newspapers copied them. As he waited nervously for a response from Redpath, he reassured himself that, even if all other options failed, he might still have a bright future if he remained on the Indianapolis newspaper's staff.[176] Nineteenth-century journalists were highly respected. Through public service and ties of personal loyalty, they often became leading citizens within the communities in which they worked.[177]

Because it was the best lecture agency in the country, the Redpath Bureau seldom represented people who had not already developed a national reputation. Although unknown outside the Midwest, Riley put together his letter and collected his references with so much care that the Bureau could not ignore his potential. On the strength of his recommendations from Burdette and other prominent men, its agents agreed to add his name to their list of clients for the 1881–1882 season.[178]

Nevertheless, they did so rather tentatively. They were not sure that there would be a single call for Riley to perform and told him not to get his hopes up too high. Moreover, because he was not well known, getting engagements required an effective publicity campaign for which Riley, not the Bureau, was primarily responsible. An employee of the Bureau advised Riley that he had to develop his own publicity circular and that printing and postage costs would come out of his own pockets.[179]

With so much riding on making a good impression for his first season with this agency, Riley immediately went to work on advertising flyers and a new lecture program.[180] In addition to his endorsement from Burdette, Riley strategically included in his circular recommendations from Albert Gallatin Porter, governor of Indiana; Benjamin Harrison, who was then a U.S. senator; and the managing editors of the *Indianapolis Journal* and the *Indianapolis Sentinel,* the city's two major political newspapers.[181] Within a few weeks, because of his connections in the press, Riley received much publicity about being under Redpath Bureau management.[182]

Having succeeded in getting the Bureau's representation, Riley's spirits were again uplifted. "Everything is bright and particularly promising," Riley reported to Bottsford at the beginning of September.[183] He told her that he was hard at work and enjoying all his endeavors. Although he preferred poetry, the humorous articles he wrote for the *Journal* grew in popularity. Riley's editorial pieces drew readers to the paper, and it sold as never before. New was delighted; and Elijah W. Halford, the managing editor, predicted that Riley's work would bring the *Journal* national exposure.[184] His future on the rostrum looked no less auspicious. Sure that the publicity he developed for his lectures would be effective in drawing the public's attention—that it would "knock 'em," he admitted that he was "feverish with impatience" for the lecture season to begin.[185]

Riley's predictions about his advertising proved accurate. The manager of the Chicago branch of the Redpath Bureau, Fred Hathaway, received requests almost daily for Riley to perform. Because communities were clamoring to engage him, Hathaway became convinced that Riley had the potential to be a "Big Card" for the agency and did everything he possibly could to advance his prospects.[186] Burdette also promoted Riley wherever he went. By November, the Bureau scheduled Riley to appear on the East Coast. At least a month's worth of engagements in the East, which included an appearance in Boston, awaited Riley at the beginning of the new year.[187]

As he became more confident of financial success, he determined that he would soon be in a position to marry Bottsford. During 1881, Riley became more serious about his relationship with her. To demonstrate his commitment, he told her that he intended to buy her the best engagement ring he could get.[188]

Nevertheless, their relationship remained rather turbulent. Riley's schedule continued not to permit him to spend much time with her. Bottsford became increasingly impatient with his long absences, and sometimes Riley did not follow through on his promises to come see her. On occasion, she dressed up and waited for him to arrive at her doorstep; but Riley did not come.[189] Perhaps in revenge for his missed appointments with her, Bottsford more than once left Riley disappointed at the train station.[190]

The geographic distance between them complicated their relationship. Sometimes their letters crossed in the mail, causing misunderstandings, especially about meeting times and dates. Although railroads greatly improved transportation in the second half of the nineteenth century, bad weather also sometimes prevented Riley and Bottsford from meeting.[191] Despite these problems and periodic disagreements, the couple continued to profess their deep abiding love and passion for one another.[192]

While Riley's professional career progressed farther and faster than ever before during 1881, this same year also brought him great personal loss. In April, a cousin's daughter succumbed to scarlet fever at the age of seven; and, in October, death struck Riley's paternal grandmother.[193] Because she had lived such a long life, Riley was ready to accept Margaret Slick Riley's passing. She was as "[g]ood as gold," and he was sure that she was in heaven with his mother.[194] Riley took the deaths of two of his friends much harder, in part because they died in their prime.[195] In May, George Harding, former editor of the *Indianapolis Herald*, with whom Riley had lived since the end of 1880, died suddenly. Following the funeral, Riley found it difficult to work or study in the rooms they had shared.[196] In November, after a long illness, Charles Philips of the *Kokomo Tribune* also passed away. Riley had been close to Philips and owed him much for promoting the "John C. Walker" poems. These two men were among those whom Riley most trusted, and their deaths left a large void in his life.[197]

Even more traumatic was the death of his younger brother Humboldt. At the end of November 1881, Riley received a telegram from his father telling him to come home immediately because Humboldt was gravely ill with typhoid fever.[198] Within days, Humboldt was dead; and Riley was overcome with regret. Only months earlier, he had escaped from Greenfield because he discovered Hum "drunker, by eleven degrees" than he himself ever was. "I didn't care to stay longer," Riley told Bottsford at the time, "and so I am here where he is not."[199] Riley's brother John described Hum as someone who "seemed to give up on life's problems as something beyond him."[200] Unlike John, who was then living in Colorado, Riley attended the funeral; but both brothers felt guilty for neglecting Humboldt and wished that they had done more to help him.[201]

Riley's schedule did not permit him a long grieving period. The frenetic pace that he kept was incompatible with traditional, social mourning practices. Riley's experience was characteristic of the time. As society industrialized and urbanized, the length of mourning was shortened more and more. People no longer had as much time to pause to honor and accept the passing of those dear to them. Mourning also became less extravagant. Burials no longer necessarily included all of the frills ordinarily associated with Victorian funeral rites.[202] During this period, some social critics complained that the new urban, industrial, capitalist order was reducing mourning to a "moment of reflection, a perfunctory gesture."[203]

Indeed, following his brother's funeral, Riley had little time to contemplate his personal loss. When he returned to Indianapolis the following week, Riley needed to find $150 to secure the booking in Boston that the Redpath Bureau negotiated for him.[204] Only a few weeks before he was scheduled to leave for the East Coast, he did not have these funds. In fact, he did not even have enough in his pockets to buy a train ticket home to Greenfield.[205] The Bureau treated him well in his first year under its management, but he received no money in advance of his performances.[206]

Finding the money necessary to finance this trip east was critical to Riley. If he did not make it to Boston during the 1881–1882 season, he would be yet another "year behind."[207] Therefore, he determined that no matter what it took he would find a way to get there: "I've been behind now long enough—So I'm going to the front—that's all!"[208]

To raise the money he needed, Riley went further into debt. Preying on Bona Bottsford's desire to see his sister happy and well cared for, Riley convinced the eldest of his fiancée's brothers to help finance him.[209] Two weeks before he was to leave for Boston, he advised the Redpath Bureau that he was ready and awaited further orders.[210] However, Riley still did not think he had enough money to make the trip wholly successful. To conceal his true economic circumstances, he wanted to go to the East Coast in style. So that he could associate with anyone he met in Boston without any personal embarrassment, Riley approached other friends, such as Albert Busch, for further loans.[211] He asked Busch for another $150 and assured him that the proceeds from his future bookings would more than enable him to pay back what he owed.[212]

Riley's friends came through, and he started to plan his strategy for Boston. By this time, he was a master of self-promotion. Although the Redpath Bureau advertised his readings in advance, Riley decided to do everything possible to assure that his appearance in the city proved an "eminent success."[213] He calculated he should arrive in Boston a few days before his performance. Armed with letters of introduction from such Indianapolis notables as John New, he would have the opportunity to "meet brother newspaper men" who might help publicize his readings.[214]

Just before Christmas, the Redpath Bureau informed Riley that he would appear in Boston on 3 January 1882, a couple of weeks earlier than anticipated. On Christmas morning he left for Canton, Ohio, where he was to perform that evening.[215] Five days later, he traveled to Boston. When he arrived at his hotel just opposite the Tremont Temple on the afternoon of 29 December, the first thing the poet saw was the famous theater's marquee, which read, "James W. Riley, the Hoosier Poet, Dialect Reader and Humorist."[216] Before setting out to explore the city, Riley immediately shut himself in his room "scrubbing and lathering and shaving."[217] He took so much care with his personal grooming because it was very important for him to make a favorable impression wherever he went. The way he looked and behaved in his first encounters with the people of Boston mattered a great deal in the image they would form of him.

Although New York had gained in importance at the end of the nineteenth century, for Riley, Boston remained the nation's cultural center because it was home to so many literary giants. He immediately took advantage of what the city had to offer. He spent his first night attending a play called *The Fool's Revenge,* starring Edwin Thomas Booth.[218] Son of Junius Brutus Booth and brother of John Wilkes Booth, Lincoln's assassin, Edwin was a member of America's most famous family of actors. Reflecting changes in tastes among theater audiences, his acting style was less flamboyant and ferocious than his father's. He was establishing himself as America's most influential Shakespearean actor; and his quiet, subtle, and intellectual portrayals of Hamlet and other characters became the paradigm for the modern stage.[219]

However, Riley claimed that he did not go to the theater solely to appreciate Booth's great acting abilities. "I went more to get [a] bird's eye view of [an] elite Bostonian audience," he wrote to Bottsford shortly following the play's conclusion, "and I must here assure you that I'll not be afraid o' facin' one, in the least."[220] Observing a Boston audience firsthand gave Riley confidence that he could succeed.

The Redpath Bureau was not so sure. Agents for the Bureau expected Riley to be older.[221] As a little-known performer from the Midwest, Riley was very aware of all the prejudices he had to overcome to be successful in this environment. He told Bottsford that he intended to "get in work" in the four days before his first readings in the city.[222] Riley was supposed to correspond with the *Journal* to supply the newspaper with stories about his experiences in Boston; but he was instead determined to spend his time meeting as many of the literati as possible. In this respect, his friendship with General Dan Macauley, formerly of Indianapolis, who had introduced Riley at his performance at the Park Theater two years earlier, was immensely helpful. Shortly after Riley's arrival in Boston, Macauley, who now managed a large printing establishment in this city, called on him at his hotel and promised to introduce him to all of his influential friends.[223]

From his past experiences, Riley understood the importance of taking advantage of such connections. During the nineteenth century, much business was conducted on this basis. The letters of introduction Riley brought with him from Indianapolis also proved invaluable. In a note to George Hitt, Riley quipped, "I was "pen sesamed' around to a wonderful extent—meeting not only notables to whom they were addressed but 'boosted' on by the *recipients* till I know everybody of the ilk."[224] Because of his charm, wit, and dapper appearance, literary notables whom Riley met gave him their direct assurances that they would attend his lecture.[225]

By visiting newspaper offices across the city, Riley took full advantage of the connections his employment at the *Journal* afforded him. He understood that reporters would be much more apt to take him seriously and to give him positive reviews if he met them before his lecture and identified himself as a colleague: "Today I have been around among the newspapers, and they seem all wonderfully disposed, and their actions promise that the hearing they will give me will be hearty, and wholesome to my future prospects."[226]

While Riley was carrying out his own publicity campaign, the Redpath Bureau effectively advertised his lecture. The agency circulated cards announcing his readings that included the text of his poem entitled "The Tree Toad."[227] Reaction to these cards helped to dispel any doubts that Riley would succeed in Boston. Even to Riley's own amazement, "The Tree Toad" excited much curiosity among the city's elite: "They think it 'very odd'—'very striking'—'very original' &c. &c. and compare it, in its novelty, as fresh as Bret Harte's stuff when he was new." Because these advertising cards caught the public's attention, the Bureau informed Riley that he was "dead certain" of an audience of two thousand people.[228]

During these first few days in Boston, Riley took time out from promoting himself to do some sightseeing. Boston Common was an easy walk from the Tremont House, where he lodged; and he also visited other tourist sites, such as the Old South Church of Paul Revere's famous ride. Boston was older than any other city Riley had ever seen, and he marveled that something of historical significance lurked around every corner.[229]

However, its parks and historic buildings were not this metropolis' only attractions for the poet. Coming to Boston gave him the opportunity to see the ocean for the first time; and the area was also home to Longfellow, whom Riley still admired more than any other writer. Against all advice, Riley was determined to try to see his idol. All along, one of the goals of his pilgrimage to the East Coast had been to find some way to meet this eminent literary figure, who, at the beginning of 1882, was still alive but in poor health. Prospects were not good, for Riley had been told that Longfellow's physicians did not permit visitors.[230]

Despite the odds against him, with Macauley as his companion, Riley went to Cambridge from Boston with the slim hope of an audience with this great man. At least, he wanted to get a good look at the place where Longfellow lived.[231] As they stood across the street from Longfellow's "quaint old mansion," Riley said that his "desires to cross the sacred threshold were too clamorous to be denied."[232] Macauley convinced Riley that he should go ahead and attempt the venture: "It may be the last chance you will ever have of seeing him, and, even if you fail, it will be a pleasure in the future to know that you once made the most daring effort, and, although repulsed, you yet had the honor of shaking hands with his doorbell."[233]

Upon his friend's urging, Riley approached the house and rang the bell. A matronly woman answered and told the two gentlemen that Longfellow was indeed receiving no visitors. In desperation, they requested that she at least present the New England poet with their calling cards, upon which they wrote that they wished to offer him their respects. Riley later said that Macauley, through the power of his charm, successfully cajoled Longfellow's housekeeper to do their bidding. She gave their cards to her employer and, within minutes, returned to tell them that he would see them.[234]

"I fetched him! O I fetched him!," Riley wrote to Bottsford, overcome with joy that Longfellow cared enough about meeting him to disobey his doctor's orders. The old New Englander seemed delighted to make Riley's acquaintance as well.[235] He smiled warmly and extended his hand to his visitors, leading them from a hallway into his private study. "It is more like freedom here," Longfellow said, "where we can talk and be content."[236]

As they stood there, Riley could barely realize that this "lovable old man," who was "medium-sized and rather sparely built . . . [was] the great poet"; but, when Riley heard his voice and observed his earnestness and his intensity, "it was easy to recognize in him the poet, artist, scholar, sage and humanitarian."[237] According to Riley, Longfellow was immaculately dressed in a black coat and snowy white shirt. Nearly seventy-five, he was in the last months of his life. The younger poet remarked that his idol's silver hair and beard were much thinner than depicted in engravings, and his facial features were not so full and rugged as in his portraits. However, Longfellow appeared very agile for a man of his age.[238]

Once seated in his study, Longfellow and Riley began to discuss poetry and dialect. "He very highly commended some views I expressed regarding the higher worth of dialect," Riley said to Bottsford, "and clapped his hands over the 'Old-fashioned Roses,' which I repeated in illustration of the real purity and sweetness which might be found in the Hoosier idiom. I can't begin to tell you the great interest he expressed."[239] Because he held this man in such awe, Riley claimed that he had never before felt so unworthy of attention or commendation. Nevertheless, he reminded the old gentleman he was the first "real poet" who gave him any encouragement; and Longfellow "most heartily offer[ed] the same again."[240]

Although Riley shared the details of this visit with some of his friends immediately after it occurred, the *Indianapolis Journal* only made quick mention of it. Riley did not publish anything in the newspaper about it until some months later, after Longfellow died.[241] When he finally wrote an account of it for the *Journal*, Riley romanticized and idealized the encounter. The article elevated Longfellow as an international figure who deserved to be honored and revered. Although he omitted what the older poet said of his work, Riley heightened his own reputation by reporting that such a man deemed him worthy enough to entertain in his own private home.[242] By doing so, Longfellow made Riley almost his equal. Soon he inherited Longfellow's position as the most-read poet in America; and, as time went by, the meeting between these two writers became almost legendary.

Many critics associated Riley with Longfellow. Because he considered the older author's works a "poetical bible," Riley emulated him when he wrote.[243] As his ardent admirer, he said that Longfellow was "the historian of the heart of all the world" and consciously attempted to follow in his footsteps.[244] In the same way that Longfellow used the cultures of Native America and New England as subjects for his popular verse, Riley brought midwestern culture alive in his poems.[245]

Through his study of Longfellow, he learned to "be artless and subdued and very tender."[246] Riley found Longfellow's poetry calming and serene: "It is like resting to read it. It is like bending with uncovered head beneath the silent benediction of the stars. It is deep and warm and generous in religious fervor; it is infinitely sorrowful, and yet so humanely comforting throughout, one can but breathe a blessing on the kindly heart from which it is poured."[247] Indeed, Longfellow believed that American literature should be "without spasms and convulsions"; and, although he supplied some satiric and irreverent poems to the newspapers, for the most part Riley conformed to this model by avoiding controversy and unpleasantness in his poems.[248] He now thought that "poetry should deal with bright and beautiful things."[249]

As an apostle of Longfellow, Riley also followed many European literary conventions. Longfellow did not think Americans should reject their "literary allegiance to Old England," and both Longfellow and Riley demonstrated "that poems with traditional metrical patterns could be huge successes with the public."[250] Most usually, poetry anthologies had a limited readership. Their sales rarely generated enough to pay the author a living wage. In this way, Riley and Longfellow were exceptional. The works of both men went through a number of editions while they were still alive.

Even before his most popular work, *The Song of Hiawatha*, appeared, Longfellow was already earning $2,000 annually from his poems. Upon its release in 1855, *Hiawatha* became a publishing phenomenon. It sold ten thousand copies in one month and another thirty thousand within a year.[251] Only the sales figures for Riley's books surpassed those of his idol. For example, at the beginning of 1893, a new Riley anthology, *Green Fields and Running Brooks,* which was not even among his best, within two months sold tens of thousands of copies.[252] Howells proclaimed that Riley's poetry was more widely read than Longfellow's *Hiawatha* and Whittier's *Snow-Bound.* Except for the case of Longfellow, Riley's popularity had no parallel among American poets. No others ever reached such a widespread audience.[253]

Riley's visit with Longfellow would be one of his happiest recollections from this first trip to Boston, but it was just one of many triumphs that he experienced there. Because the Boston-based *Atlantic Monthly* had continually rejected his work, he had expected a cool reception from the literati in this hub of culture. However, with the help of his letters of introduction, Macauley, and the Redpath Bureau, Bostonians warmed up to him quickly and received him graciously. Riley told Hitt that in a few short days he had become enchanted by the city: "What makes a place lovable is being *welcomed* to it, and made thoroughly at home. I can't begin to tell you how dear to me old Boston is! It didn't—*just at first*—seem to thoroughly appreciate the honor I was doing it by taking an engagement here.—but now it is 'catching-on,' and we're mutually looking over each other's short-comings, knowing each other better day by day."[254] Riley wrote this letter in the hours before he took the stage at Tremont Temple. His plan to familiarize Boston society with his name would reach a crescendo with this performance. However, this had not been his only purpose in arriving to the city early. As he said, he also got to know Bostonians better day by day. The time spent communicating with people in the area proved very useful to him. By learning their strengths and their "short-comings," he could adjust his program to fit his audience.[255]

Although he was sure about the material he was about to present, Riley feared that he would forget his lines. He was under a great deal of pressure. The theater was full, and the critics and literary figures whom he had cultivated were in attendance. "I'll ask you to imagine Tremont Temple, the 'crack' place of the city, literally brimmed with twenty five hundred people,—the best," Riley wrote describing the experience to Bottsford, "with gallery upon gallery, and reaches of enthusiastic auditors, so far away that without my glasses, I couldn't ever fancy where the limit was."[256] To deal with the stage fright he suffered during every performance, Riley had developed the habit of removing his spectacles: "You know I am near-sighted and without my glasses I ain't worth a cuss. Well, when I see I have a cold and critical audience I just take off my glasses and lay them on the desk. Then, the house can be just as uneasy as they like, for I can't see a thing."[257]

With his spectacles lying on a desk next to him, Riley began his lecture. As usual, he began by remarking on the nature of poetry and dialect. Because it had drawn such an overwhelmingly positive response on Redpath's advertising cards, Riley made sure to read "The Tree Toad." This dialect verse, along with others such as "Squire Hawkins's Story," was one of the selections that was particularly well received. Riley concluded his program that evening with "The Bear Story."[258]

The Tremont Temple audience responded with much laughter and applause, and Riley received uniformly good reviews. Critics commented on the originality and freshness of his material and complimented him on the style in which he presented it.[259] One reporter described Riley's character sketches as "impersonations," and others remarked that he had neither been spoiled by schools of oratory nor sounded like an ordinary elocutionist.[260] Instead, he read from the heart: "Riley is not only a genuine poet but . . . possesses the rare power in recitation of conveying his own feelings to his audience."[261] According to one review, his "fine poetic instinct, . . . keen sense of humor, good presence, . . . pleasant, flexible voice, clear, distinct utterance, and remarkable power of facial expression . . . would make him a strong card and an especial favorite with the public."[262]

Riley felt no need to be modest about his success when he related the news to Bottsford: "The papers today are, every devil of em—praising me and it shows their splendid taste. . . . The Bureau is tickled beyond expression."[263] By putting Riley on its bill of entertainers, the Redpath Bureau reinforced its reputation for having "an uncanny knack for reading the public taste."[264] The agency's owners, the Hathaways, correctly predicted that the Hoosier poet would have appeal. Now that Riley was starting to demonstrate his full potential, they were ready to promote him without reserve. The Bureau immediately extended his East Coast tour by making engagements for readings in New York. "[N]ow it [the Redpath Bureau] *knows* what my real worth is," Riley said, "and will recommend me to the continent."[265]

As Riley suggested, the Hathaways entertained the idea that they might have a real public sensation on their hands, for the poet received honors and accolades that no one had anticipated. For the large representative audience present at Tremont Temple, his lecture "was a surprise—even to those who did not know the poems were his own.... In the literary circles of Boston, he made a similar impression."266

On the day of his first appearance at this famous theater, Riley met John Boyle O'Reilly, an editor for the Boston *Pilot* and a respected author who had earlier discovered his work and recognized its worth.267 O'Reilly not only requested that Riley furnish him with as many of his poems as possible, so that he might write an article in the young author's behalf, but also invited him to an anniversary banquet at the very exclusive Boston St. Botolph Club. The Hoosier poet could not believe his good fortune: "I'm destined to meet every literary potentate of the town—and on an *equality* too. Just think of it! Men are bred and grown up here, through all gradations of development, with no other object than to work their final way into this club—and fail and fade and droop away and die without accomplishing their object—And here *I* come and sidle in and don't even try to[—] *can't-help-myself!*"268 While in Boston, Riley was also a guest at the Papyrus Club, one of the most influential literary clubs in the nation.269 A dispatch to the *Indianapolis Journal,* most probably written by Macauley, stated that these honors paid him by some of the most prominent men "in critical Boston" were more impressive than the press notices he received in the city's newspapers.270

Within days, Riley returned to Indianapolis. On the surface nothing had changed; he went back to work giving lectures closer to home and writing articles he had promised to the *Indianapolis Journal.*271 However, because he had "conquered" the East, life for the Hoosier poet was forever altered.272 Word spread about the crowds his lectures had attracted; and the manager of the Chicago Branch of the Redpath Bureau, Fred Hathaway, proclaimed Riley the "*coming* card for all [of the] United States."273

Robert Burdette, who took credit for being the first to recognize Riley's lecturing abilities, announced that his protégé had such talent that he could do no wrong on the stage: "There is nothing but pure gold about Riley, and whatever he says is worth listening to. No lecture course is complete without him."274 Such statements made Riley realize that he now had a "*real* reputation to sustain."275 He was under pressure to meet the high standards that this kind of publicity set for him. "I feel the great weight of responsibility—or rather, am just *beginning* to," he said to Bottsford.276 Demand for his readings increased; and each time he stepped onto the lecture platform, Riley realized that audiences expected more from him.

Because of the national exposure, people expected more from him as a poet as well. From Boston, O'Reilly wrote: "He has rare quality as a writer. Outside his insight into local character, he is a poet in his wide perceptions and sympathies. His work is only beginning, but it is the kind that is full of promise. Hoozierdom [*sic*] cannot hold his reputation locally. He will grow to be an American poet, or we know nothing of the signs of genius."[277] With O'Reilly's endorsement and strong support from other members of Boston's literary community, the president of the Papyrus Club invited Riley to return to the city.[278]

At the end of February 1882, only weeks after his first triumphal visit, Riley was headed back to the East Coast. This second trip, if anything, proved even more glorious. Boston's literati treated him as an important author; and, as such, he had the opportunity to meet William Dean Howells and Thomas Bailey Aldrich. Riley was just as excited to meet Aldrich as Howells, for Aldrich had recently succeeded Howells as editor of the *Atlantic Monthly*.[279]

The Redpath Bureau took advantage of this trip to book Riley for more lectures in the East. On this tour, the Hathaways arranged for him to give readings in Philadelphia with one of the most famous American humorists of the time, Henry Wheeler Shaw (Josh Billings).[280] Born in 1818, Shaw was much more experienced as a published author and lecturer than Riley. However, like his colleague, he had tried several different vocations before settling on writing and performing as a career, including riverboat owner and auctioneer. In the years following the Civil War, he published many books and traveled extensively on the lecture circuit as Billings, becoming enormously popular for his easily quoted, homespun wit and wisdom. Many similarities existed between the material of Billings and Riley. Both men used native humor in the idiomatic language of common, ordinary people.[281]

Along with Billings, the Bureau scheduled Burdette to participate in this program with the purpose of introducing Riley. Although Billings and Burdette were better known, Riley stole the show. According to a critic writing for the *Philadelphia Enquirer*, "Billings seated himself at a table at the front of the stage and[,] in his familiar style[,] read about a hundred of . . . his 'best sayings.'"[282] Apparently Billings's lecture had grown stale. This reviewer stated that the aphorisms the humorist used that evening "were among the most ancient in his budget." He admonished Billings for assuming that, "like wine, . . . [they took] on an extra merit with age."[283]

The compliments the *Enquirer* gave Riley contrasted sharply with its criticisms of Billings. Following a short introduction, which Burdette peppered with bits of dry wit, Riley came out on stage and thoroughly charmed the Philadelphia audience.[284] He repeated the program of selections that had been so successful in Boston and discussed the problems and merits of writing in dialect. At least half of the *Enquirer*'s review pertained to Riley's readings, and the critic who wrote it concluded that he "proved himself not only a poet of genuine merit, but a dialect speaker of rare ability."[285]

In Philadelphia Riley demonstrated that he could do more than just hold his own when he appeared with tried and tested performers. He also showed that his success in Boston was no fluke. Therefore, the Redpath Bureau was further convinced that he should be billed as a leading attraction. At the same time, as he recited his own poems in these high-profile lectures, Riley's work was becoming more widely known. In April, editors of *The Century Illustrated Monthly Magazine,* a literary journal almost equal in reputation to the *Atlantic Monthly,* inquired about his poems.[286]

While on this lecture tour to Philadelphia, Riley and Burdette tried but failed to see Walt Whitman at his home in Camden, New Jersey. When he finally met the "Good Gray Poet" the following autumn, Riley liked him as an individual; but, because he did not hold the author of *Leaves of Grass* in the same regard, the meeting which occurred between them did not hold the same importance for him as his encounter with Longfellow.[287]

However, Riley admired Whitman's poems that eulogized Abraham Lincoln. Influenced by his father's political ideals, Riley shared Whitman's convictions about Lincoln's assassination. The last lines of Riley's 1884 poem entitled simply "Lincoln" echo Whitman's belief that the Civil War president's death represented a decisive and transcendent moment in history.[288] In this poem, Riley compared his assassination to Christ's crucifixion:

> A peaceful life! . . . They haled him even
> As One was haled
> Whose open palms were nailed toward Heaven
> When prayers nor aught availed,
> And, lo, he paid the selfsame price
> To lull a nation's awful strife
> And will us, through the sacrifice
> Of self, his peaceful life.[289]

Although Riley admired such Whitman poems as "O Captain! My Captain," his free verse generally held little appeal for him. After Whitman's death, Riley said that he could not understand why this other poet received so much critical praise.[290]

In spring 1882, despite his increasing professional success, Riley was delinquent in paying his city taxes, and creditors threatened to take him to court.[291] Drinking also continued to be a major problem: "I am so dead-tired of this every-day agony of whiskey that I'd give the world for even a year of peace and utter rest from it. I *think* the rest is come sometimes—as I do this time, but that's what I always think, but it don't last."[292] At the end of May, Riley solemnly swore to Bottsford that he would make yet another attempt to give up "his old tendency."[293]

Riley's success solved none of his personal problems, and his contact with the sophisticated life and culture of Boston and Philadelphia filled him with disdain for his hometown. Within three years, he had grown so accustomed to city life that he no longer missed the slow pace and quiet of the village. By spring 1882, everything for Riley in Greenfield had become "dead waste": "I wouldn't be shut there again with its damned denizens for millions. God! how insignificant and coarse and insufficient they are! It don't seem that I ever came out of such a place." After visiting the town on holiday, Riley could not wait to escape back to Indianapolis.[294]

Summer 1882 promised to be very busy. As usual, he had more work than he could handle. However, Riley again thought that his luck was about to change. It seemed that this time his hard work was going to bring him the recognition and the financial security he so desired. His recent correspondence with *The Century*'s editors encouraged him to think that some of his poetry would soon be published in the magazine, and he told Bottsford that the upcoming lecture season promised to bring him at least $2,000. By telling her that he was "clean quit" of whiskey and that he was almost guaranteed a generous income in the next year, Riley again tried to assure Bottsford that they would soon be able to marry.[295]

While Riley traveled on his lectures and worked at the *Journal* in the city, Bottsford was stuck at home. With rising costs and falling prices, her family's farm continually lost money.[296] Bottsford described her surroundings as "poor," "mean," and "dreary."[297] She yearned to escape. She threatened to move away and take a job, but Riley strongly objected. He did not want his fiancée "to engage in the trials of any business . . . [that put her] at the mercy of a damned treacherous and utterly unfeeling world."[298] According to Riley's nineteenth-century attitudes about gender, women should remain safely within the family household where they were protected from the harsh and impersonal realities of the male public sphere.

Although he said he wished desperately that he could change their situation, he saw no way to do it immediately. "My *hope* of doing so seems always a year ahead," he said. Bottsford's endless complaining maddened him, and he reminded her that he "was trying hard to be brave" so that he would not drink. All he could do was reassure her that he still loved her and was doing his best.[299]

During the summer of 1882, Riley was slowly climbing out of debt.[300] To better his financial position, he continued to write more editorials and prose sketches for the *Journal* than he did poetry. As always, Riley tried to write according to what his audiences wanted; and, with the publishing revolution of the last half of the nineteenth century, the public demanded a high volume of prose fiction. The call for poetry was in its twilight.[301] At this time in his career, Riley provided prose to the *Journal* not only because it paid better than the poems did but also because he perceived that there was a broader commercial market for such material. Although he "itch[ed]" to be writing verse full time, he wanted to pull enough of these pieces together for a book.[302] However, Riley wrote prose only with great difficulty: "Now it is prose—prose—prose—that I am forced to furnish, and as I write prose only with terrible effort, I have scarcely time for long breaths between sketches."[303]

Nevertheless, Riley took some "breaths" between prose sketches to renew himself by writing poems. As he struggled to keep away from the bottle, he was also determined to follow Dana's advice and Longfellow's example to stop writing about "old introspective unpleasant themes . . . [to do] wholesomer, happier work."[304] It was at this time that he created his most enduring pseudonym, "Benjamin F. Johnson of Boone." The first poem published under this pen name, "The Old Swimmin'-Hole," appeared in the *Indianapolis Journal* on 17 June 1882.[305] Eleven more poems by "Johnson" appeared in intervals of one week to ten days between the end of June and the middle of September.[306]

Much in the same way as James Russell Lowell prefaced the "Biglow Papers," Riley introduced the "The Old Swimmin'-Hole" with a short, unsigned article designed to lead readers to think that "Johnson" really existed.[307] He wanted them to accept that an uneducated farmer had spontaneously contributed some of his verse to the *Journal* for publication upon the urging of his friends and neighbors. To make this story seem more authentic, Riley quoted the misspelled and ungrammatical letter that this mythical character supposedly wrote to accompany his poem: "Mr. Johnson thoughtfully informs us that he is 'no edjucated man,' but that he was 'from childhood up till old enugh to vote, always wrote more or less poetry, as many of an album in the neghberhood can testify.'"[308]

With "Benjamin F. Johnson," Riley repeated the same strategy to get attention and publicity that he used when writing under the name "John C. Walker" and other noms de plume. Until the last poem in the series was printed, he never admitted his authorship except to a close circle of friends and newspaper colleagues.[309] The poems and the *Journal*'s editorials respecting them drew comment. Immediately, questions were asked about this "country poet's" identity. Because Riley's publicity schemes and his writing style by now were so familiar, many people were not fooled and quickly guessed that he was "Johnson."[310]

Nevertheless, as long as there was some doubt about their authorship, the poems continued to enjoy much publicity. Riley admitted that he was determined to take full advantage of the attention he received as a consequence.[311] In fact, this series of poems became so popular with readers that he and his friend George Hitt decided they might be marketable enough to be published as an anthology. By pursuing publication of the "Johnson" poems, Riley followed the same pattern as did most professional American writers of the second half of the nineteenth century. With the exception of Henry James and William Dean Howells, almost all authors established themselves during this period by using the regional form. Regionalism was a dominant literary genre, and it was one of the easiest in which to be published because writers who had little formal education could legitimately use their own personal experiences as subjects without concern about traditional literary conventions. First-hand knowledge of the primitive and picturesque actually became valuable.[312]

However, Riley had more in mind than just marketability when he wrote the "Johnson" poems. He said that he created "Johnson" as the narrator of this series "to better carry out his dialectic idea."[313] For Riley, dialect included more than language. It encompassed an entire way of life— "not only in speech, but in every mental trait and personal address."[314] As the Hoosier author Meredith Nicholson pointed out, Riley always wrote with character in mind. With a flair for the dramatic, he often thought of his poems and sketches in terms of performance. He focused on a particular individual or type to use as a narrator in his writings and composed his poems and sketches to reflect this person's ideas, thought patterns, and mental outlook as well as his or her peculiarities of verbal expression. Therefore, the "Boone County poet's contributions [to the *Indianapolis Journal*] are printed as the old farmer is supposed to have written them, not as reported by a critical listener."[315]

Riley was just one of many authors in the late nineteenth century who gave voice to the socially disenfranchised. In this way, "Johnson" and the other rustics Riley created for his verse were not unlike Twain's Huckleberry Finn. The regional literature of the period is full of such colorful characters who inhabited worlds untouched by modern development. The semiliterate and unlettered personages presented by the authors of these works lived in culturally backward settings, where people spoke in a local vernacular and continued to adhere to old local folkways.[316]

Riley's contemporaries viewed him as an "annalist" who chronicled the simple lives of common people who resided in these small, isolated, autonomous cultural economies.[317] In this way, the regional fiction of the period became nineteenth-century ethnography. Especially when he wrote in the dialect of his native region, Riley's goal was "absolute clearness and fidelity of utterance."[318] He presented what he and other regionalist authors wrote as transparent accounts of the way people really lived: "The scene is the country and the very little town, with landscape, atmosphere, simplicity, circumstance—

all surroundings and conditions—*veritable*—everything rural and dialectic, no less than the simple, primitive, common, wholesome-hearted men and women who so naturally live and have their blessed being in . . . stories, just as in . . . life itself."[319]

For Riley, "Johnson" became the perfect instrument through which he could express his nostalgia for life in the rural Indiana village as he remembered it from childhood. With much affection, he recalled the romantic figure of a "country poet," whom he claimed he had often encountered in his youth.[320] In Riley's idealized rural world, this figure was just as common as the "country fiddler" "and just as full of good old-fashioned music." Personified as one of these bucolic versifiers, "Johnson" incorporated the qualities that Riley thought best reflected the honesty, innocence, and genuineness of people as yet unspoiled by the evils of civilization. Riley stated simply that "the purpose of this series of dialectic studies [was] to reflect the real worth of this homely child of nature, and to echo faithfully, if possible, the faltering music of his song."[321]

Riley's vision remained rooted in Thomas Jefferson's agrarian polity, and he believed that the fundamental values he communicated through "Johnson" were what made the country great. Like many other Americans, Riley sensed that these values were being lost. Through rapid corporate-capitalist industrial development, the social forces that predominated in post–Civil War America eroded local autonomy. Railroads vastly improved transportation, connecting once-isolated communities to the outside world. National industries and marketing networks emerged which began to destroy older agrarian and artisanal relationships. As a result of the growth of transportation and commerce, large cities sprang up across the country, superseded rural, small towns, and further devitalized and depleted them by drawing their populations away. Because of these developments, regions perceived as self-sufficient islands of premodern culture were disappearing into the past.[322]

Like other pieces of regional literature, the "Benjamin F. Johnson of Boone" poems served to record and memorialize colloquial language and customs before they vanished. During the Gilded Age, much of society shared the sentiments manifested in Riley's dialect poems, which was one of the reasons they became immensely popular. However, the small agrarian communities Riley idealized were never as autonomous as he and his literary colleagues described them. Furthermore, during the years of their purported demise, some local-cultural economies adapted, survived, and even flourished.[323]

Therefore, Riley and other regionalist writers participated in forming a picture of nineteenth-century America that "did not simply record contemporary reality but helped compose a certain version of modern history."[324] In essence, Riley created a mythological universe when he described the small villages of Indiana as isolated enclaves, insulated from broader cultural contact.

Regionalist fiction ignored the fact that the cultures of small towns had always evolved and interacted with the world beyond them. Such depictions were typical and served not only to mourn lost cultures but also to establish a certain account of how different cultures in the United States developed. This version of history explained how the new, urban, corporate-industrial order superseded older local cultural economies by providing plausible reasons for its rise to national dominance.[325]

Although *The Century Magazine, Harper's Monthly Magazine,* and the *Atlantic Monthly* readily published the regional fiction of such authors as Sarah Orne Jewett, Mark Twain, and George Washington Cable, Riley did not find a company willing to print the "Boone County" poems.[326] As distinctions between high and low culture began to develop, his reputation as a newspaper poet became an obstacle to his publication as a serious author. By 1882, the poet's "genius" had long been considered "essentially journalistic and diffusive."[327] There was much truth in this. The demands of his newspaper and platform work required him first and foremost to be entertaining. Moreover, to meet newspaper deadlines, Riley wrote his poems and editorials quickly in a number of different styles and on a wide variety of subjects. Because of their journalistic quality, some people classified them as unworthy of being called true literature.

In the way they readied the "Benjamin F. Johnson of Boone" anthology manuscript for submission to a publisher, Riley and Hitt made this situation worse. They clipped the poems in the series from the *Journal* and pasted each on a sheet of paper, making it obvious where they had first appeared. By doing this, they made Riley's poetry collection look undignified. Robert Clarke & Co., a well-known Cincinnati firm that Hitt approached, immediately assumed that it was of inferior quality and turned it down.[328]

Although no company was willing to accept the risk of putting out a book of Riley's poetry, Hitt believed enough in his friend that he was willing to help finance it.[329] Riley decided to call this first anthology simply *The Old Swimmin'-Hole and 'Leven More Poems.* He kept the "Johnson" pseudonym but added his own name in parentheses on the title page. Robert C. Clarke & Co. agreed to print the book as long as Hitt and Riley shared the publishing costs and as long as the company's name appeared nowhere in its pages. *The Old Swimmin'-Hole* came out in July 1883, more than one full year after publication of the first "Johnson" poem in the *Journal.*[330]

This small volume was bound in cream-colored parchment wrappers and sold for fifty cents a copy.[331] With its first review in the *Indianapolis Journal,* Riley's employers launched the book's publicity campaign, broadcasting that the anthology should have "large sales" and announcing that each poem in the collection was "perfect in itself."[332] Within a week after this notice, Riley was overwhelmed by the response: "Everything in interest of the book [is] far beyond expectations. The press West and East, is more than generous."[333] The modest little volume sold so briskly that Riley already knew that reprinting would be necessary.[334]

The Old Swimmin'-Hole also brought Riley a number of flattering commendations from leading literary figures. "I must say," Robert Underwood Johnson, an editor for *The Century Magazine,* wrote to Riley, "that there is nobody present writing who seems, to me, to get so much of the genuine human nature into a short space as you have."[335] Joel Chandler Harris, author of the Uncle Remus stories, claimed that Riley was the "only verse-builder . . . who . . . caught the true American spirit and flavor";[336] and John Hay, the writer and statesman, told Riley that he thought his poems had a "distinct and most agreeable flavor . . . entirely their own" and that he particularly liked "When the Frost Is on the Punkin" and "Wortermelon Time."[337]

Within three months, the anthology was sold out, and Riley and Hitt had each netted over eighty dollars in profit.[338] Seeing the potential for future sales, Merrill, Meigs & Company, a local Indianapolis publisher known primarily for its legal publications, became interested in the book and, during the latter part of 1883, printed a second edition.[339]

Hitt and Riley had taken a risk by paying for the first edition themselves. However, as Riley later said, he "got there just the same."[340] His first anthology's publication was his formal literary debut, and it marked an important turning point in his writing career. The success of the "Benjamin F. Johnson" collection of poems started to bring Riley national attention as an author and began a prosperous publishing relationship. This relationship would last the rest of his life and would help to make Merrill, Meigs's successor, the Bobbs-Merrill Company, the publishing powerhouse of the Midwest.[341]

With his entrée into book publishing, Riley started to overcome the handicap of his reputation as a newspaper poet. Henceforth, the editors of the country's leading literary journals took him much more seriously. Eventually, his publishers succeeded in making him best known for his poetry volumes; and the years he had spent contributing to the daily and weekly press faded into oblivion.

Nevertheless, the work Riley did and the lessons he learned as a journalist served him well. Newspapers gave him a stable source of income and employment. They enabled him to build a strong network of professional connections within the wider journalistic fraternity. They also helped to toughen him against criticism and rejection. Because of his journalistic experience he was no stranger to harsh public criticism, and became less and less sensitive to it over time. When a manuscript was rejected, instead of giving up on it he could look at it carefully to find its weaknesses, to "[s]earch, examine, rewrite, [and] simplify."[342] Through this kind of exercise, he gradually understood what he should look for in his writing before submitting a poem, prose sketch, or editorial for publication. Most importantly, the constant stream of material that he supplied to the *Journal* and other newspapers made Riley increasingly perceptive about the nature of public taste.[343]

Riley's newspaper experience brought him into contact with all phases of life. When he recalled working on a small-town newspaper, he said that "there was a little of almost everything to write."[344] Gathering local news for the *Anderson Democrat* exposed him to people from all classes in many different circumstances. Riley always credited his employment in journalism for giving him insights into human nature that he otherwise would never have been able to acquire. His years spent writing on newspapers taught him what people were really like. By writing on a variety of different themes for the *Indianapolis Journal* and other papers, he learned what they responded to in his work and was more than willing to please them. As he gained increasing national fame, the lessons he learned as a journalist served him well.[345]

ABOVE, LEFT: *Elizabeth Marine Riley, the poet's mother, ca. 1855. James Whitcomb Riley Birthplace, Greenfield, Indiana.*

ABOVE, RIGHT: *Reuben Alexander Riley, the poet's father, in his Civil War uniform, 1861. James Whitcomb Riley Birthplace, Greenfield, Indiana.*

BELOW: *Self-portrait of the poet at fourteen, 1863. Dickey Mss., InU–Li.*

LEFT: *Siblings John Andrew, James Whitcomb, Mary Elizabeth, Elva May, and Alexander Humboldt Riley, 15 December 1871. Indianapolis–Marion County Public Library Riley Collection, InHi C6040*

BELOW: *The James Whitcomb Riley Birthplace, Greenfield, Indiana, 1902. In.*

ABOVE: *Mary Alice Smith, the real "Little Orphant Annie," at the time when she was living with the Rileys, ca. 1863. James Whitcomb Riley Birthplace, Greenfield, Indiana.*

RIGHT: *"Little Orphant Annie," as depicted by Hoosier artist Will Vawter, ca. 1908. RMA.*

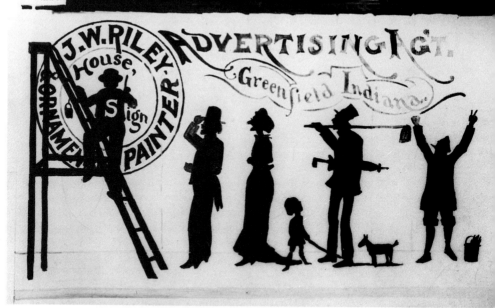

ABOVE: *"J. W. Riley Advertising Agent."* Riley used this sign to advertise his own business in Greenfield, ca. 1871. Dickey Mss., InU–Li.

LEFT: *This photograph is believed to be of the "Graphics," ca. 1873, with Riley seated at left and James McClanahan at right.* Indianapolis–Marion County Public Library Riley Collection, InHi C8125.

Riley the "Painter-Poet," ca. 1872. Indianapolis–Marion County Public Library Riley Collection, InHi C6038.

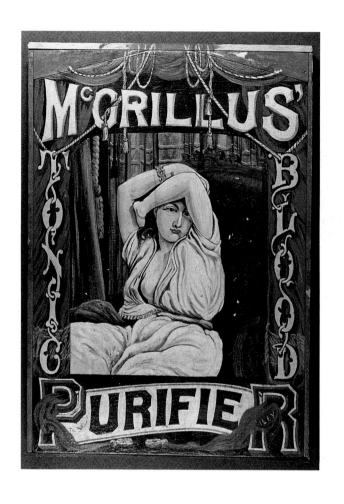

ABOVE, LEFT: *"McCrillus' Tonic Blood Purifier,"*
original sign by James Whitcomb Riley, 1873. InU-Li.

ABOVE, RIGHT: *Adelphian Band Wagon of Greenfield,*
in which Riley played the drums, 1874. In.

BELOW, LEFT: *Samuel B. McCrillus, patent medicine*
manufacturer, for whom Riley worked during 1872 and
1873. Dickey Mss., InU-Li.

BELOW, CENTER: *Martha Lukens Riley, the poet's*
stepmother, ca. 1873. Indianapolis–Marion County
Public Library Riley Collection, InHi C7651.

BELOW, RIGHT: *C. M. "Doxy" Townsend, patent*
medicine manufacturer, for whom Riley worked in
1875. Dickey Mss., InU-Li.

Riley at twenty-four, 1873. Dickey Mss., InU–Li.

ABOVE, LEFT: *Eudora Kate "Kit" Myers, Riley's first fiancée, ca. 1877. Dickey Mss., InU-Li.*

ABOVE, RIGHT: *Clara Louise Bottsford, Riley's fiancée between 1880 and 1885, ca. 1880. Dickey Mss., InU-Li.*

RIGHT: *The popular American poet Ella Wheeler Wilcox. Indianapolis–Marion County Public Library Riley Collection, C6362.*

Park Theater, Indianapolis, the first theater in which Riley lectured in 1879, Bass Photo Collection, InHi 6451.

ABOVE: *Riley working at his desk at the*
Indianapolis Journal, *ca. 1880. Dickey*
Mss., InU-Li.

RIGHT: *Riley at thirty-four, 1883.*
Indianapolis–Marion County Public
Library Riley Collection, InHi C6052.

The Riley family in front of the Old Greenfield Seminary, their home following 1874, ca. 1888. Left to right, James Whitcomb, Clarence A. Hough (Riley's cousin), Mary Elizabeth, Martha Lukens Riley, Hannah Lukens (Riley's stepsister), Elva May (Riley) Eitel, Reuben, and Henry Eitel (holding Riley's nephew, Edmund). Indianapolis–Marion County Public Library Riley Collection, InHi C6049.

ABOVE: *Bowen–Merrill Company,
Indianapolis, Bass Photo Collection,
InHi.*

RIGHT: *Riley and his manager Amos
W. Walker, 1886. Dickey Mss.,
InU–Li.*

RIGHT: *Eugene Field, James Whitcomb Riley, Edgar Wilson "Bill" Nye, February 1886. Indianapolis–Marion County Public Library Riley Collection, InHi C6044.*

BELOW: *"Great Nye & Riley Combine Moral Show," cartoon by Walter McDougall included in* Nye and Riley's Railway Guide, *1888. Indianapolis–Marion County Public Library Riley Collection, InHi C6349.*

James Whitcomb Riley and General Lew Wallace, ca. 1890. RMA.

James Whitcomb Riley and a nephew

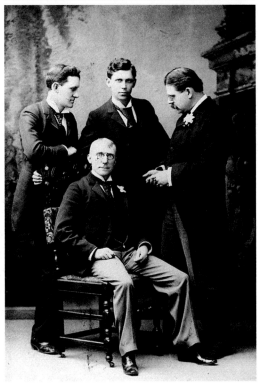

ABOVE: *Riley with nephew Edmund Eitel and writer Hamlin Garland at the poet's home in Greenfield, 1893. Dickey Mss., InU–Li.*

BELOW: *Members of the Western Association of Writers at their annual convention at Winona Lake, 1898. Dickey Mss., InU–Li.*

LEFT: *James Whitcomb Riley and Joel Chandler Harris, 1900. RMA.*

BELOW: *T. C. Steele's third portrait of Riley, 1902. InU-Li.*

Riley's portrait by John Singer Sargent, 1903. Indianapolis Museum of Art, commissioned by the Art Association of Indianapolis.

O what a joy to meet
The bookish little man
As he strolls down the street.
Musing o'er many a plan
And plot of Songs concert.—
Smoking his pipe o' Pan—
Aye, punning puns as neat
Hubbard Almost as Shakespeare can.
O what a joy to meet
The bookish little man
As he strolls down the street,
Accompanying his feet
As only poets scan.
— JWR

To—
Hewitt Hanson Howland from
his old litry friend
March 5.
1904
— James Whitcomb Riley

THIS PAGE: *Kin Hubbard caricature of Riley, March 1904, InU–Li.*

FACING PAGE, ABOVE: *Hoosier Poet Brand can label, InU–Li.*

FACING PAGE, BELOW: *Original illustration for the "Benjamin F. Johnson of Boone" poem "When the Frost Is on the Punkin," by Hoosier artist Will Vawter, ca. 1908. RMA.*

ABOVE: *James Whitcomb Riley, Meredith Nicholson, George Ade, and Booth Tarkington, 1904. In.*

LEFT: *Meredith Nicholson, Hewitt Hanson Howland, and James Whitcomb Riley, 1904. In.*

LEFT: *Riley on the way to Bobbs-Merrill Company in downtown Indianapolis, 1906. Indianapolis–Marion County Public Library Riley Collection, InHi C7652.*

BELOW: *Riley addresses assembled crowd at the dedication of the monument to Major General Henry W. Lawton in Indianapolis, 1907. In.*

Riley in top hat for the unveiling of the Lew Wallace statue in the U.S. Capitol in Washington, DC, 1910. M292, Lew Wallace Collection, C5510, InHi.

ABOVE: *Riley out in the country in his automobile, with two young admirers on the running board, ca. 1911. Indianapolis–Marion County Public Library Riley Collection, InHi C6042.*

LEFT: *The Hoosier poet on Riley Day in Cincinnati, Ohio, 1913. Indianapolis–Marion County Public Library Riley Collection, InHi, C6444.*

LEFT: *James Whitcomb Riley being presented with flowers on Riley Day, 7 October 1913. RMA.*

RIGHT: *Riley in Miami, Florida, ca. 1915. RMA.*

BELOW: *Riley and Carl Fisher on Miami Beach, Florida, surrounded by admirers, 12 March 1916. Indianapolis–Marion County Public Library Riley Collection, InHi C6446.*

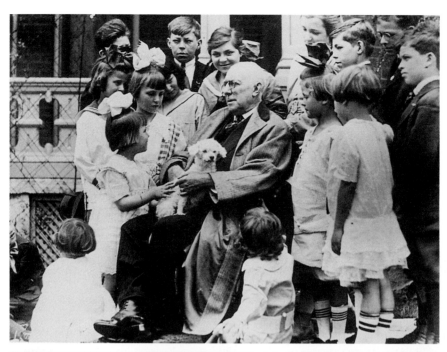

ABOVE: *Classic photo of Riley with children taken for* Indiana, The Chronicle of Your State in Pictures, *the silent film produced for the state's centennial celebration, 15 May 1916. RMA.*

BELOW: *A longer view of the same scene showing cinematographers in foreground. RMA.*

528 Lockerbie Street, Indianapolis, during the time that Riley lived there, ca. 1916. RMA.

LEFT: *Magdelena Holstein and Riley's dog, Lockerbie, 1916. RMA.*

BELOW, LEFT: *J. Marcus Dickey, Riley's personal manager, secretary, and first biographer. Dickey Mss., ca. 1918, InU-Li.*

BELOW, RIGHT: *William C. Bobbs, one of Riley's publishers, ca. 1924. RMA.*

ABOVE: *Carrying Riley's casket out of the Lockerbie Street Home, July 1916. RMA.*

BELOW: *Riley funeral cortege, July 1916. Indianapolis–Marion County Public Library Riley Collection, InHi.*

ABOVE: *James Whitcomb Riley Hospital for Children, Indianapolis, 1993. RMA.*

BELOW: *Riley's tomb at the top of Crown Hill, overlooking downtown Indianapolis, 1993. RMA.*

Realizing Ambitions

SIX

In mid-February 1889, Riley commented on his rise to fame: "Years ago it was a struggle to get anybody to publish what I wrote, even when no price was attached, then fame came upon me suddenly, and now the struggle is all the other way, to keep from overworking myself."[1] During the years in which he strove so hard for acknowledgment from the literary community, he thought that he would be able to rest after he achieved his goal. "If I had the realization of the tenth part of my *ambition*," he told Rosaline Jones in 1881, just months before his first trip to Boston, "I would be able to go to any quarter of the globe I desired to, and [have the] leisure, too, to stay as long as I desired."[2] However, he soon learned that fame came with a price and understood that "once in public favor, and the higher the favor," the more was expected from him.[3] Instead of resting, he was working harding and harder.

Riley put much of this pressure on himself because he achieved success relatively early. At forty, he was a national celebrity. Such a rise to prominence was remarkable, especially for a poet; but it did little to relieve his insecurities. Although he was only entering middle age, at times his future seemed already to be largely behind him. Therefore, he endeavored to make as much money as he possibly could at a point when he perceived that he was reaching a peak in his ability to produce poems that appealed to the public.[4] For this reason, Riley attempted to fill as many requests for his literary work as possible.

During much of the 1880s and early 1890s, he was also willing to stay away from home for months at a time while performing on the lecture circuit. For many years, lecturing enabled Riley to afford to keep on writing. In 1888, Riley told one correspondent that he would have long ago given up in despair in his effort to find an audience for his verse if he had not possessed another calling. "The successful poet must lead a dual existence," he explained. "[S]ince the majority of mankind are more in sympathy with dimes than rhymes, he must equip himself someway with means. . . . Singing alone will not pay but in the very rarest of circumstances."[5]

Although Riley's more practical calling brought him much income, lecturing was "all travel and work, . . . [and offered] little time for rest and none whatever for recreation."[6] Therefore, for Riley, giving readings became both a "wretched" and "blessed" occupation.[7] While performing created a larger demand for his literary work, it gave him less time for writing. Weeks went by when he did not have the energy or the opportunity to compose one line of verse. Especially in midwinter, traveling from hotel to hotel and from theater to theater was arduous. Long lecture tours took their toll on his health. The rigors of the circuit were so exhausting that Riley sometimes spent nearly the entire off-season recovering, without producing many poems.

Ironically, in addition to the new pressures and stresses it brought to his life, fame in some ways limited Riley's choices as an artist. While he was young and developing as a writer, he had the ability to explore many options the late nineteenth century publishing market offered. However, through the mid-1880s, as the poems from *The Old Swimmin'-Hole* and others in dialect like them quickly became the hallmarks of his career, his reputation as a regionalist poet solidified. Riley complained that the public did not permit him to write anything else.[8]

The Hoosier poet knew that the more serious and earnest he became, the less his poems were liked. His ambition caused him to want to do other kinds of work, which he believed would earn him more respect; but the literary critics as well as the rest of the public judged that his dialect poems were his best. Therefore, he was forced to write in the regionalist form to maintain not only his celebrity but also his literary reputation.[9] Limitations of time and talent prevented him from following another course.

In summer 1883, Riley thought all possibilities were still open to him. At the end of August, he contracted with Merrill, Meigs & Company for the second edition of *The Old Swimmin'-Hole*. As a result of this agreement, he reported to his brother that he would soon be able to work more leisurely. In an interview, the president of the company, Charles Meigs, later claimed that Riley indeed drove a hard bargain. The poet threatened that he would publish the book's second edition himself if he did not get 20 percent in royalties. Meigs, who thought that Riley had a brilliant future, talked his partners into accepting his demands.[10]

These generous terms never altered. During the mid-1880s, Riley sought an eastern publisher to give his work a better reputation and wider distribution; but, at that time, no other firm was willing to print his books. Guaranteed twice what most other publishing concerns paid in royalties, Riley remained loyal to Merrill, Meigs and its successors, Bowen-Merrill and Bobbs-Merrill, even after he attained national stature.[11] Although other more prestigious firms eventually printed some of his works, this company, under its various appellations, had publishing rights to a majority of his material.[12]

In part, this relationship with Merrill, Meigs was responsible for keeping the poet in Indianapolis. Only a few months before he settled his contract with the company, Riley had been preparing to move to the East Coast. The distinguished literary friends he made on lecture tours to Boston and Philadelphia convinced him that he needed to move east. In May 1883, he wrote to the publisher of *Life*, a new humorous illustrated magazine based in New York City, searching for employment. Riley wanted to be included as part of the magazine's regular staff, but he also entertained the idea of working freelance for a number of different publications.[13]

However, such inquiries led nowhere. Unlike many prominent nineteenth-century Midwest authors who eventually located in Chicago, Boston, or New York, Riley never left his native state. He was unwilling to move to New York unless he was sure of his prospects.[14] Following the publication of *The Old Swimmin'-Hole*, the reasons for changing his residence became less compelling. At the same time that his new book was selling well and receiving good reviews, one of his poems, "In Swimming-Time," was accepted by *The Century Magazine* and published in its September 1883 issue.[15] With a book in print and a poem in *The Century*, Riley's friends assured him that his future as a poet was very bright.[16] Success no longer seemed to depend on moving to a literary center. Therefore, Riley abandoned the idea of leaving home.

In fact, by the end of summer 1883, he had already achieved many of his goals. He was in demand as both a writer and lecturer. The Redpath Bureau considered him such a valuable talent that it no longer allowed him to contract independently to give readings;[17] and he had met many notable literary figures, including two of America's most important poets, Longfellow and Whitman. With the appearance of "In Swimming-Time" in the pages of *The Century*

Magazine, he joined ranks with many other writers of American regional fiction who were published in journals at the high end of the literary market.

Over the course of the next few decades, many of Riley's dialect poems would be favored with publication in these quality magazines. Much of the regional literature that appeared in the pages of these periodicals typically was not written for the people whom it described. The cultures portrayed in regional fiction were "often nonliterate and always orally based," but the end product was usually geared for a very highly literate reading public.[18] This reading public belonged to America's new high social elite.

During the second half of the nineteenth century, the United States' social, economic, and cultural world was undergoing a great deal of change. Before 1850, societal status depended primarily on one's standing within the local community. As a result of rapid corporate-capitalist industrial development, a new social elite emerged after mid-century that transcended local boundaries. People who benefited from the ascendancy of this urban, industrial economic order—inheritors of old wealth, merchants and managers who grew rich in the new corporations, and people who rose to prominence through professionalization—came together to form this social class. The new high elite was "less place-centered, more citified, more leisure-oriented, and more *culture*-oriented" than previous generations of American gentry.[19]

This more modern upper class was in the process of developing its own self-consciousness. Culture became increasingly stratified into worlds of high art for the upper classes and low art for the masses. As a result, over the course of Riley's career, fewer and fewer people from different social classes attended together mixed artistic programs that might include the works of Shakespeare and performances by singers or acrobats.[20] As these distinctions in culture became more evident, the upper classes used them as a sign of elite status. They closely associated themselves with such high culture institutions as the symphony orchestra, which featured the music of great composers, and the art museum, which was filled with classical masterpieces. *Atlantic Monthly, The Century,* and *Harper's Monthly* had a similar audience and reflected predominantly upper-class interests and preoccupations.[21]

The new social elite also distinguished itself from other segments of the population by having the luxury of leisure time and the resources to travel to Europe or spend summer in the country. "[T]he postbellum period is when the American elite perfected the regimen of the upper-class vacation."[22] This vacation type took on special significance in demonstrating this group's social superiority. While travel abroad was uncommon in 1830, it became increasingly prevalent after the Civil War. Travel for the enjoyment of scenic beauty and rustic, quaint milieus also became frequent. For example, Americans colonized summer resorts, such as the Berkshires, Cape Cod, and Martha's Vineyard.

Prominent Hoosiers retreated to such places as Lake Wawasee, located in Kosciusko County in the northern part of the state. In conjunction with the phenomenon of the vacation, touristic literature, which took the reader "to a little-known place far away" and made it visible in print, became a staple of journals aimed at the higher classes.[23]

Pieces of fiction describing European culture and rustic America appeared in tandem with articles about travel to overseas and primitive country destinations. Both served the function of demonstrating the upper classes' discerning taste. Members of this elite differentiated themselves from others by espousing the ability to receive "pleasure from the beauties of nature and art."[24] Riley's regional, dialect poems which depicted rustic scenes became a commodity for consumption by this select group of wealthy individuals and celebrated their difference from and superiority to the simple, lowly, homespun characters he described.

In turn, these poems gave Riley access to an increasingly rarefied world of culture and letters. As the son of a prominent lawyer and legislator, Riley grew up as part of the local gentry class characteristic of the village social order that existed in the antebellum period. Through the recognition he achieved, Riley developed networks that reached far beyond local or even regional boundaries. As many of the country's leading literary figures became his friends and regular correspondents, he entered a new social world that did not resemble the one from whence he came.[25] At times, this made him uncomfortable. With the publication of his first poem in *The Century* and of his first book in 1883, people increasingly came to know Riley through his poetry rather than through the face-to-face contact and daily social interchanges which were typical of life in small-town, rural America. They had little knowledge of his day-to-day existence and already began to confuse the poet with his work. In August 1883, Riley wrote, "Doubtless my work has friends but *I* have none."[26]

Riley made this situation very clear to Bottsford. Although he appreciated the kind words of his literary friends, they did not have any familiarity with his personal problems and deprivations:

> Burdette has written nearly two columns about the book [*The Old Swimmin'-Hole*]—bless him for his goodness—but he don't guess I can't pay delinquent poll-tax of four years' accumulation! Joel Chandler Harris has written to tell me I'm "The only verse builder within his knowledge who has caught the true American spirit and flavor," but he doesn't suspect for a minute that I am catching more hell to the square inch than any other "verse-builder" on the known globe! Of course I laugh as I say this,—but the grim unlovely fact remains the same.[27]

He continually complained that he always received more in compliments than he did in material rewards: "There seems nothing but praise[,] praise—praise—and never any other recompense—to pay for even respectable board—to requite old board bills—to get the very shoes I need this hour."[28]

As fall 1883 approached, despite his recent professional successes, Riley's financial circumstances changed little, leaving him feeling despondent. In his depression, Riley gave in to the temptation of alcohol. At the beginning of September, he wrote Bottsford that he had been drinking so much that he could not remember much of the last three or four weeks.[29]

Impatient with success, Riley always wanted more recognition than he received.[30] Even when Joel Chandler Harris and other literary figures praised him, he remained dissatisfied. Over the course of the next couple of years, he worked harder and was paid better than ever before. Nevertheless, he could never quite manage to get ahead economically. At times, Riley calculated that he would be able to earn enough to get himself out of debt, but his expectations continually went unmet. This situation left him feeling that the personal security and contentment for which he strove would forever be just out of his grasp.

During his bout of drunkenness in late summer 1883, Riley was in no condition to work, and the upcoming lecture season loomed uncomfortably near. Because advertisements already circulated informing local lyceum committees that he would offer a new lecture among his repertoire of possible programs, he had much to do to get ready. It usually took Riley weeks to prepare and memorize a series of new readings.[31] As he sobered up during the first weeks of September, Riley had not yet regained all of his strength and his work went slowly. He realized that he did himself much harm when he drank. With his faltering health, he was anxious, as he knew he would need every bit of physical and mental energy he could muster to make it through the next few months. Yet, if he could survive, Riley thought his efforts would be more than worthwhile. The Redpath Bureau booked him for so many engagements that he was going to be busier than ever before.[32]

By the first of October, Riley had not yet finished composing his lecture. He informed his friend John Taylor that he would be doing phenomenally well to be ready for the winter season at all. Cloistered in his room at his father's home in Greenfield away from the distractions and temptations of Indianapolis, Riley managed to complete his work just in time to go out on the road.[33] However, once the season began, he was still ill-prepared. He complained that everywhere he went the local lyceum committees wanted him to perform his new lecture, which he could not quite seem to be able to memorize. "What in God's name, is a pore kuss to do?" Riley asked Bottsford. "My memory is full o' holes, and leaks worse'n a steamer,' or any other culinary implement long since deceased."[34]

Riley wanted to excel every time he appeared on the lecture rostrum. Therefore, this situation did little to help calm his unsteady nerves. However, by mid-November, he predicted that he would soon have everything under control.[35] During this period, Riley was almost constantly on the road and did not have much time to call his own. Traveling from place to place, he could not even receive mail from his friends. Although he was always with people and enjoyed being in front of an audience once he got on stage, he found that lecturing on an extended circuit was a lonely, anxiety-ridden experience: "Nighttime I always like, for then I talk to crowds; but through the days— hurry—worry—bother—bluster—anxiety and hunger for companionship,— strangers to the right of me—strangers to the left of me—and always the spiteful and convulsive jerkings of the [railroad] car, and the din and clangor of the wheels, and the yelp of the wide-mouthed bells of passing trains[,] etc. &c. ad hysterium!"[36]

Riley described lecturing as "an awful life" which could kill "a castiron man."[37] He complained that the Bureau seemed heartless in its treatment of him. By making transportation faster and easier, railroads made lecturing commercially viable. Nevertheless, the travel involved could still be grueling. Sometimes a twelve-hour journey separated the destinations of Riley's engagements. In such instances, he would have to take a night train following his performance. Rain and snow made some trips harder than others. In midwinter, an open sleigh was sometimes the only conveyance available to transport him to some of the smaller towns. Often there was little time to rest before going out on stage. Even when he had the opportunity to get a good night's sleep, some of his hotel accommodations were far from adequate.[38]

In the various locations where Riley appeared, audiences reacted differently to selections in his repertoire. "Communities are like individuals, some are hospitable, others are distant," Riley once told a reporter. "One audience will be like a great big, good-natured boy, and you will say, 'Here's a bully;' another will have a headache, will be severe and freeze you to death."[39] People did not always welcome all of the poet's remarks. In Newark, New Jersey, he had a particularly bad experience. A minister, objecting to a portion of his program, stood up and ordered Riley to cease lecturing. Afterward, the man followed him to his hotel pressing him with further insults.[40] Although he had a few unpleasant experiences like this one, almost everywhere he went, his lecture was immensely popular; and newspapers gave him excellent reviews. He reported to Bottsford that his show was the only one of its kind.[41] Over the course of the 1883–1884 season, Riley crisscrossed the eastern half of the United States more than once. He lectured as far east as Newark and as far west as Kansas City, Missouri.[42]

At the end of March, Riley returned to Indianapolis exhausted. "It has been a long and trying season," he said to Bottsford, "and I almost wonder I'm alive."[43] Nevertheless, the suffering seemed worthwhile because of the money he earned. During February alone, his share of the receipts totaled over four hundred dollars. By the end of the season, he was almost out of debt.[44]

Free from the toils of lecturing, Riley spent the summer recuperating and putting material together for more books. As he did with *The Old Swimmin'-Hole,* Riley continued to compile materials by clipping his writings from the *Indianapolis Journal.* He then corrected the items he chose and arranged them by pasting them in position on pieces of paper. Like the popular poet Will Carleton and many other nineteenth-century writers, Riley attempted to get as much mileage out of everything he wrote as possible.[45] Hoping to get some compensation in fees from editors, he submitted poems and prose sketches for publication in newspapers and magazines. He used several of them in his original performances and finally collected his work for republication in book form.

During summer 1884, Riley had many different schemes for books in mind, some composed in prose and others in verse. Because he had long had the idea that he should compile his prose sketches, he first completed a manuscript of these short stories.[46] For this second venture into book publishing, he aspired to reach a higher literary market than he had with *The Old Swimmin'-Hole.* He wanted a "Real Book in cloth" and sought publication for his prose sketch collection from an eastern publishing house.[47] Hoping that he would act as his emissary, Riley sent his manuscript to his friend and supporter John Boyle O'Reilly, the Boston writer and editor. O'Reilly agreed to represent the Hoosier poet and took his book to J. R. Osgood & Company, a respected Boston firm.[48]

While he waited to hear about the fate of his book manuscript, Riley worked for the *Indianapolis Journal.* A steady stream of his poetry began to appear again in this newspaper. All winter long, he had had only scraps of time in which to write. Nevertheless, his journeys had inspired ideas for many poems, and the summer gave him the opportunity to bring them to full fruition.[49]

Riley's lecturing contacts also broadened. In early July, Riley received an unexpected letter from James B. Pond, an influential entertainment agent and general manager who represented some of the most successful performers on the lyceum circuit.[50] After he read it, he hastily wrote an addendum to a note to Bottsford: "Just have a letter from New York Big manager, asking how I'd like to take 100 nights' engagement, to appear jointly with Mark Twain and Chas. Dudley Warner—if same can be secured. Lordy! what a lift that would be to a man without any tobacco in his pocket! Don't speak of this—but if I *can* get that I'll never weep again!"[51] Pond approached Riley to be an equal partner with Twain and Warner. Although less familiar to today's readers than Twain, at the time, Charles Dudley Warner was a popular writer, best known for his essays, who served as a contributing editor to *Harper's Monthly*. He and Twain knew each other well from their connections in Hartford, Connecticut, and had collaborated on the book *The Gilded Age,* whose title became synonymous with this period in American history.[52]

Interestingly, Pond learned about Riley through his published poetry. He had no idea that Riley had ever appeared on the lecture circuit. "Have you ever given public readings from your works?" he asked the poet. "Have you any desire to do so?"[53] Indeed, Riley had a great desire to take Pond up on his offer, notwithstanding his preexisting contract with the Redpath Bureau, and informed Pond that arrangements for this lecture series could not be made without the consent of Fred Hathaway, the Bureau's owner and manager. Because Pond was an old friend and former business associate, he did not wish to interfere with one of Hathaway's clients. Therefore, Riley's Redpath contract prevented him from appearing with the author of *Huckleberry Finn.* Instead, George Washington Cable, the famous southern novelist from Louisiana, accompanied Twain on this tour.[54] Nevertheless, Pond saw Riley's potential and kept him in mind in case another opportunity arose to represent him.[55]

More disappointments lay ahead. By the end of the summer, Riley had spent all of the money he had earned from the previous lecture season. Although the *Journal* published poem after poem, his newspaper work did not produce enough income for him to stay ahead financially; and he was unsuccessful in getting anything published in the magazines. To get by, he had no choice but to request an advance on his earnings from the *Journal.* This situation was humiliating because, at that moment, he had nothing to offer the paper for publication. Although he desperately needed the money, for days he could find no inspiration to write.[56] "To ask for it [an advance in salary] with any grace," Riley told Bottsford, "I must take some work with me—and, as yet, I can't write a line—sat up last night for hours, but failed to raise a verse."[57]

Without funds, he retreated to Greenfield; but his surroundings there only served to depress him further: "I don't think even you [Bottsford] can guess how miserably desolate and awful everything is around us here. No wonder despair and agony boils up and bubbles and froths over the cauldron in this place sometimes!—Hell, compared, is a summer resort!"[58] Riley's stepmother was the one who made life in his father's home so uncomfortable. Bottsford urged him and his younger sister Mary to escape and come stay with her a few days at her farm. She told him that she did have an idea what it was like for him in Greenfield, referring to Riley's stepmother as an "old Jezebel."[59]

At the same time, Riley's relationship with Bottsford, which had always been turbulent, really began to deteriorate. As a consequence of his past infidelities, when Riley seemed hesitant to see her, Bottsford became convinced that there was another woman in his life. Although he wrote and visited Mary

"Haute" Tarkington, Hoosier author Booth Tarkington's older sister, by this point Riley had abandoned his flirtations with other woman.[60] While Riley enjoyed his visits with the Tarkingtons and developed a strong attachment to Booth, whom he liked to call the "The Marvelous Boy," he and Haute were never more than friends.[61] With no one else in the picture, Riley tried to reassure Bottsford that the time would soon come when they could finally marry. "God is not always going to give grief and waiting to us, my dear," Riley said, "so pray and believe with me."[62]

However, for the next several months, Riley's financial status did not change; and he was unwilling to wed until he stood on a more solid economic foundation. None of Riley's prospects for the future, including his plans for his next book, turned out as he anticipated. There was still no word from his Boston friend O'Reilly as to whether or not J. R. Osgood & Company had been favorably impressed with his manuscript of prose sketches. Therefore, while he was in Boston on other business in mid-October 1884, Charles D. Meigs agreed to talk to O'Reilly. In the end, the Boston *Pilot* editor decided that perhaps it would be better if Riley had the book published on his "own stomping grounds."[63] O'Reilly returned the manuscript and the poet gave it to Merrill, Meigs, which soon changed its name to Bowen-Merrill Company. He did not succeed in getting a more prestigious publisher for his work until 1888.[64]

The many months that Riley's book of character sketches spent in the hands of O'Reilly and Osgood had delayed its publication. Therefore, Riley continued to have to rely on meager income from other sources. To make matters worse, due to the 1884 presidential elections, the lecture business at the start of the 1884–1885 winter season was very slow. The Redpath Bureau could not find bookings for Riley before the beginning of December.[65] Because it was outside Philadelphia, his first scheduled engagement for the season actually threatened to put him further into debt. He did not have the money for a train ticket and was unsure whether or not he would be able to go. During November, he tried but failed to write enough so that he could cover the fare.[66]

At this point, Bottsford had just about reached the end of her endurance. She had waited for Riley for almost five years. Not only did he still not have enough money to marry her; he was drinking again. In fact, in fall 1884, his drinking got so bad that Mary Riley, his youngest sister, came to her for help. When Bottsford tried to intervene, he chastised her for bringing up the subject and told her that Mary should not have involved her:

> Don't ever remind me of my degradation—Mary does wrong to pain you with it, and must not. *I* know more about it than she and you and all the universe beside could comprehend. I am every minute dying with it, and if the agony of it can't be forgotten and be left behind I will drop soon. As I write I have

risen from my knees, and with the help of love and faith so long tried and tried again, I will soon rise erect, and make glad and proud the ones who still have trusted and believed.[67]

As always, Riley swore that he would be able to overcome his addiction but warned Bottsford that her nagging criticisms and doubts did him more harm than good. Nevertheless, he reiterated his love for her and prayed that she would be brave and strong.[68]

Bottsford could not help but think that Riley was finding an endless string of excuses not to legalize their liaison. Her letters became increasingly accusatory and hostile; and she was not able to shake the idea that he was romantically entangled with someone else.[69] In early winter 1884, attempting to allay her fears, he promised to marry her in the spring, after he again accumulated some money during the lyceum season. However, this plan did not satisfy Bottsford. If he did not wed her by Christmas, she threatened to create a scandal by telling people that he had dishonored her virtue.[70]

Riley did not respond well to what he characterized as letters "of abuse,"[71] threatening that they drove him to drink. After presenting what he had deemed a reasonable plan, he claimed to be baffled at her reaction:

> When I last talked with you, I made to you the noblest of proposals. I thought it wise then, as I think it wise now, and I meant it—every word. But you're going to have it different, Are you? Well, try it. To *threaten*—to so forget—to prefer infamy to honor—to desire a husband by force, after his offer to come to you of his own free choice! Surely, surely You are crazed. Christ! how I despise such littleness! Hence—as I told you before,—no threat—no devilish action or intent, design, device of any kind shall move me but to the aggressive. . . . What I could do I have done. What I can do I will. I am just as honorable as Penury permits—no more.[72]

Riley pleaded with Bottsford to look at their situation more calmly and rationally and reminded her that he was going to have to borrow the money to buy a train ticket to get to his first lecture engagement of the season in West Chester, Pennsylvania. Although he allowed that he would forgive her for her attempts to emotionally blackmail him, he warned that she had tried his patience almost to the limit.[73]

Bottsford feared that she had already lost him. In a repentant letter she wrote early in 1885, shortly after he had left on his second trip to the East Coast during the 1884–1885 season, she blamed her actions on her loneliness and misery: "O my dear—try to believe this—whatever I do—it is desperation—madness born of solitude—and despair."[74] After so many years of listening to his promises, his words sounded empty, and a mutual acquaintance had tormented her by telling her that everyone knew that their relationship was over.

She voiced her hope that soon he would be free from worry and that he would come back for her as he had pledged.[75]

But the circumstances of the coming months dealt the fatal blow to their engagement. Not long after he finally began lecturing in December 1884, Riley became ill. He missed many performances; and, because of the strain and physical hardship of traveling the lyceum circuit, he did not fully recover until the season was over.[76] By spring 1885, he was "ravenous for money."[77] His hotel and doctor bills absorbed everything he managed to earn. Instead of returning to the Bottsford farm to wed Clara, he prepared to go back out on the road during the summer months. For this tour, Riley left the Redpath Bureau's management and contracted with Amos J. Walker of the Western Lyceum Bureau, located in Indianapolis. Walker would oversee arrangements for his lecture engagements for the next several years.[78]

Because he was still not ready to marry her, Riley and Bottsford's five-year engagement ended. However, in early July, Bottsford wanted to see him one last time. In a letter, she asked him to come to her and reassured him that she would not create a scene. Although she told him that she wished to see his face and touch his hands and hair, she seemed to accept that their relationship was over and thought it would be better if they tried to forgive each other before they went their separate ways. She offered to return all of his letters and the trinkets he had given her.[79]

Despite the relatively calm resignation of this note to Riley, the breakup of their engagement devastated Bottsford. Over the years, even beyond the borders of Greenfield and Hancock County, rumors had circulated about their affair. Many people generally regarded Bottsford as Riley's mistress. During the early months of 1885, she had been happy to finally be able to tell acquaintances that they were about to marry. When their courtship ended, word spread that Riley was unwilling to make an honest woman of her.[80]

Bottsford found herself in a precarious situation. She had lost not only her reputation but also Riley's influence and direction. Although he had hesitated to permit her to work outside her family's home, when necessity made it imperative he had assisted her in finding employment. Through John New, for example, she got a job with the Indiana General Assembly during its 1883 session. Because she was Riley's fiancée, John C. Ochiltree, editor of the *Indianapolis Herald*, put her on the staff at the paper in 1885; she did not remain there after their breakup. With the Hoosier poet's support and advice, she had submitted her poems and sensational short stories to newspapers and magazines. Some of them appeared in *Frank Leslie's Illustrated Newspaper, The Chimney Corner*, the *New York Ledger*, the *Indianapolis Journal*, the *Chicago Inter-Ocean*, and the *New York Sun*.[81]

There was a real possibility that she would lose the ability to support herself; most employers would be unwilling to hire her for even the most menial of positions. None of her former success as a writer made any difference, and she certainly could not go back to being a schoolteacher. In August 1885, she wrote one last letter to the poet begging him to aid her in regaining some of her personal dignity and integrity. Surely, she said, no matter how he felt about her, he did not wish to see her languish in such infamy.[82]

Despite her pleas, Riley did nothing to help Bottsford, and she disappeared into poverty and obscurity. She eventually married a man named Wambaugh, who owned a tavern in Broad Ripple, a village north of Indianapolis on the banks of the White River. When Riley's sister Mary visited her in 1903, she found an embittered woman who had been abandoned by her husband. Only her two children brought her any joy, but their deaths preceded her own. In 1910, after she died from typhoid fever at City Hospital in Indianapolis, her obituaries made no mention of her connections to Riley or to her limited success as a writer.[83]

Although Riley wrote a letter in April 1886 saying he had just written a poem to his "new girl," no evidence exists to indicate that he ever became as deeply involved with any other woman after Bottsford.[84] From this time forward, he wrote many letters to a number of female writers. However, he most often only exchanged literary ideas with them and offered his professional advice.

While Bottsford was disgraced in some circles due to the gossip that circulated when her engagement with Riley ended in summer 1885, the poet's personal reputation remained undamaged and his professional career suffered no setbacks. Society allowed men a certain amount of sexual freedom. Therefore, their breakup did not have the same repercussions for Riley. In fact, the way he dressed and presented himself at this time made him appear very respectable. One press notice stated that he looked "like a dapper young Episcopal clergyman."[85] During the summer, Riley improved his financial situation by lecturing throughout Indiana; and, by December, Bowen-Merrill was finally ready to release his book of prose writings, which after much deliberation he entitled *The Boss Girl, A Christmas Story and Other Sketches*.[86]

As the title indicates, Bowen-Merrill intended to market *The Boss Girl* as a Christmas gift book. It was a compilation of ten short prose pieces which resembled Washington Irving's *Sketch Book*.[87] A short poem prefaced each of these tales. The company's seasonal catalog which advertised its forthcoming publication announced that it demonstrated the "two-fold ability" of "Indiana's favorite . . . Poet."[88] Bowen-Merrill banked on Riley's stature as a lecturer and the past success of *The Old-Swimmin'-Hole* to sell his new work: "Those who have read Mr. Riley's 'Old Swimmin'-Hole' or reveled in the humor of his lectures will be delighted with *The Boss Girl.*" As with the "Benjamin F. Johnson of Boone" poems, Riley's short stories purported to be a faithful and realistic presentation of life. Because they showed such insight, these "ten very interesting and pathetic character sketches" were supposedly as "true" as they were "marvelous."[89]

When it appeared in bookstores during the week before Christmas, demand was overwhelming. Two days after its release, Bowen-Merrill issued a notice to the *Indianapolis News* explaining that it was doing its best to keep retail outlets supplied: "OH YES IT'S OUT—But not enough of them. We mean that new Book by James W. Riley entitled *The Boss Girl.* The only trouble is we can't get enough of them. The bindery can't turn them out fast enough to supply one-half the demand. We are doing our very best though and expect to fill all orders tomorrow or next day at latest. Of course, we are never satisfied so still say orders respectfully solicited."[90] Within a week, the first printing of one thousand copies had sold out. The second printing was exhausted almost as quickly; and, by mid-January 1886, Bowen-Merrill had announced the third printing.[91]

Although *The Boss Girl* was extraordinarily popular throughout Indiana, it received only mixed reviews. Writing for the *Indianapolis Herald,* Robert E. Pretlow, an Earlham College–educated poet and teacher, recognized in Riley's stories many of the qualities also present in his poetry—playfulness, balance, and an eye for detail. However, according to Pretlow, too many of Riley's character sketches were weird, nightmarish, and eerie.[92] Bowen-Merrill's prospectus for *The Boss Girl* compared his stories to those of Edgar Allan Poe; and, indeed, many of them, including "A Tale of the Spider" and "An Adjustable Lunatic," may have been conscious attempts to imitate Poe's work.[93] Pretlow complained that some of them were morbid and maudlin and protested that Riley was trying in some instances to throw poetry into the form of prose. Although Riley's character sketches had some merit, Pretlow did not judge them to be entirely successful: "Nature designed him [Riley] for a poet, and when he insists upon writing prose he does so entirely on his own responsibility."[94]

Others echoed these sentiments and concluded that Riley should stick to poetry. One of Riley's friends, Donn Piatt, found the quality of the tales in *The Boss Girl* uneven. While he loved the title story and thought that it equaled anything written by Dickens in its depth of natural pathos and sentiment, he told Riley frankly that the rest of the stories were disappointing.[95] Years later, Riley conceded that his writings in prose were a source of embarrassment to him: "If it were not for the fact that my books are recorded, I never would consent to have a line of prose that I have written published. I'm sorry now that it ever got out. You know, I can't write prose. I turn out all sorts of rocky English when I try. I can't explain it, but there is something about prose that is beyond me. I seem to lose myself when I try to write it and get all tangled up."[96]

When *The Boss Girl* first appeared in December 1885, the fact that the book sold primarily in Indiana upset Riley. Although it went through several printings, it remained relatively unknown outside the state.[97] Despite all of the gains he had made in book publishing, he remained impatient and dissatisfied. A statement Riley made to Bottsford before their breakup summed up well the cause of his continued discontentment: "I am harrassed [*sic*] enough with my flickering little blaze of success because it won't burst at once into a Vesuvius of fame and pour the molten lava of my name a foot thick all over the surface of the earth."[98] Because achieving widespread fame was his primary preoccupation, Bowen-Merrill's limited distribution of *The Boss Girl* did not please him.

In early 1886, for much the same reason, Riley joined other Hoosier authors in a movement to establish an association designed to aid the development of literature in the West. He strongly shared the common belief that eastern writers and critics unfairly dominated the field of American letters, withholding recognition from meritorious writers in the western states. This very idea had hatched his Poe hoax of 1877. Since then, Riley had earned a limited amount of notoriety among people who resided in the East; but, because he was unable to get a book published by a Boston or New York firm, he still thought that prejudice was hampering his chances for national fame as a poet. Western writers had to fight the negative image that Easterners had of the population which lived beyond the Alleghenies. Books about frontier life in Indiana, in particular, including Edward Eggleston's *Hoosier Schoolmaster* and Eunice (Bullard) Beecher's *From Dawn to Daylight*, reinforced stereotypes that characterized the state's residents as boorish, backward, and uncivilized.[99]

As early as 1874, General Lew Wallace, author of *Ben-Hur*, had suggested in the *Indianapolis Journal* that western writers should form an association to overcome these problems, provide each other with encouragement, and establish a literary authority in the West to rival that of the East. But Wallace did not accept his own mandate to organize such an institution, and nothing came of his suggestions.[100]

Later, some of Riley's friends, including James Newton Matthews, a physician and poet, took up the cause. Matthews organized a poetry reading festival to bring together as many authors of verse as possible. He advertised his idea in the *Indianapolis Herald*, and it was soon suggested that the invitation should also include prose writers. Over one hundred people responded. To show his support, Riley lectured and recited some of his poems at this first meeting. The event demonstrated that those present were concerned enough about bettering the national reputation of western literature and its authors to establish a more permanent organization. They named this institution the Western Association of Writers and elected Maurice Thompson president and Riley vice president.[101]

The organization's constitution outlined a number of high-minded goals. The Western Association of Writers was to promote harmony and friendship among this literary fraternity and to impart a sense of mutual strength through encouragement of its members' professional careers. Its organizers intended meetings for the discussion of literary topics, such as dialect in literature, models of English prose and verse, and copyright issues.[102] During these meetings, they also wanted to offer ample opportunity to hear literary productions composed by its members. Because of the obstacles they faced in getting their works into print, this institution was in addition to provide an outlet for publication of quality material. Finally, the Western Association of Writers was supposed to "uphold the excellence and dignity of American literature and improve the welfare of its professional workers." This portion of the Association's constitution included a clause about protecting its members from "piratical publishers."[103]

At the next meeting, held in October 1886 in Plymouth Church in Indianapolis, Riley's appearance "called forth a storm of applause."[104] Because of his name recognition, his endorsement of this union of writers was very important. Many of those who attended hoped that their association with Indiana's most eminent literary figures, such as Riley and Thompson, would help further their own writing careers.[105] However, their presence also inspired some professional jealousy. John C. Ochiltree, editor of the *Indianapolis Herald,* complained to Benjamin S. Parker that too many of the Association's members belonged as a result of personal ambition rather than a desire to seek mutual betterment.[106]

The Western Association of Writers never met its objectives. The institution became more of a social club than a professional union. Its members did not use meetings to organize to work toward common goals. Instead, they became opportunities to come together and socialize.[107] Nevertheless, Riley took his membership seriously. Although it did not meet all expectations, his faith in it never wavered.[108] Its annual meetings, which eventually took place in northern Indiana at Winona Lake, gave him the rare opportunity to relax and commune with many other writers.

Because discussing literature and poetry was one of the few things that interested him, he craved this kind of companionship. "You see I am so starved always," he once wrote to fellow poet Rosaline Jones. "Not one in five hundred *can* talk poetry, or even listen to it, and as that's about the only thing that enthuses me, I'm, as a rule, as much out of place in society as a man in a milliner shop."[109] Therefore, the Western Association of Writers was one organization in which he could feel he truly belonged.

The Association's members were not only from Indiana. At one time, they represented fourteen central and western states. One member even came from Canada.[110] In some instances, therefore, its meetings offered Riley a chance to meet writers from other states and to see face to face people with whom he otherwise ordinarily only corresponded. Through his membership, he met such authors as Eugene F. Ware, a Kansas lawyer and politician, whose "Rhymes of Ironquill" was popular with the public and praised by Howells.[111]

William Allen White, another well-known Kansan, joined the Western Association of Writers to a great extent because of Riley's involvement. The *Emporia Gazette* editor, who became famous as a writer, social commentator, and political leader, wrote his own imitations for local newspapers after discovering Riley's dialect poems while a student at the University of Kansas. He also gave public readings of these poems. White tried to model himself after Riley and appreciated his practical approach to writing. In a letter, the poet once told the Kansas newspaperman that "the real success [of writing] depends upon *not* how it pleases the *author,* but how it pleases his *audience.*"[112] White did his best always to follow this advice. For inspiration, pictures of the Hoosier poet hung above his desk in his office at the *Emporia Gazette* and in his parlor at home.[113]

Riley proved one of the best advocates the Western Association of Writers had. Not only did his name attract members but he also constantly encouraged his writer friends to come to the Association's summer conventions, enthusing about the benefits of attending. "It's the best tonic my poetical liver has turned over," he said to Kentucky poet Madison Julius Cawein in 1890. To Lucy Salome Furman, an aspiring young novelist from Evansville, Indiana, he described his visits to Winona Lake as "a long blessed week" during which he and other writers read their works to one another.[114] Riley found these sessions very helpful and freely offered other authors his opinions and advice. Annie Fellows Johnston, another Evansville resident who attended the 1890 meeting, recalled that he was generous and gentle with beginning writers and that his presence was an inspiration to everyone.[115]

Although many of his closest friends were fellow members of the Western Association of Writers, Riley also developed strong relationships on the lecture circuit. In early February 1886, at the Grand Opera House in Indianapolis, he began his association with the humorist Edgar Wilson "Bill" Nye. Eugene Field, another humorist who was author of the popular column "Sharps and Flats," published in the *Chicago Daily News,* appeared on that first program also.[116]

This first lecture with Nye was another turning point in his career. Riley had fallen ill again in autumn 1885; and, even in Indiana, the early part of his 1885–1886 winter lyceum season had not gone particularly well. By this time, he had appeared in most towns in his native state so many times he no longer seemed a novelty. For that reason, he tried to keep his material fresh. But no matter how hard he worked preparing new readings, sometimes the turnout was small. Being billed with Nye and Field renewed the public's interest in him as an entertainer.[117]

Nye was scheduled to open the February program at the Grand Opera House. However, Riley went before the audience first to introduce him. The Hoosier poet suffered so much from stage fright before this performance that Field literally pitched him onto the stage. The theater was packed with people; and many of them waited in anticipation to see how well Riley measured up against these two other men, who, at that point, were much bigger celebrities than he was.[118] When the poet later recalled this evening spent with Field and Nye, he said it was the "pleasantest" memory of his life. The humorous exchange between Nye and Riley was so successful that they decided to become lecture partners.[119]

In February and March 1886, Riley and Nye were constantly on the road across the Midwest. Riley's admiration for his new partner grew by leaps and bounds. He told George Hitt that descriptions of Nye's performances did not do them justice: "Nye is simply superb on the stage—and no newspaper report can halfway reproduce, either the curious charm of his drollery—his improvisations—inspirations, etc. &c., or the, at times, hysterical delight of his auditors."[120]

Nye and Riley got along as well off stage as on. Riley thought that Nye was "one of the most perfect men" he ever met.[121] This humorist was always the man the poet held first in his affections. Nye was born in Shirley, Maine, in 1850, only ten months after Riley; but he spent most of his childhood on a farm in Wisconsin. As a young man, he taught school and studied to be an attorney. Like Riley, he gave up the law and, in 1876, settled in Laramie, Wyoming, where he began a career in journalism. While he was in Wyoming, he established a newspaper called the *Laramie Boomerang*. His humorous works, which were later collected into books, first appeared in this newspaper. When Riley met him, Nye had moved back to Wisconsin because of ill health. In 1887, he went to the New York City area and became a regular columnist for the *World*.[122]

Having a friend with whom to travel made working on the lyceum circuit less wearisome for Riley. For the first time in a long while, he nearly enjoyed the lecture tour experience: "With Mr. Nye for company the trials of travel are lessened till now I am almost content with what seems my principle [*sic*] mission here on earth, i.e.,—to spread over and run all around it like a ringworm."[123] On their trips together, Nye and Riley came up with idea of collaborating on a book of humorous anecdotes and poems about their journeys, entitled *Nye and Riley's Railway Guide,* which they envisioned as a parody of the tourist literature which was popular at the time. When their first tour in 1886 was over, Riley was excited about this project because he thought it would be very marketable and wanted to get right to work on it. However, the two men did not complete the *Railway Guide* until 1888.[124]

Nye planned to accompany Riley on tour at the beginning of the 1886–1887 season. Unfortunately, recurring health problems prevented him from doing so. In December 1886, Riley had no choice but to go back out on the road alone. Nye was able to join him in February 1887, when they again made a limited number of appearances together in the East and Midwest. In the meantime, without his best friend and partner at his side, he was disappointed that he had to interrupt his writing to lecture; and, to increase his frustration, Robert Underwood Johnson, assistant editor of *The Century Magazine,* was suddenly very eager to publish his work.[125] "Have I told you about *The Century?*" Riley asked James Matthews as he was about to leave Indianapolis to go out on the lyceum circuit. "It is fairly caressing me."[126]

Because of his background, Johnson made almost all decisions for *The Century* respecting the inclusion of material received from western writers. As an Indiana native and graduate of Earlham College, Johnson was more familiar with authors from this part of the country than most other editors who worked in New York or Boston, and also more sympathetic. Before Johnson showed an interest and published a Riley poem in *The Century* in 1883, no other eastern magazine editor had taken a second look at the Hoosier poet's writings. However, since then, *The Century* had not published any more of his poems; and fall 1886 marked the first time that Johnson actively solicited him for material.[127]

In other words, although Johnson had already introduced him to *The Century's* readers, his pursuit of Riley's work at the end of 1886 represented a significant break in the poet's writing career. *The Century's* editor immediately accepted two of his dialect poems and asked for more. Riley was astounded by what the magazine paid him for these contributions.[128] Unfortunately, Riley's lecture schedule stood in the way of providing the editor with the quality work he wanted. During the 1886–1887 lecture season, the poet remained away from home for nearly eight months; and, as usual, while he was traveling, he did not have much time to concentrate on his writing.[129] Understandably, he earmarked the best compositions he wrote during this time for *The Century;* one of his best loved poems, "The Old Man and Jim," was among them.[130]

Johnson was not only responsible for making Riley a member of the group of America's most elite professional writers by publishing his work in *The Century* but also gave him a prominent position in the movement to establish an international copyright law. Without such a law, American publishers had to pay American writers for their articles and books but could print the works of foreign authors for nothing. This put American authors at a competitive disadvantage. Instead of printing their writings, U.S. publishers rapidly pirated foreign works in cheap reprint editions. Facing this unfair competition, publication in periodical literature presented about the only way for American writers to earn a living by their pens alone.[131]

At *The Century,* Johnson became heavily involved in organizing writers to lobby Congress in favor of instituting a copyright bill or treaty that would safeguard their interests. In 1884, he asked Riley to be the movement's advocate in Indianapolis, by this time an important and prosperous city. Johnson wanted the Hoosier poet not only to communicate with other writers but also to get the *Indianapolis Journal* to publicize the issue and give its endorsement.[132]

The lobby which Johnson helped to establish became known as the International Copyright League. Such prominent American authors as James Russell Lowell, William Dean Howells, Oliver Wendell Holmes, and Mark Twain were members. In fall 1887, the League organized an authors' reading to benefit the cause. The League's executive committee planned a two-day event to take place at Chickering Hall in New York City. In early November, Johnson invited Riley to come and read selections from his works.[133]

The Hoosier poet was honored to be selected and lucky to be well enough to attend. He had been ill for weeks. Only one month before the copyright meeting, he had been stricken with what Dan Paine, editor of the *Indianapolis News,* characterized as a "stroke of paralysis."[134] Paine feared that his friend might be permanently disabled. The poet had lost control of the muscles of the right side of his face and could not close his right eye, giving him a twisted and distorted countenance. He did his best to keep the nature of his symptoms from the newspapers. However, he could not perform and had to cancel several lecture dates.[135] Riley was very fortunate to recover in time to be able to go to New York for the Copyright League's exclusive event.

When he received the program for these authors' readings from Johnson and learned who was going to introduce him, Riley was overwhelmed: "Ain't that a great, big, and all-swelled-up honor for the little bench-legg'd Poet out o' this blessed Hoosier Nazareth? Only think of it!—Introduced by Jas. Russell Lowell, to thousands of the crowned heads of the strictly elite literary eye-and-ear auditor of that Athens."[136] Serving as chairman of the event, Lowell headed a long list of American literary giants scheduled to be present whom Riley held in awe.

After finding out he was to appear with the chief, living representatives of American literature, the poet wrote back to Johnson telling him he would do all he could to live up to expectations.[137] Of the authors invited to participate in this benefit, Riley was the least known. He saw this occasion as a great opportunity but knew there was much pressure on him to demonstrate that he deserved to be chosen. On 28 and 29 November 1887, the two days that the Copyright League's benefit readings took place, Riley indeed shared the stage with an amazing group of authors, which included not only James Russell Lowell, but also Oliver Wendell Holmes, John Greenleaf Whittier, George William Curtis, Richard Henry Stoddard, Samuel L. Clemens, Edward Eggleston, Richard Malcolm Johnston, George Washington Cable, and Henry Cuyler Bunner. According to one observer, "no more remarkable gathering of literary men had ever appeared in America."[138] These authors "sat on stage in regular rows, like beauties in a museum."[139] They were on display almost like national art treasures, to be viewed and admired from a distance.

By the end of the 1880s, Lowell, Holmes, and Whittier were living legends who represented an older generation of New England writers. People associated them with Emerson, Longfellow, and Hawthorne. Their presence at the copyright readings connected the event to a period in the history of American letters which was cherished by many.[140]

Born in the 1820s, Stoddard and Curtis continued the New England tradition. The benefit was not the first time that they had appeared in the company of such auspicious figures as Lowell, Whittier, and Holmes. As the editor of *Harper's Weekly,* Curtis was known as a cultural arbiter throughout the literary community. He participated in the Brook Farm experiment, wrote widely admired books, and used his position at *Harper's* to advance the national movement for civil service reform. Stoddard was a poet and literary critic whose home was a center of cultural life in New York. He counted Hawthorne and Melville among his many important friends.[141]

Johnston, Eggleston, and Clemens represented an older generation who came to national attention by writing regionalist fiction. While Eggleston and Clemens wrote about the Midwest, Johnston told stories about country life in Georgia through the character he developed named "Philemon Perch." Riley and Cable, who were among the youngest writers to attend, followed in this same tradition, exposing the quaint charms of their respective native regions. The most junior of the group, Bunner, edited *Puck* magazine. By writing sketches about New York, he transferred the local-color story from the countryside to the city. These tales brought alive scenes from the urban landscape in much the same way as stories that described more rural environments.[142]

On the first day in the schedule of readings, Riley was last on the program. As chairman of the event, Lowell began the proceedings before the enthusiastic audience that filled Chickering Hall. Although his poems lent themselves to being read aloud, Lowell rarely performed them in public; and, when he did, the results were usually rather disappointing. He gave this benefit dignity and respectability, but his readings lacked the energy of those by some of the younger writers. For this reason, Clemens, who followed Lowell at the podium, was considered the star reader of the event. Next on this afternoon program was Eggleston. After his reading from an unpublished manuscript came presentations by Stoddard and Cable.[143]

Then Riley, "the stranger and the success of the occasion[,] was introduced."[144] When the Hoosier poet finally took the platform, the day's program had already run long. Some had started to leave the auditorium, but Riley brought them back to their seats.[145] He recited "When the Frost Is on the Punkin'," a "Benjamin F. Johnson of Boone" poem, and sent the audience into roars of laughter with "The Educator," a character sketch "of an eastern school teacher whose brains had been developed at the expense of the rest of him."[146]

The *New York Times* called Riley the "hit of the afternoon."[147] Other New York City newspapers were just as generous with their praise.[148] A reviewer for the New York *World* remarked that Riley greatly resembled his frequent lecture partner Bill Nye and reported that his readings were successful because he "sunk the author in the actor."[149] According to the *World*'s article, the Indiana poet even outshone Clemens, "from whose mouth it appeared, nothing unfunny could possibly issue."[150] "The fun of Mark Twain," this reviewer commented, "shriveled up into a bitter patch of melancholy in the fierce light of Mr. Riley's humor."[151] Not "more than tolerably well known to the fashionable audience" at the start of this event, he literally overnight gained recognition among the most respected literary people of his age.[152]

The following day Chickering Hall was filled beyond capacity. Nearly two hundred people did not have seats. They lined up around the walls of the auditorium waiting to hear the second group of eminent authors speak.[153] Seven more authors, including Howells and Curtis, performed. At the end of this program, the audience expected Lowell to read letters from authors who were unable to attend, such as Henry James and Robert Louis Stevenson.[154] Instead, he closed the ceremonies by paying "a graceful tribute" to Riley and flattered the poet by asking him to read once more:

> I want to thank the audience for its kind attendance and its earnest attention, without which these readings could not have been a success. I also wish to thank Mr. Riley, who has so generously consented to favor us again today with one of his delightful poems. Since yesterday's reading I have been enjoying a book of Mr. Riley's poems, and I have been so impressed with the tenderness and beauty of the more serious ones, that I hope he will repeat one of them now. But whether it be one of these or something else, I am sure it will be something good.[155]

Riley then stood up and recited two dialect poems, including "Nothin' to Say," which he narrated in character as a poor farmer. With this poem, in particular, Riley made a deep impression. Newspapers reported that it brought much of the audience to tears.[156] The *New York Sun* claimed that during this reading made even some of the forty-five authors on the stage "wipe their eyes and clear their throats."[157]

Edmund Clarence Stedman, one of the late nineteenth-century deans of American critics and scholars, said that he knew of no other recent dialect poem with such an undertone— "none in which a homely dramatis persona's heart is laid open by so subtle, indirect, absolutely sure & tender a process."[158] In "Nothin' to Say," Riley gradually unfolded the story of a widowed parent's struggle to raise a child by himself. At the beginning of the poem, the narrator has learned that his young daughter intends to marry. He does not approve of the match but has "nothin' to say" because "[g]yrls . . . in love . . . giner'ly has their way!"[159] He is reminded of the circumstances surrounding his marriage to the girl's mother, recalling that her parents objected to him and that he had to run away with her to wed her.

Life on the farm did not suit the wife. She died before their daughter was even one year old. Although she does not remember her mother, the girl has grown to be much like her. Especially in times like this, the farmer wishes his wife were still alive. Alone, he feels powerless to prevent his child from marrying. Because of his own past history, he says over and over that he has "nothin' to say;" but he has really said much. He has many misgivings about his daughter's decision to leave home. By repeating her mother's mistakes, the farmer is afraid that his daughter may be destined for her same unhappy fate.[160] Riley's New York auditors had great sympathy for the goodhearted farmer, seeing his hopes for a secure future for his daughter shattered. At the same time, the poem permitted them to identify themselves as superior to this lower-class character, who is unable to control his child's actions and stop her from making an unwise match.

Riley's success in New York had been greater than he anticipated. The other authors present were universally friendly to him, and their reaction to his readings was almost "*beyond description*": "the reception met with here is worth years of any man's life to overtake. Then to have those old white-haired laureates crowdin' round a fellar [*sic*], at the close—the audience still applauding and damp-eyed as the old immortals shaking and wrenching themselves in such names as Chas. Dudley Warner, George William Curtis, together with notable divines from all quarters."[161] Riley was particularly gratified by Lowell's public praise of his upcoming book, *Afterwhiles,* which Bowen-Merrill had readied for the 1887 Christmas season.[162]

Having taken Chickering Hall by storm, Riley returned to Indianapolis triumphant. As his picture appeared in all of the New York City newspapers following this event, not only his name but also his face became much more recognized throughout the eastern part of the country.[163] Upon his return home, people clamored to see him. He spent so much time trying to please his friends and fans that he had little time to write. "The whole town—and state too,—has been upside down about the N.Y. success," Riley wrote to Nye, "and in consequence I've just been giving my full time to shaking hands and trying to look altogether unswollen by my triumph—if I may so term it. But you've positively no idea of the general and continued rejoicing of the press and friends."[164] The prominent place he took alongside names such as Lowell in reports about the International Copyright League readings brought pride to the natives of his home state.

They had reason to be proud. The benefit did much to make Riley a national celebrity. Immediately, the exposure he received in the national press affected his lecturing and publishing career. Amos Walker, Riley's lecture manager, congratulated him on his success and excitedly told him that it would give him "a big boom in the east" for the winter lyceum season.[165] Previously, just as many of his poems were rejected as accepted by the magazines. Now, the editors of *The Century* complained when they had nothing of his to print.[166] Because of his popularity, Riley could afford to terminate his regular employment at the *Indianapolis Journal.*

There did not seem to be an end to Riley's good fortune. Bowen-Merrill's release of *Afterwhiles,* the book that had so favorably impressed Lowell, coincided with reports about his stellar performance. The first printing sold out in less than a month.[167] Although *The Boss Girl* had also disappeared from bookstore shelves quickly, it had been only a local bestseller. With Riley's endorsement from the highest ranks of America's literati, this new volume also attracted purchasers outside Indiana. In New York, Nye commented that there was a "thirst" for Riley's poetry: "Every where people are falling over each other in a mad rush for your book."[168]

Although regional in tone and setting, because they captured a national sense of moral purpose and sentiment, volumes of Riley's poetry became bestsellers upon their release throughout the country from this point on in his career. In poems such as "Nothin' to Say," he ignored social differences to demonstrate the underlying goodness of mankind, regardless of social class and background, in various life stages and circumstances. The poet avoided discussing issues that resisted idealization to bring forward aspects of American experience assumed to be available to all.[169] Through his poems, nineteenth-century readers could escape from the real social tensions of the day, which stemmed from industrialization, urbanization, capitalization, and immigration. His works had a broad appeal because they depicted a stable, autonomous world in which the relative homogeneity of the farm and small village prevailed.

While the city in the American imagination symbolized everything corruptible in society, the rural communities which Riley described represented all that was good and true about life in the United States.

During the last years of the nineteenth century, Riley became a publishing phenomenon; prestigious publishers outside Indianapolis began to court him.[170] His performances only served to add to his literary popularity. By 1888, Riley was a national favorite on the lecture circuit. After fifteen years of struggle, the poet was finally reaping the success he so much desired. "The whole country wants you," remarked Riley's friend James Matthews in spring 1888. "I have been asked a hundred times if you would be here. You have reached fame's topmost rung (are more talked about than any literary character before the public)." Riley was now the wealthiest working poet in America, earning approximately $20,000 in 1888–1889. Only a few authors, including Riley's friends Joel Chandler Harris, Mark Twain, and Robert Burdette, made more.[171]

In March 1888, a second opportunity to publicize the International Copyright League's cause took Riley to Washington, D.C., where he met President Grover Cleveland and performed with Twain, Howells, Eggleston, Charles Dudley Warner, Thomas Nelson Page, and Clarence Edmund Stedman. The Hoosier poet again appeared last on the program. This time, however, he did so not because he was little known but because the event's organizers wanted to ensure a strong ending for their show. Riley did not disappoint them. The *Chicago News* reported that he got all of the applause.[172]

After a long evening's performance, the authors attended a dinner reception at the White House. Riley made the Washington society columns. President Cleveland was entirely taken with Riley. He repeatedly told a mutual friend that he would like to see him again.[173] Within a matter of months, Riley had managed to be accepted not only into the nation's uppermost literary circles but also into the company of society's highest elite. As his friend Matthews said, the Hoosier poet had indeed already reached the top rungs of fame.

This White House dinner reception was just the first of Riley's many encounters with American presidents. Because his work espoused values presumed to be held by the majority of the nation, he was welcomed by both Democratic and Republican incumbents of this office. Although they can in many ways be characterized as conservative, Riley's poems were not seen as being partisan. Moreover, as an individual, the poet was little interested in political issues. "I found out long ago that politics was a mystery which nobody ever could comprehend," he once said, "and so I just quit thinking about it altogether."[174]

Ironically, he had worked for nearly a decade at the *Indianapolis Journal*, considered the most staunchly Republican newspaper in Indiana. Consequently, a majority of his Indianapolis friends belonged to this party. They told him that he, too, was a Republican; but he always said that if that were true it was only because his father had been one before him. In part, Riley's distaste for politics was probably a reaction to Reuben's continual heavy involvement in this realm.

The presidential election of 1888 proved the exception to the poet's disinterest. He drew the line at writing campaign poetry but threw his support behind his friend Benjamin Harrison. By the time Harrison ran for president, Riley had known him a long time. Like all nineteenth-century partisan newspapers, the *Journal* was a political nerve center. Harrison often dropped by the newspaper's business offices to join informal afternoon gatherings of a coterie of journalists and influential Republican party members which included Riley, despite his general indifference to politics.[175]

Together with these men, Riley boosted Harrison's candidacy. They formed the Harrison Marching Society, which later became the Columbia Club, the most important political institution of its kind in Indianapolis. Because of his new-found prominence, the poet's endorsement of Harrison proved an asset to the Republican presidential ticket. Riley was already Indiana's most beloved citizen. Even at home, his popularity far outstripped the future president's, and the unswerving loyalty and affection that people had for him made his words in favor of Harrison's candidacy meaningful. During an era marked by machine politics and corruption, Indiana had a widespread reputation for political fraud and vote tampering.[176] In the national press, Riley claimed that Harrison was not a typical politician. He depicted his friend as a warmhearted, sincere, and honest gentleman who did not engage in the "usual political clap-trap."[177]

When election day came, he made a special trip home to vote. At this time, Indiana was a political swing state. Neither the Democrats nor the Republicans were dominant, so both parties made special efforts to get people out to the polls. The state's population was passionate about politics, and the strife it engendered was strong.[178] In 1888, Harrison's name on the presidential ticket intensified the excitement surrounding the election. Riley found the turbulent atmosphere it created in Indianapolis distasteful and vowed never to participate actively in politics again: "Political havoc here is simply awful. Watch this way and hearken, the terribel [sic] heat of it throbs throughout the building, till the windows jar and jocund headache stands tip-toe on the final top of my plug hat. I long for peace. . . . I will put my shattered system back in my hind pocket and deliberately sit down on it, then will not hunger for my name among the list of prominent Reformers. I shall register hereafter as plain Denis and accept no gratitude."[179]

The 1888 presidential election affirmed Indiana's emergence as a state worthy of attention. Between 1880 and 1896, only New York placed as many men on national political party tickets. The state also played an important role in radical politics. Riley's friend Eugene V. Debs, one of the founders of the American Socialist Party, called Indiana home. In 1901, this party held its first convention in Indianapolis. During the late nineteenth and early twentieth centuries, Indiana experienced burgeoning industrial growth and became a center of labor union activity. Hoosiers belonged to labor unions in great numbers, and many of these organizations set up headquarters in Indianapolis. At the same time that Indiana gained prominence through its economic and political ascendancy, some argued that the state was becoming a leading literary hub because it had produced so many of the recognized authors of the time, including Riley, Eggleston, and Wallace.[180]

Once in the White House, Harrison filled his administration with prominent men from his native state who worked in his campaign. It was rumored that Riley, too, would be rewarded for his active support. Shortly following the election, the *New York Press* reported that Riley's appointment as poet laureate of the United States was all but assured. However, the U.S. Congress did not establish this position until 1985.[181] Nevertheless, Riley's status as a prominent cultural figure grew with a Hoosier in the presidency.

Harrison's election to office coincided with the commencement of one of Riley's most popular lecture seasons. For this series of readings, he resumed his partnership with Bill Nye. Riley also renewed his contact with James Pond. During winter of 1888–1889, Nye and Riley toured the country together for five months under the lecture impresario's management. Their grueling schedule took around the South, East, and Midwest. They performed seven days a week and rarely appeared in the same city two nights in a row.[182]

The Nye-Riley show was a great success. Early in the tour, one reviewer proclaimed that they brought the American public the best entertainment it had encountered since Artemus Ward's time; and another reported that theirs was the most enjoyable program that people would see that season. Nye informed Riley that they now ranked with the greatest of American platform performers, including Henry Ward Beecher. They drew crowds in almost every location. In some bigger cities, they were so popular that their show sold out, and hundreds had to be turned away. Even in some towns noted for poor turnouts, they drew large audiences.[183]

Pond explained Nye and Riley's appeal by saying that their program was not really a lecture, in the strictest sense of the term. The entertainers intended their show for pure fun and enjoyment. Riley's dialect poems and character sketches were interspersed with Nye's humorous anecdotes. To keep their presentation flexible, their program never announced the exact selections they would choose to recite during any particular show. Instead, they listed categories that gave them options for every one of their performances. For example, each night Riley recited "THE POETRY OF THE COMMONPLACE" while Nye gave readings from one of his "LITERARY GEMS, GIVEN WITHOUT NOTES AND NO GESTURES TO SPEAK OF."[184] They designed their program this way not only so that they were free to vary their presentations, but also so that they could shorten or lengthen their performances at will. "That programme, too, is a craftily arranged affair," Riley commented to Nye, "quite compressible, or elastic, . . . just what we want in that particular."[185] The poet kept thirty or forty of his poems memorized and generally decided what to recite "according to the inspiration of the moment and the temper of the audience."[186]

From his experiences on the lyceum circuit, Riley learned "that people would rather be entertained than instructed in something profound enough to require mental effort."[187] Although the lyceum and Chautauqua lectures were established for the purpose of educating the public, toward the turn of the twentieth century their cultural value as vehicles for instruction diminished as they increasingly became a medium for entertainment. At the same time, the content of lecture programs in general became less intellectually demanding. Riley admitted that his performances were hardly academic but insisted that laughter was just as wholesome as knowledge. On stage, he always behaved more like an actor than an educator. As did some other lecturers of the day, most notably Leland Powers, when Riley recited from his works, he took on the personas of different characters simply by changing his voice and mannerisms. In doing so, he helped bring about a change in attitudes toward the theater in the United States. As a result of this performance style, theater and play productions gradually became more accepted throughout the country.[188]

Local lyceum committees wanted to turn a profit so they bypassed booking talent they perceived might be too highbrow in favor of performers such as Nye and Riley, who were broadly promotable. Because their names were well recognized nationally, one newspaper article surmised that many in attendance came to the Nye-Riley show out of curiosity to see what these two men looked like in person.[189] Outside the theater, because of their high-profile celebrity status, people wanted to know more about them as individuals. Reporters dogged their steps to write about their private lives.

This phenomenon was part of the revolution in entertainment that occurred during the last decades of the nineteenth century. During the antebellum period, people provided their own amusements. Those who participated as performers were also often part of the audience, and the private was not split from the communal. Following the Civil War, entertainment became more broadly publicized and spectatorial. Performers became marketable commodities. Spectators could vicariously enjoy the lives of these personalities by reading about them in the newspapers. As celebrities, therefore, Nye and Riley's private lives became part of their allure. One reporter described the Nye-Riley lectures as a circus because of all the excitement and publicity they generated. In each town they visited, journalists not only revealed Riley's opinions and attitudes about writing and lecturing but also described many of his personal habits and idiosyncrasies. They reported that the poet ate breakfast "when the ordinary man is taking lunch," that he had "a decided liking for oyster stews, with plenty of crackers, and mince pie and cheese," and that he constantly chewed tobacco between meals. Beyond this, newspapers went on to disclose his habit of carrying an umbrella no matter what the weather, his superstition about the number thirteen, and his refusal to take a hotel room above the first floor because of his fear of fire. Many reporters commented on his poor sense of direction. Nye always made fun of Riley because he could not keep his geographical bearings. Making an allusion to phrenology, which many people of the time thought accurately indicated an individual's mental faculties and character, Nye used to say that, when God got to the place where the "bump of locality" ought to be while he was creating the poet, he had no more gray matter at hand; so he put in mayonnaise instead.[190]

Because of their popularity, during the course of their 1888–1889 tour, Nye and Riley were regularly joined on stage by other leading authors and lecturers, such as George Washington Cable and Richard Malcolm Johnston.[191] In Boston at the end of February 1889, Mark Twain introduced the pair to a large Tremont Temple audience. That evening, Riley performed "The Old Soldier's Story."[192] Twain later paid tribute to the Hoosier poet in an article called "How to Tell a Story," printed in *Youth's Companion*. He argued that the comic tale was a distinctly American literary form and contended that the success or failure of such creations depended almost totally on presentation. According to Twain, Riley had a perfect sense of comic timing with this character sketch. "The result is a performance which is thoroughly charming, and delicious," Twain said. "This is art—and fine and beautiful, and only a master can compass it."[193] Although the tour was profitable and Nye and Riley continued to enjoy each other's company, by mid-April 1889 the rigors of the schedule had taken their toll. Performing night after night without any respite, Riley was having trouble with his voice; Nye was suffering from severe back problems. The New York *World* humorist's ill health caused the cancellation of the last month of engagements. Riley later recounted that they plunged into a six-month lecture calendar and attempted to take on eight months of work.[194]

The poet returned to Indianapolis utterly exhausted and spent most of summer 1889 recuperating. Riley wrote little during his travels or during the months immediately after. However, his name was not absent from the literary pages of newspapers and journals. Between the last months of 1888 and the first months of 1889, three books containing his works came out in quick succession. The prestigious British firm Longmans, Green published a volume of Riley poems entitled *Old-Fashioned Roses* toward the end of 1888; and the Dearborn Publishing Company, based in Chicago, timed the release of *Nye and Riley's Railroad Guide*, which the authors had worked on for over a year, to coincide with the beginning of their lecture tour. Finally, Bowen-Merrill made *Pipes o' Pan at Zekesbury* available to readers at the beginning of 1889. As with other volumes which included Riley's writings, these books contained pieces that first appeared in newspapers or magazines.[195]

All three of these publications were very popular. However, in some ways they were geared toward different audiences. Because it appeared in bookstores at the same time that Nye and Riley's lecture tour was being highly publicized, the *Railway Guide* sold most quickly. The authors intended the book purely for entertainment. They filled it with light, humorous material designed to attract a broad readership. Critics all agreed that the *Guide* was effective; but some commented that the Hoosier poet's comical writings did not necessarily represent his greatest literary work.[196]

In contrast, to appeal to sophisticated British readers, for *Old-Fashioned Roses*, Riley took great care to choose only poems which he thought best demonstrated his talents as a writer. Although the book included some dialect poetry, Riley also put in a selection of sonnets and other poems in standard English, such as "The Days Gone By," "The Little White Hearse," and "The Serenade." The poet was pleased with *Old-Fashioned Roses* not only because Longmans, Green was the publisher but also because it was so attractively printed. Riley thought it was his best book; and, of the volumes published in this short period, it included the highest quality poems.[197]

Riley and his Indianapolis publisher, Bowen-Merrill, intended the third of these books, *Pipes o' Pan of Zekesbury*, for his more established American literary audience. The pieces presented in this book were a mixture of Riley's characteristic prose sketches and dialect poetry, which were familiar to readers from his many newspaper contributions. Zekesbury was a fictional Indiana town full of odd Hoosier characters. The sketch that Riley included as an introduction to the book resembled selections from Washington Irving's *Sketch Book*.[198] However, it lacks the subtleties of the work of the earlier author. According to reviews in the *Boston Advertiser*, *New York Tribune*, and *Chicago Herald*, the character sketches in *Pipes o' Pan of Zekesbury* again demonstrated that Riley was, at best, a mediocre writer of prose. They concluded that the Hoosier poet sacrificed quality for quantity in this book and that even some of the dialect poems in the volume were uninteresting.[199]

These less than positive reviews did not deter sales. There was a seemingly never-ending demand for Riley's writings, but editors at Bowen-Merrill would have to wait almost a full two years before the poet provided them with material for another book.[200] Lecture dates and ill health prevented him from writing and compiling poetry anthologies.

Although only months earlier he had vowed never again to undertake another extensive lecture tour, Riley went back on the road with Nye the following fall. At this point, Riley had not yet fully recovered from the previous season; but he could not pass up the possible profits that his renewed association with the humorist promised to bring.[201] This second tour with Nye was supposed to last six months and was to take them as far east as Boston, as far north as Toronto, and as far west as San Francisco. However, this time, Pond promised that he would not crowd in as many engagements, so that the two performers would not be overworked. In the informal, unwritten contract negotiated by Riley's brother-in-law, Henry Eitel, the lecture impresario stated that he would not book the pair for more than six appearances per week. Eitel had married the poet's sister Elva May early in 1884. He was an organizer of the Union Trust Company and served as vice president of Indiana National Bank in Indianapolis. As a banker, he provided Riley with the practical business sense in handling money matters that the poet lacked. Nevertheless, at the end of 1889, Eitel was too trusting of Pond. Pond convinced Eitel that the poet would end the season in pretty good condition and with more money than the year before.[202]

While Nye and Riley's first lecture tour had been remarkably successful, the 1889–1890 season fared even better. They packed houses everywhere; and people had to be turned away in Chicago, Cincinnati, and other towns and cities.[203] This tour was also no less grueling than the first. Attempting to wrest as much money from their shows as possible, Pond reneged on the promised one free day per week. Instead, he either scheduled Nye and Riley to travel on long trips or went ahead and booked them in theaters on their days off. Therefore, as in the past, they had very little opportunity for rest.[204]

For four months, Nye and Riley performed throughout much of the United States and Canada without any apparent incident. However, things deteriorated when Riley began to feel exploited. Although Pond promised Riley he would earn more money than he had the year before, he did not make him an equal economic partner in the show as he did with Nye. Pond gave Nye a percentage of the net proceeds from their appearances, but paid Riley a set fee of $60 per night. Because the lecture combination was so successful, Pond and Nye profited more from the tour than the Hoosier poet.

Moreover, a standing contract required Riley to give half of his lecture income to his old manager, Amos Walker of Indianapolis. Riley's relationship with Walker had soured when he signed on to work with Pond. As a result, Henry Eitel had taken over Riley's business affairs. Although he suspected that

Walker had long been cheating his brother-in-law, Eitel was unable to extricate the poet from his compact with him.[205]

Riley began to drink again. For nearly a year, he had stayed away from liquor the majority of the time; but, during the first weeks of the 1889–1890 tour, the temptation of the bottle became too great. The pressures of his punishing lecture schedule with Nye intensified the idea that he was being used and worsened his mental and physical state.

Determined to continue to earn as much as he could from his binding agreement with Riley, Walker traveled with the tour as the poet's personal manager. When problems began to arise, it was Walker's duty to ensure that Riley was sober enough every night to go out on stage. Time and again, Walker confiscated whiskey which he found in his charge's valise and pockets. He shadowed Riley and tried to prevent hotels from sending liquor to his room. Despite Walker's close surveillance, in Madison, Wisconsin, in mid-January, the poet got too drunk to perform. Riley's companions covered for him by saying that he had fallen ill; and newspaper reporters who were aware of his weakness for alcohol were kind and kept the reason for his failure to appear on stage with Nye out of the press.

Two weeks later, in Louisville, Kentucky, the poet was not so lucky. Riley became so inebriated following an evening program that he was unable to travel to Bowling Green for the next engagement. Because his partner's drinking had become troublesome, Nye canceled the rest of the tour with several weeks still left in the schedule. The reasons for the abrupt breakup could not be kept quiet. The *Louisville Courier* and the *Louisville Post* portrayed Riley as a habitual drinker, printing details about how the Hoosier poet had tricked a hotel bartender into sending drink after drink up to his room and describing how he had been found sprawled on a bed in a drunken stupor. Newspapers across the country picked up the story.[206]

When Riley read some of these newspaper articles alone in his Louisville hotel room, he thought he would die of shame: "I just rolled over, with my face agin' the wall and sobbed the plastern loose. Nobody there but *me,* you know; and being there in such poor company, I just thought die I would!"[207] Henry Eitel came to rescue his brother-in-law and take him home to Indianapolis. With reporters, he immediately jumped to Riley's defense, trying to counteract the negative newspaper stories by explaining that the poet had been victimized by overzealous managers who ruined his mental and physical health by over-working him for their own profit.[208] In these statements emerged ideas that tended toward defining alcoholism as a disease rather than a moral flaw. Eitel characterized Riley less as a sinner than as an artist whose nervous temperament made him prone to drink. Learning of the mitigating circumstances, the public became more sympathetic to his plight.

Nevertheless, society still predominantly viewed alcoholism as a moral problem. Therefore, when Riley was well enough to leave Louisville, he thought that he was ruined. To escape speaking to journalists, he and Eitel left their hotel surreptitiously and took a night train. As they approached Indianapolis, Riley could not help but think how different his homecoming had been after the International Copyright League's benefit reading just a little more than two years earlier. Then, a crowd of his friends and admirers had greeted his train congratulating him on his success. Now, in shame and disgrace, he was sneaking into the same train station under the cover of darkness.[209]

During all of the years he struggled for fame, Riley never realized that it could have negative consequences. As long as he toiled in relative obscurity, he could keep his privacy intact. With the national celebrity he achieved at the end of the 1880s, he became a public figure whose image was just as commodified as his literary works. Newspaper stories that revealed his personal ideas and private habits helped to promote him as a writer and entertainer and led to bigger book and ticket sales, but the same reporters who bolstered his career by describing attractive aspects of his personality were just as interested in revealing damaging details about him that he did not want known. Stories about Riley's drinking binge exposed him to the public at one of his lowest moments. His notoriety opened him up to such scrutiny. As one newspaper reporter said, had Riley never risen to eminence as an American poet, members of the press who dug "away at his private character would have been the last to acknowledge his existence."[210]

Because fame and fortune did not bring him the inner peace and happiness he expected, Riley continued to say that his life was ill-fated. Following the disastrous end of his partnership with Nye, the poet and his promoters worked hard to take back control of his image. Riley attempted to reclaim his private life and keep the innermost aspects of himself hidden from view. To accomplish this, in public, he differentiated his own personality less and less from the characters people saw him portray on stage and in his poems.

However, this was not what Riley had envisioned for himself as a writer. He had always developed characters for his performances on the lecture platform; but he also wanted to be considered a serious, well-rounded poet who wrote sonnets in standard English just as well as humorous verse in dialect. Because he achieved his reputation through his dialect poetry, his readers and publishers did not readily accept his other compositions. Therefore, the folksy, unassuming persona he created through his writings in dialect was both a blessing and a curse. It brought him wealth and recognition and provided him with a public mask. However, it also limited his scope. From now on, he would have little opportunity to expand himself as an artist.

Preparing a Legacy

SEVEN

At the beginning of 1892, Riley still aspired to do something greater than what he had already achieved. He thought that he was capable of composing a serious literary masterpiece, and announced that he had in his mind the seeds of an idea for his first epic poem, which would address the issue of labor in the city of Pittsburgh. Although this poem would be set in an urban environment, he intended to idealize the lives of ordinary industrial workers in the same way he did the rural farmer: "As much heroism is displayed daily in these great Pittsburgh workshops as in a nightly sally from a castle in olden times. Not all music is found in babbling brooks and singing birds."[1]

But over the course of the next year, Riley came to the realization that he was incapable of producing such a major literary work. "I could not write an epic, I am quite sure," he told a Los Angeles reporter in December 1892. "Sustained efforts of length are not my forte. I may write on a great subject, but not write a great poem. I would take it piecemeal, touching many sides and points, and completing a number of small poems. Lyrics, songs are what I produce. My own feelings incline me to serious writing; my public exact of me the dialect."[2] Although critics of the day both at home and abroad called him a genius, in these statements Riley now renounced the idea that he was a major poet.[3]

Like other late nineteenth century writers, such as Henry James and Sarah Orne Jewett, the poet organized a hierarchy of artistic merit in his mind. He shared with them the idea that masters of literary art successfully took on sustained projects that dealt with deep issues and emotions. Major authors wrote long books and poems that touched on the universal. Their writings expressed human themes that transcended local experience or revealed larger patterns of societal change.[4]

According to such understandings about what constituted great literature, the genre in which Riley excelled, by contrast, could only appear to be minor. His poems and sketches are short; and, because of his desire to "lead the human in pleasant places, cheer him by holding up to him only the bright the beautiful and the good," the emotional range of his writings is limited.[5] Moreover, the poet's repeated attempts to alter his image as a regional poet failed. Riley asserted that dialect, as the truest and most natural form of human expression, had been present in literature "since the beginning of all written thought and utterance" and argued that the languages of Shakespeare and Chaucer were nothing but an earlier form of this type of speech. In the future, nineteenth-century literature written in dialect form might prove equally worthy. Riley thought much of it would become classic over the lapse of time.[6] In the same vein as Chaucer, Riley saw himself as a chronicler of common life; but his argument has not elevated his own work to a higher status. Although he contended that dialect represented a natural language to convey "a positive force of soul, truth, dignity, beauty, grace, purity and sweetness," the world Riley created in his Hoosier dialect poems was self-contained and static.[7]

If left to himself, Riley admitted that he would compose serious verse. However, he decided that he did more good writing poetry that reached the multitudes than did other authors who wrote in an erudite style that few understood. Because of his own popularity, he refused to believe that the American public's interest in poetry was waning. Instead, he criticized authors for writing only for themselves and sophisticated literary critics. According to this point of view, a majority of writers mistakenly disregarded the business end of their affairs. "It's the people who make literature," Riley asserted.[8] Anything they did not like would "prove to be false, factitious, unhuman documents."[9]

Therefore, Riley thought it a useless endeavor to produce literary works that did not interest the public. He molded his poetry and his public persona to create products that would sell and measured his accomplishments as a "literary worker" by his commercial success and overwhelming popularity. Ironically, the poet used his poems in dialect, which he described as being natural and true, to create an image of himself which did not reflect reality. The author participated in establishing myths about himself that still persist.

Following the scandal that broke up his partnership with Nye in February 1890, Riley did not know if his career would continue. "Can tell nothing of coming possibilities," Riley wrote to A. H. Dooley. "My future, like Mr. [Artemus] Ward's, seems to be largely behind me."[10] The poet did not deny that he was culpable in the matter. However, he claimed that his forbearance had been exhausted following a long series of abuses by his managers, and that accounts of his drunken behavior were grossly exaggerated. According to Riley, the newspaper stories represented a deliberate attempt at character assassination. He challenged people to judge for themselves if there existed anything dishonorable in his life and writings and further asserted that those who knew him best understood that many aspects of the reports about his drunkenness were untrue. During his first week back in Indianapolis, he remained in seclusion, recuperating at the home of his sister Elva and her husband, Henry Eitel. Although he tried to repair the damage done to his reputation, Riley thought that he might not ever again have the courage to face an audience.[11]

Newspapers continued to print articles about the affair. While some confirmed reports about Riley's behavior which first appeared in the Louisville dailies, a large number of them accepted the idea that these stories had been sensationalized. At the same time, a great deal of sympathy for the poet began to emerge. His friends rallied around him. They admitted that Riley was fond of whiskey but denied that drinking was the primary cause of his current crisis. According to the *Indianapolis News,* Riley was recovering not from alcohol intoxication but from pneumonia. This article took his word that he was the victim of a plot to blacken his reputation. By reporting that the poet was suffering from the "effects of la grippe and the excitement and fatigue of travel," the *Indianapolis Journal* also downplayed alcohol as the source of the poet's problems.[12]

Although many newspapers did not refute that Riley's dissipation had in part precipitated the scandal, a majority of the stories that appeared following initial reports about the incident did not portray him as morally depraved. Because of his "genuine poetic temperament," he was "easily depressed and easily elevated."[13] According to this point of view, preexisting psychological and physical susceptibilities made Riley vulnerable to alcohol. This explanation deflected blame away from the poet and reflected the gradual intrusion of medical language into the discourse of moral reform.[14]

As one Boston reporter put it, nobody wanted to believe any bad stories about Riley. Acknowledging that the poet had his share of human frailties, most people chose to think that his drinking habit was not as bad as the press first depicted it.[15] Riley's call for the public to judge him by his work was a masterstroke. He had already endeared himself to thousands who only knew him through his writings. Many people could not reconcile the drunk described by the newspapers with the author of such wholesome, innocent poems as "An Old Sweetheart of Mine," "Out to Old Aunt Mary's," and "The Bear Story."[16]

The Indianapolis Literary Club further reinforced the idea that attacks on Riley's character were undeserved. By planning a large reception in his honor, the Club's members wished to demonstrate that they stood by the poet. Even in New York, the actions of this institution carried weight because many of the most respected men of Indianapolis belonged, including President Harrison, John New, and Charles W. Fairbanks. Along with these important political figures, the Literary Club counted Riley among the most distinguished persons on its membership rolls.[17]

Those who belonged to the organization protected Riley not only because he was one of their own but also because he brought so much positive attention to Indiana. In other parts of the country, the state did not have the best of reputations. By gaining national status as a writer and celebrity, Riley raised Indiana's esteem. In his poems, he ennobled its inhabitants, whom many regarded as backward and uncivilized, and glorified aspects of its landscape, which many considered dull and unremarkable. In a sense, members of the Literary Club defended Riley in the same way that they defended Indiana. The poet was already part of the state's image, and the prominent men in the Club's ranks did not want to lose the best spokesman that it had ever had.

Riley later recalled the Literary Club's reception as the most beautiful thing that ever happened in his life.[18] In a short speech before the nearly one hundred people who assembled for the event, he apologized for his behavior: "I cannot find words to express my sincere thanks for this expression of your confidence. I hope I shall not abuse it in the future as I have to some extent in the past. I shall hope the better to deserve it. I really cannot thank you; I run out of language when I attempt it."[19] The Hoosier poet was forever grateful for his friends' demonstration of support; and, in return, he vowed to show them that they had not misplaced their trust. He never again allowed his drinking to interfere with his career.

Much to his amazement, Riley emerged from this scandal more popular than ever. His friends in the press and the Indianapolis Literary Club helped him to turn it around in his favor by regaining the public's sympathy. "Have not lost a friend I had," he wrote to Rosaline Jones, "and evidently (from my mail), have gained hundreds."[20] The editors of *The Century* maintained their interest in his work and urged him to complete as soon as possible a book manuscript for publication by the journal's parent company. Overwhelmed with requests for poems and lectures, Riley could suddenly command his own price for every line he wrote and for every public engagement he accepted. Within a month after stories about the poet's drunken behavior broke in Louisville, he returned to that city with his head held high as a guest speaker at the prestigious Bluegrass Club. By the end of March, Riley was ready to begin taking limited lecture engagements. He appeared in Colorado and visited his friend Myron Reed, who at that time was pastor of the First Congregational Church of Denver.[21]

However, Riley had not heard the end of negative stories. Throughout spring 1890, some newspapers continued to indict him for his past drunken behavior; and, in May, the affair again rose to the surface when Amos Walker sued the poet for breach of contract. To compensate him for the money he had lost due to the cancellation of lecture dates at the end of the 1889–1890 Nye-Riley tour, this general entertainment manager wanted $1,000 in damages. Riley hired his friend William P. Fishback, a prominent Indianapolis lawyer, to represent him. Although the case drew much publicity, it is unclear how the matter was eventually settled.[22]

At the end of 1890, Riley again became the subject of negative press. This time, rumors spread that Nye had sued the Hoosier poet for $20,000.[23] Although the humorist informed Riley that he and Pond had lost a great deal of money because of the premature end of their lecture tour, Nye never filed any lawsuits against him.[24] Riley presumed that Walker maliciously planted these lies in an effort to justify his own case against the poet and to sway public opinion, so that accounts of his "drunkenness and imbecility [would spread] all over the United States once more."[25] However, the public's sympathy remained with Riley. Since the amount of money Nye was supposedly suing for was then considered exorbitant, these rumors only reinforced the idea that Riley had been the victim of the affair.

Despite reports to the contrary, Riley and Nye remained close friends. Only months after they separated, Nye said that he never expected again to have such enjoyable times as he had experienced during their combined lecture tours. Nevertheless, the two men appeared together only one more time on stage. In April 1891, Riley introduced Nye when he performed at the Grand Opera House in Indianapolis. Although they never partnered again, they corresponded regularly until the famous humorist's death in February 1896.[26]

Riley always remembered his friend with much fondness, calling him "the best and kindliest of men." Nye had consistently welcomed Riley as part of his family. The poet was a frequent visitor to his home and became very close to his wife. His children affectionately called him "Uncle Sidney"—a name they borrowed from some of the poems he composed for them, his niece and nephew, and children of his other friends.[27]

Several of these "Uncle Sidney" poems appeared in Riley's book *Rhymes of*

Childhood, published by Bowen-Merrill during the last weeks of 1890. Although a majority of the poems in this anthology had previously been in newspapers and magazines, some of them had never before appeared in print.[28] With *Rhymes of Childhood,* Riley firmly established himself as a children's poet. Although he had been published in such magazines as *Wide Awake* and *St. Nicholas* and was already well known for such poems as "Little Orphant Annie" and the "The Raggedy Man," *Rhymes of Childhood* marked the first time that Riley devoted an entire volume to juvenilia. After reading this volume, Clarence Edmund Stedman compared him to Robert Louis Stevenson and said that he had "more of a beneficent Pied Piper in . . . [his] composition than any other living poet."[29]

Riley thought that his approach to children's literature was novel. He contended that he described "*real*" children, who were otherwise absent from the world of letters, with all of their "*dialectic imperfections.*"[30] He took children as he naturally found them, not the "'cultured' child but him of smudgy face and grimy paw."[31] In his mind, the natural language of these children was a form of dialect just like that of the backwoods Hoosier. The poet objected to literature in which all children, even "ragamuffins," spoke using the most accurate grammar instead of the actual language in which they normally communicated. In this way, literature supposedly misrepresented their character: "[It] . . . takes Nature's children and revises and corrects them till 'their own mother doesn't know them.'"[32]

From the 1820s, when American author and reformer Lydia Maria Child founded *Juvenile Miscellany,* America's first juvenile periodical, the social mission of much children's literature in the United States included providing behavioral models for parents and children, stimulating a desire for education, and bridging the gap between the upper and lower classes.[33] To meet these goals, Riley thought that authors presented children who were "fondly and exactingly trained by parents however zealous for . . . [their] overdecorous future." They were false, stilted, "namby-pamby" beings who maintained none of "the lawless though wholesome spirit" of the genuine child.[34]

As did many other late nineteenth century Americans, the Hoosier poet "idealized the child's capacity for unrepressed emotional and imaginative experience."[35] In this view, yet untaught in an increasingly demanding web of social conventions, children were more morally innocent and more spontaneous than adults. They could teach people to lead fuller, more creative, and more authentic lives. According to Riley, training in the social graces spoiled children because it forced them to become increasingly inhibited as they grew farther and farther from nature to become cultivated men and women.

The Hoosier poet linked such cultivation to corruption and deceit: "The more cultivated you become . . . the more grammatical you speak . . . [t]he more affected you become . . . and the bigger liar."[36] Like Riley, many people believed that the increased sophistication and luxury that came with the material progress made possible by the second industrial revolution also brought the seeds of moral degradation. As more and more Americans lived in cities and ceased to be producers who labored with their hands, cultural critics feared that the country was losing its vitality. They warned that the nation was in decline. Too much economic success produced a lazy, soft population and corrupted it through the excesses it made available.[37]

By encouraging the loss of innocence and sincerity, Riley thought that much of nineteenth-century American children's literature inculcated the wrong values. It gave future generations models of propriety in etiquette and language which actually hastened the trend toward overcivilization and moral deterioration. In contrast, the "real" children in his poems provided an antidote to these problems. "We don't want to teach children," he once said. "They want to teach us. We need their ideas."[38] The Hoosier poet thought that these "real" children "*wholesomely* and amusingly *instruct*" others by demonstrating a "native love for 'Both man and bird and beast.'" They exhibited a natural piety, innocence, and purity that his readers could emulate.[39]

Although Riley thought that his concept of recording the language of the lisping child and transcribing the memories of childish thought was revolutionary, in reality, his poems only reinforced the values of the dominant white Anglo-Saxon Protestant society.[40] Moreover, he was not the sole author to create child characters who spoke in dialect. Most notably, Twain published *The Adventures of Tom Sawyer* in 1876 and *Huckleberry Finn* in 1884. Nor did recognized authors of children's literature always write in standard English. For example, Riley's good friend Joel Chandler Harris composed the famous "Uncle Remus" and "Brer Rabbit" stories in African-American dialect.

In the most famous of his children's poems, "Little Orphant Annie" and "The Raggedy Man," Riley introduced poor characters who existed on the margins of society. Although they were from the lower classes, Riley used these characters to reinforce dominant social values. In essence, "The Raggedy Man" is the personalization of the basic middle-class American belief "that the individual is on his or her own, free from the weight of the past, from tradition, from family."[41] When asked if he would like to grow up to be a rich merchant like his father, the narrator in the "Raggedy Man" responds that he wants to be like the title character.[42] The boy has this aspiration because he sees that the "Raggedy Man" is free from following social convention and free also to determine his own fate.

Orphans are ubiquitous in children's literature; Riley's "Orphant Annie" is hardly an original character. By definition, "Annie's" status as an orphan emphasizes the idea that she has nothing to rely on but herself. Although still a child, Riley suggests that she is much more grown up, independent, and worldly wise than the other children in the household. Through her own self-discipline, inner-direction, industry, merit, and talent, like the "Raggedy Man," she is ultimately the only one responsible for her own destiny.[43]

However, the poem "Little Orphant Annie" is more multi-dimensional than "The Raggedy Man." Demonstrating the contradictory facets of human nature, "Little Orphant Annie" goes beyond simple individualism to dictate a need for a social conscience. The title character tells the children who are listening to her tale that they should follow the instructions of their parents and teachers and be charitable toward others:

> You better mind yer parunts, an' yer teachurs fond an'dear,
> An' cherish them 'at loves you, an' dry the orphant's tear,
> An' he'p the pore an' needy ones 'at clusters all about,
> Er the Gobble-uns'll git you
>   Ef you
>   Don't
>   Watch
>   Out![44]

In these last statements of the poem, Riley warned about the consequences if people ignored their social responsibilities. Helping those who were less fortunate was among those obligations.

Although he did not openly confront the terrible urban poverty produced by industrial capitalism, the poet saw the need to find a way to defuse the potential for class conflict, which was certainly a nineteenth-century "Gobble-un" that threatened to destroy the social order. Like much American children's literature of this period, "Little Orphant Annie" offered solutions to poverty rooted in the restoration of the communal ethic present in the preindustrial village. This ethic dictated that those who were more prosperous should "he'p the pore an' needy ones 'at clusters all about." Therefore, in the preindustrial universe Riley created in his work, the plight of figures such as "Orphant Annie" and the "Raggedy Man" naturally came to the attention of the parents of the poems' child narrators.[45]

Riley's characters are not given handouts. Instead, they become almost like part of the family. Class differences seem to be erased as "Orphant Annie" fascinates the other children in the household with her "witch-tales" and as the "Raggedy Man" plays "horsey" with them and tells them rhymes.[46] In this way, the Hoosier poet suggests that distinctions in class which subvert the principle of human solidarity are unnatural.

However, at the same time, he does not question the idea that each member of the household has his or her proper place. The principles of mutual obligation and reciprocity bind the rich and poor together. In Riley's poems, the persons who give charity expect some deference in return. The "Raggedy Man" works for the narrator's "Pa" doing outdoor chores; and "Orphant Annie" washes dishes, dusts the hearth, and bakes bread "to earn her board-an'-keep."[47]

In "Little Orphant Annie" and the "Raggedy Man," Riley extolled the virtues of individualism and self-reliance which helped prepare children to participate in an industrial capitalist society. However, in his attempt to reconstruct the community life of the countryside and to resurrect a system of class relations that relied on mutual dependency, he also rejected modern industrial capitalist culture. A large number of Riley's poems for adults as well as children betrayed the same contradictions in ideology and reproduced the same conflicting attitudes that were present in American society at large.[48]

Many of these contradictory sentiments stemmed from the Gilded Age society's inability to deal with the realities of industrial development. Riley's depictions of childhood life especially offered adults a vicarious escape from the social, moral, and sexual anxieties of the age in which he lived. For this reason, even his children's poems had a strong appeal to men such as John Hay and Mark Twain. The Hoosier poet's *Rhymes of Childhood* came home, Hay commented, to the "hearts of those who grew up . . . [as he did] in small western towns."[49] Twain called this same volume a "charming book" which lamented his "lost youth" as no words of his own could.[50] These and other Riley poems created a nostalgic vision that linked versions of childish innocence to the simplicity and virtue connected to images of earlier periods in the nation's history.

Rhymes of Childhood found admirers abroad as well. At the beginning of 1891, at Riley's request, George Hitt, who at the time was serving as Vice-Consul General of the United States in London, hand delivered the book to Rudyard Kipling.[51] The Hoosier poet had discovered the British author a few months before this new anthology was published. Although Kipling was only in his twenties, Riley saw a "spoor of genius clean through" whatever he did and was eager to correspond with him.[52]

When he visited Kipling in London, Hitt discovered he was already familiar with Riley through his verse which had appeared in *The Century Magazine*. Kipling was so impressed with *Rhymes of Childhood* that he dedicated a poem to Riley. The Hoosier poet immediately reciprocated by composing a poem in Kipling's honor.[53] Although they did not meet until two years later, from this point forward the two men regarded each other as friends. Through the years, Riley's admiration for Kipling grew. He thought that this author was one of the most talented and versatile writers he ever encountered: "There is no subject that he cannot master. There is no field in which he fears to stray. He writes for the children and he writes for posterity; he writes of the sea and of the land; of Nature and of civilization, and he is equally at home in them all."[54]

The Hoosier poet's verse resonated with Kipling because it echoed ideas about uncorrupted childish innocence which emerged in both England and the United States during the first part of the nineteenth century. The English author William Wordsworth's poems, such as "Intimations of Immortality from Recollections of Early Childhood," most widely popularized this romantic view of this life stage.[55] Like Riley, Kipling perceived that children were "very near to God" and thought that their primitive innocence was universal, transcending all geographic boundaries.[56] On both sides of the Atlantic, the growing demands of adulthood made memories of childhood an attractive and alluring escape from the anxieties and tensions of everyday, modern life.[57]

Within a few months after his first correspondence with Kipling, Riley traveled to England with his friends Myron Reed and William P. Fishback. At the end of May 1891, with great anticipation, the trio left New York to sail to the British Isles. In the late nineteenth century, the European tour especially became a mark of upper-class status through which Riley and other members of the social elite distinguished themselves from other segments of the population.[58] The Hoosier poet intended this voyage as a literary pilgrimage. After arriving in Liverpool, he and his party headed to Dumfries, Scotland, to visit the home and burial place of the poet Robert Burns.[59]

From the time that he was a boy, Burns had been one of Riley's favorite authors. In the speeches he gave to introduce his readings, the Hoosier poet often compared his work to that of this eighteenth-century Scottish author. He claimed that the American vernacular he used was similar to Burns's Scotch dialect and implied that his poems were equal to the other writer's in worth and value.[60]

This comparison became almost commonplace. Because they both wrote in dialect, the Hoosier poet's contemporaries saw many similarities between the two poets. As the son of a poor tenant farmer, Burns was also regarded as a simple, naive individual who expressed himself with the same "charming *naivete* . . . [and] honesty of purpose" as Riley without including anything artificial or unreal.[61] When asked to pay tribute to Riley for a Western Writer's Association dinner held in his honor in 1888, Richard Watson Gilder, an editor for *The Century,* supposed that he was about the "hundredth man" who said that Riley had done for the Midwest what Burns had done for his own countrymen generations earlier.[62] Indeed, Gilder assessed this situation accurately. Throughout his career, people often referred to Riley as the "American Burns" not only because he wrote in his native dialect but also because he made the dull midwestern landscape come alive with beauty in the same way Burns transfigured the often gray and dreary Scottish countryside.[63]

Because of Burns, Riley had romanticized Scotland. However, he was not a good traveler and, when he arrived there, immediately yearned for the comforts of home. After visiting the houses in Dumfries where Burns had spent his last years, the Hoosier poet said that he understood why he had died so young. He complained to Henry Eitel that it rained almost constantly; and yet Scottish natives seemed not to notice: "[T]heir actions suggest to us . . . that the climate is exquisitely, *radiantly* dulcet and divine."[64] Unused to the damp climate, Riley came down with a terrible cold.

In part because of his illness, Riley and his travel companions remained in Scotland for over two weeks. The Hoosier poet had to abandon his plans to see "Shakespeare's old haunts;" but he did not altogether give up sightseeing. In addition to going to places connected to Burns, he and his friends saw the Scottish home of the essayist and historian Thomas Carlyle and the churchyard made famous by English poet Thomas Gray. Throughout their journeys in Scotland, Reed and Riley engaged in lively discussions about the literary works of Gray, Milton, and Goethe.[65]

At the end of June, after stopping in Edinburgh and York, Riley, Reed, and Fishback finally went to London. Here they met up with George Hitt, who acted as their guide. While in the British capital, Riley wrote to Henry Irving, a famous British actor, to request an audience with him. The poet had met Irving in New York a few years before. In March 1888, along with Mark Twain, he had attended a dinner held in the actor's honor at the fashionable Delmonico's restaurant. On this occasion, Riley had recited some of his poetry. His performance so impressed Irving that he remarked that "[t]he American stage lost a great actor when Riley refused to take the profession seriously as a life work."[66]

In response to Riley's letter reminding him of these events, Irving invited him to the theater. When the play was over, the actor asked Riley to dine with him. For the next few weeks, Irving introduced the Hoosier poet in London's most fashionable drawing rooms and made him a favored guest at the Savoy Club, to which many distinguished members of London's artistic and professional society belonged. Night after night, Riley recited his poetry for Irving's coterie of friends. The eminent critic and Shakespearean scholar Joseph Knight and a famous French actor named Coquelin were particularly impressed by his readings. Riley brought Knight to tears, and Coquelin could not stop talking about the poet's dramatic talent.[67]

Although Irving and Coquelin praised Riley for his natural ability performing before an audience, the poet claimed that he had given up the idea of an acting career because directors of the plays in which he appeared in Greenfield as a young man would not permit him any liberties in his interpretations of his roles.[68] The poet found the melodramatic style that predominated in the American theater during much of the nineteenth century false and unnatural. Because of their "fanciful presentations and descriptions of murder and suicide," he especially disliked the way Shakespearean tragedies were staged.[69]

While he was in London, Irving presented "one of the most marvelous performances" Riley had ever seen.[70] During the closing decades of the nineteenth century, Irving played his roles in a quieter, more subtle style that abandoned the histrionics which exemplified the dramatic fashion of earlier periods.[71] Riley agreed with the idea of portraying characters in this more natural manner. However, performing in plays would have been too restrictive for Riley. His one-man shows gave him complete autonomy. During his programs, he had the freedom to perform as many roles as he wished in any way he chose. As he recited his works, Riley captivated his audiences with one impersonation after another. When speaking of the poet as a public reader, George Hitt once observed, "one never thinks of him other than in the character he presents."[72]

Despite Riley's success in London society, he soon wearied of being a tourist and foreign guest. Although he found that many things he saw pleased him, Riley complained that his travel companions hurried him too much at each of the historic sites they visited for him to truly enjoy them.[73] In late July 1891, the poet grew so homesick that he decided to cut his European tour short and return home: "What I want is my way—not the world's.—Fact is I've been poutin'—trampin' on my lower lip, and kindo' 'makin' eyes' at Misery—since she at least is constant upon the least encouragement. . . . But I'm not going to encourage her any longer, but am going home instead with a glad heart, as I ought to."[74] "Truth to tell I find myself a far better citizen than foreigner," he told one of his correspondents upon his return to his native soil.[75] The Hoosier poet never traveled across the Atlantic again.

After being in Great Britain for much of the summer, Riley did not undertake a large lecture schedule during the 1891–1892 season. Although he enjoyed reading from his own works once he got out on stage, the travel became too much for him. Moreover, he regretted that he had not dedicated more of his time in the past several years to composing poetry. "I have been the greater part of my life trying to catch a train with my valise fatiguing my muscles," Riley said at the beginning of 1892, "my tongue hanging out from exhaustion and my stomach disconcerted from depot sandwiches. I now know that all this has been a mistake and I am going to rectify it. I have ceased lecturing or reading, except at intervals, and am devoting my time to writing."[76]

During the spring of that same year, Riley made some public appearances, including a joint program with George Washington Cable in Chicago, a lecture in Baltimore where he was introduced by Richard Malcolm Johnston, and a reception at the White House and National Press Club. However, for the most part, he kept his promise to himself throughout most of 1892.[77]

Although he fully committed himself to writing, at this point, Riley was already beyond his most prolific period and had written nearly all of his most famous poems. Because he reaped a good income from his publications and occasional lectures, economic need no longer drove him to write. He did not have to depend on getting new poems published in magazines to earn a living. In other words, he had the luxury of writing only when he felt inspired. However, as a consequence, he and his publishers constantly had to cull old material to keep on printing new books. Repackaged again and again, a large number of Riley's verses appear in many different volumes of his works.[78]

When *Neghborly Poems* was published at the end of 1891, a critic working at the *Chicago Tribune* recognized that several of the poems in this anthology were among his earliest productions and criticized him for including them: "[N]ow that riper and richer creations have made him famous we cannot understand how he [Riley] reconciles with his literary conscience his course in republishing these cruder efforts."[79] The reviews of many of Riley's later anthologies echoed these sentiments.

Riley's detractors expressed the opinion that all works in dialect constituted bad writing. Moreover, they said that Riley's dialect writings only served to disguise the fact that he was no poet. His skill in using the Hoosier vernacular concealed that his subjects were trite and not worth the time bestowed upon them. If the poet wrote only in straight English, his worst critics contended, no one would read his poems.[80]

When *Armazindy* was published by Bowen-Merrill in 1894, Riley gave his enemies plenty of ammunition to use against him. Such poems as "The Little Dog-Woggy" and "Jargon-Jingle" were identified as "drivel." Even some critics who usually praised him accused Riley of dumping into this book writings that should have been relegated to the dustbin, and of trading on his fame to trick the public into purchasing his inferior work. All of these articles insinuated that Riley ignored considerations of artistic merit in the name of making money.[81]

Just as insulting to Riley was the suggestion that he was a "worn-out genius."[82] Although it was true that much of the inferior work in his anthologies dated from his earliest writing days, some of it was original to the books published in the 1890s and 1900s; and, in general, the quality of the Hoosier poet's poems deteriorated during the last part of his career. As early as 1892, even his old friend Albert W. Macy noticed that the average quality of his work did not reach his former standards. Some critics thought that Riley, blinded by his own success, did not recognize the mediocrity of some of his creations.[83]

Despite these criticisms, Riley's books continued to sell at the rate of about forty thousand copies a year; and most went through several editions.[84] For a poet, such popularity was exceptional; and his publishers did everything they could to take advantage of it. To increase sales, with Henry Eitel's cooperation, William C. Bobbs of the Bowen-Merrill Company coordinated Riley's public readings with the publication of his books; and, between 1891 and the time of his death, a book of Riley's verse appeared on the literary market almost every year. *Poems Here at Home*, published in 1893 by the Century Company, which included many of Riley's most liked and most representative works, was among the best of them.[85]

During the last decades of his life, Riley became more involved in compiling books than in writing new material. He was an active participant in choosing which poems were to be included in each volume and was a careful editor. The Hoosier poet insisted that each of his poems be printed just as he intended. For Riley, the spelling of words in dialect, the use of italics, and the repetition of words, which in his mind made his characters seem more authentic and real, held much importance. He was always careful to spell words in Hoosier dialect exactly as he thought they were pronounced and made sure that his characters did not use vocabulary that would be unfamiliar to someone of their class and circumstances.[86]

Riley was also interested in the way his books were printed and illustrated. Because he painted his Hoosier characters as the poet saw them, Will Vawter, a Greenfield resident, was Riley's favorite for creating the illustrations to accompany his poems. However, other artists produced drawings for his books. In 1897, when the Century Company chose Charles Relyea, who was from outside Indiana, to illustrate *The Rubaiyat of Doc Sifers*, Riley asked him to come to the state to visit him. He wanted to make sure that Relyea represented the Hoosier landscape accurately and that he did not caricature his characters.[87]

Although most of his poems had first been printed in newspapers, some of them, including "An Old Sweetheart of Mine," "His Pa's Romance," "The Raggedy Man," and "Little Orphant Annie," were eventually republished as fully illustrated gift books. The most noteworthy of these gift books were illustrated by Howard Chandler Christy, who became famous for his illustrations of beautiful girls at the turn of the century. Christy's paintings and drawings appear in "An Old Sweetheart of Mine" and "Out to Old Aunt Mary's."[88] These gift books, aimed at the upper literary market, especially marked Riley's growing prestige.

In 1897, almost two decades before his death, Arthur H. Scribner approached Riley about publishing a standard version of his texts. Scribner perceived that there would be a demand for a complete and uniform edition of the poet's works. Because Riley had more than one publisher, up to this point his anthologies were unavailable in one type of binding and format. Moreover, a standard version of Riley's works would not repeat many of the most popular poems that appeared over and over again in several of the other publishers' books. After securing legal agreements with the Century and Bowen-Merrill companies, during the second half of 1897, Scribner's republished *Afterwhiles* as the first volume of the set, which became known as *The Homestead Edition.* By the beginning of 1898, Scribner's had already printed three of the ten volumes planned. The rest were published at intervals through 1914. In the end, the first complete edition of Riley's works comprised a total of sixteen volumes.[89]

Publication of such an edition signified that the Hoosier poet was reaching the end of his writing career. In 1900, Bowen-Merrill followed Scribner's with its own uniform version of his complete works and, in 1913, published the comprehensive *Biographical Edition*, which was edited by Riley's nephew Edmund Eitel.[90] Because his works were considered worthy of such treatment, these standard collections, especially the highly detailed *Biographical Edition*, indicated Riley's high stature in the world of American letters. Few authors have seen such editions of their works published during their lifetimes.

At the turn of the century, other factors reflected the prestige of Riley's poetry in the literary community. Although some critics questioned the value of his poems, his supporters argued that the fact that so many thousands read them and enjoyed them proved their worth as literature.[91] He came closer than any other American to being "a national poet" because people of all classes read him "without distinction of education or social sympathies."[92] His writings reached "a greater number of people, a wider diversity of classes than any other American poet."[93] Publication of each new Riley book was an event. Although the contents of these books held no surprises, people rushed out to buy them.[94]

During the last decade of the nineteenth century, English teachers across the country incorporated Riley's works into their curricula. Literary clubs read and talked about his poems. Even students in the Ivy League studied Riley in American literature surveys.[95] In 1902, through the influence of William Lyon Phelps and Henry Beers, Yale University was the first to offer Riley an honorary degree. Other honorary university degrees followed. In 1904, the University of Pennsylvania made him an honorary Doctor of Letters; and, in his home state, Wabash College and Indiana University awarded him similar titles.[96]

Riley's peers in the arts also gave him prestigious accolades. In 1908, the National Institute of Arts and Letters elected him to its membership. The American Academy of Arts and Letters did the same in 1911; and, in 1912, conferred on him its medal for poetry. Late nineteenth century literary figures and critics who admired Riley and belonged to these organizations, such as Bliss Perry and William Dean Howells, thought that his poems would always have a place in the American literary canon.[97]

Riley influenced other authors, including Hamlin Garland, William Allen White, and Edgar Lee Masters. He also had the distinction of being one of the first to discover Paul Laurence Dunbar. When James Matthews brought Dunbar to his attention in November 1892, Riley said, "Certainly he *deserves* applause, . . . there's the making of a very novel type of poet in him—a credit not only to his own race but Freedom's everywhere."[98] With the encouragement of Riley and Howells, Dunbar was among the first African Americans to break into the ranks of professional authors. Riley admired Dunbar's talent and accomplishments and, after his death in 1906, was proud to pay tribute to him. He and Benjamin S. Parker held him up as an example to demonstrate that African Americans were not inferior.[99]

Closer to home, Riley became known as the dean of Hoosier writers. Having known Booth Tarkington from the time he was a child, he very early recognized his talent and played an instrumental role in helping start his literary career. Another aspiring young Hoosier author, Meredith Nicholson, came to Riley's attention when he sent a few poems to the *Indianapolis Journal*. Riley paid a visit to the law office where he clerked to offer encouragement. Nicholson remembered that morning as one of the brightest moments of his life. The two men became close friends. In 1914, Nicholson based a novel called *The Poet* on Riley's life. George Ade also held Riley up as a model. He said that the Hoosier poet was the most interesting and entertaining mortal with whom he ever consorted for hours at a time.[100]

Although his books were bestsellers, the Hoosier poet made at least twice as much money reading his works in public. Despite his promise to devote himself to his writing, lecturing was so profitable that Riley could not resist going back on the road, as long as his health permitted it. He saw the income which he earned on the lecture platform as an investment in his future and therefore put up with the inconveniences and discomforts of travel.[101] Between 1892 and 1903, he made a number of very successful lecture tours.

In fall and winter 1892, Riley made his first appearances on the West Coast as part of a three-month schedule of readings. This tour was not only the first time that he saw the Pacific Ocean but also the first time that he had lectured extensively since the breakup of his partnership with Nye in February 1890. During the previous season, he had been careful not to crowd himself with lecture dates. Because of past unpleasant experiences, as he prepared to go back out on the road he was panicked and overwhelmed with dread.[102]

However, Riley had less to fear than during previous lecture seasons. The Hoosier poet was no longer at the mercy of ruthless lyceum bureaus or greedy general managers. Henry Eitel was now directing all of Riley's business affairs, protecting his brother-in-law so that he would not be exploited and keeping tight control of his bookings.[103]

He also hired William C. Glass, a lecture manager from New York, to travel with the poet to handle all of his personal affairs during his journey and to do everything he could to make Riley's tour more pleasant. With Glass along, Riley did not have to worry about figuring out any of his travel details. This personal manager took such good care of all of Riley's concerns on the road that the poet joked that he could even do his meditating for him. He affectionately called Glass his "mascot" and made humorous references to his name by calling him his "Venetian-ware" or "fragile" manager.[104]

Riley started his western tour in Davenport, Iowa, and then went to Denver. From Denver, he and Glass traveled by train for two days before reaching Los Angeles. By this time, people all across the country knew Riley through his poems. Although he had never been to California before, a *Los Angeles Times* article called him "the poet of America" and stated that he needed no introduction to the city's inhabitants.[105]

Everywhere Riley went, the welcome he received was almost overpowering. Large audiences greeted him at theaters and responded positively to his performances. They sometimes left him large floral displays and demanded several encores. At each stop of his tour, prominent citizens vied to honor the poet. In San Francisco the Pacific Union Club gave him a reception, and at Stanford University he was the guest of David Starr Jordan, who had known the poet since Jordan's days as president of Indiana University. Riley also visited poet Joaquin Miller, a friend of Bret Harte and author of *Songs of the Sierras,* at his home in Oakland. Miller so liked the Hoosier poet that he once wrote, "The hell of life is it has but few Jim Rileys."[106]

However, not all members of San Francisco's artistic community welcomed him so warmly. Ambrose Bierce could find nothing redeeming about Riley and his poetry. He wrote a scathing piece criticizing his work in his column for the *San Francisco Examiner,* "Prattle," in which he sarcastically stated that he hoped that Riley would be "arrested and returned forthwith to his reservation in Hoop-pole county, Indiana."[107] Making a direct reference to *The Hoosier School-Master* by mentioning "Hoop-pole" county, Bierce presented Riley as an ignorant, uncivilized backwoodsman, like the characters in Eggleston's novel, who had no notion of what poetry really was. Riley wrote off Bierce's attack as the inevitable "counter-comment" to the overwhelmingly positive press he received while on tour in the West.[108]

In spring 1893, toward the end of Riley's next series of lectures which took him through the southern states, Douglass Sherley, a Louisville, Kentucky, millionaire, joined Riley and Glass on the road. Although Sherley often introduced himself as "a stout, obscure person whom . . . Riley's manager discovered," he had actually known the poet for quite some time. Sherley was one of the many acquaintances, including Madison Cawein and Young E. Allison, that Riley had made on his lecture-tour visits to Louisville during the 1880s.[109]

Until he got to know him, Riley had not been favorably disposed to his new partner. Sherley fancied himself a writer but had not been able to get any of his work accepted by a reputable publisher. Because of his financial circumstances, he could afford to publish his stories himself. Riley had questioned his writing ability and was suspicious of his wealth. Some critics said that Sherley's writing style was stilted and that his plots were highly improbable. Nevertheless, he was a big, burly man with a pleasing disposition, who could win over audiences with his charm. When he first performed with him in April 1893, Riley realized that Sherley had much appeal and asked the Louisville man to read with him for the remainder of the season. Through 1894, the two men continued to be stage partners. The Hoosier poet was almost completely responsible for Sherley's emergence as a public lecturer, and he sought to diminish the prejudices that existed in the literary community against him.[110]

Sherley's jovial companionship enlivened Riley's travels. In contrast to the Hoosier poet, who disliked the harried schedule and called lecturing a "tedious travail," his partner thrived on the opportunity to travel and meet new people.[111] While Riley was constantly homesick and preferred to retire to his hotel room as soon as they arrived in a new town, Sherley already seemed to know everybody and spent most of his time outside the lecture hall socializing. Occasionally his eternal good nature irritated Riley. No matter what unpleasant conditions they faced, nothing seemed to bother Sherley. He was always "just as fresh as a rose on the road," and Riley was usually "well fagged with it all."[112]

During their second season together during the winter of 1893–1894, Riley and Sherley lectured in the Midwest and the East. The poet bragged that they had the "best houses of any attraction on the road."[113] In December, Riley had to interrupt their tour to hurry to the deathbed of his father. At age seventy-four, Reuben died at his home from complications of pneumonia. Tragically, Riley arrived in Greenfield thirty minutes after his father had taken his last breath.[114]

Reuben's death increased the acrimony between the Riley siblings and their stepmother. Because of her stinginess, the children thought that Mattie had not treated their father as well as she could have during his last illness. In addition, she inherited the bulk of the estate. Each of Reuben's children received only one of his belongings by which to remember him. Riley took a watch that he had given to his father as a gift.[115]

Partially disabled from his service in the Civil War, Reuben had become very feeble in his last years and was unable to work. Before Social Security, as with many elderly people, little money came into his household. Reuben and his wife's surroundings became shabby and rundown, and they had no money for proper medical care. In part so that he could be close to his father and take care of him, only months before Reuben's death Riley had purchased the house where he was born on the National Road in Greenfield, intending to spend summers there with members of his family, leading a simpler, small-town life and hoping thereby to rejuvenate himself and his poetry.[116]

Riley spent only one season in the Greenfield house while his father was still alive, and unfortunately the opportunity to resolve the many issues with his father never arose. Although he desperately tried to win his approval, the poet thought that his father never understood him. Reuben lived to see his second son become a famous poet, but Riley claimed that he never could comprehend what people saw in his writings.[117] By buying back the childhood home his father had lost, the poet wanted to demonstrate his success in terms that Reuben could understand.

Although he never had a wife and children, during his last years Riley tried to be the kind of good family man he thought his father wanted him to be. Following the death of his brother John, he refurnished his home in Greenfield and permitted his sister-in-law Julia to live there. The poet was especially close to his youngest sister Mary; and, after she left her husband in the early 1900s, Riley provided for her and her daughter, Lesley Payne.[118]

The Hoosier poet was always an affectionate, doting uncle. In 1909, he employed his nephew Edmund Eitel as his personal secretary and, in 1912, gave him a wedding gift of $50,000.[119] He was particularly involved in making decisions about Lesley Payne's future. With his sister Mary, Riley was very interested in "most thoughtfully and shrewdly" planning every move that they made in his niece's behalf.[120] When Lesley demonstrated musical talent, Riley bought her an expensive violin and sent her and her mother to Europe so that she could study with the best masters of the instrument.[121] Instead of becoming the object of his family members' charity, as his father once thought he would, Riley ultimately provided them with financial security. He showed concern for their well-being and was often very generous and indulgent with his gifts.

After his father's funeral, Riley soon resumed lecturing with Sherley. In January 1894, they headed toward the East Coast. At a reception in Riley's honor in Boston, Riley met Edward Everett Hale, the clergymen and author; Thomas Wentworth Higginson, a biographer of Longfellow and editor of Emily Dickinson's poems; and poet Louise Chandler Moulton.[122] On the road, the Hoosier poet's schedule was now always filled with such events. He complained that people made too many demands on him. When he arrived in a city for an engagement, countless messages and invitations awaited him; but all Riley wanted was some rest and peace and quiet. Social situations often made him uncomfortable, and he did his best to avoid them: "Everybody wants me to go everywhere, and I don't know where to turn or what to *try* to do—for I know it won't work—not for me. In consequence people are getting mad at me in regiments.... Reached here about 12 last night, and kept up till 3 with already accumulated worries of messages—directions to remain awake till clubs should break and yield up their ever-sleepless members wanting still to go some'rs else."[123]

The most noteworthy appearances of Riley and Sherley's East Coast tour were with Twain in New York City, in late February and early March 1894. Although he knew that Riley could easily upstage him, because he was near bankruptcy Twain reluctantly agreed to share the stage with Riley and Sherley for two nights at Madison Square Garden for a fee of $250 a night and only on condition that Riley present nothing but serious material. Because of bad weather, a third engagement featuring the three writers was added at Chickering Hall.[124]

Although he was disappointed that he could not read his humorous poems and sketches because of Twain's restrictions, Riley related that "each entertainer was in his best trim." Many of the city's most illustrious residents, including William Dean Howells, attended.[125] As Twain feared, however, the Hoosier poet received more attention and applause for his performances than he did. One year later, the author of *Huckleberry Finn* referred to these readings with Riley as "unspeakable botches."[126]

While he was still in New York, Riley became too ill to continue his lecture schedule with Sherley. He returned to Indianapolis to recuperate. In years past, while he was in the city, he usually stayed at the Denison Hotel. In 1893, the poet took up residence at the home of Charles and Magdelena Holstein at 528 Lockerbie Street, as a paying guest. Holstein was a graduate of Harvard Law School who had served as a U.S. Assistant Attorney, but many people considered him a poet in his own right. He was a good friend of Riley's and regarded him highly.[127]

Ironically, in 1880, thirteen years before he moved there, Riley had written a poem about the street where he would live for the last twenty-three years of his life. The Lockerbie Square area was one of the first subdivisions in Indianapolis settled outside the original 1820 Indianapolis mile square. The Hoosier poet was attracted to this neighborhood, with shady streets "nestled away / From the noise of the city and the heat of the day." Although he could well have afforded a large, opulent home of his own, because of his insecurities, Riley may have preferred to save his money. Moreover, living modestly better fit his image. The Holstein house was comfortable, but not opulent. When he visited Indianapolis in 1913, Theodore Dreiser decribed it as "about as old and homely as it could be ... but, shucks, who cares. Let the senators and the ex-presidents and the beef packers have the big places. What should the creator of 'Old Doc Sifers' be doing in a great house, anyhow?"[128]

"Lockerbie Land," as Riley called the Holstein house, provided him with the kind of home environment he craved. When he was away, he wrote the "Lockerbies" many letters and wistfully thought of the "fireside and bright lights and glad faces" that would greet him upon his return.[129] Riley came to be like a member of the immediate family. Even before he moved in permanently, he referred to Magdelena's mother Charlotte Nickum, who also lived there, as his second mother.[130]

He had a special respect and affection for Magdelena. Because of her many admirable qualities, he nicknamed her "St. Lockerbie." Like many other women of her class, she spent much of her time doing charity work. Her special interest was a small settlement house called the Katherine Home, which she helped to establish in 1893. Sometimes at the expense of her own health, Magdelena went out of her way to help the less fortunate in the Indianapolis community.[131] After she was widowed, Magdalena's friendship with Riley may have turned into something more serious. Holstein and Riley continued to live together in Indianapolis and, in the 1910s, were companions on winter sojourns to Miami. After Riley died, Magdelena did not live alone at 528 Lockerbie Street very long. She survived him by only three months.[132]

From spring 1894 through summer 1896, Riley remained in Indiana, dividing his time between the Holstein home and his summer residence in Greenfield. During this time, he was happy and relieved not to have to take any lecture bookings. "I've lost all heart in peregrinations about the world reading—reading—reading from my own works from one season's end to the other!" he told Louise Chandler Moulton in December 1895. "It's awful enough to listen to—but think—think . . . what a hyper-super awful thing it is to be mouthing it eternally!"[133] At the beginning of 1896, although he did not say that he would never perform in public again, Riley announced that he had decided to retire from the stage.[134]

However, his retirement from the platform did not last long. In summer 1896, Marcus Dickey, an old acquaintance then living in Colorado, convinced him to return to the lecture circuit. A Hoosier native, Dickey met the poet when he was an instructor at the Fairmount Academy in north central Indiana. During the early 1890s, he was such an admirer of Riley that he used his poetry in his classroom. A few years before he took control of the Hoosier poet's readings, Dickey left teaching to become a lecture manager. In the past, he had boosted the public speaking careers of such men as Henry Watterson, the famous editor of the *Louisville Courier-Journal*.[135]

As director of the Colorado Springs Lyceum Bureau, Dickey arranged for a very limited schedule of readings for Riley, which lasted only a few weeks in early fall 1896. He advertised this short tour to four Colorado cities as the poet's last.[136] However, it was just the first of several lecture seasons that Dickey planned for the Hoosier poet. From this point forward, serving not only as his lecture manager but also as his personal secretary and official biographer, Dickey's name was closely associated with the Hoosier poet's.

Unlike some of his past managers, such as Walker and Pond, Dickey could be trusted. He took extreme care to fulfill all arrangements as he promised.[137] Although Eitel continued to handle Riley's finances, Dickey organized each minute detail of a tour and was Riley's "very shadow," who personally saw that he was deprived of nothing.[138] Dickey was against "the social side show" that had accompanied many of Riley's public appearances. Whenever possible, he eliminated receptions and banquets from the poet's schedule and permitted him to sleep in the afternoon so that he would be fresh for each evening performance. Riley usually recognized that the social affairs that remained in his itinerary were necessary for "growing friends and enthusiasm everywhere."[139]

During the late 1890s and early 1900s, Dickey worked closely with Riley, Eitel, and Bobbs in the careful coordination of the the poet's readings with marketing for his books. They created elaborate advertising materials which not only publicized his lectures but also included excerpts from his poems and illustrations from his anthologies. Their large-scale publicity campaigns declared that Riley was a great performer and that there was a larger demand for his "poems than for those of any other poet." They informed the public that thousands purchased his volumes for holiday and birthday gifts. Their advertising brochures, sent out to the towns and cities where he lectured, featured effusive press notices from around the country that emphasized his popularity on the stage. These brochures also contained endorsements from prominent authors, such as Howells and Twain, and from famous actors of the time, such as Joseph Jefferson. In addition, Bowen-Merrill included a list of every book of Riley's that the company had published, with a short description of each. In other words, each page of these pamphlets broadcast the many ways in which the Hoosier poet was the object of insatiable and universal demand. Publicity campaigns like these, which also made full use of the national press, became typical for best-selling authors throughout the second half of the nineteenth century. As president of the company that would eventually take his name, Bobbs, in particular, was a leading figure in the publishing industry for developing strategies to market popular literature for wide distribution.[140]

In Riley's case, these strategies worked extraordinarily well. The Hoosier poet's books outsold all of Bowen-Merrill's other titles; and, in the many communities where he performed, his public readings were major social events. Never before and never again was such an effort so successful. By the end of the century, announcements of his lectures created stampedes at the box office. The treasurer of an Atlanta theater where Riley lectured in spring 1899 claimed that he had never seen anything like it. On the first day that tickets went on sale, crowds gathered in front of the theater box office before it opened; and a steady stream of customers came throughout the day.[141] The situation in Atlanta was certainly not unique. Even in East Coast cities such as Boston, tickets for his lectures sold very quickly. Riley's readings packed theaters, and hundreds often had to be turned away.[142]

Despite the ever-growing public enthusiasm for Riley, his lecture tours in the late nineteenth century were not as extensive as those he undertook in the 1880s. To minimize the discomforts of travel, Dickey attempted to avoid booking lecture dates at long distances from each other. On longer tours, he managed Riley's calendar so that he could go home for brief breaks. Short tours usually focused on a particular geographic area. For example, in winter 1897, the poet visited eight cities along the Missouri River; and, in winter 1898–1899, he made appearances in the East. Between 1896 and 1903, none of Riley's tours lasted more than three months.[143] No longer was the poet the victim of a manager who sat "in his office with a railroad guide and map" and sent him "every place he could push his infernal pencil."[144] Dickey assumed an important place on Riley's management team, strategically planning his public tours to maintain his popularity in different parts of the country without severely overtaxing him.

Although Riley told Charles Holstein that he only grew more subject to homesickness as he grew older, the material rewards of his readings made the inconveniences he suffered while he was away from Lockerbie Street more bearable. By the early 1890s, his regular lecture fee was already $150. During his last couple of years on the platform at the turn of the century, he was receiving $250 per engagement. In comparison, when he joined the lyceum circuit in 1879, he had earned only $25 plus expenses per night. At the time of his last lecture tour in 1903, Riley was a very wealthy man. While he was out on the road, he made over $1,000 a week.[145]

Because his program had changed little since the 1880s, the Hoosier poet was constantly surprised that he could continue to draw such large crowds:

> I have found in the . . . invariably packed houses and warm welcomes . . . a continual surprise. . . . *And* to save me I can't understand it: Eight times now have I tremulously faced Kansas City audiences—twice this time—and been *recalled at last number* even—every instance,—when it seems to me, every man, woman and child in the entire *Riley-ridden* municipality might repeat every harrowing word of my brazen, old and bald, and tottering and babbling meanderings from A to Izzard![146]

Through experience, Riley found that only about one in fifty of his compositions lent themselves to oral presentation. He kept forty of these memorized for his lectures. After performing in some cities on several different occasions, part of his audience invariably had attended his readings before. When he went out on stage in 1897 and 1898, Riley still feared that his popularity would diminish if he did not give something new to those people who had already heard him but, at the same time, did not want to disappoint those who expected to hear only their old favorites.[147]

With each new series of lectures, Riley increasingly recognized that his audiences did not want him to recite anything that they had not heard from him before. Although repeating the same selections over and over again grew tiresome, his audiences' applause and acclaim helped him to retain some of his enthusiasm for his performances: "Have not been boring you with papers *daily,* for every one of 'em reviews my selections by *name,* and the *sight* of these is almost as nauseating as the *sound* of 'em. Still new audiances [*sic*] and their evident approval of the old programme makes some mysterious shift to keep life in it."[148]

As they sat in theaters, his many admirers waited for him to recite the familiar selections that they expected to hear—"The Raggedy Man," "Out to Old Aunt Mary's," "An Old Sweetheart of Mine," "Little Orphant Annie," and "The Old Man and Jim." These poems are the ones for which he is still best known; and, if they were not on his program, his audiences sometimes pressed him for encores until he read them. By the end of the nineteenth century, Riley and his lectures had become an American institution.[149]

Although he never again went out on the lecture circuit following 1903, Riley continued to recite poetry at special events. During the last part of his career, he was sometimes called "the poet laureate of America" or the "People's Poet laureate;" and, on many occasions, he served unofficially in this capacity.[150]

Because nineteenth-century public meetings characteristically combined political speeches with the reading of poetry and religious passages, Riley often read from his work on Decoration Day and other observances of patriotic holidays. Throughout his career, he wrote several poems for such occasions; and, by the 1890s, he had long been a regular participant in local civic celebrations. However, starting with the World's Columbian Exposition, held in Chicago in 1893, the Hoosier poet took a role in the commemoration of events that had significance beyond the local level.

The 1893 World's Columbian Exposition celebrated not only the anniversary of Columbus's arrival to the New World but also the rise in importance of Chicago and the Midwest. As evidence of Indiana's growing prominence within the nation, exposition officials declared one day of the fair "Indiana

Day." With President Harrison, Lew Wallace, and Governor Claude Matthews, Riley represented the state on this occasion. His appearance drew just as much attention as that of the president; and, while other poets who read their work during various special programs throughout the exposition went practically unnoticed, Riley's audience greeted him with enthusiasm and applause. He received so much press coverage from the event that, shortly after the exposition was over, James Matthews wrote: "[H]ave you [Riley] escaped the fuss and flurry of the summer incident—to the World's Fair and your waxing fame? I catch a glimpse of your distinguished self in the papers frequent[ly], and wonder if my old friend is fortunate enough to preserve his balance in the midst of the riotous lionizing that everywhere besets him."[151]

Following the Exposition, Riley read poems for a select group of events which celebrated America's greatness. Although he was not very political, Riley admitted that he could be "a trifle patriotic."[152] He regretted that he had been too young to fight in the Civil War and too old to take part in the Spanish American War.[153] His patriotic poetry demonstrates that he had an untrammeled faith in the values upon which the nation had been founded and in the strength, self-reliance, and individualism of the American people.

"The Name of Old Glory," which he delivered at the 1901 Pan-American Exposition and the dedication of Indiana monuments at the Shiloh Battlefield, glorified the sacrifices that men made for their country in battle. Reading at Shiloh particularly moved the poet. For Riley, the monuments he saw there manifested the fine spirit of both the North and the South in the Civil War. He spoke of the conflict between the states as a war for union instead of a war of rebellion and hoped that through such commemorations the remaining differences between the two sides would be reconciled.[154]

In 1902, Riley read "The Soldier" at the dedication of the Soldiers and Sailors Monument in Indianapolis. Like "The Name of Old Glory," "The Soldier" honored American veterans who had died during war without ambivalence or reservation. While this poem lamented the loss of the Civil War victims, it also brought consolation and redemption by promising the hope of eternal life and by redirecting emotions to the monument that in some measure is a replacement for the war dead it mourns:

> And, even so, The Soldier slept.—Our own!—
>   The Soldier of our plaudits, flowers and tears,—
> Oh this memorial of bronze and stone—
>   His love shall outlast *this* a thousand years!
> Yet, as the towering symbol bids us do,—
>   With soul saluting, as salutes the hand,
> We answer as The Soldier answered to
>   The Captain's high command.[155]

In addition to mourning the common soldier, Riley also wrote poems elegizing such military leaders and statesmen as Indiana Governor Thomas Hendricks, President Benjamin Harrison, and Major General Henry Lawton, which he read at dedications of monuments erected in their honor.[156] John Philip Sousa set to music "America," written after President McKinley's assassination; and, in 1910, the Hoosier poet recited a poem at the unveiling of the statue of General Lew Wallace in the U.S. Capitol in Washington, D.C.[157]

Although during the last years of his active career he was in demand to read at such events, these elegies are weak pieces of poetry—so poor that, in 1890, his friend the writer Robert Burns Wilson urged him to "let the patriotic poeto-political ex-president bones–business alone."[158] But Riley ignored the advice. He is not well known for this form; but, in fact, he produced a large number of poems lamenting the deaths of family members, famous poets, friends, and acquaintances.[159]

Most of these poems simply repeated stock elegaic conventions and mortuary formulas, and even at the time, some people thought that they were artificial and insincere. In 1892, one critic declared that Riley's elegies of Whittier, Tennyson, and First Lady Caroline Scott Harrison were "affected," "mechanical obituaries" which contained no genuine sentiment.[160] To bring solace to his readers, even in "Away," one of Riley's better poems in this genre, he blandly states: "I can not say, and will not say / That he is dead.—He is just away."[161]

As with many typical elegies written during this period, these poems seem to be "person empty."[162] At a time when the pressures of capitalist society were suppressing and shortening traditional mourning rituals, the modern elegist reacted against them. Starting with the works of such poets as Thomas Hardy, elegies became more personal, complex, and detailed. In contrast, Riley continued to shape his elegies to order grief and to abstract and objectify the dead. His representations tend to be categorical and universal. Writing about individuals, Riley remained, like his predecessors, a poet who transmuted death into the promise of cyclical renewal. In these poems, he rarely displayed much ambivalence about loss and readily translated grief into consolation.[163]

In a broader sense, Riley's poems that mourn the passing of the rural scene are also elegies. While he self-consciously composed the larger proportion of his elegies for people as public discourse designed to help cure bereavement, his poems about the loss of the rural world of his youth are more deeply personal and thus more effective. Especially in "The Old Swimmin' Hole," Riley repudiated the onslaught of capitalist, industrial development. The old diving logs where he used to play are buried under the railroad bridge, and the trees that used to shade him are gone.[164]

While most of his elegies to people end with hope, in poems such as "The

Old Swimmin' Hole," the Hoosier poet did not so easily find solace. His sorrow remained unresolved as he wished he "could strip to the soul, / And dive off in . . . [his] grave like the old swimmin' hole."[165] Although all of Riley's elegies follow conventions common to elegies, such as a present-past-present/future pattern, Riley became a much more modern writer in his poems about the passing of the nineteenth century. In "Out to Old Aunt Mary's" and "The Old Swimmin' Hole," he was aware that he stood poised between two different eras. These poems can easily be seen as an expression of Riley's revolt against the emerging impersonal, industrial, capitalistic society governed by the socioeconomic laws of exchange, equivalence, and progress.[166]

In poems like "The Old Swimmin' Hole," Riley consciously inserted himself into his depictions of rural America. While his poems which portrayed the simple life of country dwellers seemed to have a never-ending appeal at the end of the nineteenth century, he feared what would happen to his own reputation when that world vanished in the twentieth. At the turn of the century, he sensed that country life was "doomed" and, like Hardy, associated "his mourning work with a threatened rural outlook."[167] As he elegized his small-town, rural roots, he also contemplated his own mortality as an artist. He connected the waning fortunes of poets to the destruction of old sensibilities and values caused by the incursion of rapid corporate-capitalist industrial development.[168]

Despite all of the public attention, honors, and accolades he received, Riley never escaped from the notion that he might not deserve them and that he had never accomplished what he set out to do. At the same time, he distrusted people who appeared to be trying to ingratiate themselves with him. He questioned his friends' sincerity when they praised his work, fearing that they lied to avoid offending him instead of giving their honest criticisms.[169]

Moreover, by "earning his board by the sweat of his dialect," Riley sometimes doubted that he had written truly great poetry and suspected that in the future his literary renown might fade.[170] Fears of mortality, failure, and rejection both plagued and motivated him. "A number of years ago . . . ," he said to a reporter at the end of 1897, "I made a scratch hit and since then I have been trying to keep people thinking they were right in their first judgment."[171] Although it was against his nature, he worked very hard because he was jealous of his reputation; but, periodically, his desire to prove to himself and to the world that his success was not a temporary fluke drove him to the point of nervous exhaustion. Throughout his life, Riley's frenzied work periods were followed by self-immobilizing, self-punishing depression.

At the turn of the century, satisfying the constant demand to lecture and to publish more books continued this cycle. At times, his many literary contracts threw him almost into a mental panic. Overwhelmed by his duties and obligations, he often found it absolutely necessary to work far into the night. Riley's friend Erasmus Wilson, a Pittsburgh columnist, told him that he was not obliged to keep his publisher's presses running, but to no avail.[172] Almost every year during the 1890s and early 1900s, his self doubts pushed him to work so hard that he made himself ill. He became so anxious and nervous that he had trouble eating and sleeping; and it was at these times when Riley was still most tempted to drink.[173]

The poet's doctors treated him repeatedly for nervous prostration, then commonly labeled neurasthenia. He was in good company; other prominent sufferers included William James, Henry Adams, and Thomas Bailey Aldrich. Modern psychiatrists would classify various neurasthenic symptoms as a number of different conditions. However, in the nineteenth century, this disease was a convenient catchall for many types of ailments, including dyspepsia, insomnia, hopelessness, paralyzing self-doubt, and a "desire for stimulants and narcotics." At one time or another Riley suffered from all of these symptoms.[174] Such eminent physicians as Silas Weir Mitchell, who was acquainted with Riley and specialized in the treatment of neurological disorders, believed that neurasthenia was a product of the post–Civil War era. They cited the new pressures engendered by industrialization and urbanization as its most likely causes, and noted that it most frequently attacked cultivated city dwellers with sensitive temperaments. According to this viewpoint, the strains of modern life were too much for people who, like Riley, suffered from nervous illness.[175] In his case, long years of hard drinking and physically punishing lecture tours exacerbated the situation.

According to most doctors of the time, the only remedy for Riley's maladies was complete rest. He sometimes spent months at a time in bed.[176] During the early 1900s, like many other wealthy nineteenth-century Americans, he also took advantage of the rest cures offered at spas with mineral water springs. In late summer 1901, the poet spent a month at Lithia Springs resort outside Atlanta and continued his vacation from work by visiting Joel Chandler Harris while he was in the area.[177]

Not surprisingly, such rest cures often exacerbated the patient's symptoms.[178] During long periods of illness, with a lack of distractions, Riley became increasingly anxious, self-absorbed, and distressed. He characterized himself as "an uninteresting invalid" and complained that he was not permitted to attend to his "most crying duties."[179] Confined to his room and warned not to write, he expressed his complete frustration with the helplessness and isolation that he felt in a letter to Madison Cawein in 1906: "Your recent and good letter has been answerless because of illness from which only now I am recovering—with friends, doctor and attendants all warning me that every attempt at, or thought of, anything like work must be avoided at the peril of my life! Well, this page may kill me, but as I'll die if I don't write it, please *know* how sincere is my desire to be of service to you and my regret over my utter helplessness in the matter."[180]

Even when he was not bedridden, Riley found it increasingly difficult to work. As early as 1899, he complained that he could no longer force his mind to function enough to produce poems on command: "The youth and elasticity is gone clean out of it, and it now seems to fit the demand like the slack, limp lasting of an old shoe."[181] Because his fans perceived him to be perpetually childlike, he became obsessed by each physical sign of his loss of youth. He continued to recycle his old poems in new anthologies rather than admit to the public that he was no longer able to produce. Although he was only in his fifties, with those whom he knew personally he enumerated endlessly the infirmities of age, including "vanishing teeth," "weird eyesight," and "thickening hearing," and began to think of himself as an old man.[182]

The deaths of several friends intensified his obsession with his own mortality. With some of his Lockerbie Street neighbors, including the Indiana artist R. B. Gruelle, Riley went so far as to participate in seances in an attempt to communicate with the dead.[183] At times he had morbid thoughts that he belonged with them rather than among the living. "Of late months I have been steadily saying good-by to outgoing friends," he wrote in 1901 to Henry Van Dyke, the writer, clergyman, and Princeton University professor, "till it is growing rather a lonesome life I'm lagging in—this side of it,—so many dear fellows over *There.*"[184]

Following 1900, Riley experienced fewer and fewer long periods of good health. With the exception of a trip to Mexico with Indiana businessman William Fortune in 1906, and a trip to Washington, D.C., for the unveiling of the Lew Wallace statue in 1910, for several years after he finished his last lecture tour in 1903, ill health prevented Riley from traveling far from home.[185] By 1908, he described himself as a semi-invalid who had a "tendency . . . to get rattled over easy."[186] His years of hard living had caught up with him. He became increasingly feeble and was easily tired out. Walking was an effort, and he lost weight. In June 1910, he wrote to Madison Cawein that he was feeling very poorly. As he customarily did in much of his correspondence, he listed his many infirmities but also said that he thought he might expire at any moment. Riley took to his bed but, in the stifling summer heat, got no better. On 10 July 1910, he suffered a severe stroke that paralyzed his right side.[187]

The Riley family managed to keep the news out of the press for a month, hoping that he would make a quick recovery. When the story finally broke in the national papers in August, Riley was still quite sick. He had very little use of his right arm and leg. He had trouble talking and was only able to walk with the help of a nurse. His inability to use his writing hand was a source of great distress to him. His recovery was very slow, and his doctors warned that he might have another attack at any time.[188]

During much of the next year, Riley rarely left the Lockerbie Street home. Wanting to make sure that he left Indianapolis a legacy before he died, in 1911, he made a gift of property at the northwest corner of St. Clair and Pennsylvania streets in Indianapolis to the State Board of School Commissioners for construction of a new city library.[189] At about this time, Riley was slowly but surely getting better. He purchased an automobile and hired a chauffeur so that he could more easily go out. As he toured Indianapolis and the surrounding countryside, his car became a familiar sight.

His progress seemed to become more rapid after he started spending winters in Miami upon the invitation of Indianapolis automobile industrialist Carl G. Fisher. After his first winter in Miami in 1913, Riley could walk with a cane unaided. During the winters of 1914, 1915, and 1916, he continued to go to Florida accompanied by Magdelena Holstein. His niece Elizabeth Eitel sometimes went along as his secretary.[190]

Although Riley's output had diminished greatly even before his stroke, William C. Bobbs found it difficult to accept that his star writer's productive life was essentially over. In 1911, he urged George Ade to encourage Riley to dictate a series of semi-autobiographical short stories about his early life in Indiana. However, the poet was still too unwell for such an undertaking and resisted dictating any new poems or stories. Between 1910 and 1916, he wrote only five more poems.[191]

Bobbs-Merrill nonetheless kept the Riley publishing machine going. The profits the company reaped from his poetry were simply too great for it to give them up. Before his stroke, Riley had always been heavily involved in compiling each of his anthologies. Now, that responsibility fell primarily to Bobbs-Merrill editor-in-chief Hewitt Hanson Howland and Riley's nephew, Edmund H. Eitel. Otherwise, the process remained little changed.

With much thought, Howland made selections for the Riley anthologies which appeared between 1911 and 1916. Two of these, *The Lockerbie Book* and *The Hoosier Book*, contained what the editor considered the best of Riley's poems. Both were bound in gilt stamped or moroccan leather covers. The former included his best poems in standard English, and the latter included his best verse in dialect. Just before publication, he passed each volume that he prepared along to Riley for his final approval. Eitel operated in a similar fashion. Hired by Bobbs-Merrill in 1913, he continued to take care of Riley's correspondence and became chief editor of the *Biographical Edition* of his uncle's works. While he compiled the *Biographical Edition*, he consulted with Riley and gathered biographical material and notes on each poem, prose sketch, and article his uncle had written.[192]

With new books still being published, Riley's poetry remained very much in the public eye. Several different composers set his poems to music, and Thomas Edison and Selig Polyscope Company held the motion picture rights to such poems as "Little Orphant Annie," "An Old Sweetheart of Mine," and "Out to Old Aunt Mary's."[193] Starting in 1912, consumers could purchase records of the poet reading some of his most familar works, including "When the Frost Is on the Punkin," "The Raggedy Man," "The Happy Little Cripple," and "On the Banks of Deer Crick."[194] These recordings so captured the fancy of Hoosier author Theodore Dreiser that he listened to them over and over again.[195]

At this point, the poet's own celebrity had long ago surpassed that of his work. Riley was one of the most recognizable men in America. His bespectacled face was caricatured in magazines and newspapers, and manufacturers used his image to sell a number of different products. For example, in the mid-1890s, because he was a constant user of tobacco, a southern Indiana company introduced the James Whitcomb Riley cigar. "Hoosier Poet" also became a brand name for canned fruits, vegetables, and coffee. Greeting cards and postcards were available containing lines from his poems.[196]

Riley's Lockerbie Street house became a mecca for visitors to Indianapolis. When he made his cross country trip to his home state in 1915, Dreiser asked his traveling companion, the illustrator and Indiana native Franklin Booth, to show him the Hoosier poet's home. Many of Riley's friends from the literary and publishing world, including Meredith Nicholson, Booth Tarkington, William Allen White, Bliss Carman, Bliss Perry, and Robert Underwood Johnson, often came to visit him there.[197]

Important nineteenth-century artists painted the poet. Riley's friend T. C. Steele, who established his early career painting wealthy Indianapolis citizens, did his portrait on three different occasions.[198] In 1903, the proceeds of a benefit reading for the Indianapolis Art Association made it possible for Riley to be immortalized by John Singer Sargent, the most sought after portraitist in the English-speaking world at the turn of the century. The Art Association's commission of the famous portraitist reflected the desire of Indianapolis residents to make Riley an equal with other prominent writers who had also been Sargent's subjects. As one of these subjects, Riley joined a select group of people in late nineteenth century high society. In May 1903, *The Century Magazine* requested that this portrait appear in one of its issues alongside Sargent portraits of John Hay and Silas Weir Mitchell, under the title "Three Men of American Letters."[199]

In 1911, Minnie Belle Mitchell, the wife of a Greenfield newspaperman, who would later become one of the poet's biographers, spearheaded a movement through the Indiana Federation of Literary Clubs for the celebration of his birthday in all the state's schools. As a result, until 1968, children throughout Indiana regularly read Riley's poems in their classrooms on his birthday. While he was still alive, the celebration of 7 October was a major statewide event.

In 1912, Riley responded to this honor by writing in his own shaky hand a letter to Indiana schoolchildren. As he usually did on public occasions, he used language that accentuated his own modesty:

> It may be well for you to remember that the day you are about to celebrate is the birthday of many good men, but if I may be counted the least of these I will be utterly content and happy. I can only thank you and your teachers with a full heart and the fervent hope that the day will poore [*sic*] an equal glory to us all.

Despite his ill health, Riley continued to perpetuate the illusion of youthfulness by identifying himself with the recipients of his short epistle:

> *To the very little Children:* I would say—be simply your own selves, and though even parents, as I sometimes think, do not seem to understanding us perfectly, we will be patient with them and love them no less loyaly [*sic*] and very tenderly. Most truly your hole [*sic*] friend and comrade.[200]

Riley's real feelings about these birthday observances remain unclear, as even on this occasion he was responding to the public as he calculated he should.

Between 1911 and 1915, the Indianapolis schools' celebration culminated in front of the Lockerbie Street home, where people gathered to catch a glimpse of the poet and children serenaded him and presented him with flowers.[201]

Each succeeding year, this celebration grew until, in 1915, U.S. Secretary of the Interior Franklin K. Lane called for its national observance.[202] The *Indianapolis Star* claimed that more than one million school children paid homage to the poet "in one of the most unique nation-wide birthday celebrations ever held."[203] In addition, prominent citizens of Indianapolis honored Riley with elaborate displays of their admiration and affection. Organizers of these birthday celebrations in 1915 attempted to elevate him and his work to high cultural levels. To commemorate the event, they commissioned American sculptor Lorado Taft to create a medallion of the poet. The popular composer Ward Stephens set some of Riley's poems to music; and, at the Murat Theater the afternoon of his birthday, ballet dancers, including some celebrated Russian performers who had belonged to Anna Pavlova's company, interpreted these compositions in a public program.[204]

That same evening, four hundred attended a banquet honoring the poet at the Claypool Hotel in downtown Indianapolis. During the last decades of the nineteenth century and the first of the twentieth, large banquets commemorating distinguished people and special events were an institution. Over long tables heavily laden with food, they celebrated the country's vitality and material progress; and the themes of the laudatory after-dinner speeches, which were a part of the banquet ritual, reinforced dominant cultural values.

The organizers of Riley's banquet bequeathed him this honor because they perceived that he had succeeded in establishing a cultural identity for Indiana of which they could be proud. Because of his wide renown, awards, and acclaim, men like Fairbanks and Ade no longer thought that they had to be ashamed to call themselves Hoosiers. Because he gave them pride of place, in their eyes, Riley could do no wrong. This special dinner gave its instigators the opportunity to display the state's importance and wealth and to show that its citizens' accomplishments and tastes were equal or even superior to those of the cultivated elite who lived in the large eastern cities. Therefore, these prominent Indiana politicians, businessmen, and authors invited some of the most respected people in literature and in public life, not only in Indiana, but from the nation as a whole. Imitating similar banquets tendered to Mark Twain and William Dean Howells, they wanted it to "surpass anything of the kind attempted in the United States."[205]

Among those who attended this special banquet were former Vice President Charles W. Fairbanks, U.S. Senators Albert J. Beveridge and John W. Kern, *Atlantic Monthly* publisher Ellery Sedgwick, *North American Review* publisher George W. Harvey, and the writer and journalist William Allen White.[206] In their after-dinner speeches, these distiguished gentlemen paid tribute to Riley and to the state that produced him. By this time, the poet's life had almost become legend. From a small country village, he had "gone steadily onward and upward" until he was known everywhere.[207] Fairbanks, Kern, Beveridge, Harvey, Ade and others held Riley up as the perfect American type, whose Hoosier roots exemplified everything worthwhile that the country had to offer. His native state gave him the material for his life's work and "an unlimited quantity of good, hard. . . , common sense."[208]

Speech after speech defined Riley as the quintessential self-made man. For example, Kern, who had been acquainted with the poet since his sign painting days, remembered him as a "fair-haired, jolly, rollicking young man, scarcely out of boyhood, without friends, unhonored, with no capital save industry and ability." Now, Kern claimed hyperbolically that he was "honored by all of the people of the world as no other man of his time."[209] Similarly, Fairbanks stated that "[h]e made his way by the force of his genius."[210] According to these versions of his life story, Riley was wholly responsible for his fate and had succeeded because of his own hard work, self-reliance, merit, and talent. Through his accomplishments, he affirmed a world view that provided many Americans with meaning and purpose.[211]

These speakers merged Riley's personality with the characters and sentiments present in his best known poems. They asserted that his life was an "open book."[212] As he did just a few months later when he wrote the script for the silent film commemorating the centennial of Indiana's statehood, George Ade proclaimed that "Riley revealed the Hoosiers to themselves" and described him as "the triple extract of all that is worth while in the make up of . . . [a] native son."[213] Because Ade and his contemporaries thought that life was more typically American in Indiana than it was elsewhere in the United States, in their minds, these same qualities more broadly revealed the best in the American character.

Riley was a man who upheld simple homely virtues. He was an "unfettered democrat" who rejected elitist social conventions and social display but who also understood "men and affairs." Everything in his life was "useful" and "honorable," and he did not hesitate to defend his principles.[214] Despite his wealth and fame, he belonged to the common people and chose to dwell among them, where he could "feel their heart beats and share with them their joys and bear with them their sorrows."[215] He was "generous, kindly, considerate, [and] sympathetic."[216] In the end, the banquet's speeches raised Riley up to be a saintly, almost Christ-like being in whose character was exemplified all the republican virtues upon which the United States had been founded. Fairbanks even went so far as to characterize him as an "uncrowned King" who was the "idol" of "young America."[217]

At the time of this banquet, Riley's mythification was already complete. His poems came to define what it meant to be a Hoosier; and, in turn, by carefully aligning himself with his characters, his audience thought that his poems were a transparent expression of his personality. In this process, the signifier had become the signified. His image itself was synonymous with Indiana: "Where men say Indiana, they say Riley also, as an eloquent synonym—a complete definition of the kindliness and wholesomeness of . . . Hoosier people."[218]

The 1915 Riley Day celebrations represented the culmination of the poet's career. At this time, he seemed healthier than he had been in years. He told a *New York Times* reporter that he felt like a boy again and that he was "enjoying life in spite of the war in Europe."[219] Seeing him in such good health and spirits, this reporter surmised that Riley would live many years more. However, in reality, like the nineteenth-century world that had made his rise to fame possible, Riley's life was at its end. During the weeks and months that followed, he never picked up his pen to write seriously again. Instead, he spent his days taking long drives in his car with his chauffeur; and friends such as Nicholson and Howland frequently visited him.

The poet lived long enough to spend one more winter in Miami; and, in May 1916, he returned to Indiana to take part in Ade's centennial film. Only two months later, on the morning of 22 July, he suffered another violent stroke. During the course of that hot summer day, he recovered enough to laugh and joke with family and friends. As he had following Riley's first stroke in 1910, his doctor, Carleton B. McCulloch, thought that Riley might survive; but the poet did not prove that resilient. He died peacefully before sunrise the next morning at the age of sixty-six.

Epilogue

In a *New York Times* article printed one month before the 1915 Riley Day celebration, a reporter commented that neither an autobiography nor a biography of the Hoosier poet had ever been published, although some Chicago authors who were well acquainted with him had at one time attempted to write his life story. When he found out, Riley was reportedly mortified. "He protested and asked his friends to leave him alone, saying his life was too commonplace to interest any one."[1] By claiming to be too ordinary to merit a biography, he wanted to give the impression that despite everything he had achieved he remained modest and unassuming. This newspaperman noted that Riley did not even like to be quoted because "[i]t seem[ed] so conceited."[2]

In reality, more than fifteen years before this interview appeared, the Hoosier poet had commissioned his personal manager and secretary, Marcus Dickey, to write his authorized biography. In 1915, Dickey's manuscript was as yet uncompleted. Three or four other people had come forward wanting to write books about the Hoosier poet's life; and, in each of these instances, Riley did indeed protest against their publication. However, he did so not because he thought that his life was unworthy of such treatment but because he wanted control over what was written. Learning of the authorized biography in progress, these other authors respected Riley's wishes.[3]

Having also acted as his personal manager and secretary, when, in 1899, he took on the task of writing Riley's biography, Dickey already knew him better than almost anyone else. He even lived next door to the poet for a while so that he could be in constant touch with him and meet his every demand. For the next two decades, Dickey spent a great deal of his time researching and writing what would become a two-volume work about Riley's life (Bobbs-Merrill published the first volume in 1919, the second in 1922). He doggedly pursued everyone with whom the poet ever exchanged letters so that he would have both sides of their correspondence from which to draw. He interviewed friends and family and took Riley out into the country to visit early childhood playmates in the hope of stimulating memories of the poet's early life.[4] On these trips, as Dickey quietly stood by taking notes, Riley and his old friends "talked old times, smoked pipes, and 'chewed tobacco and spit black.'"[5]

After the second volume of his biography appeared on the market, George Hitt told Dickey that he had portrayed their friend "in a way . . . he would have approved."[6] Behind the scenes, Dickey had been instrumental in elevating Riley's public reputation for many years; and, because of his long personal association with the poet, he did nothing to dispel the image that he had helped to create. Convinced that Riley was a true poetic genius, his official biographer idealized Riley's life in his books about him.[7] However, in his private notebooks, Dickey recorded some cogent observations that captured, in a way his biography did not, Riley's many complexities.[8]

At one point, Dickey concluded that Riley was "what [Ralph Waldo] Emerson would call a ludicrous contrast to all he has written."[9] There was much truth to this. Riley was a man of many contrasts and contradictions. The Hoosier poet liked to say that "civilization had not knocked all the edges off of him yet."[10] From statements like this one, people commonly confused the artist with his work and assumed that he was "what his poems show[ed] him to be—a great big boy."[11] Riley made the public believe that he was true to everything he wrote: "you feel, in reading his verse, that there is one of the honestest souls that ever uttered itself in that way. . . . The simplicity, the sincerity of everything Mr. Riley utters at once touches the heart."[12]

To his readers, he seemed common, plain, humorous, childlike, and tenderhearted—little different from "Benjamin F. Johnson of Boone," the "country poet" whom he had created for *The Old Swimmin'-Hole and 'Leven More Poems.* Many people were convinced that he was this pure and uncomplicated man who possessed a natural piety that enabled him to express genuine human feelings and passion.[13] In their minds, the poet retained a certain innocence which brought him nearer to God than most of the rest of the adult population. They saw in his work an implicit faith in God's providence which was free from uncertainty.

Riley's agnosticism belied his public persona. Religion did not offer him the same moral certainty as it had his ancestors: "there is nothing *reliable:* Am far less skeptical about a God in Heaven than a friend on earth. We *know* the one *here* will not (*cannot*, I suppose) deal fair: We do *not know* the Other will not.—Therefore, I grow fonder and fonder of—God,—even though *He* remains a divine abstract."[14] The Hoosier poet never attended church regularly. In his opinion, the church had grown narrowminded, conformist, and intolerant. He had little sympathy for the orthodoxy of organized religion and disliked the sanctimoniousness of many members of established congregations. He said that orthodoxy as a condition of worship and Christian living would not stand in the day of judgment.[15] These opinions reflected a general blurring of social and cultural boundaries that, during the late nineteenth century, weakened the conviction that certain principles and standards of conduct were inviolable.[16] In a secularizing society, Riley had trouble finding a firm anchor for his beliefs.

Little did people know that the man who provided readers with tender, pure, wholesome, and safe reading sprinkled his conversations with his friends liberally with vulgarities, told off-color jokes and stories, often drank to excess, and sometimes associated with women of questionable morals. To get what he wanted, he was calculating, hypocritical, and sometimes dishonest. A master at manipulating public opinion, he knew how to ascertain quickly what people wanted to hear. Throughout most of his adult life, he very selectively chose what he told people about himself and carefully shaped his statements so that they thought he was the character he professed to be.

Riley's contemporaries often exalted his supposed ignorance. Some critics remarked that book learning had fortunately neither ruined his spontaneity nor his artlessness. His poetry was natural and unaffected. It required "none of the discontent of deep thought . . . [and was] a welcome relief from the burden of cultured song."[17] They characterized Riley as a talented, primitive artist who had a knack for acquiring knowledge not found between the covers of books. As Riley's contemporaries misunderstood his religious tendencies, so they also underestimated his knowledge of the poetic craft.[18]

However, other critics, such as Ambrose Bierce, attacked Riley for having little background in the study of poetics. According to their viewpoint, the Hoosier poet relied too much on dialect. It concealed the fact that many of his subjects were trite and "cover[ed] up faulty construction . . . and ungainliness of structure."[19] At times, critics claimed that his writings were not truly poems at all.[20] Many of them would have been surprised to learn that he was hardly an uneducated country bumpkin.

Because he lacked a lengthy formal education, Riley understood his scholastic weaknesses.[21] In order to better his writing skills, he devoted himself to the study of poetry. In contrast to what was commonly known about his knowledge of literature, he could quote verse from a variety of different sources, including the works of Elizabethan, early American, and Victorian authors. His friends often heard him reciting lines from William Shakespeare, Robert Burns, or Algernon Charles Swinburne; and some of his less popular poems in standard English imitated Henry Wadsworth Longfellow, Edgar Allan Poe, Bret Harte, Joaquin Miller, and Alfred Tennyson.[22]

In many ways, Riley's life was an American fairytale. The poet demonstrated that the United States was truly a land of fresh starts. All odds were against his success, for how could anything be expected of a boy from the small town of Greenfield, Indiana, "who cared nothing for school, and deserted it at the first opportunity, to take up a wandering life."[23] He emerged as an example of the self-made man who, in the popular imagination, possessed "neither intellectual brilliance nor unusual physical prowess."[24] In interviews, Riley always said that his persistence and hard work were the most important factors in his eventual success; but there was actually more to the story.

When he left Greenfield to travel across Indiana as an advance man for Doc McCrillus, he freed himself from the weight of the past, from tradition, from family. Going to places where no one knew him, he soon discovered that personal identity was fluid—that it could be redefined. In preindustrial society, the family, the community, and the church provided stable foundations for the definition of selfhood. As society became more mobile, impersonal, and secularized, personal identity seemed to depend less on the social and moral values instilled and internalized in youth. Instead, people learned to change their attitudes and behavior in reaction to the needs and demands of others.

Riley's experiences as an itinerant sign painter and patent medicine show performer turned him into the consummate showman who learned how to manipulate appearances to further himself. He had an indomitable will to overcome obstacles, and used every means he could think of, including tricks and hoaxes, to draw the public's attention and forward his literary career. To promote himself professionally and personally, he was acutely aware that he shifted his psychological stance to fit diverse circumstances. In essence, his concept of selfhood consisted of a series of manipulable social masks. Sometimes he even called his various "selves" by name.[25] As Bottsford once told his sister Mary, Riley was always "an actor first and last."[26] In many ways, his life became a series of performances through which he remade himself.

In his youth, he looked decidedly bohemian, with his flamboyant mustache, shabby Prince Albert coat, trousers that bagged at the knee, a broadbrimmed felt hat, and cane. When older, Riley decided to alter his appearance to be accepted by good society. He became fashionable, polished, and sophisticated. According to the *New York Times,* he was probably "the most fastidious poet in the history of literature": "No Lord Byron soft collars or Edgar Allan Poe flowing ties, or long, uncut hair for him. His clothes are neat and plain and of the latest fashion. His cuffs always protrude from the coat sleeve a precise distance. His shoes shine like a mirror, his cravat looks as though it had never been worn before. And every hair on his head looks as though it knew its own particular groove."[27]

As he rose to prominence, Riley grew to have more and more in common with the cultural and social elite who lived in the United States' major cities rather than with the people with whom he grew up in Greenfield. The wandering, bohemian "painter-poet" operating on the margins of society eventually became the respectable, national literary figure who was accepted in the highest ranks. Although he never moved to New York or Boston, Riley corresponded and became friends with some of the nation's leading literary figures. He also met internationally known artists and statesmen. The poet performed for presidents; the celebrated British actor Henry Irving admired his talents; and John Singer Sargent, best known for his portraits of the rich and famous, painted him.

On the surface, the Hoosier poet seemed to be free of the self-doubts and anxieties that plagued much of modern industrial society at the end of the nineteenth century. He avoided unpleasant subjects in his poems, and those that dealt with death and loss rarely failed to hearten and console. As did many other writers of the period, Riley tempered his realism. In the majority of his works, he followed middle-class standards of propriety that accorded with predominant, middle-class Protestant values. His pen was "as clean as his purpose."[28] The poet intended his writings to uplift his readers by evoking emotions that would call them to high purposes and make them want to be better human beings.[29]

Because the great majority of his literary work expressed a steadfast cheerfulness, his poetry ironically earned him the nickname "Sunny Jim."[30] However, by nature, Riley was pessimistic. According to the poet, he was never happy unless he was perfectly miserable. He thought that he drew disasters to himself and was never quite satisfied with what he accomplished.[31]

When his mother died in 1870, Riley lost the one parent who understood him. Reuben Riley was strict and emotionally unavailable to his children; and, no matter how wealthy and successful he became, the Hoosier poet never felt that he won his acceptance and approval. In his desire to prove that he was worthy of his father's love, Riley often worked himself into a state of nervous prostration. "Seems to me I either burn and flame and glare and glare, or else am sodden ashes," he once told Clara Bottsford in the early 1880s.[32] He was sometimes "blue to desperation." During these periods, he just had to "flee away."[33] Too often, he turned to alcohol in an attempt to escape from his problems.

After he achieved nationwide recognition as a poet and performer, this pattern of behavior continued. Because he thought they would bring him the happiness and inner peace that always seemed to elude him, in his youth, Riley wanted fame and fortune more than anything else. However, when he reached these goals, he soon realized that fame had its own personal costs: "Dad-burn this thing of always belonging to the world at large! What I've always wanted, and at last got, I find is just exactly what I don't want."[34] Instead of relieving his anxieties, when he gained celebrity, they seemed only to multiply because he felt that he had to meet the public's expectations of him both personally and professionally.

Insecure about his fame, Riley worked harder than ever to broaden and retain it. Ironically, his rise to national prominence came through a literary genre that ultimately limited the height of his reputation. Regional writing was the easiest course by which nineteenth-century writers, such as Riley, who had little formal education could establish themselves professionally. Unfortunately, this genre also ensured that his work, by today's standards, earns him only minor status. Following the established form that regional literature took at this time, the majority of Riley's writings consist of short sketches and poems. His only poem of any major length outside this genre, *Flying Islands of the Night*, was a critical failure. None of his works penetrate below the surface of any issues of social gravity, and the emotional range of his poetry is relatively narrow. "[H]e does not rouse us with 'the thunder of the trumpets of the night,' or move us with the deep organs of tragic grief." Instead, the feeling and tone of Riley's poetry is mitigated to a "tender pathos, kindred to his humor."[35]

Moreover, in his literary works, Riley failed to make his rural Indiana village a microcosm of the broader American experience. Many people believed that his pen was "a camera, which truthfully and accurately . . . caught the vivid distinctness of the reflected light of the country cornfields and meadows, and the sweetness, pathos, and humor of rural life"; but the picture he created was only a fictive snapshot.[36] Instead of capturing the larger world within a local framework, his poems depict a static, self-contained world removed from participation in broader national patterns of societal change. In reality, the poet "produced a real-sounding yet deeply fictitious America that was not homogenous yet not radically heterogeneous either and whose diversities were ranged under one group's normative sway."[37]

Riley's poetry was part of a literary genre that recognized the plurality of America without acknowledging the foreign ethnic groups associated with modern industrialization. The Hoosier poet attempted to recapture a time and place when life seemed more genuine and authentic. Much of Riley's work expressed his own persistent desire to free himself from paralyzing self-doubt and anxiety which he perceived to be caused by the technological advance and material progress of modern society. In his dialect poems, he restored the relative homogeneity of the rural village and idealized life on the farm. By avoiding the cultural anxieties of the upper and middle classes instead of confronting them, Riley's writings represented an escape for his nineteenth-century readers from real threats to the white Anglo-Saxon Protestant domination of American society.

Although he would have liked to have written serious verse in standard English, Riley continued to compose dialect poetry because his audiences demanded it of him and the literary critics judged these works to be his best. This fact put Riley into a double bind. He could not risk displeasing his readers and losing their favor, but his status as a regional poet lessened his ability to be considered as a great classic artist. In the end, he chose to continue to be a bestselling author:

> I would rather have the assurance that I had pleased the rank and file of the people, the common run, than to please all the erudites in the world. The good Father of us all made the world for the generality of mankind, for the great consensus, and not for the few.[38]

At the same time, he was never quite satisfied with his literary achievement.[39] The Hoosier poet was more prescient about what his ultimate position in the world of letters might be than were many of his contemporaries who predicted that his "simple, heartfelt poetry would one day stand at the head of American classics."[40]

At the turn of the century, Riley was accepted as a poet with high literary prestige. Students in classrooms on the prairie and in the Ivy League read Riley poems, and leading critics of the period held him in high regard. For many members of the literati, his works exemplified the American experience. They captured the essence of what they thought was a characteristically American small-town, rural way of life and expressed fundamental values rooted in a Jeffersonian vision of an agrarian polity. Denying growing diversity, critics presumed these values were held by the majority of the nation.

Riley's unprecedented popularity as a poet alone led many critics and authors at the turn of the century to believe that he would forever retain a place in the American literary canon. "Perhaps no one except his publishers, taught by experience how hard it is to sell poetry," a *New York Sun* reporter once said, "is fully alive to the extraordinary success of Mr. Riley from a commercial point of view."[41] His writings reached an even wider audience than those of either

Whittier or Longfellow; and booksellers made the comment that there was a greater demand for his poems than for the works of any other one poet, living or dead.[42] In exploring the commercial development of the publishing industry in the United States following the Civil War, scholars have assumed that poetry was always a literary genre that attracted only highly educated readers who were members of the social elite.[43] As a poet, Riley is exceptional because he had such a broad appeal. Like many writers of fiction, who like him were driven by a need for money, he kept his eye on the demands of the popular market and succeeded in finding a mass audience. He achieved his wealth and fame by becoming an exponent of small-town traditions and virtues at a time of explosive industrial and commercial change. Ironically, he did this with the aid of modern consumer marketing techniques.

In the process, the Hoosier poet became a national celebrity. Along with his publishers and managers, Riley ably promoted his name and image until his face and figure were known almost everywhere. When he was made a literary star, the individuals who profited from his celebrity overlooked his frailties and protected him. People like Bobbs and Dickey helped him to create his Hoosier persona to maximize their returns on their investment in him. This creative management of his reputation and image in many ways anticipated Hollywood.

Because he "added luster to the reputation of the state," Indiana's political and economic leaders also stood by Riley "through thick and thin."[44] On a conscious or unconscious level, his poetry diverted attention from the real agents of cultural change, such as urbanization and industrialization. He provided Indiana a picture of calm, stability, and assurance, at a time when his contemporaries in the Hoosier state were Eugene V. Debs and Theodore Dreiser. The rural environment Riley depicted was not only free from a potentially unruly mob of lower-class immigrants who could with their ideas poison the entire pool of urban American workers but also lacked agents of corruption that threatened society from within. This conception of the region contributed greatly to the public's demand for Riley's poetry and helps to explain why he was embraced by the middle class and upper middle class establishment.

By the time of his death, in his home state, Riley had reached a status approaching sainthood. He had become Indiana's ambassador to the rest of the United States and, for that matter, to the rest of the English-speaking world. For this reason, Riley's tomb stands at the highest point in the city of Indianapolis; and other landmarks, including his birthplace in Greenfield, serve to help remind the state's citizens of his legacy. With his gift to the Indianapolis–Marion County Public Library, he revealed how important he thought it was that future generations of children have free access to the world of books.

Most notably, in 1921, a stalwart group of Riley's friends came together to establish a lasting memorial in his name. In the minds of these men, the poet's work depicted more than just a sense of Indiana's cultural identity. One of his most enduring subjects was the world of the child. Riley said that he gave "real children" a voice—not the children of the privileged in society, but common, ordinary children who often struggled to survive in the midst of overwhelming poverty.[45] After discussing several options for their memorial to the poet, the incorporators of this association responded to a new consciousness that arose in Indiana and across the nation at the end of the nineteenth century about the state of the health of the children whom Riley described.

With the contributions of more than forty-four thousand Hoosiers, the James Whitcomb Riley Memorial Association built and continues to support the state's only children's hospital, at the Indiana University Medical Center. In 1954, the Association's commitment to the welfare of children expanded when it established Camp Riley for Youth with Physical Disabilities at Bradford Woods, an Indiana University camping and outdoor recreational facility located just south of Indianapolis. In addition, this organization owns the poet's Lockerbie Street home and maintains it as a museum. Riley's Indianapolis residence has gained wide recognition as a fine example of Victorian preservation; and, because of the Association's efforts, Riley Hospital and Camp Riley have become fine facilities through which thousands of lives have been saved and thousands of physically disabled youth have returned home to become productive members of society. Therefore, the poet's legacy is unique because of what his name symbolizes for the children of his home state.

In a larger context, although his image has faded, Riley still touches important aspects of the American psyche. His poetry sets Midwesterners, and especially Hoosiers, apart from Southerners and Easterners, defends their regional culture, and gives them their own identity. His verse describes sturdy pioneer ancestors who, in the face of many hardships, brought civilization to the frontier. This pioneer type, whose common sense and wisdom Riley elevated over big-city sophistication, continues to help define the way these early settlers' descendants think about themselves. He upheld their love of home and country and celebrated their genuine goodness, natural piety, primitive vigor, and rugged individualism. Furthermore, Riley's underlying messages speak to a public longing for what it perceives to have been a simpler, more moral past. Today, people are still searching to recapture this fictional, golden world where individuals did not experience modern anxieties and where traditional virtues and values always stood firm.

Abbreviations and Short Title List

Primary Sources

(Repositories abbreviated in the text)

CSmH   The Henry E. Huntington Library, San Marino, California

In   Indiana Division, Indiana State Library, Indianapolis
                    L135 James Whitcomb Riley Collection
                    L123 Benjamin Stratton Parker Collection

In-Ar   Indiana State Archives, Indiana Commission on Public Records, Indianapolis

InHi   Indiana Historical Society, Indianapolis
                    M98 William H. English Collection
                    M240 James Whitcomb Riley Collection
                    M628 Edmund H. Eitel Collection
                    M660 Indianapolis/Marion County Public Library James
                          Whitcomb Riley Collection

InU-Li   The Lilly Library, Indiana University, Bloomington
            Manuscripts:
                    Appleton Century Mss.: Appleton-Century Publishing
                          Company
                    Bobbs-Merrill Mss.: Bobbs-Merrill Publishing Co.
                    Bottsford Mss.: Correspondence, James Whitcomb Riley
                        to Clara Louise Bottsford

Brunn. Mss.: Correspondence, James Whitcomb Riley
to Elizabeth D. Kahle

Callahan Mss.: Correspondence, James Whitcomb Riley
and Lillian Callahan Richards

Dickey Mss.: Papers and letters of John Marcus Dickey

Evans Mss.: Papers and letters of Walter E. Evans,
employee of Bobbs-Merrill Co.

Fairbanks Mss.: Papers of Charles Warren Fairbanks

Hitt Mss.: Papers and letters of George Cooper Hitt

Holstein Mss.: Correspondence, James Whitcomb Riley
and Charles and Magdelena Holstein

Jameson, M., Mss.: Correspondence, James Whitcomb
Riley and Mary Booth Tarkington
Jameson and Newton Booth
Tarkington

Macy Mss.: Correspondence, Albert William Macy and
David Laurence Chambers

Mitchell Mss.: Letters relating to James Whitcomb Riley
and his family by Minnie Belle Mitchell,
John Fowler Mitchell, and Elsie D.
Mitchell

Payne, L. Mss.: Papers of Lesley Payne

Riley Mss.: Correspondence and papers of James
Whitcomb Riley

Riley II. Mss.: Correspondence, James Whitcomb Riley
and Meredith Nicholson

Riley III. Mss.: Correspondence and papers of James
Whitcomb Riley

Riley IV. Mss.: Manuscripts by or about James
Whitcomb Riley

Riley V. Mss.: Correspondence and writings of James
Whitcomb Riley

Riley VI. Mss.: Transcripts of letters of James Whitcomb
Riley, collected by John Marcus Dickey

Printed Materials:

LPS2700: Miscellaneous printed materials regarding
James Whitcomb Riley

RMA   James Whitcomb Riley Memorial Association, Indianapolis.
Misc. materials regarding James Whitcomb Riley and his family

Secondary Sources

Biographical Edition	James Whitcomb Riley, *The Complete Works of James Whitcomb Riley*, biographical edition, Edmund H. Eitel, ed., 6 vols. (Indianapolis: Bobbs-Merrill Co., 1913)
Complete Works	James Whitcomb Riley, *The Complete Works of James Whitcomb Riley,* memorial edition, 10 vols. (New York: P. F. Collier & Son Company, 1916)
Crowder	Richard Crowder, *Those Innocent Years: The Legacy and Inheritance of a Hero of the Victorian Era, James Whitcomb Riley* (Indianapolis: Bobbs-Merrill Co., 1957)
Dickey—*Maturity*	Marcus Dickey, *The Maturity of James Whitcomb Riley* (Indianapolis: Bobbs-Merrill Co., 1922)
Dickey—*Youth*	Marcus Dickey, *The Youth of James Whitcomb Riley* (Indianapolis: Bobbs-Merrill Co., 1919)
Mitchell	Minnie Belle Mitchell, *James Whitcomb Riley As I Knew Him* (Greenfield, Indiana: The Old Swimmin' Hole Press, 1949)
Phelps	William Lyon Phelps, ed., *Letters of James Whitcomb Riley* (Indianapolis: Bobbs-Merrill Co., 1930)
Russo	Anthony J. Russo and Dorothy R. Russo, *A Bibliography of James Whitcomb Riley* (Indianapolis: Indiana Historical Society, 1944)

Notes

Preface

1. Booth Tarkington, "Mr. Riley," *Collier's* 58 (30 Dec. 1916): 4.

Prologue

1. *Indianapolis Star,* 23 July 1916; *Indianapolis News,* 24 July 1916.

2. Ibid.; "Entire State Pays Tribute to Riley," *Indianapolis Star,* 7 Oct. 1911; "Riley Day Souvenir Section," *Indianapolis Star,* 8 Oct. 1915; "Riley Day Celebration Will Be Nation Wide," *Indianapolis News,* 4 Oct. 1915.

3. "Thousands Expected to Pass Riley Bier," *Indianapolis Star,* 24 July 1916, p. 1.

4. "Tears Fall as Throngs View Face," *Indianapolis Star,* 25 July 1916; "Silent Tribute Arranged to Show Love of People for Indiana's Poet," *Indianapolis News,* 24 July 1916; "Lockerbie Bids Good-by to the Poet," *Indianapolis News,* 25 July 1916.

5. Ibid.

6. "Memorial to Riley Is Being Discussed," *Indianapolis News,* 26 July 1916. For a history of the Riley Memorial Association see Elizabeth J. Van Allen and Omer H. Foust, *Keeping the Dream* (Indianapolis: Riley Memorial Association, 1996).

7. Martin Ridge, "Introduction," in Frederick Jackson Turner, *History, Frontier, and Section, Three Essays* (Albuquerque: University of New Mexico Press, 1993), pp. 1–2, 11–13; H. W. Brands, *The Reckless Decade: America in the 1890s* (New York: St. Martin's Press, 1995), pp. 1–2, 20–23; Paul Boyer, *Urban Masses and Moral Order in America, 1820–1920* (Cambridge: Harvard University Press, 1978), pp. 121–22; Alan Trachtenberg, *The Incorporation of America: Culture and Society in the Gilded Age* (New York: Hill and Wang, 1982), pp. 14–15; Larzer Ziff, *The American 1890s* (New York: Viking Press, 1966), pp. 21–22; Andrew R. L. Cayton and Fredricka J. Teute, eds., *Contact Points: American Frontiers from the Mohawk Valley to the Mississippi* (Chapel Hill: University of North Carolina Press, 1998).

8. Brands, *The Reckless Decade,* pp. 1–2, 41; Trachtenberg, *The Incorporation of America,* pp. 36–37.

9. John Hay to James Whitcomb Riley (hereafter JWR), 15 Dec. 1890, Riley Mss., InU-Li; "Not without Honor," *Indianapolis News,* 9 Jan. 1892; [enclosure], William Dean Howells to John Marcus Dickey, 2 Feb. 1918, Dickey Mss., InU-Li.

10. Howells, "The New Poetry" in *North American Review* 168 (May 1899): 588.

11. Ibid.

12. Howells quoted in Trachtenberg, *The Incorporation of America,* p. 189.

13. Trachtenberg, *The Incorporation of America,* pp. 186, 191–92; Ziff, *The American 1890s,* p. 31; "An Evening with a Poet, James Whitcomb Riley, the 'Hoosier Poet,' Lectures at the Exchange Hall," *Kansas City Journal,* 2 Feb. 1884.

14. "Riley Talks Entertainingly," *Dayton Daily News,* 23 Feb. 1901; "The Genial Hoosier," *Detroit Free Press,* 8 Mar. 1893.

15. "Riley Talks Entertainingly."

16. Howells quoted in Ziff, *The American 1890s,* p. 31.

17. Eugene V. Debs, "Riley, The Hoosier Poet and Interpreter," in *Pastels of Men* (New York: Pearsons 25¢ Library, 1919), p. 16.

18. Clara E. Laughlin to JWR, 24 June 1897, Riley Mss., InU-Li.

19. Henry Augustin Beers, "The Singer of the Old Swimmin' Hole" in *The Connecticut Wits and Other Essays* (New Haven: Yale University Press, 1920), p. 31. Beers omitted the hyphen after "Swimmin'" in his title.

20. Ibid., pp. 33–34.

21. Ibid., p. 32.

22. Walt Whitman, "One's-Self I Sing," *Leaves of Grass* (New York: Vintage Books/Library of America, 1992), p. 165.

23. Ibid.; David Reynolds, *Walt Whitman's America: A Cultural Biography* (New York: Alfred A. Knopf, 1995), pp. 50–51, 326–27, 467–68; Ziff, *The American 1890s,* p. 12.

24. Beers, "The Singer of the Old Swimmin' Hole," pp. 34–35.

25. Frederick L. Paxson quoted in Clifton J. Phillips, *Indiana in Transition: The Emergence of an Industrial Commonwealth, 1880–1920* (Indianapolis: Indiana Historical Society, 1968), p. 362.

26. Ibid.

27. Phillips, *Indiana in Transition,* pp. 361–62; John Bodnar, "Introduction: Ethnic History in America and Indiana," in Robert M. Taylor and Connie McBierney, eds., *Peopling Indiana: The Ethnic Experience* (Indianapolis: Indiana Historical Society, 1996), p. 5.

28. Ronald Weber, *The Midwestern Ascendancy in American Writing* (Bloomington: Indiana University Press, 1987), p. 15.

29. Arthur Shumaker, *A History of Indiana Literature, With Emphasis on the Authors of Imaginative Works Who Commenced Writing Prior to World War II* (Indianapolis: Indiana Historical Society, 1962), pp. 4–5.

30. Glenway Wescott quoted in Weber, *The Midwestern Ascendancy in American Writing,* p. 16.

31. JWR to E. S. Martin, 22 May 1883, Riley Mss., InU-Li.

32. JWR to Madison Julius Cawein, 23 Oct. 1891, L 135, In.

33. "The Hoosier Poet, James Whitcomb Riley's Views on American Poetry," *Marlborough Express,* 3 Dec. 1888.

34. T. C. Steele to JWR, Munich, 6 June 1884, Riley Mss., In-Li.

35. "An Evening with a Poet, James Whitcomb Riley, the 'Hoosier Poet,' Lectures at the Exchange Hall"; "Mr. Riley in Town," *Fort Wayne Sentinel,* 16 May 1899.

36. Ibid.; "Dave Martin as an Uncle, James W. Riley Talks of His Boyhood," *Oakland Weekly Times,* 15 Dec. 1892.

37. "An Evening with a Poet, James Whitcomb Riley, the 'Hoosier Poet,' Lectures at the Exchange Hall"; "Mr. Riley in Town."

38. "Hoosier Poet Comes to Town," *Pittsburgh Chronicle Telegraph,* 26 Oct. 1903; "Mr. Riley Here," *Richmond Palladium,* 15 May 1899; "Dialect in Its Purity," *Chicago Morning News,* 1 Nov. 1886.

39. JWR to Thomas Wentworth Higginson, 9 Dec. 1891, L 135, In.

40. JWR to May L. Dodds, 19 Aug. 1896, Riley Mss., InU-Li; William Dudley Foulke, "Indianapolis Now the Hub from Which American Literature Radiates," *Indianapolis Star,* 9 Oct. 1915; "Talk with Hoosier Poet," *Chicago Herald Times,* 22 Oct. 1900.

41. "Talk with Hoosier Poet."

42. "American Poets Snubbed," *Pittsburgh Dispatch,* 1 Jan. 1892; "An American Poet," *Washington, D.C. Evening News,* 8 Mar. 1893; Erasmus Wilson, "The Quiet Observer," *Pittsburgh Commercial Gazette,* 28 June 1898; "A Child-World," *Literary World,* 3 June 1897; "Riley's Recent Poems," *Memphis Commercial,* 27 Oct. 1892; "James Whitcomb Riley's Verse, *Green Fields and Running Brooks," New York Times,* 30 Jan. 1893.

43. Ambrose Bierce, "Prattle," *San Francisco Examiner,* 17 Dec. 1892.

44. Ibid.; "Mr. Perry's Address, Editor of Atlantic Monthly Speaks at Butler College," *Indianapolis Sentinel,* 8 June 1901.

45. Weber, *The Midwestern Ascendancy in American Writing,* p. 11.

46. "Talk with Hoosier Poet."

47. "A Chat with Whitcomb Riley," *Chicago Herald,* 17 Feb. 1888; "Dana and Riley," *Milwaukee Sentinel,* 25 July 1888.

48. "Talk with Hoosier Poet"; Trachtenberg, *The Incorporation of America,* p. 194.

49. "Talk with Hoosier Poet"; "Has No Favorite Book or Poem," *Lincoln Daily Star,* 4 Dec. 1903.

50. Ibid.

51. "Talk with Hoosier Poet"; "Hoosier Poet Comes to Town."

52. "Mr. Riley Here," *Richmond Palladium,* 15 May 1899; Trachtenberg, *The Incorporation of America,* pp. 194–95.

53. Thomas Strychacz, *Modernism, Mass Culture, and Professionalism* (New York: Cambridge University Press, 1993), p. 11.

54. "Mr. Riley in Town."

55. Ibid.

56. Rachel Bowlby, *Just Looking: Consumer Culture in Dreiser, Gissing and Zola* (New York: Methuen, 1985), p. 9.

57. "A Chat with the Poet Riley," *Los Angeles Express,* 5 Dec. 1892.

58. "Talk with Hoosier Poet."

59. JWR to Dodds, 19 Aug. 1896; "Riley Waited for Mood; Humor Took Odd Turns," *Indianapolis News,* 24 July 1916.

60. Attorney General Richard Olney quoted in Boyer, *Urban Masses and Moral Order in America,* p. 127; "Riley Waited for Mood."

61. "Riley Waited for Mood."

62. "Mr. Riley's New Book," *Indianapolis News,* 6 Oct. 1894.

63. Whitman, *Leaves of Grass* [1855], p. 26; Reynolds, *Walt Whitman's America,* pp. 5, 518, 538, 587–89; Beers, "The Singer of the Old Swimmin' Hole," p. 33; "Riley Day Celebration Will Be Nation Wide," *Indianapolis News,* 4 Oct. 1915.

64. *Indiana, The Chronicle of Your State in Pictures in Connection with Indiana Centennial,* L808 Motion Picture, Indiana Historical Commission, In-Ar.

65. Dickey to JWR, 4 Mar. 1904, Riley Mss., InU-Li.

1. *A Child-World*

1. JWR to Edith M. Thomas, 10 Aug. 1903, Riley Mss., InU-Li.

2. Thomas to JWR, 3 Sept. 1903, Riley Mss., InU-Li.

3. JWR to Thomas, 18 Sept. 1903, Riley Mss., InU-Li.

4. Emma Lou Thornbrough, *Indiana in the Civil War Era, 1850–1880* (Indianapolis: Indiana Historical Society, 1966), p. 362; Phillips, *Indiana in Transition*, pp. 135, 324, 339.

5. JWR to Thomas, 18 Sept. 1903, Riley Mss., InU-Li.

6. JWR to J. N. Matthews, 16 Mar. 1891, Riley Mss., InU-Li.

7. "Dave Martin as an Uncle, James W. Riley Talks of His Boyhood"; George M. Anderson, "The Fires That Feed Genius," *Success* (Feb. 1901): 617.

8. Russo, p. 66.

9. Lydia Hoyt Farmer, "Flashes from Literature," *Boston Ideas,* 2 Jan. 1897.

10. Ibid. Although *A Child-World* can be read as one continuous poem, it is actually divided into a number of individual poems that function as chapters.

11. JWR, "The Good, Old-Fashioned People," *Complete Works,* VIII: 2068–69; JWR quoted in Dickey, "Memories of James Whitcomb Riley," n.d., unpublished manuscript, p. 16, Dickey Mss., InU-Li.

12. Phelps, p. 207.

13. [enclosure], Howells to Dickey, 2 Feb. 1918, Dickey Mss., InU-Li.

14. Ibid.; Weber, *The Midwestern Ascendancy in American Writing*, p. 5.

15. [enclosure], Howells to Dickey, 2 Feb. 1918; Beers, "The Singer of the Old Swimmin' Hole," pp. 34–35; Priscilla Ferguson Clement, *Growing Pains: Children in the Industrial Age, 1850–1890* (New York: Twayene, 1997), p. 1.

16. The Rileys moved into their expanded home sometime between January and September 1854. The *Family Friend,* a newspaper then published in Greenfield, stated in the issue of 6 Sept. 1854 that twenty-six new homes had been completed in the town since January of that year, and the Rileys' was among them (*Family Friend,* 6 Sept. 1854). JWR, "The Child-World," *Complete Works,* VII: 1711–1716. "The Child-World" forms the introduction to the volume, *A Child-World. A Child-World* appears in its entirety at the beginning of this volume of this edition of *Complete Works* (VII: 1710–1841); records copied from the Riley Family Bible, RMA. Clement, *Growing Pains,* p. 64.

17. Material on Reuben A. Riley, n.d., Folder 3, M628, InHi; John H. Binford, *History of Hancock County, Indiana, From Its Earliest Settlement by the Pale Face in 1818 down to 1882* (Greenfield, Ind.: King & Binford, 1882), pp. 25–27, 172; Dickey—*Youth,* pp. 14–15; Crowder, pp. 24–25; Mitchell, p. 14.

18. Binford, *History of Hancock County, Indiana,* pp. 26–28; Crowder, p. 24.

19. Binford, *History of Hancock County, Indiana,* p. 181; JWR, "The Child-World."

20. JWR, "The Child-World," *Complete Works,* VII: 1711.

21. Ibid., VII: 1711–12.

22. JWR, "The Old Home-Folks," *Complete Works,* VII: 1726.

23. Ibid.

24. JWR, "The Child-World," *Complete Works,* VII: 1712–13.

25. Ibid.

26. Ibid., VII: 1713–15.

27. JWR, "The Old Home-Folks," *Complete Works,* VII: 1726–27.

28. Ibid., VII: 1724, 1726.

29. Ibid., VII: 1717; JWR to John Riley, 12 Feb. 1896, Riley Mss. IV, InU-Li. Records copied from the Riley Family Bible, n.d., RMA. Martha Celestia was born in Greenfield on 21 Feb. 1847. The family Bible record states that she died of "scarletina" on 4 Sept. 1851.

30. JWR, "The Old Home-Folks," *Complete Works,* VII: 1717; "D. M. Bradbury writes," Fall 1916, M660, InHi; JWR to John Riley, [Spring 1872], 14 May 1872, M660, InHi; JWR to Elizabeth D. Kahle, 6 May 1879, Brunn Mss., InU-Li; Mitchell, p. 33.

31. JWR, "The Old Home-Folks," *Complete Works,* VII: 1718–20.

32. Ibid., 7: 1720; Elva May (Riley) Eitel to JWR, 26 Dec. 1903, Riley Mss., InU-Li.

33. JWR, "The Old Home-Folks," *Complete Works.* VII: 1721; Mitchell, pp. 36–37; John Riley to JWR, 15 Mar. 1896; Lesley Payne to Governor Roger D. Branigan, 20 July 1967 (copy), RMA.

34. JWR, "The Old Home-Folks," *Complete Works,* VII: 1721–22; Mitchell, pp. 34–35.

35. JWR, *Complete Works,* VII: 1764–1839; John Riley to JWR, 15 Mar. 1896; Dickey, Interview with Almon Keefer, 20 June 1913, M628, InHi; Lydia Hoyt Farmer, "Flashes from Literature."

36. JWR, "The Old Home-Folks," *Complete Works,* VII: 1717.

37. Marianne W. McKinney, "Performing Arts," in David J. Bodenhamer and Robert G. Barrows, eds., *Encyclopedia of Indianapolis* (Bloomington: Indiana University Press, 1994), pp. 143, 149.

38. JWR, "The Child-World," *Complete Works,* VII: 1712; Binford, *History of Hancock County, Indiana,* p. 27. The danger of malaria was greatly reduced when these wetlands were later drained. Early settlers considered the swamp and marsh land around Greenfield almost worthless. When they were drained, they were found to be the most productive agriculturally.

39. JWR, *Complete Works,* X: 2790–92; JWR, "Our Little Girl," *Complete Works,* I: 138; JWR, "When Our Baby Died," *Complete Works,* II: 471; JWR, "The Little White Hearse," *Complete Works,* IV: 890.

40. Clement, *Growing Pains,* p. 80; Samuel H. Preston and Michael R. Haines, *Fatal Years: Child Mortality in Late Nineteenth-Century America* (Princeton: Princeton University Press, 1991), pp. 3–6.

41. Elliott West, *Growing Up with the Country: Childhood on the Far Western Frontier* (Albuquerque: University of New Mexico Press, 1989), p. 232.

42. Binford, *History of Hancock County, Indiana,* pp. 41, 180–81, 184.

43. Ibid., pp. 180–82.

44. Thornbrough, *Indiana in the Civil War Era,* pp. 332–33.

45. Ibid., pp. 181, 185; R. A. Riley to "Dear Brother," 6 Apr. 1856, M628, InHi.

46. Ibid.

47. "Little Orphant Annie," *Complete Works,* V: 1169; "The Raggedy Man," "Our Hired Girl," *Complete Works,* VI: 1458, 1462; "The Hired Man and Floretty," *Complete Works,* VII: 1757; "The Hired Man's Faith in Children," "The Hired Man's Dog Story," "The Raggedy Man on Children," "'Lizabeth-Ann on Bakin'-Day," *Complete Works,* VIII: 1462, 1968, 2222, 2236, 2237. William R. Hough (Riley's cousin) confirmed in his discussions with Edmund Eitel (Riley's nephew) that the Rileys usually employed

hired help (interview with Judge Willliam R. Hough, 30 July 1914, M628, InHi). John Riley listed Mary Loehr, Lizzie Damanschitt, Mary Walsh, Jane Sturk, Emma Corson, and War Barnett as some of the domestics who served at one time or another in the Riley home (John Riley to JWR, 15 Mar. 1896).

48. Clement, *Growing Pains,* p. 126.

49. "The Old Home-Folks," *Complete Works,* VII: 1722–23.

50. Ibid.; John A. Riley to JWR, 23 Feb. 1896, Riley Mss., InU-Li.

51. Hamlin Garland, "Real Conversations.—IV. A Dialogue Between James Whitcomb Riley and Hamlin Garland," *McClure's Magazine* 2 (Feb. 1894): 231; "His Rhymes," *Cleveland Leader,* 4 Jan. 1898; JWR to Joe S. Riley, 30 Dec. 1895, Riley VI. Mss., InU-Li.

52. Ibid.; Edmund Eitel to William C. Bobbs, 18 June 1912, M628, InHi.

53. Index of Ancestry, M628, InHi; Holman to Edmund Eitel, 1 Oct. 1914, M628, InHi; Holman to Eitel, 7 Oct. 1914, 17 Mar. 1915; Holman to Maude M. Wells, 24 Feb. 1915; M628, InHi.

54. Index of Ancestry, M628, InHi; Holman to Edmund Eitel, 1 Oct. 1914, M628, InHi; Holman to Eitel, 7 Oct. 1914, 17 Mar. 1915, M628, InHi.

55. Interview with Joe S. Riley, 11 Aug. 1914, M628, InHi; Index of Ancestry, M628, InHi. Information on John Slick, Folder 14, M628, InHi; John Slick Riley to Grand Nephew [Edmund Eitel], 8 May 1911, M628, InHi.

56. Notes by himself—R. A. Riley, n.d., M628, InHi; John Slick Riley [Document Signed], n.d., M628, InHi; J. S. Riley to Dickey, 10 Dec. 1901, Dickey Mss., InU-Li. Riley's father, Reuben, and his uncle John disagreed about when they moved with their parents to Ohio and Indiana. John said that they left Pennsylvania in 1821 and then moved to Indiana eight years later in 1829. Reuben thought that the family traveled to Ohio in September 1825 and came to Randolph County in 1833.

57. Notes by himself—R. A. Riley, n.d.; Notes on Reuben Riley, n.d.; Interview with Joe S. Riley, 11 Aug. 1914; M628, InHi. Margaret Riley's funeral notice states that she passed away at the home of her son Dr. A. J. Riley of Muncie, Indiana (Funeral Notice of Mrs. Margaret Slick Riley, M628, InHi). John Slick Riley attended medical school at Mississippi State University (John Slick Riley [Document Signed], n.d.; "Pilot Point Has Practicing Physician More Than One Hundred Years Old," *Dallas Morning News,* 21 Dec. 1913). Jacob Piatt Dunn, *Greater Indianapolis: The History, the Industries, the Institutions and the People of a City of Homes,* 2 vols. (Chicago: Lewis Publishing Co., 1910) 2: 1211.

58. Ibid.; Interview with JWR, 29 July 1914, M628, InHi; "The Old Home-Folks," *Complete Works,* VII: 1718–19.

59. John Riley to JWR, 15 Mar. 1896, Riley Mss., InU-Li.

60. Edmund Eitel to Mrs. Charles E. Gage, 22 Aug. 1913; Notes on conversations with Mr. [Samuel] Mendenhall, Mr. Thornburg, Mrs. Willard Haynes, n.d., Dickey Mss., InU-Li.

61. Ibid.; Edmund Eitel to Philip Kabel, 20 Dec. 1913, M628, InHi; Notes collected by Philip Kabel of Winchester, Ind., n.d., M628, InHi.

62. Ibid.

63. Notes by himself—R. A. Riley, n.d., M628, InHi; Notes collected by Philip Kabel of Winchester, Indiana, n.d., M628, InHi; Notes on conversations with Mr. [Samuel] Mendenhall, Mr. Thornburg, Mrs. Willard Haynes, n.d., Dickey Mss., InU-Li.

64. Notes collected by Philip Kabel of Winchester, Indiana. n.d., M628, InHi. Notes on Elizabeth Marine, n.d.; Records copied from Marine Family Bible; Conversation with Samuel Mendenhall, 13 Dec. 1913; RMA.

65. Genealogist Alfred Holman reported that the French origins of the Marine family were impossible to prove because he could not find the name of the person or persons whe had first emigrated from France (Holman to Edmund Eitel, 26 Aug. 1913, RMA). Jonathon and Mary Charles Marine, Riley's great-grandparents, were Quakers who married in England and emigrated to Maryland (Notes on Jonathon Marine; Holman to Eitel, 11 Sept. 1913; RMA).

66. Notes on Marine Family, M628, InHi; Records copied from Marine Family Bible, Elizabeth Peelle to Edmund Eitel, 14 Apr. 1913, RMA.

67. Interview with Anna Jane Hopkins Dustman, 3 May 1915, History Files, RMA; Notes gathered by Philip Kabel on Elizabeth Marine, n.d., History Files, RMA; *History of Wayne County*, 2 vols. (Chicago: Inter-State Publishing, 1884), II: 412–13.

68. Auto-Ride with Riley, 9 Sept. 1913, History Files, RMA.

69. Clement, *Growing Pains*, p. 41.

70. Alice Thornburg to Edmund Eitel, 12 July 1913, History Files, RMA.

71. Ibid.; W. P. Marine to Edmund Eitel, 15 Feb. 1912; Interview with Anna Jane Hopkins Dustman, 3 May 1915; RMA; Notes on the Marine Family, n.d., M628, InHi.

72. Garland, "Real Conversations," p. 231; Notes on the Marine Family, n.d., M628, InHi.

73. JWR, "The Old Home-Folks," *Complete Works*, VII: 1723.

74. Clement, *Growing Pains*, pp. 38–39.

75. Ibid., With Mr. Riley, 1 Aug. 1914, M628, InHi; [William R.] Hough, The Boy's Mother, M660, unpublished mss., n.d., InHi.

76. Interview with William R. Hough, 30 July 1914, Folder 3, M628, InHi; Dickey, Interview with Almon Keefer, 20 June 1913, Folder 14, M628, InHi; Clement, *Growing Pains*, p. 39.

77. "A Noble Character, Death of Capt. R. A. Riley, Father of James Whitcomb Riley," *Indianapolis Journal*, 7 Dec. 1893; Dickey, Interview with Almon Keefer, 20 June 1913, Folder 14, M628, InHi; The Boy's Mother, by Judge Hough, n.d., M660, InHi; Margaret Decker to Edmund Eitel, 4 Jan. [?], M660, InHi. For examples of Elizabeth Marine Riley's poems see Riley Mss., InU-Li.

78. Clement, *Growing Pains*, p. 39.

79. The Boy's Mother, by Judge Hough, n.d., M660, InHi.

80. Notes by himself—R. A. Riley, n.d., M628, InHi; R. A. Riley, Folder 3, Box 69, M98, InHi.

81. Ibid; Justin E. Walsh, *A Biographical Directory of the Indiana General Assembly*, 2 vols. (Indianapolis, Indiana: Select Committee on the Centennial History of the Indiana General Assembly, 1984), 1: 331; Reynolds, *Walt Whitman's America*, pp. 66–68.

82. Entries for 1, 18, 23 Dec. 1845; 16 Jan. 1846, *Journal of the House of Representatives of the State of Indiana, 30th Session of the General Assembly* (Indianapolis, 1845); Entries for 4, 5, 7, 12, 20 Dec. 1848; 9, 13, 16 Jan. 1849, *Journal of the House of Representatives of the State of Indiana, 33rd Session of the General Assembly* (Indianapolis, 1849); Binford, *History of Hancock County, Indiana*, p. 384; Walsh, *A Biographical Directory of the Indiana General Assembly*, 1: 331; R. A. Riley, Folder 3, Box 69, M98, InHi; Notes by himself—R. A. Riley, n.d., M628, InHi.

83. "A Noble Character"; R. A. Riley to "Dear Brother," 6 Apr. 1856.

84. Lesley Payne to Governor Roger D. Branigan, 20 July 1967; JWR, "The Old Home-Folks," *Complete Works,* VII: 1730; Payne to Branigan. Dickey, Notes on JWR, Nov. 1902, Notes on JWR, n.d., Dickey Mss., InU-Li; Interview with Hough; John Riley to JWR, 15 Mar. 1896.

85. Interview with Hough; Binford, *History of Hancock County, Indiana,* p. 380.

86. Interview with Hough.

87. "A Noble Character."

88. Mildred Stoler, "Insurgent Democrats of Indiana and Illinois in 1854," *Indiana Magazine of History* 33 (Mar. 1937): 12; R. A. Riley to "Dear Brother," 6 Apr. 1856.

89. Ibid.; Charles Zimmerman, "The Origin and Rise of the Republican Party in Indiana from 1854 to 1860," *Indiana Magazine of History* 18 (1917): 219, 228, 235; Thornbrough, *Indiana in the Civil War Era.* pp. 54–66.

90. Stoler, "Insurgent Democrats," p. 7; Carl Fremont Brand, "History of the Know-Nothing Party in Indiana," *Indiana Magazine of History* 18 (1922): 63.

91. Ibid., p. 20–22; Zimmerman, "The Origin and Rise of the Republican Party," p. 234; John A. Riley to JWR, 15 Mar. 1896; Mildred Stoler, "The Democratic Element in the New Republican Party in Indiana," *Indiana Magazine of History* 36 (Sept. 1939): 185–86.

92. Stoler, "The Democratic Element," pp. 186, 188–89, 203; Zimmerman, "The Origin and Rise of the Republican Party," pp. 234, 247; John A. Riley to JWR, 15 Mar. 1896.

93. "A Noble Character"; Stoler, "The Democratic Element," p. 203; Dunn, *Greater Indianapolis,* 2: 1211; "Three Richmonds in the Field!/The Fourth in Embryo!!/ Republicanism Jubilant!!" *Greenfield Sentinel,* 7 Aug. 1857.

94. Ibid., Reynolds, *Walt Whitman's America,* pp. 155–56; Gregory Clark and S. Michael Halloran, "Introduction: Transformations of Public Discourse in Nineteenth-Century America" in Clark and Halloran, eds., *Oratorical Culture in Nineteenth-Century America: Transformation in the Theory and Practice of Rhetoric* (Carbondale: Southern Illinois University Press, 1993), p. 24.

95. Reynolds, *Walt Whitman's America,* pp. 155–56.

96. "James Whitcomb Riley" (promotional brochure) (Indianapolis: Bobbs Merrill, [1900]); "Was Born a Genius," *South Bend Tribune,* 6 Oct. 1900.

97. "Three Richmonds in the Field"; "Two Reports of Capt. Riley's 3-hour Speech," *Indianapolis Sun,* 27 Aug. 1878.

98. "Riley's Chief Ambition," *New Haven Register,* 16 Nov. 1898.

99. "Three Richmonds in the Field"; Muster Rolls of the 8th Regt., In-Ar; R. A. Riley, et al. to Gov. [Oliver P.] Morton, 19 Apr. 1861, Correspondence 8 Regt., Folder A, 16 Apr. 1861–19 July 1865, In-Ar; 8th, History of Regt., Correspondence 8 Regt., Folder C., 21 Apr. 1861–13 July 1865, "A Noble Character."

100. Reuben Riley to Albert Gallatin Porter, 19 Oct. 1862; Reuben Riley to Oliver P. Morton, 8 Dec. 1862, 16 Dec. 1862; R. A. Riley to Adjutant General Noble, 18 May 1863, AG Civil War, Muster Rolls of the 90th Regt (5th Cavalry), Recruits, Correspondence, In-Ar; Payne to Branigan, 20 July 1967.

101. Muster Rolls of the 5th Cavalry, 90th Regiment, In-Ar; History of Company "G" 5th Indiana Cavalry from the 30th day Oct. 1862 to the 1st day of May 1865, Folder 2, Box 187, AG Civil War, In-Ar; Ann Turner, *Guide to Indiana Civil War Manuscripts* (Indianapolis: Indiana Civil War Centennial Commission, 1965), pp. 281–82.

102. Thornbrough, *Indiana in the Civil War Era*, p. 177; R. A. Riley to [Elizabeth Riley], 7 Mar. 1863, M628, InHi; John Riley to JWR, 15 Mar. 1896.

103. JWR, "Where Is Mary Alice Smith?," *Complete Works*, X: 2564–76; Mitchell, pp. 87–90; Calvin Oliver Power, Introduction Explaining Rediscovery of "Little Or-phant Annie" [Mary Alice Smith], [ca. 1917], HM44514, CSmH. Oliver, whose correspondence with Mary Alice Smith appears in this collection, states that Smith told him that she was born in Liberty, Indiana (Union County) in 1850. She also told him that her parents were still alive during the time she lived at the Riley home and that they did not die until after her marriage to John Wesley Gray in 1868. Clement, *Growing Pains*, p. 126.

104. Special Field Orders, No. 114, Headquarters Department of the Ohio, Knoxville, E. Tennessee, 22 Dec. 1863, Box 186, Civil War, Muster Rolls of the 90the Regiment (5th Cavalry), Recruits, Correspondence; History of Company "G" 5th Indiana Cavalry; In-Ar; Walsh, *A Biographical Directory of the Indiana General Assembly*, 1: 331; R. A. Riley to [Elizabeth Riley], 29 Apr. 1864; M628, InHi.

105. "Hoosier Poet Is a Wichita Visitor," *Wichita Daily Beacon*, 8 Dec. 1903.

106. R. A. Riley to [Elizabeth Riley], 21 Sept. 1869, M628, InHi.

107. "Hoosier Poet Is a Wichita Visitor"; "James Whitcomb Riley," *Tacoma News*, 2 Jan. 1893; [John] Marcus Dickey, "What JWR Thought of Farming," *Farm and Fireside* (Oct. 1925): 4.

108. Dickey, Notes on JWR, Nov. 1902, n.d., Dickey Mss., InU-Li; "Dialect in Its Purity," *Chicago Morning News*, 1 Nov. 1886.

109. "Dialect in Its Purity"; R. A. Riley to "Dear Brother," 6 Apr. 1856; Dickey, Notes on JWR, Feb. 1900, Dickey Mss., InU-Li.

110. Interview with Joe S. Riley, 11 July 1914, M660, InHi.

111. Clement, *Growing Pains*, pp. 151–52; Rose Mitchell [Mrs. H. H.] Gregg to Dickey, 14 Apr. 1902, Dickey Mss., InU-Li.

112. JWR, "The Barefoot Boy," *Complete Works*, IV: 915.

113. For examples of just a few of these poems see JWR, "Our Boyhood Haunts," *Complete Works*, VII: 1948; JWR, "Kingry's Mill," *Complete Works*, V: 1210–13; "The Songs of Yesterday," 3: 618–21; and "The Old Swimmin'-Hole," 3: 798. Payne to Branigan, 20 July 1967; Mitchell, pp. 22–23; Jackson Lears, *Fables of Abundance* (New York: Basic Books, 1994), pp. 43–44.

114. JWR, "The Old Home-Folks"; JWR to John Riley, 12 Feb. 1896, Riley IV. Mss., InU-Li; John A. Riley to JWR, 15 Mar. 1896. The letter that Riley wrote to the widow of his friend Edgar Wilson Nye reflects the same ideas (JWR to Mrs. E[dgar] W[ilson] Nye, 10 Mar. 1897, Riley Mss., InU-Li).

115. JWR, "Flying Islands of the Night," *Complete Works*, II: 297–383; JWR, "Away," *Complete Works*, IV: 1001; "The Flying Islands of the Night," *Indianapolis Herald*, 14 Sept. 1878.

116. Clint Hamilton to Edmund Eitel, 14 Apr. [19—], M660, InHi; Mitchell, pp. 54–60.

117. Interview with Anna Jane Hopkins Dustman; JWR, "When We First Played 'Show,'" *Complete Works*, VIII: 1986–88; Mitchell, pp. 56, 67–69.

118. JWR, "When We First Played 'Show.'"

119. John Riley to JWR, 15 Mar. 1896; JWR, "The Old Home-Folks," *Complete Works*, VII: 1736–38; Mitchell, pp. 63–66, 68–69.

120. JWR, "The Old Home-Folks," VII: 1738; Interview with Joe S. Riley; John

Riley to JWR, 15 Mar. 1896 Jacob B. Loehr to Dickey, 9 Apr. 1902, Dickey Mss., InU-Li.

121. John Riley to JWR, 15 Mar. 1896; James B. Townsend to Dickey, 5 Jun 1901, Adelphian Dramatic Club Programs, 28–29 Jan. 1871, scrapbook 2, box 14, PS2700, InU-Li. Riley performed a medley of tunes accompanied on the piano by his friend Nellie Millikan.

122. JWR, "Poetry and Character" [n.p., n.d.]; JWR, "The Drum," *Complete Works,* III: 625; "Your Violin," *Complete Works,* III: 790; "My Fiddle," *Complete Works,* III: 848; "Her Light Guitar," *Complete Works,* IV: 894.

123. John Riley to JWR, 15 Mar. 1896; Dickey, Notes on JWR, n.d., Dickey Mss., InU-Li.

124. Clint Hamilton to Edmund Eitel, 14 Apr. [19—].

125. JWR, "St. Lirriper," *Complete Works,* VII: 1840.

126. Ibid.; JWR, "Christmas Season," *Complete Works,* VIII: 2133; JWR, "God Bless Us Everyone," *Complete Works,* 2: 484; JWR to Joel Chandler Harris, 31 Dec. 1902, Riley VI. Mss., InU-Li; JWR to Louise Chandler Moulton, 14 Apr. 1899, Riley VI. Mss., InU-Li; JWR to Fellow-Pilgrim [Edith M. Thompson], 28 Nov 1907, Riley V. Mss., InU-Li.

127. JWR, *Complete Works,* VII: 1719, 1724, 1728, 1732–33; Crowder, pp. 30–31.

128. Loehr to Dickey, 9 Apr. 1902, Dickey Mss., InU-Li.

129. JWR on school, n.d., M660, InHi; Dickey, Interview with Almon Keefer, Notes on JWR, Apr. 1901, Dickey Mss., InU-Li.

130. Clement, *Growing Pains,* pp. 87–88.

131. Binford, *History of Hancock County, Indiana,* p. 38; Thornbrough, *Indiana in the Civil War Era,* pp. 461–74; Crowder, pp. 31–32.

132. "The Hoosier Poet," *Lafayette Comet,* 8 Nov. 1885; Rose Mitchell [Mrs. H. H.] Gregg to Dickey, 14 Apr. 1902, Dickey Mss., InU-Li; John Riley to JWR, 15 Mar. 1896; Mitchell, p. 45.

133. "The Hoosier Poet."

134. Clement, *Growing Pains,* pp. 90, 92.

135. "The Hoosier Poet."

136. A text of "The Educator," or "The Object Lesson" as Riley also called it, may be found in the *Complete Works,* IX: 2480–84.

137. Roger Galeshore, "JWR and His Children," *Success* (Dec. 1903): 721.

138. "The Youth of JWR," *Boston Evening Transcript,* 8 Nov. 1919; Clement, *Growing Pains,* p. 164.

139. "A Noble Character"; Dickey, Notes on conversation with Judge Offutt, n.d., Dickey Mss., InU-Li; Dickey, Notes on JWR, n.d., Dickey Mss., InU-Li.

140. Interview with Julia Wilson Riley, 20 Jan. 1913, M628, InHi; Payne to Branigan, 20 July 1967.

141. Payne to Branigan, 20 July 1967; *Indianapolis News,* 29 July 1893; Trachtenberg, *The Incorporation of America,* p. 162.

142. Ibid; Interview with Julia Wilson Riley.

143. "A Trio of Funnymen," *Indianapolis Journal,* 17 Nov. 1895.

144. Ibid.

145. Ibid.; Dickey, Interview with Almon Keefer, Notes on JWR, Apr. 1901, Dickey Mss., InU-Li.

146. "A Trio of Funnymen."

147. Clement, *Growing Pains,* p. 38.

148. Ibid.; Mitchell, pp. 70–71. Riley was especially close to Nellie Millikan Cooley, with whom he corresponded until she died in 1878. Thomas Earl Williams holds that Nellie Millikan was the only woman that Riley truly loved (*James Whitcomb Riley: The Poet as Flying Islands of the Night* [Greenfield, Ind.: Coiny Press, 1997], but there is no evidence for this. Millikan married George Cooley and left Greenfield to go with him to Belleville, Illinois. The extant correspondence between Riley and Millikan Cooley suggests no romantic involvement. Millikan seemed to be sisterly in her attitude toward Riley and encouraged him with his work, and in one letter Riley expressed an interest in Clara Louise Bottsford, to whom he later became engaged (George B. and Nellie M. Cooley to JWR, 12–[1]3 Jan. 1877, Riley Mss., InU-Li; Nell Cooley to JWR, 23 Apr. 1877, Riley V. Mss., InU-Li; JWR to Nellie Cooley, 28 Oct. 1877, Riley VI. Mss., InU-Li).

149. Correspondence of the Fifth Cavalry (90th Regiment) of Indiana Volunteers, 26 Aug. 1862, InU-Li; Dickey, Notes on JWR, n.d., Dickey Mss., InU-Li; *In Honor of JWR, A Meeting of the Indiana State Teachers' Association* (Indianapolis: Bobbs-Merrill, 1905), p. 51.

150. *In Honor of JWR, A Meeting of the Indiana State Teachers' Association* (Indianapolis: Bobbs-Merrill, 1905), p. 51; "Was Born a Genius."

151. *In Honor of JWR, A Meeting of the Indiana State Teachers' Association,* p. 51; "Was Born a Genius"; George Ade, "Riley and His Friends," *Saturday Evening Post* 263 (27 Sept. 1930): 141. Sensational dime novels typically "appeared as yellow-covered pamphlets emblazoned with large black lettering and melodramatic woodcuts picturing violent or erotic scenes (Reynolds, *Walt Whitman's America,* p. 204).

152. *In Honor of JWR, A Meeting of the Indiana State Teachers' Association,* p. 51; "Was Born a Genius"; Dickey, Memories of JWR, n.d, p. 25, Dickey Mss., InU-Li. Clement, *Growing Pains,* pp. 92, 94.

153. Mitchell, p. 76; Weekly Report, Jas. W. Riley, signed by John W. Lacey, Riley Mss., InU-Li; Crowder, pp. 48–49; *Hancock Democrat,* 13 Jan. 1870, 20 Jan. 1870, 3 Mar. 1870.

154. "James Whitcomb Riley," *Indianapolis Journal,* 5 Feb. 1892.

155. "Riley," *Portland* [Indiana] *Commercial-Review,* 27 Nov. 1903.

156. Beers, "The Singer of the Old Swimmin' Hole," pp. 36–37.

157. "A Trio of Funnymen"; Interview with Anna Jane Hopkins Dustman.

158. "A Trio of Funnymen"; "Autobiography of a Poet," *Indianapolis Journal,* 5 Jan. 1890.

159. Dickey, Notes on JWR, n.d., Dickey Mss., InU-Li.

160. Minnie Belle Mitchell to Mrs. Jesse Johnson, n.d., Mitchell Mss., InU-Li.

161. JWR, "The Child-World," *Complete Works,* VII: 1711.

162. JWR, "Proem," *Complete Works,* VII: 1710. Italics in original.

163. Beers, "Singer of the Old Swimmin' Hole," pp. 36–37; "The Youth of JWR," *Boston Evening Transcript,* 8 Nov. 1919.

2. In Search of a Voice

1. Garland, "Real Conversations," p. 219; Meredith Nicholson to JWR, 5 Nov. 1894, Riley Mss., InU-Li.

2. Ibid.

3. Ibid., pp. 219, 234.

4. Ibid., p. 222; JWR, "Poetry and Character."

5. E. F. Ware to JWR, 15 June 1891; Meredith Nicholson to JWR, 5 Nov. 1894, Riley Mss., InU-Li; Bierce, "Prattle"; Booth Tarkington, "Mr. Riley," *Collier's* 58 (30 Dec.1916): 4.

6. Garland, "Real Conversations," p. 223; Ella Page Brown Goodson to Dickey, Sterling, Kansas, 16 Nov. 1902; Dickey Mss., InU-Li; "The Poet from Hoosierdom," *Kansas City Times,* 28 Feb. 1892; "Riley and Hilarity," *Lexington Express,* 11 Aug. 1888. (This article represents one of the best examples of a complete misrepresentation of Riley's life during his early career).

7. Garland, "Real Conversations," pp. 223, 234; "Was Born a Genius"; "Riley and Hilarity," *Lexington Transcript,* 11 Aug. 1888; "The Poet and Hoosierdom," *Kansas City Times,* 28 Feb. 1892; Ade, "Riley and His Friends," p. 10.

8. JWR to Milton Crowell, May 1870, Riley Mss., InU-Li; Crowell to Dickey, 23 Nov. 1902, Dickey Mss., InU-Li.

9. Irvin Walker to JWR, 14 Sept. 1871, Riley Mss., InU-Li.

10. Dickey, Riley's Words and Incidents, n.d., Dickey Mss., InU-Li; Wm. Hammel to Crowell, 29 May 1870, Riley Mss., InU-Li.

11. JWR, "I Am Sitting Now and Sighing," 23 Sept. 1870, [unpublished poetry] Riley III. Mss., InU-Li.

12. JWR to John Riley, 14 [July] 1871, M660, InHi; John Riley to JWR, 23 Feb. 1896, Riley Mss., InU-Li.

13. JWR to John Riley, 14 [July] 1871.

14. JWR to Mellie Ryan, 25 Nov. 1870, Riley VI. Mss., InU-Li.

15. Ibid.; JWR to Ryan, 8 Dec. 1870, Riley VI. Mss., InU-Li.

16. JWR to Ryan, 25 Nov. 1870, 8 Dec. 1870.

17. R. A. Riley to JWR, 19 Dec. 1870, M628, InHi.

18. Ibid.; JWR to Ryan, 25 Nov. 1870, 8 Dec. 1870.

19. JWR quoted in Dickey—*Youth,* p. 74.

20. "The Poetic Path," *Lafayette Journal,* 23 Apr. 1885; Dickey, Notes on JWR, n.d., Dickey Mss., InU-Li; Crowder, p. 51; JWR, "The Same Old Story," *Complete Works,* I: 30; Biographical Edition, I: 393.

21. Adelphian Dramatic Club Programs, 1870–1873, scrapbook 2, box 14, PS2700, InU-Li; Chronological Notes on JWR, M660, InHi.

22. JWR to Crowell, May 1870.

23. "James Whitcomb Riley," *Indianapolis Herald,* 18 Apr. 1885.

24. *Child of Waterloo,* 6 Apr. 1870, Adelphian Dramatic Club Programs, 1870–1873; Lee O. Harris quoted in Dickey, Notes on JWR, n.d., Dickey Mss., InU-Li; "Was Born a Genius."

25. *The Chimney Corner,* 31 Dec. 1873, Adelphian Dramatic Club Programs, 1870–1873; *Harper's Weekly,* 9 Jan. 1892; [notation], JWR to Nellie Cooley, 28 Oct. 1877, Riley VI. Mss., InU-Li; Mitchell, p. 126.

26. Irvin Walker to JWR, 18 July 1871, Riley Mss., InU-Li.

27. Ibid.

28. Thornbrough, *Indiana in the Civil War Era,* pp. 690–91; John S. Gentile, *Cast of One: One-Person Shows from the Chautauqua Platform to the Broadway Stage* (Urbana: University of Illinois Press, 1989), pp. 4–5.

29. JWR quoted in Dickey, "A Quiet Religion," n.d., Dickey Mss., InU-Li; Crowder, p. 66.

30. Garland, "Real Conversations," p. 223; Dickey, Notes on JWR, n.d., Dickey Mss., InU-Li.

31. Garland, "Real Conversations," p. 223; Dickey—*Youth*, p. 77; Crowder, p. 55.

32. Garland, "Real Conversations," p. 224; "The Poetic Path."

33. JWR to John Riley, [Spring 1872], [May] 1872, 14 May 1872, [1872], M660, InHi; Crowder, pp. 55–56; JWR, "Man's Devotion," *Complete Works*, I: 42; Biographical Edition, I: 395.

34. JWR to John Riley, [May 1872].

35. JWR to John Riley, 14 May 1872; Crowder, p. 57; JWR, "A Ballad," *Complete Works*, I: 45; Biographical Edition, I: 396.

36. JWR to John Riley, 14 May 1872, JWR to John Riley, [Spring 1872]; JWR to "Dear Brother" [John Riley], [1872]; JWR to John Riley, [1872].

37. JWR to John Riley, [1872].

38. Ibid., 31 May 1872, M660, InHi.

39. Ibid.

40. Ibid.; Obituary of Dr. Samuel B. McCrillus, *Anderson Herald*, 13 Feb. 1901; Doc McCrillus Advertisement, n.d., no. 4, box 6, PS2700, InU-Li; Dickey—*Youth*, p. 112; Lears, *Fables of Abundance*, pp. 40–41.

41. Dickey, Notes on JWR, Feb.-Mar. 1900, Dickey Mss., InU-Li; JWR to John Riley, 18 June 1872, M660, InHi.

42. Elva May Riley to John Riley, Wednesday [*sic*] 4 1872, M660, InHi; JWR to John Riley, 14 [July] 1871, M660, InHi.

43. JWR to John Riley, 18 June 1872.

44. Ibid.; "Riley the Painter Poet," *Anderson Herald*, 19 July 1872.

45. Ibid.; Dickey—*Youth*, pp. 111–12, 116–18.

46. Lears, *Fables of Abundance*, p. 42.

47. JWR to John Riley, [Summer] 1872, M660, InHi; JWR to John Riley, [Nov. 1872] M660, InHi; Dickey—*Youth*, p. 113–14.

48. JWR, "Regardin' Terry Hut," *Complete Works*, V: 1181–83.

49. Lears, *Fables of Abundance*, pp. 42, 54.

50. Ibid., p. 43.

51. Ibid., pp. 44–45.

52. Ibid., p. 42–45; Dickey, "Riley, the Medicine Man," *Tile and Till* 14 (May 1928): 38.

53. Lears, *Fables of Abundance*, p. 42.

54. Garland, "Real Conversations," p. 224.

55. Ibid.; Dickey—*Youth*, pp. 135–37.

56. Garland, "Real Conversations," p. 224.

57. Lears, *Fables of Abundance*, pp. 46, 55.

58. JWR to John Riley, 23 Oct. 1872, M660, InHi.

59. Ibid., 20 Aug. 1872, M660, InHi.

60. Ibid., 23 Oct. 1872, M660, InHi.

61. Ibid., [Spring 1871 or 1872], [1872], M660, InHi; E. A. Brininstool, *Los Angeles Express*, 15 Dec. 1911.

62. Dickey, Interview with daughter of Mrs. H. E. Whitmore, Notes on JWR,

Anderson, Feb. 1901, Dickey Mss., InU-Li; Goodson to Dickey, 16 Nov 1902; Dickey Mss., InU-Li.

63. JWR to John Riley, [Nov. 1872]; Dickey, Notes on JWR, n.d., Dickey Mss., InU-Li; Dickey—*Youth*, p. 150–51; Crowder, p. 61; Williams, *The Poet as Flying Islands of the Night*, p. 282.

64. Interview with daughter of Mrs. H. E. Whitmore, Notes on JWR, Anderson, Feb. 1901, Dickey Mss., InU-Li; Dickey—*Youth*, p. 150–55.

65. Ibid.

66. Ibid.; Dickey, Notes on JWR, Nov. 1902, Dickey Mss., InU-Li.

67. [JWR to Mooresville] *Enterprise*, 24 Apr. 1873, Riley Mss., InU-Li.

68. Ibid.; Thornbrough, *Indiana in the Civil War Era*, pp. 362, 536.

69. [JWR to Mooresville] *Enterprise*, 24 Apr. 1873, Thornbrough, *Indiana in the Civil War Era*, pp. 411, 414–15.

70. [JWR to Mooresville] *Enterprise*, 24 Apr. 1873.

71. Ibid.; Thornbrough, *Indiana in the Civil War Era*, pp. 362, 555.

72. JWR to [John Riley], [17 Feb. 1873], M660, InHi; S. B. McCrillus, diary entry, 17 Jan. 1873, Dickey Mss., InU-Li.

73. Ibid.; Riley & McClanahan Advertising Company (business card), no. 6, box 6, PS2700, InU-Li.; Dickey—*Youth*, p. 132.

74. JWR to [John Riley], [17 Feb. 1873]; Goodson to Dickey, 16 Nov. 1902, Dickey Mss., InU-Li.

75. Goodson to Dickey, 16 Nov. 1902; Dickey—*Youth*, p. 132; "James Whitcomb Riley," *Hancock Democrat*, 23 June 1887; T. A. Wickersham to JWR, 22 Apr. 1876, JWR to John Riley, 7 Aug. 1873, M660, InHi; The Graphic Advertisers (business card); Garland, "Real Conversations," p. 224. Authors such as Walt Whitman were regular contributors to the New York *Daily Graphic* and *Weekly Graphic* in the early 1870s (Reynolds, *Walt Whitman's America*, pp. 516–17).

76. Goodson to Dickey, 16 Nov. 1902; Dickey—*Youth*, p. 132; Garland, "Real Conversations," p. 224; "The Poetic Path."

77. Reynolds, *Walt Whitman's America*, pp. 143, 432.

78. Garland, "Real Conversations," p. 224; "Riley and the Graphics," *Indianapolis Journal*, 26 Dec. 1889.

79. Dickey—*Youth*, pp. 132–33; Lears, *Fables of Abundance*, p. 294.

80. JWR to John Riley, 7 Aug. 1873; Material on Reuben Riley, M628, InHi.

81. JWR to John Riley, 7 Aug. 1873, 29 Aug. 1873, 8 Sept. 1873; 29 Sept. 1873, M660, InHi.

82. JWR to John Riley, 7 Aug. 1873; Lears, *Fables of Abundance*, pp. 63–74.

83. JWR to John Riley, 29 Sept. 1873.

84. JWR to John Riley, 7 Aug. 1873, "Riley and the Graphics," *Indianapolis Journal*, 26 Dec. 1889; Lears, *Fables of Abundance*, pp. 63–74.

85. JWR to John Riley, 29 Sept. 1873; JWR to Angie Williams, 14 Feb. 1876, Riley VI. Mss., InU-Li.

86. JWR to John Riley, 7 Aug. 1873; Dickey—*Youth*, pp. 142–43.

87. JWR to John Riley, 15 Oct. 1873, 18 Oct. 1873, 26 Oct. 1873, M660, InHi.

88. JWR to John Riley, 26 Oct. 1873.

89. JWR to John Riley, 26 Oct. 1873.

90. Ibid.

91. Ibid.

92. Jack London quoted in Edward Behr, *Prohibition: Thirteen Years That Changed America* (New York: Arcade Publishing, 1996), p. 50.

93. JWR to [John Riley], [17 Feb. 1873]; 16 Nov. 1873, M660, InHi; Garland, "Real Conversations," p. 224.

94. JWR to [John Riley], 16 Nov. 1873.

95. JWR to [John Riley], 17 July 1872; 7 Aug. 1873; JWR, "The Stepmother," *Complete Works*, V: 1241.

96. John A. Riley to JWR, 23 Feb. 1896; JWR, "The Mother Sainted," *Complete Works*, III: 715–16.

97. Mattie [Martha] C. Riley to JWR, 18 Oct. 1875; Riley Mss., InU-Li.

98. Ibid.; Dickey, Interview with Almon Keefer, 20 June 1913, M628, InHi; Roger Price, "James Whitcomb Riley in 1876," *Indiana Magazine of History* 35 (June 1939): 137.

99. Mattie C. Riley to JWR, 4 Apr. 1892, Riley Mss., InU-Li; Mary Riley to John Riley, 6 Jan. 1888, M660, InHi; S. A. Wilson to John Riley, 8 Dec. 1893, M660, InHi; Henry Eitel to John Riley, 18 Dec. 1893, M660, InHi; Henry Eitel to Julia Riley, 31 Dec. 1893, M660, InHi.

100. Adelphian Dramatic Club Programs, 1870–1873.

101. James H. McClanahan to JWR, 26–7 Nov 1873, Riley Mss., InU-Li; Fanny P. Brown to Edmund Eitel, 21 May 1913, M660, InHi; Crowder, pp. 63–64; JWR, "At Last," *Complete Works*, I: 52–53; Biographical Edition, I: 399; C. E. McGeachy to JWR, 20 June 1874, Riley Mss., InU-Li; The *Danbury News* published seven Riley poems between 25 Feb. 1874 and 15 Aug. 1874 (Russo, p. 281).

102. Ronald Weber, *Hired Pens: Professional Writers in America's Golden Age of Print* (Athens: Ohio University Press, 1997), pp. 111, 134.

103. Ibid., pp. 54–55.

104. "The Hoosier Poet, James Whitcomb Riley's Views on American Poetry," *Marlborough Express*, 3 Dec. 1888; Price, "James Whitcomb Riley in 1876," p. 130.

105. John J. Skinner to Dickey, 3 Sept. 1901, no. 2, box 20, PS2700, InU-Li; Brown to JWR, 20 May 1876, Riley Mss., InU-Li; JWR to John Riley, Greenfield, 1 Apr 1875, M660, InHi; Garland, "Real Conversations," p. 224; Crowder, pp. 66–67.

106. JWR to Alonzo Hilton Davis, 16 Apr. 1885, M660, InHi; Irvin Walker to JWR, 22 Feb. 1874, Riley Mss., InU-Li.

107. JWR to Samuel L. Clemens, 31 Dec. 1890, Riley VI. Mss., InU-Li; JWR to Jas. H. Burke, 8 Sept. 1886, Riley IV. Mss., InU-Li; Crowder, 64–65.

108. Gentile, *Cast of One*, pp. 3, 8–9.

109. Ibid., pp. 3–5.

110. Ibid., 6–10.

111. Ibid., pp. 10–11; Dickey—*Youth*, pp. 98–99.

112. Garland, "Real Conversations," p. 224.

113. Adelphian Dramatic Club Programs, 1870–1873.

114. JWR to [John Riley], 1874, M660, InHi; Crowder, p. 64.

115. JWR to [John Riley], 1874; Crowder, pp. 65–68.

116. O. P. Moore to Dickey, 9 Dec. 1902, Dickey Mss., InU-Li; Dickey, Notes on JWR, n.d., Dickey Mss., InU-Li; Crowder, pp. 65–68.

117. Ibid.

118. M. C. Chomel, "An Interview with James Whitcomb Riley," *The Lamp* (Dec. 1903): 289.

119. Chronological Notes on the Life of James Whitcomb Riley, M660, InHi; Crowder, pp. 65–67; JWR, "Tradin' Joe," in *The Complete Works*, 1: 76–80; Biographical Edition, I: 401.

120. JWR to John Riley, 1 Apr. 1875, M660, InHi.

121. Dickey, Notes on JWR, Nov.-Dec. 1899, Dickey Mss., InU-Li; Weber, *The Midwestern Ascendancy*, p. 28.

122. Ibid.; JWR, "Mr. Hammond's Parable" or "The Dreamer," *Complete Works*, VII: 1777–80; Biographical Edition, IV: 558.

123. Dickey, Notes on JWR, Nov.-Dec. 1899, Dickey Mss., InU-Li; Crowder, p. 67; "The Poetic Path."

124. "The Hoosier Poet," *Columbus Ohio Press*, 5 Dec. 1898.

125. JWR to Alonzo Hilton Davis, 16 Apr. 1885; A. W. Macy, Reminiscences, n.d., M660, InHi; "Riley's Dream, Pure Politics," *Buffalo Enquirer*, 1 Nov. 1898; Price, "James Whitcomb Riley in 1876," p. 131; JWR, "An Old Sweetheart of Mine," *Complete Works*, I: 90. First published in the *Indianapolis Journal* on 28 Feb. 1887, this poem appeared in *Pipes o' Pan* (1888), *An Old Sweetheart* (lithograph ed.), 1891); *Love Lyrics* (1899), *An Old Sweetheart of Mine* (Howard Chandler Christy, ed., 1902), and *The Lockerbie Book* (1911) (Biographical Edition, I: 404).

126. A. W. Macy, Reminiscences, n.d., M660, InHi.

127. JWR to Alonzo Hilton Davis, 16 Apr. 1885; "The Poetic Path"; Townsend to Dickey, 5 June 1901.

128. Garland, "Real Conversations," p. 224; "The Poetic Path"; "Was Born a Genius"; JWR to Alonzo Hilton Davis, 16 Apr. 1885.

129. Garland, "Real Conversations," p. 224; "The Poetic Path"; "Was Born a Genius"; JWR to Alonzo Hilton Davis, 16 Apr. 1885; Townsend to Dickey, 5 June 1901.

130. "The Poetic Path," *Lafayette Journal*, 23 Apr. 1885; JWR to John Skinner, 14 Sept. 1875, Riley IV. Mss., InU-Li.

131. Ibid.; "Early Times on Brandywine," *Indianapolis Press*, 23 July 1900; Townsend to Dickey, 5 June 1901.

132. Townsend to Dickey, 5 June 1901; JWR to John Skinner, 14 Sept. 1875.

133. Townsend to Dickey, 5 June 1901; "The Poetic Path."

134. Townsend to Dickey, 5 June 1901; JWR to John Skinner, 14 Sept. 1875; Lears, *Fables of Abundance*, p. 42.

135. Lears, *Fables of Abundance*, p. 42.

136. Ibid.; Townsend to Dickey, 5 June 1901; JWR to John Skinner, 14 Sept. 1875.

137. Tocqueville quoted in Lawrence Levine, *Highbrow/Lowbrow: The Emergence of Cultural Hierarchy in America* (Cambridge: Harvard University Press, 1988), p. 17.

138. Levine, *Highbrow/Lowbrow*, pp. 16–37; Reynolds, *Walt Whitman's America*, p. 156.

139. Levine, *Highbrow/Lowbrow*, pp. 13–16.

140. JWR to John Skinner, 14 Sept. 1875.

141. Ibid.; Peter Burke, *Popular Culture in Early Modern Europe* (New York: New York University Press, 1978), pp. 186–89; Lears, *Fables of Abundance*, pp. 17–26.

142. Lears, *Fables of Abundance*, p. 24; Edgar Lee Masters, "James Whitcomb Riley, A Sketch of His Life and an Appraisal of His Work," in *Century Magazine* 114 (Oct. 1927): 704.

143. Lears, *Fables of Abundance,* p. 23; Masters, "James Whitcomb Riley, A Sketch," p. 704.

144. Masters, "James Whitcomb Riley, A Sketch," pp. 704–5.

145. Ibid.

146. JWR to John Skinner, 7 Oct. 1875, Riley IV. Mss., InU-Li; Will Hammel to JWR, 31 Oct. 1875, Riley Mss., InU-Li; Townsend to Dickey, 5 June 1901; Garland, "Real Conversations," p. 224; "Was Born a Genius."

147. Townsend to Dickey, 5 June 1901; Garland, "Real Conversations," p. 224; "Was Born a Genius."

148. JWR to John Skinner, 7 Oct. 1875; "Was Born a Genius."

149. Ibid.

150. Townsend to Dickey, 5 June 1901.

151. JWR to Kate, 1 Sept. 1872, Riley Mss., InU-Li; Dickey, "An Unmarried Man," unpublished manuscript, n.d., pp. 1–2, Dickey Mss., InU-Li. Kate's last name is unknown. However, she may well have been Kate Myers, a woman from Anderson to whom Riley was later briefly engaged.

152. JWR to Ryan, 25 Nov 1870; JWR to Ryan, 8 Dec. 1870; JWR to John Skinner, 14 Sept. 1875, 7 Oct. 1875, Riley IV. Mss., Lilly Library; JWR to Angie Williams, 14 Feb. 1876, Riley VI. Mss., InU-Li; Dickey, "An Unmarried Man," p. 1.

153. JWR to Skinner, 14 Sept. 1875, 7 Oct. 1875; "Riley's Dream, Pure Politics," *Buffalo Enquirer,* 1 Nov. 1898.

154. Dickey, "A Whimsical Poet" [unpublished manuscript], n.d., p. 9, Dickey Mss., InU-Li; JWR to Kahle, 14 Aug. 1879, Brunn Mss., InU-Li; JWR to Rosaline E. Jones, 22 Aug. 1880, Riley Mss., InU-Li.

155. Goodson to Dickey, 16 Nov. 1902; Townsend to Dickey, 5 June 1901; JWR to J. N. Matthews, 23 Nov. 1887, Riley Mss., InU-Li.

156. JWR to Kate, 1 Sept. 1872.

157. Dickey, "An Unmarried Man," p. 1; JWR to John Skinner, 14 Sept. 1875.

158. JWR to John Skinner, 14 Sept. 1875.

159. Ibid.; JWR to Edith T. Mediary, 26 Nov. 1907, Riley Mss., InU-Li.

160. JWR to John Skinner, 7 Oct. 1875; "Was Born a Genius."

161. C. M. Townsend, 1875, Riley Mss., InU-Li; J. Jackson to JWR, 13 Feb. 1876, Riley Mss., InU-Li.

162. JWR to B. S. Parker, 21 June 1875, 31 Aug. 1875, 23 Oct. 1876, Riley Mss., InU-Li; Parker to JWR, 16 Oct. 1876, Riley Mss., InU-Li; Lee O. Harris to JWR, 27 Oct. 1876, Riley Mss., InU-Li.

163. Dame Durden [Eda L. Brown] to JWR, 6 July 1876; Brown to [Florence Mae Eberhart], 5 Aug. 1876; Riley Mss., InU-Li; Biographical Edition, I: 408. Riley called Brown "Dame Durden," which was John Jarndyce's pet name for Esther Summerson in Dickens's *Bleak House* (Arthur L. Hayward, *The Dickens Encyclopedia* [Edison, N.J.: Chartwell, reprint 1995, first published 1924], p. 47).

164. Dickey—*Youth,* pp. 288–89; Brown to JWR, 5 May 1876, 20 May 1876, 22 Nov. 1876, Riley Mss., InU-Li; JWR to Brown, 22 Nov. 1876, Riley Mss., InU-Li.

165. JWR to Parker, 23 Oct. 1876, 12 Dec. 1876, Riley Mss., InU-Li; Weber, *Hired Pens,* p. 111.

166. T. A. Wickersham to JWR, 22 Apr. 1876, 8 Nov. 1876; Riley Mss., InU-Li; [Brown] to JWR, 22 Nov. 1876, Riley Mss., InU-Li; JWR to [Brown], 28 Nov. 1876, Riley Mss., InU-Li; McClanahan to JWR, 10 Dec. 1876; Riley Mss., InU-Li.

167. Brown to JWR, 5 May 1876, 20 May 1876, Riley Mss., InU-Li.

168. Ibid., 6 July 1876, 3 Aug. 1876, 13 Feb. 1877, Riley Mss., InU-Li; Mc-Clanahan to JWR, 9 Jan. 1877, Riley Mss., InU-Li.

169. [Brown] to JWR, 22 Nov. 1876, Riley Mss., InU-Li; [Brown] to JWR, 27 Feb. 1877, Riley Mss., InU-Li.

170. [Brown] to JWR, 22 Nov. 1876; [Brown] to JWR, 28 Nov. 1876, Riley Mss., InU-Li. McClanahan to JWR, 10 Dec. 1876; Riley Mss., InU-Li.

171. Ibid.

3. Rising Ambition

1. "A Poet Talks of Success," *Chicago Daily News,* 17 July 1897.

2. Ibid.; "The Poetic Path."

3. JWR to Evelyn E. Silverman, 22 Oct. 1915, Riley VI. Mss., InU-Li; "Riley Loves Longfellow," *Rochester Herald,* 2 Nov. 1898; "Riley in Omaha," *Omaha World Herald,* 19 Nov. 1897.

4. "A Poet Talks of Success."

5. "The Hoosier Poet, James Whitcomb Riley's Views on American Poetry," *Marlborough Express,* 3 Dec. 1888.

6. JWR to [Brown], 28 Nov. 1876; JWR to Henry W. Longfellow, 20 Nov. 1876; quoted in Dickey—*Youth,* p. 318; Reynolds, *Walt Whitman's America,* p. 341; "Biographical Notes," in *American Poetry, the Nineteenth Century,* 2: 920–21. In addition to "In the Dark," Riley sent "A Destiny" ("The Dreamer") and "If I Knew What Poets Know" to Longfellow (Biographical Edition, I: 412–13).

7. JWR to [Brown], 28 Nov. 1876; Wickersham to JWR, 8 Nov. 1876, 3 May 1877, 9 May 1877, Riley Mss., InU-Li; McClanahan to JWR, 10 Dec. 1876, 9 Jan. 1877; Riley Mss., InU-Li.

8. JWR to [Brown], 28 Nov. 1876; "James Whitcomb Riley," *Hancock Democrat,* 23 June 1887.

9. JWR to [Lee O. Harris], 26 Oct. 1876, in Phelps, pp. 10–11.

10. JWR to [Brown], 28 Nov. 1876.

11. Longfellow to JWR, 30 Nov. 1876 Riley Mss., InU-Li; JWR to Parker, 5 Dec. 1876, in Phelps, p. 12; "A Poet Talks of Success," *Chicago Daily News,* 17 July 1897.

12. Parker to JWR, New Castle, 5 Dec. 1876, Riley Mss., InU-Li; *Hancock Democrat,* 7 Dec. 1876.

13. *Hancock Democrat,* 7 Dec. 1876; JWR to John Riley, [Nov 1872]; Albert W. Macy to JWR, 18 Dec. 1876, Riley Mss., InU-Li. Will J. Ethell to JWR, 17 Dec. 1876; Riley Mss., InU-Li.

14. Parker to JWR, 5 Dec. 1876; Weber, *Hired Pens,* p. 79; Richard Brodhead, *Cultures of Letters: Scenes of Reading and Writing in Nineteenth-Century America* (Chicago: University of Chicago Press, 1993), p. 79.

15. Longfellow to JWR, 30 Nov. 1876; Charles Phillips to JWR, 24 Aug. 1879, Riley Mss., InU-Li.

16. The *Indianapolis Journal* represented the interests of the Republicans while the *Indianapolis Sentinel* represented the interests of the Democrats. In 1870, the *Indianapolis News* began publishing as a daily journal without political affiliation. Aside from these three major newspapers, several others were published in the state capital. However, many of them were only short-lived (Ann Mauger Colbert and David G.

Vanderstel, "Journalism," in Bodenhamer and Barrows, eds., *Encylopedia of Indianapolis*, pp. 95–98).

17. JWR to Parker, 12 Dec. 1876; "A Chat with Whitcomb Riley," *Chicago Herald*, 17 Feb. 1888; Biographical Edition, I: 415–17, 6: 19; Crowder, p. 76.

18. JWR, "A Remarkable Man"; *Complete Works*, IX: 2311–30; Lears, *Fables of Abundance*, pp. 99–101.

19. JWR, "A Remarkable Man."

20. Whitman quoted in Lears, *Fables of Abundance*, p. 55.

21. JWR, "A Remarkable Man"; Lears, *Fables of Abundance*, pp. 55, 99–101.

22. JWR to Lee O. Harris, 12 Mar. 1877, Riley VI. Mss., InU-Li; Dickey, Notes on JWR, n.d., Dickey Mss., InU-Li. Martindale purchased the *Journal* in 1875. Appointed judge of the Common Pleas Court for Henry, Madison, Hancock, Rush, and Decatur counties by Governor Morton, Martindale was probably already familiar with Reuben Riley and his family (Will Cumback and J. B. Maynard, eds., *Men of Progress. Indiana. A Selected List of Biographical Sketches of the Leaders in Business, Professional and Official Life* [Indianapolis: Indianapolis Sentinel Co., 1899], pp. 162–65).

23. D. M. Bradbury to JWR, 21 Feb. 1877, Riley Mss., InU-Li. E. B. Martindale to JWR, 27 Feb. 1877, Riley Mss., InU-Li.

24. Martindale to JWR, 8 Mar. 1877; Biographical Edition. I: 404–5.

25. JWR to Martindale, 10 Mar. 1877, Riley Mss., InU-Li.

26. Ibid.; JWR to Parker, 12 Dec. 1876, Riley Mss., InU-Li.

27. Dunn, *Greater Indianapolis*, 2: 1211; Frank Riley to Neff [JWR], 22 Mar. 1877, Riley Mss., InU-Li.

28. JWR to Lee O. Harris, 12 Mar. 1877; JWR to John Riley, 7 Apr. 1877, 11 Apr. 1877, Riley Mss., InU-Li; W. H. Sidall to JWR, 4 Apr. 1877, Riley Mss., InU-Li; Garland, "Real Conversations," p. 226; "The Poetic Path."

29. *Anderson Herald*, 27 Apr. 1877; Dickey, Notes on JWR, Feb.-Mar. 1900, Dickey Mss., InU-Li; Dickey—*Youth*, p. 334; Crowder, p. 77.

30. Sally Foreman Griffith, *Home Town News: William Allen White and the Emporia Gazette* (New York: Oxford University Press, 1989), pp. 7, 34.

31. Dickey—*Youth*, p. 334.

32. "JWR Dead; Stroke of Paralysis Is Fatal to Famous Indiana Poet," *Cincinnati Enquirer*, 23 July 1916.

33. "Poet and Story Teller," Lansing Michigan, *State Republican*, 1 Nov. 1893.

34. Ziff, *The American 1890s*, p. 148.

35. Griffith, *Home Town News*, pp. 19–20.

36. JWR to Samuel L. Clemens, 31 Dec. 1890; JWR to Parker, 23 Oct. 1876.

37. Griffith, *Home Town News*, pp. 20–21.

38. Ibid.

39. Ibid., p. 68.

40. Ibid., pp. 24–25.

41. Ibid., pp. 32–34; Dickey—*Youth*, pp. 334–35; Crowder, p. 78; "James Whitcomb Riley Dead; Stroke of Paralysis Is Fatal to Famous Indiana Poet," *Cincinnati Enquirer*, 23 July 1916; Ziff, *The American 1890s*, p. 148.

42. JWR to "Andy," 24 May 1877, Riley III. Mss., InU-Li; Dickey—*Youth*, pp. 334–35; Crowder, p. 78; William R. Cagle, "James Whitcomb Riley, Notes on the Early Years," *Manuscripts* 17 (Spring 1965): 6.

43. Wm. Hammel to JWR, 9 Apr. 1877, Riley Mss., InU-Li; JWR to Luther

Benson, June 1877, quoted in Dickey, Notes on JWR, Feb.-Mar. 1900, Dickey Mss., InU-Li.

44. [Brown] to JWR, 22 Nov. 1876; Brown to JWR, 10 Feb. 1877, 13 Feb. 1877, 27 May 1877, Sat. Eve., 1877, Riley Mss., InU-Li; Brown McClanahan to Florence [Eberhart], 7 June 1878, Riley Mss., InU-Li.

45. JWR to Kate, 1 Sept. 1872; JWR to [Kate Myers], 15 Sept. 1877, Riley Mss., InU-Li; Kit [Kate Myers] to JWR, 20 Sept. 1877, Riley Mss., InU-Li. Unfortunately, few letters exist from Riley's relationship with Myers. Myers's brother destroyed most of the letters that Riley wrote to her during the time of their betrothal (Jessie Tremont Croan to Edmund Eitel, [1913], Riley III. Mss., InU-Li).

46. Dickey—*Youth*, pp. 288–311; JWR to [Myers], 15 Sept. 1877; JWR to [Ella Wheeler Wilcox], 19 Aug. 1880, [1 Sept. 1880], 30 Nov. 1880, Riley III. Mss., InU-Li.

47. Brown to JWR, 3 Aug. 1876, 10 Feb. 1877, 27 Feb. 1877, Riley Mss., InU-Li.

48. JWR to L. D. Kahle, 23 Aug. 1879, Brunn Mss., InU-Li.

49. Brodhead, *Cultures of Letters*, pp. 49–50; Lois W. Banner, *American Beauty* (New York: Alfred A. Knopf, 1983), pp. 45–65.

50. JWR to [Wilcox], 19 Aug. 1880, Riley III. Mss., InU-Li.

51. JWR to John Riley, 11 Apr. 1877; "The Poetic Path"; James Whitcomb Riley, Dory Biddle, comp., *Riley's First Poems* (Anderson, Indiana: privately printed, 1901), p. v. Selma N. Steele, Theodore L. Steele, and Wilbur D. Peat, *The House of the Singing Winds* (Indianapolis: Indiana Historical Society, 1966), p. 14.

52. Biddle, comp., *Riley's First Poems*, p. v.; "The Poetic Path."

53. Garland, "Real Conversations," p. 226; Lee O. Harris to JWR, 12 June 1877, Riley Mss., InU-Li; Cagle, "James Whitcomb Riley, Notes," p. 6.

54. Lee O. Harris to JWR, 12 June 1877.

55. "James Whitcomb Riley Dead; Stroke of Paralysis Fatal"; *Anderson Herald*, 18 May 1877.

56. Garland, "Real Conversations," p. 226; Dickey—*Youth*, p. 361; Crowder, p. 78; Cagle, "James Whitcomb Riley, Notes," pp. 6–7.

57. Garland, "Real Conversations," p. 226," "The Poetic Path"; Dickey—*Youth*, p. 361.

58. W. H. Sidall to JWR, 4 Apr. 1877, Riley Mss., InU-Li; JWR to ed. *Kokomo Dispatch* [J. O. Henderson], 23 July 1877, Riley Mss., InU-Li.

59. JWR to J. O. Henderson, 23 July 1877.

60. J. O. Henderson to JWR, 23 July 1877, Riley Mss., InU-Li.

61. Ibid.; Griffith, *Home Town News*, pp. 13–14.

62. Griffith, *Home Town News*, p. 14.

63. Dickey—*Youth*, p. 368.

64. JWR to J. O. Henderson, 26 July 1877, Riley Mss., InU-Li.

65. Ibid.; "Posthumous Poetry," *Kokomo Dispatch*, 2 Aug. 1877; J. O. Henderson to JWR, 3 Aug. 1877, Riley Mss., InU-Li.

66. "Posthumous Poetry," *Kokomo Dispatch*, 2 Aug. 1877; J. O. Henderson to JWR, 3 Aug. 1877, Riley Mss., InU-Li; "Biographical Notes," in *American Poetry, the Nineteenth Century*, 1: 1020.

67. "Posthumous Poetry," *Kokomo Dispatch*, 2 Aug. 1877; "Biographical Notes," in *American Poetry, the Nineteenth Century*, 1: 1020–21.

68. J. O. Henderson to JWR, 3 Aug. 1877, Riley Mss., InU-Li.

69. JWR to J. O. Henderson, 4 Aug. 1877, Riley Mss., InU-Li.

70. Ibid.; JWR to Mrs. D. M. Jordan, July 1877, Riley VI. Mss., InU-Li; JWR to J. O. Henderson, 26 July 1877; JWR to Mrs. D. M. Jordan, July 1877, Riley VI. Mss., InU-Li; Biographical Edition, I: 429.

71. JWR to J. O. Henderson, 26 July 1877; JWR to Henderson, 4 Aug. 1877; Biographical Edition, I: 429.

72. JWR to J. O. Henderson, 6 Aug. 1877, Riley Mss., InU-Li; Cagle, "James Whitcomb Riley, Notes on the Early Years," p. 10.

73. JWR to J. O. Henderson, 6 Aug. 1877; Biographical Edition, I: 431.

74. JWR to J. O. Henderson, 6 Aug. 1877.

75. JWR to D. M. Jordan, July 1877; JWR to J. O. Henderson, 4 Aug. 1877, 6 Aug. 1877; Benjamin S. Parker and Enos B. Heiney, eds., *Poets and Poetry of Indiana: A Representative Collection of the Poetry of Indiana During the First Hundred Years of Its History as Territory and State* (New York: Silver Burdett, 1900), pp. 438–39.

76. JWR to J. O. Henderson, 6 Aug. 1877. For an example of Riley's previous deceptions, see the blind sign painter story in chapter 2.

77. J. O. Henderson to JWR, 9 Aug. 1877, 13 Aug. 1877, Riley Mss., InU-Li; JWR to Henderson, 10 Aug. 1877, Riley Mss., InU-Li; Paul G. Henderson to Paul Lemperly, 29 July 1937, Riley Mss., InU-Li; "Biographical Notes," in *American Poetry, the Nineteenth Century,* 2: 915–16; Cagle, "James Whitcomb Riley, Notes on the Early Years," pp. 7, 10. Cagle lists the *New York Sun* and *New York Herald* publication date as 9 Aug. 1877. In reality, the *Herald* article appeared on 5 August and the *New York Sun* article on 7 August.

78. J. O. Henderson to JWR, 9 Aug. 1877, 13 Aug. 1877; JWR to Henderson, 10 Aug. 1877.

79. J. O. Henderson to JWR, 16 Aug. 1877, Riley Mss., InU-Li.

80. Will M. Croan to JWR, 20 Aug. 1877, Riley Mss., InU-Li; JWR to C. B. Foote, 26 Nov. 1886, Riley Mss., InU-Li; Cagle, "James Whitcomb Riley, Notes on the Early Years," p. 11.

81. Will M. Croan to JWR, 20 Aug. 1877; JWR to J. O. Henderson, 27 Aug. 1877, 31 Aug. 1877, Riley Mss., InU-Li; Cagle, "James Whitcomb Riley, Notes on the Early Years," p. 11.

82. J. O. Henderson to JWR, 25 Aug. 1877, Riley Mss., InU-Li.

83. JWR to J. O. Henderson, 31 Aug. 1877; Garland, "Real Conversations," p. 226.

84. JWR to J. O. Henderson, 27 Aug. 1877, Riley Mss., InU-Li.

85. J. O. Henderson to JWR, 28 Aug. 1877, Riley Mss., InU-Li.

86. "The Alleged Poe Poem-card from Mr. J. W. Riley," *Indianapolis Journal,* 30 Aug. 1877; JWR to the Public, 29 Aug. 1877, Riley Mss., InU-Li.

87. JWR to Editor [Indianapolis] Sentinel, [30] Aug. 1877, Riley Mss., InU-Li. Riley simply signed this letter with a "W."

88. J. O. Henderson to JWR, 28 Aug. 1877; JWR to J. O. Henderson, 31 Aug. 1877; Kit [Kate Myers] to JWR, 20 Sept. 1877; Will M. Croan to JWR, 9 Oct. 1877, Riley Mss., InU-Li.

89. Garland, "Real Conversations," p. 226.

90. JWR to [John M.] Anderson, 25 Oct. 1877, Riley VI. Mss., InU-Li; "The Revenges of an Unappreciated Genius," *Cincinnati Commercial,* 10 Oct. 1877.

91. JWR to [John M.] Anderson, 25 Oct. 1877.

92. Ibid.

93. Ibid.; JWR to J. O. Henderson, 6 Aug. 1877, 10 Aug. 1877; "The Alleged Poe

Poem-card from Mr. J. W. Riley"; JWR to J. O. Henderson, 27 Aug. 1877; Parker, "J. W. Riley," *New Castle Mercury,* 7 Sept. 1878.

94. J. O. Henderson to JWR, 3 Aug. 1877; JWR to Henderson, 31 Aug. 1877.

95. Dickey, "A Hoodoo from Hoodooville," unpublished manuscript, n.p. n.d., p. 1, Dickey Mss., InU-Li; "Plagiarism or Reincarnation," *Chicago Tribune,* 16 Dec. 1894; D. M. Jordan, "James W. Riley, A Sympathetic Note of the Life and Work of Our Poet," *Indianapolis Journal,* 9 Feb. 1885; J. H. Tedford to James H. Burke, *Iowa Record News,* 19 Aug. 1916; Dickey—*Youth,* p. 368; Crowder, p. 28.

96. Foote to JWR, 11 Nov. 1886; JWR to Foote, 26 Nov. 1886; Garland, "Real Conversations," p. 226; John Patterson to JWR, 21 Oct. 1891, Riley Mss., InU-Li; Paul G. Henderson to Paul Lemperly, 29 July 1937; Alfred Russel Wallace, "An Unpublished Poem by Edgar Allan Poe," *Fortnightly Review* (Feb. 1904): 329–32; Alfred Russel Wallace, *Edgar Allan Poe; a series of seventeen letters concerning Poe's scientific erudition in Eureka and his authorship of Leonainie* (New York: privately printed, 1930).

97. Parker to JWR, 15 Sept. 1878, Riley I Mss., InU-Li; Jordan to JWR, 5 Sept. 1877, Riley Mss., InU-Li; JWR to Foote, 26 Nov. 1886; Garland, "Real Conversations," p. 226; Cagle, "James Whitcomb Riley, Notes on the Early Years," p. 11.

98. Ibid.

4. Exploring Literary Possibilities

1. Anderson, "The Fires That Feed Genius."

2. Ibid.; Russo, p. 278.

3. Brodhead, *Cultures of Letters,* p. 80.

4. Dickey, Diary entry, 26 Mar. 1891, Dickey Mss., InU-Li; Dickey, Notes on JWR, n.d., Dickey Mss., InU-Li.

5. JWR to Jones, 4 Aug. 1880, Riley Mss., InU-Li; Mr. Riley Here," *Richmond Palladium,* 15 May 1899; Brodhead, *Cultures of Letters,* pp. 80–81; Trachtenberg, *The Incorporation of America,* pp. 194–95.

6. JWR to Parker, 24 Apr. 1883, Riley Mss., InU-Li; JWR to Jones, 4 Aug. 1880; Brodhead, *Cultures of Letters,* pp. 80–81; Janet Gray, ed., *She Wields a Pen: American Women Poets of the Nineteenth Century* (Iowa City: University of Iowa Press, 1997), p. xxxiii.

7. "The Hoosier Poet," *The New York Critic,* 21 Nov. 1891.

8. Brodhead, *Cultures of Letters,* p. 80; Gentile, *Cast of One,* pp. 10–21.

9. JWR to J. O. Henderson, 4 Sept. 1877, Riley Mss., InU-Li; Crowder, pp. 81–82.

10. Ibid.; Hammel to JWR, 9 Apr. 1877; JWR to Benson, June 1877; Ade, "Riley and His Friends," p. 9.

11. JWR to [Kit Myers], 15 Sept. 1877.

12. Behr, *Prohibition,* p. 21.

13. The word "alcoholism" first appeared in an 1849 study by the Swedish doctor Magnuss Huss (Jean-Charles Sournia, *A History of Alcoholism,* trans. Nick Hindley and Gareth Stanton [Cambridge: Basil Blackwell, 1990], pp. 45, 96).

14. Dickey, Notes on JWR, Nov. 1902, Dickey Mss., InU-Li.

15. Behr, *Prohibition,* p. 26.

16. Nicholas O. Warner, "Temperance Morality and Medicine in the Fiction of Harriet Beecher Stowe," in David S. Reynolds and Debra J. Rosenthal, eds., *The Serpent in the Cup: Temperance in American Literature* (Amherst: University of Massachusetts Press, 1997), p. 141.

17. Sournia, *A History of Alcoholism*, p. 106; Behr, *Prohibition*, pp. 24–26; Charles E. Rosenberg, *The Care of Strangers: The Rise of America's Hospital System* (New York: Basic Books, 1987), p. 305.

18. JWR to [Kit Myers], 15 Sept. 1877.

19. Kit [Myers] to JWR, 24 Sept. 1877, Riley Mss., InU-Li.

20. Miscellaneous quotes and anecdotes, no. 3, box 20, PS2700, InU-Li; Dickey, Notes on JWR, Nov. 1902, Dickey Mss., InU-Li. In early October, Will Croan was the last to mention Myers's name in any of Riley's correspondence dating from this period (Croan to JWR, 9 Oct. 1877).

21. Biographical Edition, I: 409–33; J[ohn] M. Anderson to JWR, Cincinnati, 26 Oct. 1877; "The Revenges of an Unappreciated Genius."

22. JWR to Charles H. Philips, 30 Sept. 1877; Philips to JWR, 24 Sept. 1877; Dickey, Notes on JWR, Nov.-Dec. 1899, Dickey Mss., InU-Li.

23. JWR to Nellie Cooley, 28 Oct. 1877, Riley VI. Mss., InU-Li.

24. JWR to Bottsford, 19 Mar. 1880, Bottsford Mss., InU-Li.

25. JWR to Cooley, 28 Oct. 1877; Crowder, p. 82.

26. Schedule 3.—Productions of Agriculture in Sugar Creek Township, in the County of Hancock in the Post Office: Palestine, Indiana, 27 Oct. 1870, In-Ar; Schedule 2.—Productions of Agriculture in Sugar Creek Township in the County of Hancock in the State of Indiana, 3 June 1880, In-Ar; Hancock County Marriage Index, 1836–1920, In-Ar; Binford, *History of Hancock County, Indiana*, p. 310; Thornbrough, *Indiana in the Civil War Era*, pp. 393–94.

27. Binford, *History of Hancock County, Indiana*, p. 310; Robert M. Taylor Jr., J. Kent Calder, Elizabeth Van Allen, "Dear Dream: The Love Letters of James Whitcomb Riley and Clara Louise Bottsford," in *Traces of Indiana and Midwestern History* 7 (Fall 1995): 4; Crowder, pp. 82–83.

28. JWR to Jack [John] M. Anderson, 13 Nov. 1877, Riley VI. Mss., InU-Li; Lee O. Harris to JWR, 9 Dec. 1877; Jack [John] M. Anderson to JWR, 20 Dec. 1877.

29. JWR, *Complete Works*, I: 238; Biographical Edition, I: 435.

30. David S. Reynolds, "Black Cats and Delirium Tremens: Temperance and the American Renaissance," in Reynolds and Rosenthal, eds., *The Serpent in the Cup*, pp. 26–27.

31. Karen Sánchez-Eppler, "Temperance in the Bed of a Child: Incest and Social Order in Nineteenth-Century America," in Reynolds and Rosenthal, eds., *The Serpent in the Cup*, p. 60.

32. JWR, *Complete Works.*, I: 252; Biographical Edition, I: 436; Benson to JWR, 1 Jan. 1878, Riley Mss., InU-Li.

33. "Benson Out-Bensoned," *Anderson Democrat,* 13 July 1877; JWR to Parker, 28 Jan. 1879, Riley Mss., InU-Li.

34. Benson to JWR, 1 Jan. 1878; "The Poet Riley, Sued by Luther Benson for a Debt of $60," *Cincinnati Enquirer,* 21 Feb. 1892; H. M. Johnson to JWR, 3 Jan. 1878, Riley Mss., InU-Li; Crowder, p. 83.

35. Samuel Richards to JWR, 11 Jan. 1878, Riley Mss., InU-Li; Parker to JWR, 15 Sept. 1878.

36. JWR to Editor of *Scribner's Monthly* [Josiah Gilbert Holland], 18 Jan. 1878, Riley Mss., InU-Li; Editor *Scribner's Monthly* to JWR, 22 Jan. 1878, Riley Mss., InU-Li.

37. JWR to John M. Anderson, 13 Nov. 1877; "An Indiana Poet," *Kokomo Tribune,* 30 Aug. 1879.

38. Reynolds, *Walt Whitman's America*, pp. 134; 368–75; 433.

39. Brodhead, *Cultures of Letters*, pp. 76–84; Lears, *Fables of Abundance*, p. 274.

40. JWR to Martindale, 11 Jan. 1878, Riley Mss., InU-Li.

41. Ibid.

42. JWR to [Bottsford], 9 May 1878, Bottsford Mss., InU-Li.

43. Reynolds, *Walt Whitman's America*, p. 167; Gentile, *Cast of One*, p. 24.

44. Clark and Halloran, eds., "Introduction," in *Oratorical Culture in Nineteenth-Century America*, p. 9; Reynolds, *Walt Whitman's America*, pp. 166–68, 582; Gentile, *Cast of One*, pp. 19–24.

45. Gentile, *Cast of One*, p. 52; Dickey—*Maturity*, p. 18.

46. Paul H. Gray, "Poet as Entertainer: Will Carleton, James Whitcomb Riley, and the Rise of the Poet-Performer Movement," in *Literature in Performance* 5 (Nov. 1984): 2–4.

47. Robert Carl Martin, "The Early Lyceum, 1826–1845," Ph.D. diss., Northwestern University, 1953, quoted in Gentile, *Cast of One*, pp. 18–19 (brackets are Gentile's).

48. Redpath Lyceum to JWR, 29 July 1881, Riley Mss., InU-Li; H. M. Johnson to JWR, 3 Jan. 1878; JWR to J. O. Henderson, 24 Jan. 1878, Riley Mss., InU-Li; Philips to JWR, 31 Jan. 1878, Riley Mss., InU-Li.

49. JWR to J. O. Henderson, 24 Jan. 1878.

50. Ibid.

51. James B. Pond quoted in Gentile, *Cast of One*, p. 24.

52. JWR to J. O. Henderson, 24 Jan. 1878; Levine, *Highbrow/Lowbrow*, pp. 21, 30–33; Gentile, *Cast of One*, p. 6; Reynolds, *Walt Whitman's America*, p. 162.

53. J. O. Henderson to JWR, 5 Feb. 1878, Riley Mss., InU-Li.

54. Thornbrough, *Indiana in the Civil War Era*, p. 393.

55. Philips to JWR, 31 Jan. 1878, 2 Feb. 1878, 5 Feb. 1878, Riley Mss., InU-Li.

56. "Riley's Recitations," *Kokomo Dispatch*, 7 Feb. 1878; Henderson quoted in Dickey—*Maturity*, p. 20.

57. "A Select Reading," *Kokomo Tribune*, 7 Feb. 1878.

58. Gentile, *Cast of One*, p. 21.

59. Philips to JWR, 18 Feb. 1878, Riley Mss., InU-Li.

60. JWR to E. Shirk of the Tipton Lecture Association, 25 Feb. 1878, Riley Mss., InU-Li; M. V. B. Newcomer to C. S. W. Pettijohn, Riley Mss., InU-Li; Dickey—*Maturity*, p. 22; Crowder, p. 84.

61. N. R. Halling to JWR, 13 May 1878, Riley Mss., InU-Li; *Hancock Democrat*, 16 May 1878.

62. Nan Johnson, "The Popularization of Nineteenth-Century Rhetoric: Elocution and the Private Learner" in Clark and Halloran, eds., *Oratorical Culture in Nineteenth-Century America*, pp. 139–42.

63. "The Pioneers' Old Settlers' Reunion at Oakland," *Indianapolis Journal*, 5 Aug. 1878.

64. Ibid.; JWR, "A Child's Home—Long Ago," *Complete Works*, II: 289.

65. Levine, *Highbrow/Lowbrow*, pp. 29–30; Reynolds, *Walt Whitman's America*, pp. 154–56.

66. Colbert and Vanderstel, "Journalism," in Bodenhamer and Barrows, eds., *Encyclopedia of Indianapolis*, pp. 95–98.

67. JWR to Lee O. Harris, 10 Dec. 1877; Biographical Edition, I: 434–49, 2: 475–507; Dickey—*Maturity*, p. 23.

68. John A. Riley to JWR, 16 Apr. 1878, Riley Mss., InU-Li.

69. JWR to Charles E. Gard, 22 Aug. 1878, Riley Mss., InU-Li; Frederick J. Antczak and Edith Siemers, "The Divergence of Purpose and Practice on the Chautauqua: Keith Vawter's Self-Defense," in Clark and Halloran, eds., *Oratorical Culture in Nineteenth-Century America*, pp. 213–14; Gentile, *Cast of One*, p. 69.

70. JWR to Charles E. Gard.

71. JWR to Parker, 19 Mar. 1878, Riley Mss., InU-Li; Parker to JWR, 23 Mar. 1878.

72. JWR to Lee O. Harris, 10 Dec. 1877.

73. Dickey—*Maturity*, pp. 35–36.

74. Ibid., pp. 34–35.

75. Ibid., pp. 34–35; JWR, "Respectfully Declined Papers of the Buzz Club," no. 2, *Indianapolis Herald*, 15 June 1878.

76. JWR to Parker, 13 Sept. 1878, Riley Mss., InU-Li; Robert L. Patten, "Introduction," in Charles Dickens, *The Pickwick Papers* (New York: Penguin Books, 1972), pp. 11–30.

77. JWR, "The Respectfully Declined Papers of the Buzz Club, no. 4," *Indianapolis Saturday Herald,* 24 Aug. 1878; JWR to Charles Warren Stoddard, 19 Nov. 1891, in Phelps, p. 147; Russo, pp. 37–39.

78. Richard Hovey to JWR, 25 Dec. 1894, Riley Mss., InU-Li; John Clark Ridpath, "Foreword," in *Flying Islands of the Night* (Indianapolis: Bowen-Merrill, 1891); Ignatius Donnely to JWR, 26 Nov. 1891, Riley Mss., InU-Li; Grace Greenwood to JWR, 16 Nov. 1891, Riley Mss., InU-Li; "Biographical Notes," in *American Poetry, the Nineteenth Century*, 2: 892–93.

79. Levine, *Highbrow/Lowbrow*, pp. 17, 22; JWR, "The Respectfully Declined Papers of the Buzz Club, no. 4." British critics and Shakespearean scholars were among those who most readily accepted Riley's play. After reading "Flying Islands," Ignatius Donnely remarked that Riley "should have lived in the Elizabethan age"; and Joseph E. Knight thought it was "Exquisite!" (Ignatius Donnely to JWR, 26 Nov. 1891; Knight to JWR, 26 Dec. 1891, Riley Mss., InU-Li).

80. JWR, "Flying Islands of the Night," *Complete Works*, II: 297–383.

81. R. A. Foakes, "Introduction," in William Shakespeare, *A Midsummer Night's Dream,* The New Cambridge Shakespeare ed. (New York: Cambridge University Press, 1984), p. 40.

82. JWR to Parker, 13 Sept. 1878; JWR to John Hay, 2 Dec. 1891, Riley Mss., InU-Li.

83. JWR to Parker, 13 Sept. 1878; William Hazlitt quoted in Foakes, *A Midsummer Night's Dream*, pp. 24–25.

84. JWR quoted in Mitchell, pp. 158–59.

85. Foakes, *A Midsummer Night's Dream*, pp. 26, 40; Madison J. Cawein to JWR, 10 Nov. 1891, Riley Mss., InU-Li.

86. Greenwood to JWR, 17 Nov. 1891.

87. Foakes, *A Midsummer Night's Dream*, pp. 23, 26–27, 40–41. Thomas Williams identifies this darker interpretation of Riley's play and uses it to construct the conceptual framework for his book *James Whitcomb Riley: The Poet as Flying Islands of the Night*. Although it is true that "Flying Islands" does illustrate certain aspects of Riley's personality, Williams unfortunately overstates his case by making "Flying Islands" *the* key to understanding the poet. He claims that "'Flying Islands of the Night'. . . bears great sense as an autobiographical exposition under the circumstances of its writing" (p. 64). Williams analyzes each character in the play as a different part of Riley's character.

However, in several instances, the book makes it sound as if Riley suffered from dissociative personality disorder. For example, Williams states, "Riley's play character Jucklet deviously arranged for Riley to come to great fame in the way that the scheming, ludicrous minstrelsy of this character would do such a thing" (p. 114). Although it is true that "Flying Islands" is enlightening, it alone cannot explain everything about Riley's personality as Williams suggests at the beginning of his book. Williams himself demonstrates that his own argument is flawed by including chapters entitled "Mr. Bryce" (one of Riley's characters from the "Buzz Club") and "Bud," which represents Riley's inner-child, neither of which appears in "Flying Islands of the Night."

88. JWR, "Flying Islands of the Night," *Complete Works*, II: 302.

89. Ibid., II:.318–20, 336–39.

90. Ibid., II: 323–24.

91. Ibid., II: 323–25.

92. Ibid., II: 336–39.

93. Ibid., II: 346–52.

94. Ibid., II: 374–81.

95. Ibid., II: 380–83.

96. JWR to Benson, June 1877; JWR to [Wilcox], 19 Aug. 1880.

97. Williams, *The Poet as Flying Islands of the Night.*

98. JWR, "Flying Islands of the Night," *Complete Works*, II: 323–24.

99. Although Williams identifies Nellie Cooley as the model for Dwainie (*The Poet as Flying Islands of the Night*, pp. 170–84), she may actually represent the best characteristics of a number of women he knew, including his mother, Cooley, Kit Myers, and Clara Bottsford.

100. JWR to [Bottsford], 28 May 1878, Bottsford Mss., InU-Li.

101. JWR, "Flying Islands of the Night," *Complete Works*, II: 299.

102. JWR to [Bottsford], 3 June 1878, Bottsford Mss., InU-Li.

103. Ibid.; JWR, "Flying Islands of the Night," *Complete Works*, II: 337.

104. *Indianapolis News*, 26 Aug. 1878.

105. Parker, "J. W. Riley."

106. JWR to Parker, 13 Sept. 1878; Russo, p. 39.

107. Colbert and Vanderstel, "Journalism," in Bodenhamer and Barrows, eds., *Encyclopedia of Indianapolis*, p. 98; Dunn, *Greater Indianapolis*, 1: 403.

108. Dunn, *Greater Indianapolis*, 1: 403.

109. Ibid., 1: 402–3.

110. Griffith, *Home Town News*, p. 42.

111. Ibid., p. 47; "Flying Islands of the Night," *People*, 21 Sept. 1878.

112. Griffith, *Home Town News*, p. 47; "Flying Islands," *People*, 31 Aug. 1878; "Flying Islands," *People*, 7 Sept. 1878; "Flying Islands of the Night," *Indianapolis Herald*, 14 Sept. 1878; "A Poet Criticizes a Poet," *Indianapolis Herald*, 14 Sept. 1878; "The War of Poets," *People*, 5 Oct. 1878; "The Poetic War," *Indianapolis Herald*, 12 Oct. 1878; "Unconscious Plagiarism," *People*, 26 Oct. 1878; "End of the Poetic War," *Indianapolis Herald*, 19 Oct. 1878; Russo, p. 39.

113. Dickey, among others, claims that a review of the poem which appeared in the *Herald* on 14 Sept. 1878 signed by Riley's friend W. C. C. Cooper was actually written by Riley (Dickey—*Maturity*, p. 37).

114. "Flying Islands of the Night," *Indianapolis Herald*, 14 Sept. 1878.

115. Ibid.; see chapter 3.

116. "Flying Islands of the Night," *People*, 21 Sept. 1878; Russo, p. 39; Dickey— *Maturity*, pp. 36–38.

117. "The Poetic War," *Indianapolis Herald*, 12 Oct. 1878.

118. Ibid.

119. Parker, "J. W. Riley"; Parker to JWR, 15 Sept. 1878, Riley Mss., InU-Li.

120. Parker, "J. W. Riley"; Parker to JWR, 15 Sept. 1878.

121. Frank R. Stockton to JWR, 18 Jan. 1892, Riley Mss., InU-Li.

122. Parker to JWR, 15 Sept. 1878.

123. Parker, "J. W. Riley."

124. Johnson, "The Popularization of Nineteenth-Century Rhetoric," p. 148.

125. Levine, *Highbrow/Lowbrow*, pp. 46–47; Ignatius Donnely to JWR, 26 Nov. 1891. Donnely (1831–1901) was a member of the U.S. House of Representatives (1863–1869). He also wrote *The Great Cryptogram* (1888), a book intended to prove that Francis Bacon authored plays attributed to Shakespeare (*Webster's New Biographical Dictionary* [Springfield, Mass.: Merriam Webster, 1983]).

126. "Dana and Riley," *Milwaukee Sentinel*, 25 July 1888.

127. [enclosure] *New York World*, 9 Dec. 1891, in JWR to Madison Julius Cawein, 9 Dec. 1891, Riley Mss., InU-Li.

128. Ibid.; Cawein to JWR, 12 Dec. 1891, Riley Mss., InU-Li.

129. "The Flying Islands of the Night," *New York Independent*, 7 Jan. 1892.

130. Hay to JWR, 30 Nov. 1891, Riley Mss., InU-Li.

131. Knight to JWR, 26 Dec. 1891, Riley Mss., InU-Li. "Joseph Knight was editor of *Notes and Queries*, dramatic critic of the *Globe* (London), biographer of Dante Gabriel Rossetti, author of *Life of David Garrick*, etc." (Phelps, p. 139).

132. JWR to Howells, 19 Jan. 1892 in Phelps, p. 157.

133. Cawein to JWR, 12 Dec. 1891.

134. Ibid.; Brodhead, *Cultures of Letters*, pp. 80–81, 157–59.

135. JWR to Thomas Bailey Aldrich, 27 Oct. 1896 in Phelps, pp. 208–9.

136. Russo, p. 39; *Pittsburgh Commercial Gazette*, 18 Dec. 1891.

137. Martindale to JWR, 1 Oct. 1878, Riley Mss., InU-Li.

138. Weber, *Hired Pens*, p. 134.

139. Brodhead, *Cultures of Letters*, p. 52. The increase in circulation was indeed startling. Brodhead points out that before the mid-nineteenth century if a book sold five or six thousand copies it was a "decided hit."

140. JWR to Mary Hartwell Catherwood, 16 Sept. 1879, Riley VI. Mss., InU-Li.

141. JWR to Kahle, 21 Feb. 1879, Brunn Mss., InU-Li.

142. Paul Gray, "Poet as Entertainer: Will Carleton, James Whitcomb Riley, and the Rise of the Poet-Performer Movement" in *Literature in Performance* 5 (Nov. 1984): 7.

143. JWR to George S. Cottman, 29 Jan. 1879, Riley Mss., InU-Li.

144. Ibid.; JWR to Kahle, 21 Feb. 1879.

145. "An Indiana Poet," *Kokomo Tribune*, 30 Aug. 1879; *Indianapolis Journal*, 6 Sept. 1903; JWR to Samuel Richards, 16 Feb. 1879, Riley Mss., InU-Li; JWR to Eugene Bundy, 8 Apr. 1879, Riley VI. Mss., InU-Li.

146. Interview with Charles Martindale, n.d., Dickey Mss., InU-Li.

147. JWR to Bundy, 8 Apr. 1879.

148. JWR to Kahle, 21 Feb. 1879.

149. JWR to Parker, 22 Mar. 1879, Riley Mss., InU-Li.

150. JWR to Parker, 28 Jan. 1879; "An Indiana Poet," *Kokomo Tribune*, 30 Aug. 1879.

151. Ibid.; "Ingersoll Take-Off," *Kokomo Tribune*, 18 Jan. 1879.

152. Dickey, Notes on JWR, n.d., Dickey Mss., InU-Li; Reynolds, *Walt Whitman's America*, pp. 469, 525, 581.

153. "An Indiana Poet," *Kokomo Tribune*, 30 Aug. 1879.

154. Paul Gray, "Poet as Entertainer," p. 5; Gentile, *Cast of One*, p. 52.

155. "The Poetic Path."

156. JWR to Philips, [Mar. 1879], Riley VI. Mss., InU-Li.

157. JWR quoted in Biographical Edition, II: 483–84.

158. "Make Home Attractive," *Kokomo Tribune*, 22 Mar. 1879.

159. Ibid.

160. Dunn, *Greater Indianapolis*, 1: 518.

161. Biographical Edition., II: 484; JWR to Jacklet (John M. Anderson), 27 Sept. 1879.

162. Brodhead, *Cultures of Letters*, pp. 83–84.

163. Philips to JWR, 14 June 1879.

164. Ibid.

165. JWR, "Tom Johnson's Quit," *Complete Works*, II: 448–50.

166. Behr, *Prohibition*, pp. 31, 36–45, 48–49. The Anti-Saloon League was established in 1893.

167. Ibid., pp. 36–44, 52.

168. Reynolds, "Black Cats and Delirium Tremens," pp. 26–30. In a letter written to Riley in late summer 1879, *Indianapolis News* editor Dan Paine told the poet that Benson had been on "big bender" (Paine to JWR, 16 Aug. 1879, Riley Mss., InU-Li). Riley parodied Benson in some of his early lectures and in a newspaper story entitled "Benson Out-Bensoned" (*Anderson Democrat*, 13 July 1877; JWR to Parker, 28 Jan. 1879, Riley Mss., InU-Li).

169. Twain quoted in Reynolds, "Black Cats and Delirium Tremens," p. 29.

170. Reynolds, "Black Cats and Delirium Tremens," p. 29. Other authors who used this character type included Herman Melville and George Lippard.

171. JWR, "Tom Johnson's Quit."

172. Ibid.

173. Reynolds states that, according to one estimate, 80 percent of the people who took the temperance pledge in 1840 had started drinking again by 1848 ("Black Cats and Delirium Tremens," p. 29).

174. JWR to [Kit Myers], 15 Sept. 1877; JWR to Bottsford, 10 Feb. 1881, Bottsford Mss., InU-Li; JWR to Bottsford, 29 May 1882, Bottsford Mss., InU-Li, Bottsford Mss., InU-Li; Dickey, Notes on JWR, Nov. 1902, Dickey Mss., InU-Li; Ade, "Riley and His Friends," p. 9.

175. Ibid.; Philips to JWR, 17 June 1879, Riley Mss., InU-Li; Robert Burdette to Philips, 19 June 1879, Riley Mss., InU-Li.

176. "The Kokomo Tribune," promotional pamphlet (Kokomo, Ind.: T. C. Philips, Publishers, [1880]). Sarah T. Bolton (1820–1893) was another Indiana poet. She resided in Indianapolis and was most famous for the poem "Paddle Your Own Canoe" which was set to music and became a very popular song (Parker and Heiney, eds., "Biographical Notes," *Poets and Poetry of Indiana*, pp. 419–20; Dunn, *Greater Indianapolis*, 1: 504–5).

177. "Burdette's Compliment to JWR," *Kokomo Tribune*, 5 July 1879.

178. "Who Is John C. Walker?," *Kokomo Tribune*, 19 July 1879; "John C. Walker's Boon—Guess Who He Is?," *Kokomo Tribune*, 26 July 1879.

179. *Indianapolis Herald,* 26 July 1879.

180. Shumaker, *A History of Indiana Literature,* pp. 310–19; Jeannette Vanausdall, *Pride and Protest: The Novel in Indiana* (to be published by the Indiana Historical Society), pp. 51–52; Maurice Thompson quoted in the *Cincinnati Gazette,* 26 July 1879.

181. Philips to JWR, 12 July 1879.

182. JWR to Jacklet [John M. Anderson], 27 Sept. 1879.

183. Ibid.; JWR to Catherwood, 2 Apr. 1878, Riley Mss, InU-Li; JWR to Kahle, 14 Aug. 1879, Brunn Mss., InU-Li.

184. Shumaker, *A History of Indiana Literature,* pp. 303–4; Vanausdall, *Pride and Protest,* pp. 28–30.

185. Ibid.; *New Castle Mercury,* 21 Feb. 1880; Catherwood to JWR, 3 July 1879; JWR to R[ichard] W[atson] Gilder, 23 Apr. 1888, Riley Mss., InU-Li; Gilder to JWR, 9 May 1888, Riley Mss., InU-Li; Catherwood to JWR, 10 May 1888, Riley Mss., InU-Li; "Literary Women of Indiana, Mary Hartwell Catherwood," *Indianapolis Journal,* 10 July 1892.

186. Catherwood to JWR, 19 June 1879, 23 June 1879, 28 June 1879, Riley Mss., InU-Li.

187. Emma Cole to Hum Riley, 10 Sept. 1876, 13 Sept. 1876; Riley V., Mss., InU-Li; Mary Riley to JWR, 4 May 1877, Riley V., Mss., InU-Li; Elva May Riley to JWR, 28 May 1877, Riley Mss., InU-Li; JWR to [Jim] "Meeks," 12 Nov. 1878, Riley Mss., InU-Li.

188. JWR to Catherwood, 16 Sept. 1879, Riley VI. Mss., InU-Li.

189. JWR to Kahle, 6 May 1879.

190. JWR to Kahle, 29 Jan. 1879.

191. JWR to Kahle, 23 Aug. 1879, Brunn Mss., InU-Li.

192. Kahle to JWR, 7 Mar. 1880, Riley Mss., InU-Li.

193. JWR to Kahle, 10 Oct. 1879, Brunn Mss., InU-Li.

194. Ibid., 14 Aug. 1879.

195. Ibid., 23 Aug. 1879.

196. Kahle to JWR, 7 May 1881, Riley Mss., InU-Li.

197. JWR to Kahle, 10 Oct. 1879.

198. Ibid., 23 Aug. 1879.

199. Erna Olafson Hellerstein, Leslie Parker Hume, and Karen M. Offen, eds., *Victorian Women: A Documentary Account of Women's Lives in Nineteenth-Century England, France, and the United States* (Stanford, Calif.: Stanford University Press, 1981), p. 118; Peter Gay, *Education of the Senses* (New York: Oxford University Press, 1984), p. 169–70.

200. Gay, *Education of the Senses,* p. 194.

201. Ibid., p. 207.

202. Ibid.; pp. 169–71, 200–2.

203. JWR to Kahle, 23 Aug. 1879.

204. JWR to Kahle, 14 Aug. 1879.

205. Bottsford to JWR, 2 July 1879, Riley Mss., InU-Li; JWR to Bottsford, 7 Apr. 1880, Bottsford Mss., InU-Li.

206. JWR to Howard [Singleton] Taylor, 4 Sept. 1879, Riley VI. Mss., InU-Li.

207. JWR to Catherwood, 16 Sept. 1879.

208. Philips to JWR, 24 Aug. 1879.

209. Ibid.

210. Maurice Thompson, quoted in the *Cincinnati Gazette,* 26 July 1879.

211. Paine to JWR, 16 Aug. 1879, Riley Mss., InU-Li.

212. Philips to JWR, 27 July 1879, 8 Sept. 1879, Riley Mss., InU-Li; J[ohn] O. Hardesty to JWR, 30 Aug. 1879; Catherwood to JWR, 3 Sept. 1879, Riley Mss., InU-Li.

213. Common-Sense Literary Bureau to JWR, 18 Sept. 1879, Riley Mss., InU-Li.

214. JWR to Catherwood, 16 Sept. 1879.

215. H[enry] W[illiam] Taylor to JWR, 21 Oct. 1879, Riley Mss., InU-Li; Parker and Heiney, eds., "Biographical Notes," *Poets and Poetry of Indiana*, p. 457.

216. Gentile, *Cast of One*, p. 10.

217. Brodhead, *Cultures of Letters*, pp., 52–53, 67.

218. Ibid., p. 69; JWR to Catherwood, 16 Sept. 1879.

219. Common-Sense Bureau to JWR, 26 Sept. 1879, Riley Mss., InU-Li; JWR to Secretary C[ommon]-S[ense] Bureau, 29 Sept. 1879, Riley Mss., InU-Li; JWR to John [Newton] Taylor, 30 Sept. 1879, Riley VI. Mss., InU-Li.

220. This theater opened in 1859 and was originally called the Metropolitan. It had only recently been renamed when Riley appeared there. The only other major theater in Indianapolis, the Academy of Music, burned down in 1877 (McKinney, "Performing Arts," p. 149).

221. "J. W. Riley the Poet," *Indianapolis Herald*, 8 Oct. 1879.

222. "The Riley Testimonial," *Indianapolis Journal*, 16 Oct. 1879.

223. Ibid.

224. "J. W. Riley the Poet," *Indianapolis Herald*, 8 Oct. 1879.

225. Ibid.

226. George C. Hitt, "Mr. Riley as a Public Reader," *Book News Monthly* 23 (Mar. 1907): 439–40; "How Authors Read," *St. Louis Republic*, 5 Jan. 1893, *Pittsburgh Leader*, 15 Jan. 1893.

227. [enclosure] Howells to Dickey, 2 Feb. 1918, Dickey Mss., InU-Li.

228. "J. W. Riley the Poet," *Indianapolis Herald*, 8 Oct. 1879.

229. Tom J. Kemp to Dickey, 14 Apr. 1902, Dickey Mss., InU-Li.

230. JWR to Howard S. Taylor, 4 Sept. 1879.

231. "Riley's Lecture at the Park Theater," *Indianapolis News*, 17 Oct. 1879.

232. Clark and Halloran, eds., "Introduction," in *Oratorical Culture in Nineteenth-Century America*; Antczak and Siemers, "The Divergence of Purpose and Practice on the Chautauqua," pp. 211–12.

233. *Indianapolis Herald*, 18 Oct. 1879.

234. "The Hoosier Poet, James Whitcomb Riley's Views on American Poetry," *Marlborough Express*, 3 Dec. 1888.

235. Meredith Nicholson quoted in *In Honor of JWR, A Meeting of the Indiana State Teachers' Association* (Indianapolis: Bobbs-Merrill, 1905), pp. 31–32.

236. Gentile, *Cast of One*, pp. 19, 46.

237. "Riley's Lecture at the Park Theater," *Indianapolis News*, 17 Oct. 1879.

238. Levine, "Highbrow/Lowbrow," p. 46; Johnson, "The Popularization of Nineteenth-Century Rhetoric," pp. 140–43.

239. Ibid.; *Indianapolis Herald*, 18 Oct. 1879.

240. *Indianapolis Herald*, 18 Oct. 1879.

241. Johnson, "The Popularization of Nineteenth-Century Rhetoric," pp. 142–43.

242. "Riley's Lecture at the Park Theater," *Indianapolis News*, 17 Oct. 1879. The "Germlish" poem referred to is probably "Leedle Dutch Baby," first published in the *Indianapolis Journal* 28 June 1879 (Biographical Edition, III: 487).

243. Ibid.

244. Dickey—*Maturity,* p. 98; JWR to Kahle, 22 Nov. 1879, Brunn Mss., InU-Li.

245. JWR to Kahle, 1 Sept. 1879; JWR to Bottsford, 14 Nov. 1879, Bottsford Mss., InU-Li.

246. "The Hoosier Poet, James Whitcomb Riley's Views on American Poetry," *Marlborough Express,* 3 Dec. 1888; Interview with Charles Martindale, n.d., Dickey Mss., InU-Li; David Rank to Edmund Eitel, 5 Nov. 1915, M660, InHi.

247. Interview with Charles Martindale, n.d., Dickey Mss., InU-Li; Rank to Edmund Eitel, 5 Nov. 1915, M660, InHi.

248. "Nellie Bly on the Wing," *New York World,* 4 Nov. 1888.

249. JWR to Kahle, 22 Nov. 1879; Interview with Charles Martindale, n.d.

5. Newspaper Poet

1. "The Genial Hoosier," *Detroit Free Press,* 8 Mar. 1893.

2. Ibid.

3. Ibid.

4. Ibid.

5. Ibid.; Brodhead, *Cultures of Letters,* chapter 2.

6. "The Genial Hoosier," *Detroit Free Press,* 8 Mar. 1893.

7. Ibid.

8. JWR to John Taylor, 29 [Nov.] 1879, Riley Mss., InU-Li.

9. James Madison, "Economy," in Bodenhamer and Barrows, eds., *Encyclopedia of Indianapolis,* pp. 62–63; Robert M. Taylor, Jr., et al., *Indiana: A New Historical Guide* (Indianapolis: Indiana Historical Society, 1989), pp. 382–83; Dunn, *Greater Indianapolis,* pp. 345–47.

10. Madison, "Economy," pp. 63–64; James Divita, "Demography and Ethnicity," in Bodenhamer and Barrows, eds., *Encyclopedia of Indianapolis,* p. 55.

11. Taylor, et al., *Historical Guide,* p. 384; Elizabeth Brand Monroe, "Built Environment," in Bodenhamer and Barrows, eds., *Encyclopedia of Indianapolis,* p. 26.

12. Taylor, et al., *Historical Guide,* p. 384.

13. Divita, "Demography and Ethnicity," p. 53; Monroe, "Built Environment," pp. 23, 25, 29; Taylor, et al., *Historical Guide,* p. 383–84.

14. JWR to Bottsford, 21 Nov. 1879, Bottsford Mss., InU-Li.

15. Ernestine Bradford Rose, *The Circle: The Center of Indianapolis,* reprint (Indianapolis: Crippin, 1971), pp. 23–24.

16. Ibid., p. 11; Robert Burdette to JWR, 15 Jan. 1905, Riley V. Mss., InU-Li.

17. Ibid.

18. JWR to Bottsford, 2 Dec. 1879, Bottsford Mss., InU-Li.

19. Ibid., 29 Nov. 1879.

20. Bottsford to Riley, 2 July 1879, Riley Mss., InU-Li. For examples of Riley's advice to Bottsford see JWR to Bottsford, 8 July 1879, 28 Oct. 1879, [6 Nov. 1879], 2 Dec. 1879, 11 May 1880, 25 May 1880, 22 July 1880, Bottsford Mss., InU-Li.

21. JWR to Bottsford, 25 May 1880, 29 Oct. 1880, Bottsford Mss., InU-Li.

22. Gay, *Education of the Senses,* p. 174.

23. JWR to Bottsford, 9 Feb. 1880, Bottsford Mss., InU-Li.

24. Gay, *Education of the Senses,* p. 280.

25. Ibid., p. 201.

26. JWR to Bottsford, 5 Jan. 1880, Bottsford Mss., InU-Li.

27. Ibid.

28. JWR, "The Werewife," *Complete Works*, II: 531. This poem appeared in the *Indianapolis Journal* on 6 Jan. 1880 (Biographical Edition, II: 499).

29. JWR to Bottsford, 5 Jan. 1880, Bottsford Mss., InU-Li.

30. Gay, *Education of the Senses*, p. 197.

31. Ibid., p. 157.

32. JWR to Bottsford, 3 Feb. 1880, Bottsford Mss., InU-Li.

33. JWR to Kahle, 2 Jan. 1880, Brunn Mss., InU-Li.

34. "Mr. Riley at Crawfordsville," *Indianapolis Journal*, 21 Jan. 1880.

35. Ibid.

36. JWR to Kahle, 2 Jan. 1880, Brunn Mss., InU-Li; Dickey, "A Magical Life," [unpublished manuscript], n.d., p. 6, Dickey Mss., InU-Li.

37. JWR to Kahle, 29 Feb. 1880, Brunn Mss., InU-Li.

38. Ibid., 27 May 1880.

39. Ibid.; JWR to Kahle, 13 Apr. 1880, Brunn Mss., InU-Li.

40. Ibid.; "Nellie Bly on the Wing," *New York World*, 4 Nov. 1888.

41. C[harles] A. Dana to JWR, 20 Mar. 1880, Riley Mss., InU-Li; Biographical Edition, II: 503.

42. JWR to Kahle, 13 Apr. 1880, 27 May 1880, Brunn Mss., InU-Li.

43. "Dana and Riley," *Milwaukee Sentinel*, 25 July 1888.

44. JWR to Kahle, 27 May 1880.

45. Dana to JWR, 30 Apr. 1880, 12 May [1880], Riley Mss., InU-Li.

46. Ibid.

47. JWR to Dana, [May 1880], Riley Mss., InU-Li.

48. Dana to JWR, 17 May 1880, Riley Mss., InU-Li.

49. JWR to Dana, [May 1880].

50. Beers, "The Singer of the Old Swimmin' Hole," p. 36.

51. "Fairbanks Tells of Riley's Early Days," *Indianapolis Star*, 8 Oct. 1915.

52. JWR, "Dream" (unpublished), 14 Sept. 1870; "Haunted" (unpublished), 6 Oct. 1870; "I am Sitting Now and Sighing" (unpublished), 23 Sept. 1870, Riley III. Mss., InU-Li.

53. JWR, "Te-Click"; JWR, "In the City Streets," *Indianapolis Journal*, 14 Feb. 1886; JWR, "The Doctrine of Depravity," *Indianapolis Journal*, 27 Feb. 1880.

54. JWR to Dana, [May 1880].

55. Griffith, *Home Town News*, pp. 175–78; Reynolds, "Black Cat and Delirium Tremens," p. 23.

56. Reynolds, "Black Cats and Delirium Tremens," p. 28; Sánchez-Eppler, "Temperance in the Bed of a Child," p. 61.

57. JWR, "On Quitting California," *Indianapolis Herald*, 16 Nov. 1878; JWR, "The Dismal Fate of Tit," *Indianapolis Journal*, 9 Jan. 1880; JWR, "In Smithes Settlement" (unpublished), n.d.; JWR, "John Golliher's Third Womern" (unpublished), 27 July 1879, JWR, "Te-Click" (unpublished), 20 Jan. 1871, Riley III. Mss., InU-Li. Even "Te-Click" which described a train crash made references to drinking: "Well, all of the boys had drunk pretty free,/And the engineer drunk as a man could be,/When he started out on his midnight run." Reynolds, "Black Cats and Delirium Tremens," p. 28; Sánchez-Eppler, "Temperance in the Bed of a Child," p. 61.

58. JWR, "The Dismal Fate of Tit."

59. Ibid.

60. Behr, *Prohibition*, p. 49.

61. Ibid., p. 7.

62. Rev. T. A. Goodwin quoted in Dunn, *Greater Indianapolis*, p. 445.

63. Ibid.; Behr, *Prohibition*, pp. 7, 11; Elva May (Riley) Eitel to John A. Riley, 18 Nov. 1890, M660, InHi.

64. Behr, *Prohibition*, p. 23; JWR, "In Smithes Settlement," "John Golliher's Third Womern."

65. Behr, *Prohibition*, p. 3. In Indiana between 1853 and 1855, temperance agitation led to passage of the state's first prohibition law. In 1856, this law was held to be unconstitutional. During the Civil War, there was little interest in the temperance cause. However, in 1868, the State Temperance Alliance was established and began organizing throughout Indiana. The Indiana Prohibition League, founded in 1876, and other temperance organizations followed. Dunn stated that the Prohibition League's efforts led to the closure of 500 saloons and 60,000 individual temperance pledges (Dunn, *Greater Indianapolis*, 1: 453–56).

66. Warner, "Temperance, Morality, and Medicine," p. 141.

67. JWR, "Afterwhiles," manuscript fragment, Riley III. Mss., InU-Li.

68. Writings, Riley III. Mss., InU-Li.

69. "Tom Johnson's Quit" appeared in *Pipes o' Pan at Zekesbury* (Indianapolis: Bobbs-Merrill, 1888) as well in collections of Riley's complete works (Biographical Edition, II: 383).

70. John New had long been a prominent member of Indiana's Republican party. At age thirty, in 1861, he was elected to the Indiana State Senate and, in 1862, served as Indiana quartermaster general under Governor Morton. In this capacity and as an officer of the First National Bank of Indianapolis, he distinguished himself as a man with excellent financial skills. President Ulysses S. Grant recognized his abilities and appointed him United States Treasurer in 1875. He held this office through 1876. He would later serve as first assistant secretary in the Department of the Treasury from 1882 to 1883, under President Chester A. Arthur, and as U.S. consul general in London from 1889 to 1893, under President Benjamin Harrison (Walsh, *A Biographical Directory of the Indiana General Assembly*, 1; 290; Dunn, *Greater Indianapolis*, 1: 412; *Commemorative Biographical Record of Prominent and Representative Men of Indianapolis and Vicinity containing Biographical Sketches of Business and Professional Men and of Many Early Settled Families* [Chicago: J. H. Beers, 1908], pp. 18–20; Cumback and Maynard, eds., *Men of Progress. Indiana*, pp. 312–14; John H. B. Nowland, *Early Reminiscences of Indianapolis, with Biographical Sketches of its Early Citizens, and of a Few of the Prominent Business Men of the Present Day* [Indianapolis: Sentinel Book and Job Printing House, 1870], pp. 371–72).

71. S. R. Henderson to JWR, 3 Dec. 1879, Riley Mss., InU-Li; JWR to Bottsford, 12 May 1880, Bottsford Mss., InU-Li.

72. Ibid.

73. *Scribner's Monthly* to JWR, 4 June 1880; JWR to editor of *Atlantic*, 10 June 1880; JWR to *Scribner's Monthly*, 14 June 1880; Editors, *Scribner's Monthly* to JWR, 14 June 1880, 28 June 1880; *Harper's Magazine* to JWR, 26 July 1880, Riley Mss., InU-Li.

74. JWR to Bottsford, 31 May 1880, Bottsford Mss., InU-Li

75. JWR to Jones, 10 July 1880, Riley Mss., InU-Li.

76. Ibid.; JWR to Kahle, 6 July 1880, Brunn Mss., InU-Li.

77. Dana to JWR, 7 July 1880, Riley Mss., InU-Li; JWR to Jones, 10 July 1880.

78. JWR to [Wilcox], 11 July 1880, Riley III. Mss., InU-Li.

79. T. J. Jackson Lears, *No Place of Grace: Antimodernism and the Transformation of American Culture, 1880–1920,* paperback ed. (Chicago: University of Chicago Press, 1994), pp. 35–36.

80. Ibid.

81. Ibid.

82. Lears, *No Place of Grace,* p. 37.

83. JWR to [Wilcox], 7 Sept. 1880.

84. "First Letter about Mr. Riley—1882," Correspondence Cincinnati Gazette, Riley Mss., InU-Li.

85. Interview with Charles Martindale, n.d., Dickey Mss., InU-Li; Ade, "Riley and His Friends," p. 10. Hitt became business manager of the *Indianapolis Journal* in 1875. He "later became part owner and remained with the paper for over twenty-five years" (Van Allen and Foust, eds., *Keeping the Dream,* p. 108). Riley met George Hitt in 1876. Through their mutual employment at the *Journal,* Hitt became one of the dearest of Riley's Indianapolis friends (Dickey to Hitt, 20 July 1923, Hitt Mss., InU-Li; Lesley Payne to John F. Mitchell, Jr., 28 June 1949, Payne, L., Mss., InU-Li).

86. JWR to Bottsford, n.d., Riley V. Mss., InU-Li.

87. JWR to Bottsford, 5 July 1880, 6 July 1880, Bottsford Mss., InU-Li.

88. Gay, *Education of the Senses,* p. 452.

89. JWR to Bottsford, 6 July 1880, Bottsford Mss., InU-Li.

90. Gay, *Education of the Senses,* p. 453.

91. Ibid., pp. 80, 453.

92. JWR to Bottsford, 5 July 1880, 6 July 1880., Bottsford Mss., InU-Li.

93. Ibid., 15 June 1880.

94. Ibid., 7 July 1880.

95. Ibid., 19 Apr. 1880.

96. Riley's first letter to Wilcox was dated 24 Feb. 1880 (Riley Mss., InU-Li).

97. JWR to Louella White, 30 Jan. 1880, 11 Mar. 1880, Riley VI. Mss., InU-Li; JWR to White, 6 Feb. 1880, 21 Feb. 1880, 20 Mar. 1880, 25 Mar. 1880, 21 May 1880, 5 July 1880, M660, InHi.

98. JWR to Bottsford, 5 Jan. 1880, Bottsford Mss., InU-Li.

99. Ibid., 7 July 1880.

100. Ibid.

101. Ibid.

102. Ibid.

103. JWR to [Wilcox], 11 July 1880,19 Aug. 1880, Riley III. Mss., InU-Li.

104. JWR to Bottsford, 22 July 1880 [enclosure], Bottsford Mss., InU-Li. Myron Reed (1836–1899) was minister of First Presbyterian Church in Indianapolis between 1877and 1884. He was one of the most influential ministers serving in the city at this time (Jacob Piatt Dunn, *Indiana and the Indianians,* 4 vols. [American Historical Society, 1919], 3: 1260). Reed discovered Riley through his early contributions to the *Indianapolis Journal.* They met at Crown Hill Cemetery on Decoration Day in May 1878 and became fast friends (Crowder, p. 86). Although Riley generally did not like organized religion, he always had much respect for Reed; and he became Riley's spiritual advisor.

105. Ibid., 12 Dec. 1880; Dunn, *Greater Indianapolis,* 1: 404.

106. JWR to Bottsford, 12 Dec. 1880, Bottsford Mss., InU-Li.

107. Ibid.; JWR to Bottsford, 19 Oct. 1880, Bottsford Mss., InU-Li.

108. JWR to Bottsford, [26 Mar. 1880], Bottsford Mss., InU-Li.

109. Grace Monk Morland to JWR, 18 Aug. 1880, 24 Aug. 1880, 30 Aug. 1880, Riley Mss., InU-Li.

110. Morland to JWR, 30 Aug. 1880, Riley Mss., InU-Li.

111. Gentile, *Cast of One,* pp. 4–5, 47.

112. Sarah Bernhardt appeared in Indiana during winter 1881 (JWR to Bottsford, 26 Feb. 1881, Bottsford Mss., InU-Li).

113. JWR to [Wilcox], 24 Feb. 1880, Riley III. Mss., InU-Li.

114. Ibid., 7 June 1880, 13 June 1880, 11 July 1880.

115. Ibid., 21 June 1880.

116. "Biographical Notes," in *American Poetry, the Nineteenth Century,* 2: 925. *Poems of Passion,* published in 1883, was her most popular anthology. It sold 60,000 copies within two years. Like Riley, Wilcox is also often criticized as an author of inept sentimental Victorian poetry (Janet Gray, ed., *She Wields a Pen,* p. 222; Paula Bennett, "Not Just Filler and Not Just Sentimental: Women's Poetry in American Periodical, 1860–1900," in Kenneth M. Price and Susan Belasco Smith, eds., *Periodical Literature in Nineteenth-Century America* [Charlottesville: University Press of Virginia, 1995], fn 22).

117. JWR to [Wilcox], 11 July 1880.

118. Ibid., 24 June 1880, Riley III. Mss., InU-Li.

119. Ibid.; 11 July 1880, 19 Aug. 1880, InU-Li.

120. Ibid., [1 Sept. 1880], Riley Mss., InU-Li; "Riley's Sour Grapes, The Meaning of His Attack on Ella Wheeler," *Milwaukee Journal,* 8 Feb. 1884.

121. JWR to [Wilcox], [1 Sept. 1880].

122. Ibid., 11 July 1880.

123. Ibid., 7 Sept. 1880, 30 Nov. 1880, Riley III. Mss., InU-Li.

124. Brodhead, *Cultures of Letters,* pp. 160–61; Gay, *Education of the Senses,* pp. 169–71, 179.

125. JWR to Wilcox, 7 Sept. 1880, 30 Nov. 1880; "Biographical Notes," in *American Poetry, the Nineteenth Century,* 2: 925; Janet Gray, ed., *She Wields a Pen,* p. 222.

126. JWR to Bottsford, 5 Jan. 1880, Bottsford Mss., InU-Li; "Riley's Sour Grapes," *Milwaukee Journal,* 8 Feb. 1884; "The Hoosier Poet, A Chat with James W. Riley," *Kansas City Star,* 2 Feb. 1884.

127. "Biographical Notes," in *American Poetry, the Nineteenth Century,* 2: 925; Janet Gray, ed., *She Wields a Pen,* p. 222.

128. "The Hoosier Poet, A Chat with James W. Riley."

129. Ibid. 130. "Riley's Sour Grapes," *Milwaukee Journal,* 8 Feb. 1884.

131. Wilcox to JWR, 6 Dec. 1906, Riley III. Mss., InU-Li.

132. Ibid.

133. JWR to Kahle, 6 July 1880, Brunn Mss., InU-Li.

134. Ibid.; Hellerstein, et al., eds., *Victorian Women,* p. 120.

135. JWR to Jones, 29 July 1881, Riley Mss., InU-Li.

136. JWR to Kahle, 6 Oct. 1880, Brunn Mss., InU-Li.

137. J. H. Tedford to James H. Burke, 19 Aug. 1916, Riley III. Mss., InU-Li.

138. "James Whitcomb Riley, A Prophet Who Is Honored at Home and Abroad," *Indianapolis News,* 25 Feb. 1891.

139. Hewitt Hanson Howland, "Riley the Humorist," *Book News Monthly* 23 (Mar. 1907): 436.

140. JWR to Bottsford, 22 Aug. 1881, Bottsford Mss., InU-Li.

141. JWR to Louise Chandler Moulton, 27 Feb. 1894, Riley VI. Mss., InU-Li.

142. JWR to J. N. Matthews, 26 July 1887, Riley Mss., InU-Li.

143. Reynolds, *Walt Whitman's America,* pp. 198–99.

144. JWR to Matthews, 26 July 1887.

145. JWR to Kahle, 6 July 1880, Brunn Mss., InU-Li.

146. Ibid., 6 July 1880, 23 June [1881]; JWR to White, 11 Mar. 1880; JWR to Matthews, 26 July 1887.

147. JWR to Wheeler, 7 Sept. 1880; JWR to Bottsford, 20 Aug. 1880; JWR to Jones, 22 Aug. 1880, Riley Mss., InU-Li.

148. JWR to Jones, 22 Aug. 1880.

149. Ibid., 19 Nov. 1880.

150. JWR to [Wilcox], 7 Sept. 1880.

151. JWR to Kahle, 6 Oct. 1880, Brunn Mss., InU-Li.

152. JWR to Bottsford, 15 Sept. 1880, Bottsford Mss., InU-Li.

153. JWR to [Wilcox], 30 Nov. 1880; JWR to Kahle, 6 Oct. 1880.

154. JWR to Bottsford, 17 Nov. 1880, Bottsford Mss., InU-Li.

155. Ibid., 8 Dec. 1880.

156. Ibid., 12 Dec. 1880.

157. JWR to Jones, 22 Dec. 1880, Riley Mss., InU-Li.

158. Ibid., 5 Dec. 1880.

159. JWR to Jones, 4 Feb. 1881. JWR started to correspond with Jones, who was married to a man named Carver, in July 1880. She was a regular contributor to the *Kokomo Tribune.* JWR to Jones, 6 July 1880; *Kokomo Tribune* [pamphlet, Kokomo, Ind.: T. C. Philips's Sons Publishers (1880)]).

160. JWR to Kahle, 6 Oct. 1881. "The Land of Used-to-Be" appeared in *Wide Awake* in Nov. 1881; and "A Nonsense Rhyme" appeared in *St Nicholas* in Nov. 1880 (Biographical Edition, II: 516, 529).

161. JWR to Bottsford, 10 Feb. 1881, Bottsford Mss., InU-Li; Parker to JWR, 4 Mar. 1881, Riley Mss., InU-Li.

162. JWR to Bottsford, 10 Feb. 1881.

163. Ibid., 1 Mar. 1881, 20 June 1881; Parker to JWR, 4 Mar. 1881. On 21 Feb., Riley told Bottsford that he had "scarcely failed a day" staying away from the bottle but had been so sick that he could hardly sit up. He said that his head looked "like a biscuit on a horse hair," and that he continued to be unsteady on his feet (JWR to Bottsford, 21 Feb. 1881, Bottsford Mss., InU-Li).

164. W. W. Loring to JWR, 27 Feb. 1881, 22 Apr. 1881; J. W. Buseck to JWR, 29 Mar. 1881, Riley Mss., InU-Li.

165. JWR to Albert Busch, 8 Apr. 1881, Riley VI. Mss., InU-Li.

166. JWR to Bottsford, [18 Apr. 1881], Bottsford Mss., InU-Li.

167. JWR to Jones, 27 Apr. 1881; Paul H. Gray, "Preparing for Popularity: Origins of the Poet-Performer Movement," in *Literature in Performance* 6 (Nov. 1985): 38–39.

168. Paul Gray, "Preparing for Popularity," pp. 38–40.

169. Ibid.

170. Ibid.

171. JWR to Kahle, 23 June [1881], Brunn Mss., InU-Li.

172. Burdette to JWR, 7 June 1881, Riley Mss., InU-Li.

173. Ibid.

174. JWR to Bottsford, 27 June 1881, Bottsford Mss., InU-Li.

175. JWR, "Summer Composition," *Indianapolis Journal,* 13 July 1881; "Giant on the Show Bills," 16 July 1881; "Old Letters," 6 Aug. 1881; "Ach Chew," 13 Aug. 1881; "Old Fiddler," 20 Aug. 1881; "Tizwin," 9 Sept. 1881; "John Boyle O'Reilly," "Sketch of Burdette at Home," 21 Jan. 1882; "An Hour with Longfellow," 29 Apr. 1882; "Entertainment Decoration Day Fund," 24 May 1882.

176. JWR to Bottsford, 25 July 1881, Bottsford Mss., InU-Li; JWR to Jones, 1 July 1881, 29 July 1881; JWR to Kahle, 10 Sept. 1881.

177. Griffith, *Home Town News,* pp. 15–16.

178. Redpath Lyceum Bureau to JWR, 29 July 1881, Riley Mss., InU-Li.

179. Ibid.

180. JWR to Bottsford, 10 Aug. 1881, Bottsford Mss., InU-Li.

181. Redpath Lyceum Bureau (circular), Oct. 1881.

182. JWR to Bottsford, 18 Aug. 1881, Bottsford Mss., InU-Li.

183. JWR to Bottsford, 4 Sept. 1881, Bottsford Mss., InU-Li.

184. Ibid.

185. JWR to Bottsford, 31 Aug. 1881, Bottsford Mss., InU-Li; JWR to Kahle, 10 Sept. 1881, Brunn Mss., InU-Li.

186. JWR to Bottsford, 10 Nov. 1881, Bottsford Mss., InU-Li; JWR to Burdette, 9 Nov. 1881, Berg Collection of American and English Literature, New York Public Library.

187. JWR to Bottsford, 8 Nov. 1881, 10 Nov. 1881, Bottsford Mss., InU-Li.

188. JWR to Bottsford, 15 Oct. 1881, Bottsford Mss., InU-Li.

189. Bottsford to JWR, 6 Oct. 1881, Riley Mss., InU-Li.; JWR to Bottsford, 8 June 1882, Bottsford Mss., InU-Li.

190. JWR to Bottsford, 5 Jan. 1880, 18 Sept. 1880, 17 Aug. 1883, Bottsford Mss., InU-Li.

191. Ibid., 8 Dec. 1880, 16 Dec. 1880, 5 July 1881, 19 Nov. 1881, 5 June 1882, 3 Oct. 1882, Bottsford Mss., InU-Li.

192. Ibid., 20 July 1881, 25 July 1881, 1 Aug. 1881, 5 Aug. 1881, 10 Aug. 1881, 26 Sept. 1881; Bottsford to JWR, [17] Aug. 1881, 6 Oct. 1881, 19 Nov. 1881, Riley Mss., InU-Li.

193. JWR to Bottsford, 7 Apr. 1881, 8 Apr. 1881, Bottsford Mss., InU-Li; JWR, "Mabel," Biographical Edition, II: 340.

194. JWR to Bottsford, 4 Oct. 1881, Bottsford Mss., InU-Li; Margaret Slick Riley died at the home of one of Riley's uncles. She was eighty-seven (Margaret Slick Riley, funeral notice, 3 Oct. 1881, M628, InHi).

195. As late as 1900, only about 4 percent of the population in the United States was over sixty-five years of age (Hellerstein, et al., eds., *Victorian Women,* pp. 452–53).

196. JWR to Bottsford, 19 Oct. 1880, 11 [May] 1881, 13 May 1881, Bottsford Mss., InU-Li.

197. Ibid., 8 Nov. 1881; Chas Philips to JWR, 28 Jan. 1881, Riley Mss., InU-Li.

198. R. A. Riley to JWR, 23 Nov. 1881, Riley Mss., InU-Li.

199. JWR to Bottsford, 20 July 1881, Bottsford Mss., InU-Li.

200. John Riley to JWR, 2 Dec. 1881, Riley Mss., InU-Li.

201. Ibid.; JWR to Jones, 2 Dec. 1881, Riley Mss., InU-Li.

202. Jahan Ramazini, *Poetry of Mourning: The Modern Elegy from Hardy to Heaney* (Chicago: University of Chicago Press, 1994), p. 10–13; James J. Farrell, *Inventing the*

American Way of Death, 1830–1920 (Philadelphia: Temple University Press, 1980), pp. 178–81.

203. Joseph Jacobs quoted in Ramazini, *Poetry of Mourning,* p. 12.

204. In a letter to Robert Burdette, Riley said that getting his Boston dates would cost him money (JWR to Burdette, 9 Nov. 1881). In mid-December, he wrote to the Redpath Bureau to say that he assumed the $150 cost for same (JWR to R[edpath] L[yceum] Bureau, 12 Dec. 1881, Riley Mss., InU-Li).

205. JWR to Bottsford, 3 Dec. 1881, Bottsford Mss., InU-Li.

206. Ibid.

207. JWR to Bottsford, 7 Dec. 1881, Bottsford Mss., InU-Li.

208. Ibid.

209. Ibid.; JWR to Bottsford, 8 Dec. 1881, InU-Li; Mrs. George (Lotta Bottsford), "A Hoosier Romance, Riley's Love Story Told," *Indianapolis Times,* 7 Oct. 1935; Cooper, "Riley, School Teacher Planned to Be Married, Sister of Girl Writes," *Indianapolis Times,* 8 Oct. 1935.

210. JWR to R[edpath] L[yceum] Bureau, 12 Dec. 1881.

211. Ibid.; JWR to Busch, 23 Dec. 1881, Riley VI. Mss., Riley Mss., InU-Li.

212. JWR to Busch, 23 Dec. 1881.

213. JWR to Bottsford, 19 Dec. 1881, Bottsford Mss., InU-Li.

214. Ibid.

215. Redpath Lyceum Bureau to JWR, 24 Dec. 1881, Riley Mss., InU-Li.

216. JWR to Bottsford, 29 Dec. 1881.

217. Ibid.

218. Ibid.

219. Levine, *Highbrow/Lowbrow,* p. 48.

220. JWR to Bottsford, 29 Dec. 1881, Bottsford Mss., InU-Li.

221. JWR to Busch, 1 Jan. 1882, Riley VI. Mss., InU-Li.

222. JWR to Bottsford, 29 Dec. 1881, Bottsford Mss., InU-Li.

223. Ibid.; JWR to Hitt, 1 Jan. 1882, Hitt Mss., InU-Li.

224. JWR to Hitt, 1 Jan. 1882.

225. JWR to Busch, 1 Jan. 1882.

226. JWR to [Bottsford], 30 Dec. 1881, Riley Mss., InU-Li. Although this letter was separated from those found in the Bottsford collection, from the text, it is clear that it is the continuation of the letter to Bottsford dated 29 December and that both were sent in the same envelope.

227. JWR to Busch, 1 Jan. 1882; JWR, "The Tree Toad," *Complete Works,* II: 485–86. This poem was first published in the *Indianapolis Herald* on 2 Aug. 1879 (Biographical Edition, II: 490–91).

228. Ibid.

229. Ibid.; JWR to Hitt, 1 Jan. 1882; JWR to [Bottsford], 30 Dec. 1881.

230. Ibid.; "An Hour with Longfellow," *Indianapolis Journal,* 29 Apr. 1882. Longfellow suffered a serious nervous attack in 1881 ("Biographical Notes," in *American Poetry, the Nineteenth Century,* 1: 1012).

231. Ibid.

232. "An Hour with Longfellow."

233. Macauley quoted in "An Hour with Longfellow."

234. "An Hour with Longfellow"; JWR to [Bottsford], 30 Dec. 1881.

235. JWR to [Bottsford], 30 Dec. 1881.

236. "An Hour with Longfellow."

237. Ibid., JWR to [Bottsford], 30 Dec. 1881.

238. Ibid.

239. JWR to [Bottsford], 30 Dec. 1881.

240. Ibid.

241. Ibid., JWR to Busch, 1 Jan. 1882, JWR to Hitt, 1 Jan. 1882, "Mr. J. W. Riley at Boston," *Indianapolis Journal*, 13 Jan. 1882; "An Hour with Longfellow" was published in the *Indianapolis Journal* in April, one month following Longfellow's death from peritonitis on 24 Mar. 1882 ("Biographical Notes," in *American Poetry, the Nineteenth Century*, 1: 1011–12).

242. "An Hour with Longfellow." Elijah W. Halford, then editor of the *Indianapolis Journal*, later recalled that when Riley returned to Indianapolis from Boston he told him that he dared not repeat what Longfellow had said to him regarding his work and the possibilities for the future (Halford to Chas. W. Fairbanks, 22 Sept. 1915, Riley III. Mss., InU-Li). However, Riley usually did not hesitate to mention that he met Longfellow and that he was the first poet of reputation to acknowledge that he had poetic talent.

243. "Riley in Omaha," *Omaha World Herald*, 19 Nov. 1897.

244. "Riley Loves Longfellow," *Rochester Herald*, 2 Nov. 1898.

245. "James Whitcomb Riley," *New York Sun*, 5 Mar. 1893; "James Whitcomb Riley," *Saint Louis Mirror*, 10 Feb. 1898; Howells, "The New Poetry," 168 (May 1899): 588; Beers, "The Singer of the Old Swimmin' Hole," p. 33; Reynolds, *Walt Whitman's America*, p. 318.

246. JWR to Jones, 1 Aug. 1882, Riley Mss., InU-Li.

247. JWR, "Poetry and Character."

248. Reynolds, *Walt Whitman's America*, p. 318.

249. "The Hoosier Poet, A Chat with James W. Riley," *Kansas City Star*, 2 Feb. 1884.

250. "James Whitcomb Riley," *New York Sun*, 5 Mar. 1893; Reynolds, *Walt Whitman's America*, pp. 318, 353.

251. Reynolds, *Walt Whitman's America*, pp. 310, 353.

252. "James Whitcomb Riley," *New York Sun*, 5 Mar. 1893. A fire at Bowen-Merrill destroyed files containing sale figures for Riley's books before 1890. According to David Laurence Chambers, president of Bobbs-Merrill (Bowen-Merrill's successor) at the time of the centennial of Riley's birth, the publisher sold over 2.5 million copies of the Hoosier poet's books between 1893 and 1949 (David Laurence Chambers, James Whitcomb Riley, 1893–1949, RMA).

253. Ibid.; Howells, "The New Poetry," 168 (May 1899): 588; Bowlby, *Just Looking*, p. 9; Reynolds, *Walt Whitman's America*, 310, 353. The only other American poet who managed to reach a broad audience was Whittier. However his sales did not match those of Riley and Longfellow. His most popular work, *Snowbound*, published in 1866, sold 20,000 copies ("Biographical Notes," in *American Poetry, the Nineteenth Century*, 2 vols. [New York: The Library of America, 1993] 1: 1030).

254. JWR to Hitt, 3 Jan. 1882, Riley Mss., InU-Li

255. Ibid.

256. JWR to Bottsford, 4 Jan. 1882, Bottsford Mss., InU-Li

257. "How Riley Does It," *Indianapolis Journal*, 11 May 1891.

258. "Tremont Temple," *Boston Journal*, 4 Jan. 1882; "End of the Bible Union Course," *Boston Globe*, 4 Jan. 1882.

259. Ibid.; *Boston Evening Transcript*, 3 Jan. 1882.

260. Ibid.

261. *Boston Evening Transcript*, 3 Jan. 1882.

262. Ibid.

263. JWR to Bottsford, 4 Jan. 1882, Bottsford Mss., InU-Li.

264. Paul Gray, "Preparing for Popularity," p. 39.

265. JWR to Bottsford, 4 Jan. 1882.

266. John Boyle O'Reilly quoted in "First Letter about Mr. Riley—1882."

267. JWR to Hitt, 3 Jan. 1882. John Boyle O'Reilly (1844–1890) was born in Ireland. In 1869, he escaped to America after being deported to Australia and sentenced to 23 years of penal servitude for enlisting in the British military with the intention of inciting revolt as a member of the Fenians (forerunners of the Sinn Fein). After coming to the United States, he joined the staff of the Boston *Pilot* in 1870. O'Reilly eventually became an owner of the *Pilot* and a naturalized American citizen. Between 1873 and 1889, he published several volumes of poetry (*Webster's New Biographical Dictionary*). Riley described him as a man with "a high round head, a bronzed face, [and] "a crisp, black moustache and an eye whose frank and generous expanse of brow command[ed] the fullest confidence." He was not a large man but was apparently solid in build. Riley wrote that he worked hard and had great powers of endurance (JWR, "John Boyle O'Reilly," *Indianapolis Journal*, 21 Jan. 1882).

268. JWR to Hitt, 3 Jan. 1882.

269. JWR to Bottsford, 4 Jan. 1882.

270. "Mr. J. W. Riley at Boston," *Indianapolis Journal*, 10 Jan. 1882. In a letter to Hitt, Riley said that Macauley would write to the *Journal* if he had time (JWR to Hitt, 3 Jan. 1882).

271. JWR to Bottsford, 20 [Jan.] 1882, Bottsford Mss., InU-Li.

272. JWR to Kahle, 18 Jan. 1882, Brunn Mss., InU-Li.

273. JWR to Bottsford, 20 [Jan.] 1882.

274. Burdette quoted in the *Hancock Democrat*, 18 Jan. 1882.

275. JWR to Bottsford, 20 [Jan.] 1882.

276. Ibid.

277. O'Reilly quoted in "First Letter about Mr. Riley—1882."

278. JWR to Bottsford, [15 Feb. 1882], Bottsford Mss., InU-Li.

279. JWR to Hitt, 26 Feb. 1882, Riley Mss., InU-Li. Aldrich (1836–1907) served as editor of the *Atlantic Monthly* between 1881 and 1890. He wrote several volumes of poetry, stories such as "Marjorie Dawe," and novels such as *Queen of Sheba* (*Webster's New Biographical Dictionary*).

280. JWR to Bottsford, [20 Feb. 1882], Bottsford Mss., InU-Li.

281. *Benet's Reader's Encyclopedia of American Literature* (New York: Harper Collins, 1991), p. 98.

282. "A Humorous Trio, Billings, Burdette and Riley Together in the Star Course," *Philadelphia Enquirer*, 7 Mar. 1882.

283. Ibid. When Riley appeared with Billings at the beginning of Mar. 1882, Billings was at the end of his career. He was almost 64 years old and would die three years later (*Benet's Reader's Encyclopedia of American Literature*).

284. "A Humorous Trio."

285. Ibid.

286. JWR to Bottsford, 6 Apr. 1882, Bottsford Mss., InU-Li.

287. Burdette again accompanied Riley on this visit to Whitman in October 1882. Although he rarely mentioned this legendary American poet, Riley was very aware of his nickname and reputation. In a letter dated 21 Oct. 1882, he simply referred to Whitman as the "Good Gray" (JWR to Howard Taylor, 21 Oct. 1882, Riley Mss., InU-Li). Whitman lived in Camden with his brother George and his sister-in-law Louisa from 1873 to 1884. George Whitman was a civil engineer and made enough money to enable Walt to live cheaply under his roof. In 1884, Whitman purchased his own cottage in Camden, where he remained until his death in 1892 (Reynolds, *Walt Whitman's America*, pp. 497–98, 546).

288. "Poets and Critics," *Scranton Truth*, 5 Apr. 1893; R. Gerald McMurtry, "Poet and President, Riley's Estimate of Lincoln," *Lincoln Herald* (Feb. 1945): 29; Reynolds, *Walt Whitman's America*, p. 440.

289. *Complete Works*, IV: 1055–56. "Lincoln" was first printed in the *Indianapolis Journal* on 26 Oct. 1884 (Biographical Edition, III: 529).

290. "Poets and Critics," *Scranton Truth*, 5 Apr. 1893.

291. John S. Spann to JWR, 15 Apr. 1882, Riley Mss., InU-Li; Demand for Delinquent Taxes, 18 Apr. 1882, Riley Mss., InU-Li.

292. JWR to Bottsford, 29 May 1882, Bottsford Mss., InU-Li.

293. Ibid., 29 May 1882, 31 May 1882.

294. Ibid., 31 May 1882.

295. Ibid., 31 May 1882, 5 June 1882.

296. Schedule 2.—Productions of Agriculture in Sugar Creek Township in the County of Hancock in the State of Indiana, 3 June 1880, In-Ar; Phillips, *Indiana in Transition*, pp. 30–31.

297. Bottsford to JWR, 6 Oct. 1881.

298. JWR to Bottsford, 16 June 1882, Bottsford Mss., InU-Li.

299. Ibid.

300. Ibid.

301. Bowlby, *Just Looking*, pp. 8–9; Weber, *Hired Pens*, p. 134.

302. JWR to Parker, 6 June 1882, Riley Mss., InU-Li.

303. JWR to Jones, 15 June 1882, Riley Mss., InU-Li.

304. JWR to Bottsford, 8 June 1882, Bottsford Mss, InU-Li.

305. [JWR], "A Boone County Pastoral," 17 June 1882.

306. "Benjamin F. Johnson of Boone," *Indianapolis Journal*, 16 Sept. 1882. For a complete list of these poems and the date upon which the *Journal* published them see Russo, p. 6.

307. Meredith Nicholson, *The Hoosiers*, centennial ed. (New York: Macmillan, 1915), p. 160.

308. [JWR], "A Boone County Pastoral," 17 June 1882.

309. "Published His Poems Under Another Name," *Indianapolis News*, 30 Sept. 1907.

310. "A Boone County Pastoral," reprinted from the *Lebanon Patriot* in the *Indianapolis Journal*, 26 June 1882; "A Guess at the Authorship," reprinted from the *Saturday Herald* in the *Indianapolis Journal*, 26 June 1882; "Thinks Mr. Johnson a Myth," reprinted from the *Richmond Palladium* in the *Indianapolis Journal*, 26 June 1882; "Benjamin F. Johnson, The Poet," *Hancock Democrat*, 7 Sept. 1882.

311. JWR to Bottsford, 3 July 1882, Bottsford Mss., InU-Li.

312. Brodhead, *Cultures of Letters*, pp. 116–18.

313. "Benjamin F. Johnson of Boone," *Indianapolis Journal,* 16 Sept. 1882.
314. JWR, "Dialect in Literature," *Complete Works,* X: 2681.
315. Nicholson, *The Hoosiers,* pp. 161–62.
316. Brodhead, *Cultures of Letters,* p. 108, 115–16.
317. Nicholson, *The Hoosiers,* p. 158.
318. JWR to Thomas Wentworth Higginson, 9 Dec. 1891, L135, In.
319. JWR, "Dialect in Literature," *Complete Works,* X: 2681.
320. Brodhead, *Cultures of Letters,* p. 120; Biographical Edition, II: 535.
321. Biographical Edition, II: 535–36.
322. Brodhead, *Cultures of Letters,* pp. 119–20.
323. Ibid., pp. 120–21.
324. Ibid., p. 121.
325. Ibid.
326. Sarah Orne Jewett (1849–1909) became a professional author by writing about remote New England villages. Mark Twain (Samuel Clemens, 1835–1910) wrote about life in Missouri and on the Mississippi River, and George Washington Cable (1844–1925) wrote about the Creoles in Louisana (Brodhead, *Cultures of Letters,* pp. 116, 122; "Biographical Notes," in *American Poetry, the Nineteenth Century,* 2: 875, 893; *Webster's New Biographical Dictionary*).
327. "Mr. J. W. Riley of Boston."
328. Dickey—*Maturity,* pp. 158–61.
329. Dickey to George Hitt, 20 July 1923, Hitt Mss., InU-Li.
330. George C. Hitt & Co., Account Book, July–Dec. 1883, Hitt Mss., InU-Li; Russo, pp. 3–4; "Dana and Riley," *Milwaukee Sentinel,* 25 July 1888; Lesley Payne to John F. Mitchell, Jr., 28 June 1949, L. Payne Mss., InU-Li.
331. George C. Hitt & Co., Account Book; Hitt to L. L. Dickerson, 13 Apr. 1938, Hitt Mss., InU-Li; Russo, pp. 3–4.
332. "Benj. F. Johnson of Boone," *Indianapolis Journal,* 21 July 1883.
333. JWR to W. D. Pratt, 30 July 1883, M660, InHi.
334. Ibid.
335. Robert Underwood Johnson to JWR, 18 Aug. 1883, Riley Mss., InU-Li.
336. Joel Chandler Harris to JWR, 3 Aug. 1883, Riley Mss., InU-Li.
337. John Hay to JWR, 7 Nov. 1883, Riley Mss., InU-Li.
338. George C. Hitt & Co., Account Book; Russo, p. 4.
339. Ibid.
340. "Dana and Riley," *Milwaukee Sentinel,* 25 July 1888.
341. "William C. Bobbs" (obituary) *Indianapolis Star,* 12 Feb. 1926.
342. Anderson, "The Fires That Feed Genius."
343. Ibid.
344. Ibid.; "Riley Is Here," *San Francisco Report,* 8 Dec. 1892.
345. "Riley Is Here," *San Francisco Report,* 8 Dec. 1892. "Poet and Story Teller," Lansing, Michigan, *State Republican,* 1 Nov. 1893.

6. Realizing Ambitions

1. *Detroit Free Press,* 15 Feb. 1889.
2. JWR to Jones, 10 Aug. 1881, Riley Mss., InU-Li.
3. JWR to Matthews, 23 July 1883, M660, InHi.

4. JWR to A. H. Dooley, 13 Feb. 1890, HM44409, CSmH. JWR to Jones, 12 Nov. 1890, Riley Mss., InU-Li.

5. JWR to Alonzo L. Rice, 17 May 1888, Riley Mss., Inu-Li.

6. *Detroit Free Press,* 15 Feb. 1889.

7. JWR to Jones, 8 Jan. 1884.

8. Ibid.; JWR to Matthews, 12 Oct. 1888, Riley Mss., InU-Li.

9. Ibid.; "Dana and Riley," *Milwaukee Sentinel,* 25 July 1888.

10. Interview with Charles Meigs, n.d., M660, InHi. There is no extant written contract between Riley and Merrill, Meigs. If such a document existed, it was destroyed in a company fire. A letter to John Riley corroborates Meigs's story. In it, Riley announces that he is to receive a very liberal royalty (JWR to John Riley, 29 Aug. 1883, Berg Collection of American and English Literature, New York Public Library).

11. When in 1890 he was asked why he did not seek publication with a top East Coast publisher, Riley responded that he was unwilling to give up the royalties he earned from Bowen-Merrill. He knew that another company might handle his books more advantageously, but his royalties seemed to make up for the drawbacks of working with an Indianapolis firm (JWR to F. M. Morris, 23 Dec. 1890, M660, InHi).

12. For example, Longmans, Green, and Co. published *Old-Fashioned Roses* in 1888; and The Century Co. published *Poems Here at Home* in 1893 (Russo, pp. 19, 46). However, the vast majority of Riley's books were published by Merrill, Meigs/Bowen-Merrill/Bobbs-Merrill. David Laurence Chambers estimated that his company published seventy-five titles by Riley. In 1949, twenty-two were still in print (Chambers, James Whitcomb Riley, 1893–1949, RMA).

13. JWR to Howard Taylor, 24 Apr. 1883, Riley Mss., InU-Li; JWR to E. S. Martin, 22 May 1883, Riley Mss., InU-Li.

14. JWR to Bottsford, 21 May 1883, Bottsford Mss., InU-Li.

15. The Century Co. to JWR, 16 Aug. 1883, Riley Mss., InU-Li. This first poem published in *The Century Magazine* is not one of Riley's characteristic dialect poems. However, it idealizes a rustic, rural scene in which children play in a "crooning creek" (*Complete Works,* IV: 953–54). In the notes of the biographical edition of Riley's works, Edmund Eitel misattributes compliments from *Century Magazine* editor Robert Underwood Johnson to Riley regarding his book *The Old Swimmin'-Hole* to this poem (Biographical Edition, III: 514; Johnson to JWR, 18 Nov. 1883).

16. Maurice Thompson to JWR, 22 Aug. 1883, Riley Mss., InU-Li; Catherwood to JWR, 24 Aug. 1883, Riley Mss., InU-Li; Parker to JWR, 15 Sept. 1883, Riley Mss., InU-Li.

17. JWR to Mrs. Emmons, 3 Oct. 1883, InU-Li.

18. Brodhead, *Cultures of Letters,* pp. 116–17, 122.

19. Ibid., pp. 123, 154–55.

20. Ibid., pp. 122–24; Levine, *Highbrow/Lowbrow,* pp. 23, 104–68.

21. Ibid.

22. Brodhead, *Cultures of Letters,* p. 225.

23. Ibid.; S. Michael Halloran, "The Rhetoric of Picturesque Scenery," in Clark and Halloran, eds., *Oratorical Culture in Ninteenth-Century America,* p. 239.

24. Hugh Blair quoted in Halloran, "The Rhetoric of Picturesque Scenery," p. 240.

25. Brodhead, *Cultures of Letters,* pp. 154–55.

26. JWR to Bottsford, 17 Aug. 1883, Bottsford Mss., InU-Li.

27. Ibid. While Riley uses quotation marks in his references to Joel Chandler Harris,

he really paraphrased the words in Harris's 3 Aug. 1883 letter (Joel Chandler Harris to JWR, 3 Aug. 1883).

28. JWR to Bottsford, 17 Aug. 1883, Bottsford Mss., InU-Li.

29. Ibid., 8 Sept. 1883, Bottsford Mss., InU-Li.

30. Ibid., 5 Mar. 1884, Bottsford Mss., InU-Li.

31. Ibid., 8 Sept. 1883; JWR to John Riley, 29 Aug. 1883.

32. JWR to Bottsford, 13 Sept. 1883, 20 Sept. 1883, Bottsford Mss., InU-Li.

33. Ibid., 1 Oct. 1883, 3 Oct. 1883, Bottsford Mss., InU-Li; JWR to J. N. Taylor, 1 Oct. 1883, Riley Mss., InU-Li.

34. JWR to Bottsford, 12 Nov. 1883, Bottsford Mss., InU-Li.

35. Ibid.; JWR to Bottsford, 17 Oct. 1883, Bottsford Mss., InU-Li.

36. JWR to Jones, 15 Nov. 1883, Riley Mss., InU-Li.

37. JWR to Bottsford, 19 Dec. 1883, Bottsford Mss., InU-Li.

38. Ibid., 25 Nov. 1883, 19 Dec. 1883, 1 Feb. 1884, Bottsford Mss., InU-Li; JWR to Jones, 1 Feb. 1884, Riley Mss., InU-Li.

39. "Talk with a Lecturer," *Louisville Journal*, 10 Apr. 1893.

40. JWR to Bottsford, 1 Feb. 1884; JWR to Jones, 1 Feb. 1884.

41. JWR to Bottsford, 25 Nov. 1883.

42. JWR to Bottsford, 8 Jan. 1884, 1 Feb. 1884, 3 Mar. 1884.

43. JWR to Bottsford, 31 Mar. 1884, Bottsford Mss., InU-Li.

44. Ibid., 3 Mar. 1884; Redpath Lyceum Bureau, Accounts of JWR lectures, Feb. 1884, Riley Mss., InU-Li.

45. JWR to Bottsford, 31 Mar. 1884; Paul Gray, "Poet as Entertainer," p. 3.

46. Riley thought he might also seek publication for *The Flying Islands of the Night*, another book of prose, and another volume of dialect poems (JWR to Hitt, 22 July 1888, Hitt Mss., InU-Li).

47. JWR to Bottsford, 31 Mar. 1884; Hitt to JWR, 23 July 1884, Riley Mss., InU-Li; John A. Riley to JWR, 31 Aug. 1884, Riley Mss., InU-Li.

48. JWR to Hitt, 22 July 1884; John A. Riley to JWR, 31 Aug. 1884; Charles D. Meigs to JWR, 13 Oct. 1884, Riley Mss., InU-Li.

49. JWR to Parker, 26 Mar. 1884, Riley Mss., InU-Li. During the 1883–1884 lecture season (Oct.-Mar.), the *Journal* only published six of Riley's poems. When the season was over, his poems again appeared weekly in the paper. Often two of his poems were printed in the newspaper on the same day (Biographical Edition, III: 514–29).

50. Gentile, *Cast of One*, p. 24; Mary Boewe, "On Stage and Off with James Whitcomb Riley and Mark Twain," in *Traces* 7 (Fall 1995): 18.

51. JWR to Bottsford, 7 July 1884, Bottsford Mss., InU-Li. Riley wrote this note on the reverse of the short letter he wrote to Bottsford on this date.

52. James B. Pond to JWR, 3 July 1884, Riley Mss., InU-Li. Warner (1829–1900) was a neighbor of Twain's in Hartford, Connecticut. In addition to serving as a contributing editor to *Harper's* (1884–1898), he was also editor of the Hartford *Courant*. In addition to *The Gilded Age* (1874), which he coauthored with Twain, he published book collections of his essays. He also contributed essays and travel literature to magazines (*Webster's New Biographical Dictionary;* Trachtenberg, *The Incorporation of America*, p. 149–50; Brodhead, *Cultures of Letters*, pp. 126, 131).

53. Pond to JWR, 3 July 1884.

54. Ibid.; Pond to JWR, 22 July 1884, Riley Mss., InU-Li.

55. Ibid. On the reverse of Pond's letter, Riley drafted his response. At this point, Twain was not yet familiar with the Hoosier poet. In her article about the relationship

between these two men, Mary Boewe contends that Pond was unable to convince the older author that Riley would be a suitable lecture partner. Although this may be true, Riley remained Pond's first choice for the combination. Riley's standing contract with the Redpath Bureau was a primary obstacle to a lecture tour involving Twain and Riley (Boewe, "On Stage and Off," p. 18).

56. JWR to Bottsford, 12 Sept. 1884, 17 Sept. 1884, Bottsford Mss., InU-Li.

57. Ibid., 17 Sept. 1884.

58. Ibid.

59. Bottsford to JWR, 18 Sept. 1884, Riley Mss., InU-Li.

60. Riley began corresponding with Mary "Haute" (Tarkington) Jameson in 1881 and continued through 1884 (Jameson, M., Mss., InU-Li; JWR to Haute Tarkington, 28 Aug. 1883;12 Sept. 1883, 22 Jul. 1884, Riley VI. Mss., InU-Li).

61. JWR to Haute Tarkington, 15 Feb. 1883, Jameson, M., Mss., InU-Li.

62. JWR to Bottsford, 29 Sept. 1884, Bottsford Mss., InU-Li.

63. Charles D. Meigs to JWR, 13 Oct. 1884, 15 Oct. 1884, Riley Mss., InU-Li.

64. The London firm Longmans, Green published *Old-Fashioned Roses* in 1888 (Russo, p. 19).

65. Redpath Lyceum Bureau to JWR, 16 Oct. 1884, Riley V. Mss., InU-Li.

66. JWR to Bottsford, [1 Nov. 1884], Bottsford Mss., InU-Li.

67. Ibid.

68. Ibid.

69. Ibid.; JWR to Bottsford, 9 Dec. 1884, Bottsford Mss., InU-Li.

70. Ibid., 9 Dec. 1884.

71. Ibid.

72. Ibid.

73. Ibid.

74. Bottsford to JWR, [Jan.] 1885, Riley Mss., InU-Li.

75. Ibid.

76. JWR to Hathaway, 20 Dec. 1884, Riley Mss., InU-Li; JWR to Jones, 2 Mar. 1885, Riley Mss., InU-Li; JWR to A[mos] J. Walker, 9 Apr. 1885, Riley Mss., InU-Li. Riley stated that his heart valves were affected, which suggests that he may have been suffering from rheumatic fever (JWR to George Payne, 21 Dec. 1884, Riley Mss., InU-Li).

77. JWR to Walker, 9 Apr. 1885.

78. Ibid.; "Mr Riley's Coming Season," *Indianapolis Herald,* 11 Apr. 1885.

79. It is unclear whether or not Riley granted this last request because his letters to Bottsford remained in her hands until after her death (Bottsford to JWR, 2 July 1885, Riley Mss., InU-Li; "Riley Love Letters Found," *New York Times,* 17 Aug. 1917; Robert M. Taylor Jr., et al., "Dear Dream: The Love Letters of James Whitcomb Riley and Clara Louise Bottsford," *Traces* 7 [Nov. 1995]: 4, 6).

80. Bottsford to JWR, 12 Aug. 1885. Ironically, Mrs. George (Lotta Bottsford) Cooper, who wrote a book and a series of articles for the *Indianapolis Times* about her older sister with the purpose of exonerating her in her role in her relationship with Riley, was one of the people from whom Clara said she was estranged: "I am not good enough to be with Geo Cooper and family. The forger and thief, Lord will justice ever be done in this world. They all fell out with me, over Jim, except Al." The tone of this letter reveals how unhappy and bitter she had become (Cooper, "A Hoosier Romance, Riley's Love Story Told," *Indianapolis Times,* 7 Oct. 1935, Cooper, "Riley, School Teacher Planned to Be Married, Sister of Girl Writes," *Indianapolis Times,* 8 Oct. 1935;

[Bottsford] Wambaugh to Mary [Riley] Payne, 3 Sept. 1903, Special Collections Dept., Alderman, Univ. of Virginia, Charlottesville, Va).

81. Bottsford to JWR, 8 Mar. 1883, 12 Aug. 1885; JWR to Bottsford, 12 Feb. 1883, Bottsford Mss., InU-Li; Binford, *History of Hancock County*, p. 310. Parker and Heiney, eds., "Biographical Notes," *Poets and Poetry of Indiana*, p. 447.

82. Bottsford to JWR, [ca. summer 1885], Bottsford Mss., InU-Li. Although this letter is undated, Bottsford mentioned Amos Walker in its text. Riley did not work with Walker until spring and summer of 1885. Bottsford to JWR, 12 Aug. 1885.

83. [Bottsford] Wambaugh to Payne, 3 Sept. 1903; *New York Times*, 17 Aug. 1917; Taylor, et al., "Dear Dream," p. 6; Cooper, "Riley, School Teacher Planned to Be Married, Sister of Girl Writes," *Indianapolis Times*, 8 Oct.1935; Death Notices, *Indianapolis News*, 26 July 1910; "Former Greenfield Woman Is Dead," *Greenfield Daily Reporter*, 25 July 1910; "Death of Clara Wambaugh," *Hancock Democrat*, 28 July 1910.

84. This letter contains the only reference to a "new girl." Her identity and the character of their relationship remain unknown (JWR to Nye, 6 Apr. 1886, Riley Mss., InU-Li). The poem Riley mentions in his letter to Nye is most probably "In the South," which was published in the *Indianapolis Journal* on 11 Apr. 1886. It begins: "There is a princess in the South / About whose beauty rumors hum" (*Complete Works*, V: 1196–97; Biographical Edition, III: 548).

85. *Indianapolis Herald*, 5 Dec. 1885.

86. Walker to JWR, [June 1885], Riley Mss., InU-Li; JWR to A. J. Walker, 18 Aug. 1885, Riley Mss., InU-Li. Elva May (Riley) Eitel to John Riley, 2 Dec. 1885, M660, InHi; *Indianapolis Herald*, 5 Dec. 1885; *The Boss Girl, A Christmas Story and Other Sketches* (book prospectus) Bowen-Merrill Co., 23 Nov. 1885, No. 4, Box 8, PS2700, InU-Li. By the time this book was published, Merrill, Meigs & Co. had become Bowen-Merrill Co. (Russo, p. 7).

87. Washington Irving's (1783–1859) *Sketch Book* was published in 1822. It included "The Legend of Sleepy Hollow," "Rip Van Winkle," and "Spectre Bridegroom" (*Webster's New Biographical Dictionary*).

88. *The Boss Girl* (book prospectus).

89. Ibid.

90. Bowen-Merrill Co. (press notice), 21 Dec. 1885; Russo, p. 10.

91. Russo, p. 11.

92. R[obert] E. Pretlow, "The Boss Girl," *Indianapolis Herald*, 20 Mar. 1886; Parker and Heiney, eds., "Biographical Notes," *Poets and Poetry of Indiana*, p. 451.

93. *The Boss Girl* (book prospectus).

94. Pretlow, "The Boss Girl," 20 Mar. 1886.

95. Donn Piatt to JWR, 6 Feb. 1886, Riley Mss., InU-Li.

96. "Riley's Old Friends," *Buffalo Express*, 30 Oct. 1898.

97. JWR to C[harles] Longman, 6 May 1888, Riley Mss., InU-Li; Russo, pp. 7–13.

98. JWR to Bottsford, 5 Mar. 1884.

99. Booth Tarkington once stated that some people never forgave Eggleston for making Hoosiers so backward and unattractive in the *The Hoosier Schoolmaster* ("Mr. Riley," *Collier's* 58 (30 Dec. 1916): 4). Eunice (Bullard) Beecher was the wife of the famous minister Henry Ward Beecher. She wrote *Dawn to Daylight* about her experiences as a preacher's wife in Indianapolis during the 1830s. This novel raised quite a controversy in this city. Indianapolis residents recognized the unflattering portrait of themselves, and the book "was effectively banned by public sensation" in this state capital (Vanausdall, *Pride and Protest*, pp. 27–28). See also Jeanette Vanausdall, "The

Story of a Western Home: Eunice Beecher in Indiana," in *Traces* 2 (Spring 1990): 16–23.

100. George A. Schumacher, "Writer's Society Formed in 1886, Result of Jealousy," *Indianapolis Star,* 19 Aug. 1934.

101. Ibid.; "The Poets Singing Bee," *Indianapolis Herald,* 18 Feb. 1886; J. N. Matthews, "The Coming Poets' Convention," *Indianapolis Herald,* 20 Feb. 1886; Richard L. Dawson, "The American Association of Writers," *The Current* 7 (29 Jan. 1887): 145.

102. Dawson, "The American Association of Writers," 146; Schumacher, "Writer's Society Formed in 1886."

103. Dawson, "The American Association of Writers," 146.

104. "The Convention of Writers at Plymouth Hall, Indianapolis," *Indianapolis Herald,* 7 Oct. 1886.

105. John C. Ochiltree to Parker, 24 July 1887, L123, In.

106. Ibid.

107. Schumacher, "Writer's Society Formed in 1886."

108. JWR to Parker, 30 June 1890, Riley Mss., InU-Li.

109. JWR to Jones, 19 Oct. 1880, Riley Mss., InU-Li.

110. Schumacher, "Writer's Society Formed in 1886."

111. JWR to Nye, 7 July 1890, Riley Mss., InU-Li; JWR to Young E. Allison, 5 July 1890, Riley Mss., InU-Li; Griffith, *Home Town News,* p. 24. Other prominent members of the Association included Frank Lebby Stanton (1857–1927), poet and editor of the *Atlanta Constitution,* and John James Piatt (1835–1917), poet, editor, and friend of Howells and Whitman (Dawson, "The American Association of Writers"; "Biographical Notes," in *American Poetry, the Nineteenth Century,* 2: 908; *Webster's New Biographical Dictionary*).

112. JWR to William Allen White, 8 Oct. 1897, Emporia State University, Emporia, Kansas; Griffith, *Home Town News,* pp. 24, 27, 140, 179.

113. Burdette to JWR, 23 Jan. 1898, M660, InHi; Griffith, *Home Town News,* p. 179.

114. JWR to Furman, 12 Jan. 1897, Riley Mss., InU-Li. In a letter to Furman, dated 2 Mar. 1893, Riley enclosed an undated clipping which identified Furman as an aspiring novelist from Evansville (JWR to Furman, 2 Mar. 1893, Riley VI. Mss., InU-Li). Riley admired her work and thought her equal in talent to Rudyard Kipling (JWR to Furman, 3 Apr. 1897, Riley Mss., InU-Li).

115. JWR to Furman, 12 Jan. 1897; Annie Fellows Johnston to Edmund Eitel, 15 Oct. 1915, M660, InHi; Parker and Heiney, eds., "Biographical Notes," *Poets and Poetry of Indiana,* p. 438.

116. "The Riley-Nye-Field Entertainment," *Indianapolis Sentinel,* 3 Feb. 1886; John H. Wrenn and Margaret M. Wrenn, *Edgar Lee Masters* (Boston: Twayne Publishers, 1983), p. 19.

117. Edmund Eitel, Notes on Conversation with William C. Bobbs, 8 Oct. 1915, M660, InHi; Robert McIntyre to JWR, 12 Sept. 1885, Riley Mss., InU-Li; JWR to Bottsford, 29 Sept. 1884. In 1895, when the president of Bowen-Merrill, Silas T. Bowen, died, Bobbs took over the company and the name was changed to Bobbs-Merrill (Van Allen and Foust, *Keeping the Dream,* p. 83; Interview with Charles Meigs, n.d., M660, InHi).

118. Edmund Eitel, Notes on Conversation with Bobbs; "Nye-Field-Riley," *Indianapolis Journal,* 5 Feb. 1886: Dickey, "Stage Fright and Other Afflictions," unpublished mss., n.d., Dickey Mss., InU-Li, pp. 5–6.

119. Ibid.; "When Three Wits Meet," *St. Paul Globe,* 22 May 1900; *Knightstown Banner,* 19 Feb. 1886.

120. JWR to Hitt., 3 Mar. 1886, Hitt Mss., InU-Li.

121. "When Three Wits Meet."

122. Ade, "Riley and His Friends," p. 10; Frank Nye to Edmund Eitel, 17 Nov. 1913, M660, InHi; *Webster's New Biographical Dictionary.*

123. JWR to Jones, 30 Mar. 1886, Riley Mss., InU-Li.

124. Nye to JWR, 5 Apr. 1886; JWR to Nye, 7 Apr. 1886, Riley Mss., InU-Li; Nye to JWR, 28 Feb. 1888, Riley Mss., InU-Li; *New York Critic,* 10 Nov. 1888.

125. Nye to JWR, 8 Nov. 1886, 28 Feb. 1888, Riley Mss., InU-Li; JWR to Matthews, 7 Dec. 1886, Riley Mss., InU-Li; Johnson to JWR, 25 Oct. 1886, 23 Nov. 1886, Riley Mss., InU-Li; Pond to JWR, 10 Jan. 1887, 10 Feb. 1887, 20 Feb. 1887, Riley Mss., InU-Li.

126. JWR to Matthews, 7 Dec. 1886.

127. Johnson to JWR, 25 Oct. 1886, 23 Nov. 1886; Parker to JWR, 28 Apr. 1883, Riley Mss., InU-Li; Parker and Heiney, eds., "Biographical Notes," *Poets and Poetry of Indiana,* p. 438. *The Century Magazine* published "In Swimming-Time" in its Sept. 1883 issue. Another Riley poem did not appear in this journal until "Nothin' to Say" was published in Aug. 1887 (Biographical Edition, III: 514, 509).

128. JWR to Matthews, 7 Dec. 1886.

129. Ibid., 26 July 1887, Riley Mss., InU-Li.

130. Edmund Eitel stated that "The Old Man and Jim" was first read on stage in Jan. 1888, at the Grand Opera House in Indianapolis (Biographical Edition, III: 561). Although it was not published by the Century Company until 1893, Johnson accepted the poem and enclosed a check for it in a letter dated 3 Jan. 1887 (Johnson to JWR, 3 Jan. 1887, Riley Mss., InU-Li). During January and February 1887, of the poems Riley sent him, Johnson also accepted "At the Literary" (JWR to Johnson, 12 Feb. 1887, Riley Mss., InU-Li). Only twelve Riley poems appeared in the *Indianapolis Journal* between December 1886 and July 1887 (Biographical Edition, III: 554–56).

131. During the early 1840s, Poe campaigned for an international copyright law in the *Broadway Journal*; and, in New York in 1843, other authors joined him in creating the American Copyright Club. Under the presidency of William Cullen Bryant, this institution organized to discredit the propaganda put out by publishers which spread the idea that, by providing American readers with plenty of cheap reading material, the benefits of literary piracy overrode the harm it did to writers. The American Copyright Club was unsuccessful in reaching its goals. Therefore, in the 1880s, American authors remained unprotected by any international copyright legislation (Weber, *Hired Pens,* pp. 14–16).

132. Johnson to JWR, 24 Jan. 1884, Riley Mss., InU-Li.

133. Ibid., 9 Nov. 1887, Riley Mss., InU-Li.

134. D[an] L. Paine to Parker, 5 Oct. 1887, Riley Mss., InU-Li.

135. Ibid.; JWR to Mrs. McKenna Neal, 12 Oct. 1887, Riley Mss., InU-Li; JWR to [Robert] McIntyre, 17 Oct. 1887, Riley Mss., InU-Li. Although there is no way to be certain, considering his full recovery, Riley most likely was suffering from Bell's palsy, a disease that causes temporary paralysis of the facial nerve, producing distortion on one side of the face.

136. JWR to Matthews, 23 Nov. 1887, Riley Mss., InU-Li.

137. JWR to Johnson, 21 Nov. 1887, Riley Mss., InU-Li.

138. L. Frank Tooker quoted in Ziff, *The American 1890s,* p. 15.

139. "Big Brains Hold a Levee: The 'Authors Readings' in Behalf of an International Copyright Law," *New York World,* 29 Nov. 1887.

140. Ziff, *The American 1890s,* p. 15.

141. Ibid., p. 16; *Webster's New Biographical Dictionary.*

142. Ziff, *The American 1890s,* pp. 16–17.

143. Ibid., p. 15; "Big Brains Hold a Levee"; *New York Tribune,* 29 Nov. 1887; "Authors Asking Justice," *New York Times,* 29 Nov. 1887; Boewe, "On Stage and Off," 18; Paul Gray, "Preparing for Popularity," 36.

144. "Big Brains Hold a Levee."

145. Nye to Matthews, 22 Dec. 1887, Riley Mss., InU-Li; Boewe, "On Stage and Off," 18.

146. Boewe, "On Stage and Off," 18; *New York Tribune,* 29 Nov. 1887. Riley also called the character sketch "The Object Lesson." He renamed it for this event (JWR to Bill Nye, 11 Nov. 1887, Riley Mss., InU-Li; *Complete Works,* IX: 2480–84).

147. *New York Times,* 29 Nov. 1887.

148. Boewe, "On Stage and Off," 18–19; "Big Brains Hold a Levee"; *New York Tribune,* 29 Nov. 1887; "Many Authors on View," *New York Sun,* 30 Nov. 1887.

149. "Big Brains Hold a Levee." This reviewer was probably none other than Nye himself. The famous humorist moved to New York by May 1887 to begin a new contract with the *New York World* (Nye to JWR, 22 Mar. 1887, Riley III. Mss., InU-Li). At this time, he was the newspaper's most popular columnist.

150. Ziff, *The American 1890s,* p. 16.

151. "Big Brains Hold a Levee."

152. Ibid.

153. *New York Tribune,* 30 Nov. 1887.

154. "Mr. Lowell's Happy Hits," *New York Times,* 30 Nov. 1887; Boewe, "On Stage and Off," 18.

155. Lowell quoted in "The Lounger," *The New York Critic,* 8 (10 Dec. 1887): 299–300.

156. "Many Authors on View," *New York Sun,* 30 Nov. 1887; "Mr. Lowell's Happy Hits," *New York Times,* 30 Nov. 1887. "Nothin' to Say" first appeared in the Aug. 1887 issue of *The Century* and was included in *Afterwhiles,* published by Bowen-Merrill at the end of 1887 (Biographical Edition, III: 509; Russo, p. 14).

157. "Many Authors on View," *New York Sun,* 30 Nov. 1887.

158. Stedman to JWR, 15 Dec. 1887, Riley Mss., InU-Li.

159. JWR, "Nothin' to Say," *Complete Works,* IV: 922–24.

160. Ibid.

161. JWR to Henry Eitel, 30 Nov. 1887, Riley VI. Mss., InU-Li.

162. Ibid., Russo, p. 14–15.

163. Mary Riley to John A. Riley, 6 Jan. 1888; "Glimpses of Noted Authors," *Indianapolis Journal,* 18 Dec. 1888.

164. JWR to Nye, 14 Dec. 1887, InU-Li.

165. Walker to JWR, 8 Dec. 1887, Riley Mss., InU-Li.

166. JWR to Mrs. McKenna Neal, 15 Nov. 1887, Riley Mss., InU-Li; William Carey to JWR, 1 Jan. 1888, Riley Mss., InU-Li.

167. Russo, p. 15.

168. Nye to JWR, 21 Dec. 1887, Riley Mss., InU-Li.

169. Ziff, *The American 1890s*, p. 18.

170. Richard Watson Gilder to JWR, 4 Feb. 1888, Riley Mss., InU-Li; C. J. Longman to JWR, 10 May 1888, Riley Mss., InU-Li.

171. Matthews to JWR, 20 Apr. 1888, Riley Mss., InU-Li.

172. "Whitcomb Riley Got There," *Chicago News*, [undated clipping], PS2700, InU-Li; Boewe, "On Stage and Off," 20–21.

173. Boewe, "On Stage and Off," 20–21; Katherine Willard to JWR, 23 Apr. 1888, 27 Aug. 1888, Riley Mss., InU-Li.

174. "Riley's Old Friends," *Buffalo Express*, 30 Oct. 1898.

175. Ibid.; *Pittsburgh Commercial Gazette*, 13 Nov. 1888; Ade, "Riley and His Friends," p. 10; Interview with Charles Martindale, n.d., Dickey Mss., InU-Li; Dickey, "Disturbed by Politics," n.d., unpublished manuscript, p. 2, Dickey Mss., InU-Li; JWR to Johnson, 10 Sept. 1888, Riley Mss., InU-Li.

176. Phillips, *Indiana in Transition*, p. 1.

177. "Whitcomb Riley on Harrison," *Pittsburgh Commercial Gazette*, 13 Nov. 1888.

178. Phillips, *Indiana in Transition*, p. 1.

179. JWR to William Carey, 5 Nov. 1888, Riley VI., InU-Li. Today, instead of "plain Denis," Riley would probably say "ordinary Joe."

180. Phillips, *Indiana in Transition*, pp. 1, 274, 343; Bodenhamer and Barrows, eds., "Preface," *Encyclopedia of Indianapolis*, p. vii; Milton Farber, "Socialist Parties and Movements," Bodenhamer and Barrows, eds., *Encyclopedia of Indianapolis*, p. 1275; *New York World*, 16 Nov. 1888; "Indiana Authors Lead," *Chicago Evening Post*, 20 Oct. 1892; Foulke, "Indianapolis Now the Hub from Which American Literature Radiates," *Indianapolis Star*, 9 Oct. 1915.

181. Phillips, *Indiana in Transition*, pp. 36–37; *New York Press*, 12 Nov. 1888. Great Britain created the office of poet laureate in 1668. John Dryden was the first to serve in this position. The United States was slow to create this official title. Between 1937 and 1984, consultants in poetry were assigned to the Library of Congress. In 1985, U.S. Congress gave these consultants the official name of poet laureate. The first poet laureate of the United States was Robert Penn Warren. Unlike their British counterparts, each U.S. poet laureate serves a one-year term.

182. Pond to JWR, 29 Aug. 1888, Riley Mss., InU-Li; Nye and Riley's Route, 1888–1889, [circular], PS2700, InU-Li; JWR to Matthews, 1 Nov. 1888, Riley Mss., InU-Li; "Dialect Writing Talk with a Master of the Art," *Rochester Herald*, 25 Dec. 1889.

183. *Washington Capital*, 18 Nov. 1888; *Atlanta Constitution*, 25 Nov. 1888; "Nye and Riley, Season of 1889," PS2700, InU-Li; Nye to JWR, 10 Oct. 1888, Riley III. Mss., InU-Li.

184. "Nye and Riley, Season of 1889," PS2700, InU-Li.

185. JWR to Nye, 13 Oct. 1888, Riley Mss., InU-Li.

186. "Dana and Riley," *Milwaukee Sentinel*, 25 July 1888.

187. "The Hoosier Poet, James Whitcomb Riley's Views on American Poetry," *Marlborough Express*, 3 Dec. 1888.

188. Ibid.; Antczak and Siemers, "The Divergence of Purpose and Practice on the Chautauqua," pp. 213, 218. Leland Powers was a popular lecturer on the Chautauqua circuit in the late nineteenth century. He became known for his theatrical readings of plays and novels. Like Riley, he changed characters without the external accoutrements of props and costume and has been noted for being influential in changing attitudes toward the theater (Gentile, *Cast of One*, pp. 44–47).

189. Antczak and Siemers, "The Divergence of Purpose and Practice on the Chautauqua," p. 218; "Humor and Sentiment," *Chicago Inter-Ocean,* 5 Feb. 1889.

190. "Bill Nye in the Toils," *Chicago Journal,* 4 Feb. 1889; "The Thirteen Superstition," *New York World,* 10 Feb. 1889; "Bill Nye Comes to Town," *St. Louis Post Dispatch,* 18 Jan. 1889; "James Whitcomb Riley," *Saint Joseph* [Missouri] *Herald,* 2 Apr. 1889; "Bill Nye in Town, He Is Accompanied by Messrs. Riley and Edwards," *Atlanta Constitution,* 5 Dec. 1888; "Nye, Riley, and Edwards," *Atlanta Constitution,* 9 Dec. 1888; "Nye and Riley's Modesty," *Indianapolis Journal,* 18 Mar. 1889; "Nye and Riley Matinee," *Philadelphia Press,* 21 Feb. 1889; "How Riley Spends His Money," *Oshkosh Northwestern,* 16 Feb. 1889; "Riley in Omaha," *Omaha World Times,* 19 Nov. 1892.

191. "A Big Four Together," *Philadelphia Press,* 9 Mar. 1889.

192. "Nye-Riley, with Mark Twain to Act as Middleman, Tremont Temple Full of Mirth," *Boston Globe,* 1 Mar. 1889; Boewe, "On Stage and Off," 21.

193. Clemens (Twain), "How to Tell a Story," *Youth's Companion* (3 Oct. 1895); Boewe, "On Stage and Off," 23.

194. "Nye and Riley May Part," *Kansas City Times,* 13 Apr. 1889; "Dialect Writing, Talk with a Master of the Art," *Rochester Herald,* 25 Dec. 1889.

195. "Dialect Writing, Talk with a Master of the Art"; Russo, pp. 19–28.

196. Russo, p. 22; *Pittsburgh Press,* 1 Dec. 1888; *New York Commercial Advertiser,* 4 Dec. 1888; *New York News,* 2 Dec. 1888; *New York Evening Telegram,* 8 Dec. 1888; *Chicago Times,* 1 Dec. 1888.

197. Dickey, Notes on JWR, 1907, Dickey Mss., InU-Li; JWR to Longman, 22 Oct. 1888, Riley Mss., InU-Li; "Old-Fashioned Roses," *The Academy,* 20 Oct. 1888; "Literature of the Day," *London Telegraph,* 23 Sept. 1891; "The Hoosier Poet's Best Work," *New York Tribune,* 3 Feb. 1889; Russo, p. 20.

198. JWR, "At Zekesbury," *Complete Works,* X: 2640–57. This story first appeared in the *Chicago Current* (24 Apr. 1886) with the title "A Waste of Genius at Zekesbury" (Russo, p. 26).

199. "The Hoosier Poet's Best Work"; "Pan in Hoosierdom," *Boston Advertiser,* 8 Jan. 1889; "Current Literature, Gems from the Garden of Poesy," *Chicago Herald,* 9 Feb. 1889.

200. Russo, p. 29.

201. "Mr. Riley Calm and Happy," *Kansas City Star,* 15 Apr. 1889; "The Hoosier Poet's Illness," *Chicago Times,* 13 Oct. 1889.

202. Henry Eitel to JWR, 5 Nov. 1889, Riley Mss., InU-Li; "Brother-in-Law of Riley in Banking Business Many Years," *Indianapolis News,* 19 Feb. 1934.

203. "Rye and Riley," *Louisville Courier-Journal,* 2 Feb. 1890.

204. "The Poet's Side of It," *Louisville Courier-Journal,* 3 Feb. 1890.

205. Henry Eitel to JWR, 21 Nov. 1888, 8 Jan. 1889, Riley Mss., InU-Li..

206. "A Bard's Bad Break," *Louisville Post,* 1 Feb. 1890; "Rye and Riley," *Louisville Courier-Journal,* 2 Feb. 1890; "Nye and Riley Dissolve, The Cause Attributed to the Personal Habits of the Indiana Poet," *Indianapolis News,* 1 Feb. 1890; "Poet Riley Makes a Statement," *Chicago Herald,* 8 Feb. 1890; *New York Dramatic Mirror,* 8 Feb. 1890; *New York World,* 10 Feb. 1890; *Philadelphia Bulletin,* 10 Feb. 1890; *Pittsburgh Bulletin,* 8 Feb. 1890; *Boston Herald,* 9 Feb. 1890; *Washington Chronicle,* 9 Feb. 1890.

207. JWR to Jap Miller, 10 Feb. 1890, Riley Mss., InU-Li.

208. "The Poet's Side of It," *Louisville Courier-Journal,* 3 Feb. 1890.

209. Warner, "Temperance Morality and Medicine," p. 140; Edmund Eitel, "Recollections of My Uncle," n.d., p. 6, M660, InHi.

210. *St. Paul Press,* 1 Mar. 1890.

7. Preparing a Legacy

1. "Writing a Poem on Labor," *Pittsburgh Dispatch,* 6 Jan. 1892.

2. "A Chat with the Poet Riley."

3. "About James Whitcomb Riley. His Simplicity and the Absence of Snobbishness," *Terre Haute Express,* 6 May 1891; "James Whitcomb Riley," *London Sun,* 10 Apr. 1892.

4. Brodhead, *Cultures of Letters,* pp. 165–69.

5. "The Genial Hoosier," *Detroit Free Press,* 8 Mar. 1893.

6. JWR, "Dialect in Literature," *Complete Works,* X: 2675–76.

7. Ibid.

8. "Dave Martin as an Uncle, James W. Riley Talks of His Boyhood"; "Hoosier Poet Comes to Town," *Pittsburgh Chronicle Telegraph,* 26 Oct. 1903.

9. "Talk with Hoosier Poet," *Chicago Times-Herald,* 22 Oct. 1900.

10. JWR to Dooley, 13 Feb. 1890, HM44409, CSmH.

11. JWR to Mrs. Frederick Baggs, 10 Feb. 1890, Riley VI. Mss., InU-Li; "Poet Riley Makes a Statement," *Chicago Herald,* 8 Feb. 1890; *Indianapolis Journal,* 8 Feb. 1890.

12. *New York World,* 10, 15 Feb. 1890; *Philadelphia Bulletin,* 10 Feb. 1890; *Pittsburgh Bulletin,* 8 Feb. 1890; *Boston Herald,* 9 Feb. 1890; *Chicago Herald,* 9 Feb. 1890; *Washington Chronicle,* 9 Feb. 1890; *New York Dramatic Mirror,* 8 Feb. 1890; "Never Say Die," *Rochester Chronicle,* 11 Feb. 1890; *Kansas City Star,* 14 Feb. 1890; *Washington Post,* 13 Feb. 1890; "A Sensible View of It," *Chicago Tribune,* 14 Feb. 1890; *Lincoln State Journal,* 14 Feb. 1890; "Very True," *Utica Press,* 17 Feb. 1890; "Nye and Riley," *Buffalo Express,* 22 Feb. 1890; *Indianapolis Journal,* 8 Feb. 1890; "In Riley's Behalf," *Indianapolis News,* 4 Feb. 1890.

13. "Never Say Die," *Rochester Chronicle,* 11 Feb. 1890.

14. Warner, "Temperance, Morality, and Medicine," p. 140.

15. *Boston Herald,* 9 Feb. 1890.

16. "Never Say Die," *Rochester Chronicle,* 11 Feb. 1890; *Boston Herald,* 9 Feb. 1890.

17. *New York World,* 15 Feb. 1890; *Kansas City Star,* 14 Feb. 1890; "A Welcome to Poet Riley," *Indianapolis Journal,* 18 Feb. 1890.

18. Edmund Eitel, "Recollections of My Uncle."

19. "A Welcome to Poet Riley."

20. JWR to Jones, 27 Feb. 1890, Riley Mss., InU-Li.

21. William Carey to JWR, 12 Feb. 1890, Riley Mss., InU-Li; JWR to John Riley, 17 Feb. 1890, Riley VI. Mss., InU-Li; JWR to Matthews, 5 Mar. 1890, Riley Mss., InU-Li; "Bluegrass Blades," *Louisville Courier-Journal,* 21 Mar. 1890; "The Hoosier Poet," *Denver Colorado News,* 25 Mar. 1890; Dunn, *Indiana and the Indianians,* 3: 1260.

22. John C. Briggs to JWR, 18 May, 15 June 1890, Riley Mss., InU-Li; "James Whitcomb Riley Sued, Amos Walker, the Poet's Former Manager, Wants $1000 Damages," *Chicago Evening News,* 14 May 1890; "James Whitcomb Riley Sued," *Chicago Inter-Ocean,* 15 May 1890; "Jim Riley Sued," *Louisville Courier-Journal,* 15 May 1890.

23. "Bill Nye Sues James Whitcomb Riley for $20,000," *Chicago News,* 10 Dec. 1890; *Chicago Times,* 12 Dec. 1890; *Chicago Herald,* 12 Dec. 1890; *Chicago Evening Journal,* 12 Dec. 1890; *Washington Star,* 12 Dec. 1890; *Laramie Boomerang,* 12 Dec. 1890; *New York Press,* 13 Dec. 1890; *Washington Post,* 13 Dec. 1890.

24. Nye to JWR, 18 July 1890, [Jan.] 1891, Riley III. Mss., InU-Li.

25. "Riley's Letter Written on the Trouble" [JWR to Nye], [1890], Riley Mss., InU-Li.

26. Pond to JWR, 4 Sept. 1890, Riley Mss., InU-Li; JWR to Nye, 5 Mar. 1891, Riley Mss., InU-Li; Nye to JWR, 17 Mar. 1891, Riley Mss., InU-Li; [Clara] Mrs E. W. Nye to JWR, 22 Feb. 1896, Riley Mss., InU-Li.

27. Nye to JWR, [Jan.] 1891, 7 June 1888, Riley Mss., InU-Li; JWR to [William] Carey, 6 Mar. 1896, Riley Mss., InU-Li; "Mr. Riley in Repose," *Kansas City Times,* 7 Dec. 1903; F[rank] W. Nye to Edmund Eitel, 18 Aug. 1913, Riley III. Mss., InU-Li.

28. Russo, p. 29. Several of the "Uncle Sidney" poems appeared in this volume. In particular, Riley wrote "Max and Jim," which was published in *Rhymes of Childhood,* for Nye's sons Max and Frank; the latter went by the nickname Jim (Biographical Edition, IV: 407). In a letter to Riley in January 1891 following this book's release, Nye said, "The pride of my children over the fact that they are 'in a book' may be better imagined than described" (Nye to JWR, [Jan.] 1891).

29. Stedman to JWR, 29 Dec. 1890, Riley Mss., InU-Li.

30. JWR to Johnson, 3 June 1890, Berg Collection of American and English Literature, New York Public Library.

31. "Riley's Rhymes of Childhood," 14 Dec. 1890.

32. JWR, "Dialect in Literature," *Complete Works,* X: 2686.

33. Carolyn L. Karcher, "Lydia Maria Child and *The Juvenile Miscellany:* The Creation of an American Children's Literature," in Price and Smith, *Periodical Literature in Nineteenth-Century America,* p. 90. Child (1802–1880) was born in Medford, Massachusetts. She edited *Juvenile Miscellany* between 1826 and 1834 and the *National Anti-Slavery Standard* between 1841 and 1843. She was active in the movements for abolition and women's suffrage and authored novels, children's books, and social reform literature (*Webster's New Biographical Dictionary*).

34. JWR, "Dialect in Literature," *Complete Works,* X: 2686–87; JWR to Kate Douglas Wiggin, 30 Mar. 1891, CSmH.

35. Lears, *No Place of Grace,* p. 146.

36. "The Hoosier Poet Arrives," *Kansas City Star,* 27 Feb. 1892.

37. Lears, *No Place of Grace,* pp. 26–27.

38. "Riley's Chief Ambition," *New Haven Register,* 16 Nov. 1898.

39. JWR to Johnson, 3 June 1890.

40. Karcher, "Lydia Maria Child and *The Juvenile Miscellany,*" p. 91; Clara E. Laughlin, "James Whitcomb Riley as a Poet of Childhood," *The Book Buyer* 17 (Oct. 1898): 181.

41. Isaac Kramnick, quoted in Karcher, "Lydia Maria Child and *The Juvenile Miscellany,*" p. 99.

42. JWR, "The Raggedy Man," *Complete Works,* VI: 1461.

43. Karcher, "Lydia Maria Child and *The Juvenile Miscellany,*" p. 99.

44. JWR, "Little Orphant Annie," *Complete Works,* V: 1171.

45. Ibid.; Karcher, "Lydia Maria Child and *The Juvenile Miscellany,*" pp. 102–3.

46. JWR, "Little Orphant Annie," *Complete Works*, V: 1169–70; JWR, "The Raggedy Man," *Complete Works*, VI: 1458–60.

47. Ibid.

48. Lears, *No Place of Grace*, pp.17–32, 74–75; Karcher, "Lydia Maria Child and *The Juvenile Miscellany*," p. 106.

49. Lears, *No Place of Grace*, p. 25, 150–51; Hay to JWR, 15 Dec. 1890, Riley Mss., InU-Li.

50. Mark [Clemens] to JWR, 29 Dec. 1890, Riley Mss., InU-Li.

51. Hitt to JWR, 21 Jan. 1891, Riley Mss., InU-Li. In 1889, President Harrison appointed Hitt Vice-Consul General and John New Consul General of the United States in London (Cumback and Maynard, eds., *Men of Progress*, pp. 312–14; Van Allen and Foust, eds., *Keeping the Dream*, p. 108).

52. JWR to Cawein, 11 May 1890, 13 Jan. 1891, HM44385, CSmH.

53. Hitt to JWR, 21 Jan. 1891, Hitt Mss., InU-Li. The text of this Kipling poem may be found in a letter dated 20 Jan. 1891 and in the notes to the Biographical Edition (Kipling to JWR, 20 Jan. 1891, Riley Mss., InU-Li, Biographical Edition, IV: 513). JWR, "To Rudyard Kipling," *Complete Works*, VI: 1479–80.

54. "Riley's Old Friends," *Buffalo Express*, 30 Oct. 1898.

55. Lears, *No Place of Grace*, p. 145

56. Kipling to JWR, 20 Jan. 1891, Riley Mss., InU-Li; Biographical Edition, IV: 513; Lears, *No Place of Grace*, p. 145.

57. Lears, *No Place of Grace*, p. 146.

58. Brodhead, *Cultures of Letters*, p. 125; JWR to George Smith, 26 May 1891, Riley Mss., InU-Li.

59. JWR to George Smith, 26 May 1891, Riley Mss., InU-Li; Extracts from the Diary of William P. Fishback, 27 May 1891, 5 June 1891, no. 2, box 20, PS2700, InU-Li. Known as the Scottish national poet, Burns (1759–1796) lived in Dumfries from 1791 until his death in 1796 (*Webster's New Biographical Dictionary*).

60. "An Evening with a Poet, James Whitcomb Riley, the 'Hoosier Poet,' Lectures at the Exchange Hall," *Kansas City Journal*, 2 Feb. 1884; JWR, "Poetry and Character" [n.p., n.d.], no. 10, box 6, PS2700, InU-Li; "James Whitcomb Riley, A Treasury of Country Tales—His Ideas on Dialect," *Rochester Democrat Chronicle*, 14 Apr. 1888; "A Humorous Trio, Billings, Burdette and Riley together in the Star Course," *Philadelphia Enquirer*, 7 Mar. 1882; Katherine R. Beeson, *Literary Indiana* (Indianapolis: Bobbs-Merrill, 1925), p. 18.

61. Charles W. Stoddard to JWR, 25 Feb. 1893, Riley V. Mss., InU-Li.

62. Gilder to M. L. Andrews, 16 Oct. 1888, Riley Mss., InU-Li.

63. "Riley-Cable Entertainment," *Chicago News*, 13 Jan. 1892; Albert J. Beveridge quoted in *In Honor of JWR, A Meeting of the Indiana State Teachers' Association* (Indianapolis: Bobbs-Merrill, 1905), pp. 10–11; Garland, "Real Conversations," p. 234; "About James Whitcomb Riley. His Simplicity and the Absence of Snobbishness," *Terre Haute Express*, 6 May 1891; "The Hoosier Writer's Works in Prose and Verse—An Appreciation," *New York Times*, 6 May 1899.

64. Extracts from the Diary of Myron Reed, 6 June 1891, M660, InHi; JWR to Henry Eitel, 9 June 1891, Riley VI. Mss., InU-Li.

65. Ibid.; JWR to Smith, 26 May 1891; Extracts from the Diary of William P. Fishback, 8, 11, 12, 15, 24 June 1891. "Elegy Written in a Country Churchyard" is Thomas Gray's (1716–1771) most famous poem (*Webster's New Biographical Dictionary*).

66. Extracts from the Diary of William P. Fishback, 24, 29 June 1891; JWR to Irving, 29 June 1891, Riley Mss., InU-Li; Boewe, "On Stage and Off": 21; Dickey—*Maturity*, p. 369.

67. JWR to Irving, 1 July 1891, Riley Mss., InU-Li; JWR to Cawein, 3 July 1891, Berg Collection of American and English Literature, New York Public Library; JWR to William Carey, 13 Dec. 1891, Riley Mss., InU-Li.

68. *Cincinnati Times Star,* 8 Apr. 1893.

69. "The Genial Hoosier,"*Detroit Free Press,* 8 Mar. 1893.

70. JWR to Helena Stallo Vinton, 16 July 1891, Riley Mss., InU-Li.

71. Levine, *Highbrow/Lowbrow,* p. 48.

72. Hitt, "Mr. Riley as a Public Reader": 440.

73. JWR to Cawein, 3 July 1891.

74. JWR to Vinton, 27 July 1891, Riley Mss., InU-Li.

75. Ibid., 24 Aug. 1891, Riley Mss., InU-Li.

76. "Our Bobby Burns," *St. Louis Evening Star,* 26 Jan. 1892.

77. "Riley-Cable Entertainment," *Chicago News,* 13 Jan. 1892; "Washington—Mar. 31.—James Whitcomb Riley," *Louisville Commercial,* 1 Apr., 1892; Johnston, "Introduction of JWR in Baltimore," [28 Mar. 1892], Riley Mss., InU-Li.

78. "Indiana's Poet, Long Silent, Sings Again," *Chicago Times-Herald,* 13 Oct. 1900; Russo; Dickey, "A Home-Loving Poet," n.p., n.d. [unpublished manuscript], p. 16, Dickey Mss., InU-Li.

79. "*Neghborly Poems,"* *Chicago Tribune,* 24 Oct. 1891.

80. "Poetry of the United States," *The Atheneum,* 3 Mar. 1893; Bierce, "Prattle."

81. *Atlanta Constitution,* 18 Nov. 1894; "*Armazindy,"* *Milwaukee Sentinel,* 12 Nov. 1894; "Riley's New Verse," *New York Times,* 12 Oct. 1894.

82. "*Armazindy,"* *Milwaukee Sentinel,* 12 Nov. 1894.

83. Macy to JWR, 8 Nov. 1892, Riley Mss., InU-Li; "Riley's Recent Poems," *Memphis Commercial,* 27 Oct. 1892; "Riley's New Poems," *San Francisco Chronicle,* 11 Nov. 1894; *Atlanta Constitution,* 18 Nov. 1894; "Selling His Books," *Crawfordsville Journal,* 12 Apr. 1901. For example, "Jargon-Jingle" and "The Youthful Patriot," both originally published in *Armazindy,* have little merit as poems (Russo, pp. 54–57; *Complete Works,* VI: 1645, 1664).

84. Russo; "A Volume of Riley's Verse," *New York Times,* 12 Nov. 1893; "James Whitcomb Riley," *New York Sun,* 5 Mar. 1893.

85. "A Volume of Riley's Verses," *New York Sun,* 12 Nov. 1893; Edmund Eitel, Memories of My Uncle, 23 Jan. 1914, M660, InHi. For example, *Poems Here at Home* included "The Old Man and Jim," "Bereaved," "Down to the Capital," "Fessler's Bees," and "Squire Hawkin's Story" (Russo, pp. 46–50).

86. JWR to Carey, 21 Sept. 1890, n.d., HM6194, HM6232, CSmH; JWR to Carey, 14 July 1892, 17 May 1893, Riley Mss., InU-Li; JWR to Thomas Wentworth Higginson, 9 Dec. 1891, L135, In; JWR to Lucy Furman, 14 Feb. 1893, Riley Mss., InU-Li; JWR to Charles Scribner's Sons, 10 Sept. 1897, Riley Mss., InU-Li; JWR to Scribner, 21 Feb. 1901, Riley Mss., InU-Li.

87. JWR to Carey, 29 May 1897, Riley Mss., InU-Li; JWR to Relyea, 6 Sept. 1897, Riley Mss., InU-Li; JWR to Scribner's, 4 Sept. 1897, Riley Mss. VI., InU-Li; JWR to R. U. Johnson, 27 July 1901, Riley Mss., InU-Li; JWR to Edith M. Thomas, 4 Sept. 190; "JWR and His Works," *Detroit Tribune,* 20 Oct. 1898.

88. Christy (1873–1952) accompanied American troops to Cuba during the Span-

ish American War. He became famous for the Christy Girl which appeared in *Scribner's* as an illustration called "The Soldier's Dream" (Walter Reed, ed., *The Illustrator in America, 1900–1960s* [New York: Reinhold, 1966], p. 50). Russo, pp. 90, 98. Other illustrators of Riley's works included Gustave Baumann, Ethel Franklin Betts, Edward Windsor Kemble, and Charles M. Relyea (Russo, pp. 46, 69, 71, 93, 103, 109, 113, 140–42, 156).

89. Scribner to JWR, 22 May 1897; Charles Scribner's Sons to [—] [advertising flyer], 17 Nov. 1897, no. 2, box 19, PS2700, InU-Li; JWR to Stedman, 14 Feb. 1898, Riley Mss., InU-Li; Russo, p. 223.

90. Russo, pp. 224–25.

91. Wilson, "The Quiet Observer." "Whitcomb Riley's 'Home Folks,'" *Chicago Times-Herald,* 14 Oct. 1900; *James Whitcomb Riley* (Indianapolis: Indiana School of Journalism Teachers' Club, 1898); *San Francisco Argonaut,* 27 Oct. 1902.

92. "James Whitcomb Riley," *New York Sun,* 5 Mar. 1893.

93. *San Francisco Argonaut,* 27 Oct. 1902.

94. Ibid.

95. William Lyon Phelps to JWR, 7 Dec. 1900, Riley Mss., InU-Li; Wilson, "The Quiet Observer"; "Whitcomb Riley's 'Home Folks,'" *Chicago Times-Herald,* 14 Oct. 1900; *James Whitcomb Riley* (Indianapolis: Indiana School of Journalism Teachers' Club, 1898).

96. Anson Phelps Stokes to JWR, 13 May 1902, Riley Mss., InU-Li; Jesse Y. Burk to JWR, 6 Jan. 1904, Riley Mss., InU-Li; William Lowe Bryan to JWR, 10 June 1907, InU-Li; Chronology, M660, InHi. Wabash College, located in Crawfordsville, Indiana, made Riley an honorary Doctor of Literature in 1903; and Indiana University awarded him with an honorary Doctor of Law degree in 1907.

97. Chronology, M660, InHi; JWR to the Institute of Arts and Letters, [ca. 30 Jan. 1912], Riley VI. Mss., InU-Li; Howells, "The New Poetry," in the *North American Review* 168 (May 1899): 588; "Mr. Perry's Address, Editor of Atlantic Monthly Speaks at Butler College," *Indianapolis Sentinel,* 8 June 1901; Phelps to JWR, 17 May 1906, Riley III. Mss., InU-Li. In 1898, to further literature and fine arts on the U.S., the American Social Science Association founded the National Institute of Arts and Letters. From 1904 to 1976, the American Academy of Arts and Letters formed a section of this organization. In 1976, the two merged to create the American Academy and Institute of Arts and Letters. Membership is limited to 250 U.S. citizens.

98. JWR to Matthews, 28 Nov. 1892, Riley Mss., InU-Li; JWR to Dunbar, 22 Nov. 1892, Riley VI. Mss., InU-Li; JWR to C. D. Higgins, 8 June 1916.

99. Parker to JWR, 10 Feb. 1906, Riley Mss., InU-Li; Eugene F. Ware to JWR, 14 May 1897, Riley Mss., InU-Li; JWR to C. D. Higgins, 8 June 1916; Brodhead, *Cultures of Letters,* p. 117.

100. "Riley Is Most Loved Man in State," *Marion Daily Chronicle,* 28 Apr. 1910; Albert J. Beveridge quoted in *In Honor of JWR, A Meeting of the Indiana State Teachers' Association* (Indianapolis: Bobbs-Merrill, 1905, p. 11); JWR to Carey, 15 Oct. 1895, Riley IV. Mss., InU-Li; Tarkington to JWR, 30 Oct. 1895; Ade, "Riley and His Friends," 9; Nicholson, *The Poet* (New York: Houghton Mifflin, 1914); Nicholson, "Address by Meredith Nicholson at Manual Training High School, Oct. 6, 1911" (Indianapolis, 1911). See Riley II. Mss., InU-Li for Nicholson's correspondence with JWR.

101. JWR to Kipling, 4 Mar. 1893, Riley Mss., InU-Li; JWR to Nye, 11 May 1892, Riley Mss., InU-Li.

102. JWR to Nye, 11 May 1892; JWR to Carey, 21 Sept. 1891, Riley Mss., InU-Li.

103. JWR to Pond, 20 July 1892, M240, InHi.

104. JWR to "Grandpa" [George Smith], 21 Nov. 1892, Riley VI. Mss., InU-Li; JWR to "Lockerbies" [Charles and Magdelena Holstein, John and Charlotte Nickum], 17 Nov. 1892, Holstein Mss., InU-Li; JWR to [Magdelena] Holstein, 11 Jan. 1893, Holstein Mss., InU-Li.

105. *Los Angeles Times,* 4 Dec. 1892.

106. JWR to [Smith], 17 Dec. 1892, Riley Mss., InU-Li; "Mr. Riley Home Again," *Indianapolis Journal,* 20 Jan. 1892; Miller to JWR, 20 Jan. 1893. "Biographical Notes," in *American Poetry, the Nineteenth Century,* 2: 905–6.

107. Bierce, "Prattle." Eggleston set his novel *The Hoosier School-Master* in fictional "Hoopole" county. For more on this subject, see George Blakey, "Hoopole County, Hard to Find, Harder to Forget," in *Traces* 7 (Fall 1995): 41–47.

108. Ibid.; JWR to [Magdelena] Holstein, 30 Dec. [1892], Holstein Mss., InU-Li.

109. "The Hoosier Poet's Readings," *Washington Star,* 2 Mar. 1893; JWR to Nye, 14 June 1893, Riley Mss., InU-Li; JWR to Cawein, 14 Aug. 1890, Riley VI. Mss., InU-Li.

110. JWR to "Squidjicum" [Magdelena Holstein], 10 Apr. 1893, Holstein Mss., InU-Li; JWR to Nye, 14 June 1893; JWR to Carey, 15–16, 1894, Riley Mss., InU-Li; "Riley's Full House," *Minneapolis Journal,* 14 Nov. 1893; "The Hoosier Poet's Readings," *Washington Star,* 2 Mar. 1893.

111. JWR to Magdelena Holstein, [15 Apr.] 1893, Holstein Mss., InU-Li; JWR to Smith, 11 Feb. 1894, Riley Mss., InU-Li.

112. JWR to Magdelena Holstein, [15 Apr.] 1893, 25 Oct. 1893, 18 Nov. 1893, Holstein Mss., InU-Li; JWR to Charles [Holstein], 13 Feb. 1894, Holstein Mss., InU-Li.

113. JWR to [George Smith], 3 Nov. 1893, Riley Mss., InU-Li.

114. "A Noble Character," *Indianapolis Journal,* 7 Dec. 1893.

115. Elva May (Riley) Eitel to Mrs. John (Julia) Riley, 31 Dec. 1893, M660, InHi; Henry Eitel to John Riley, 18 Dec. 1893.

116. [Martha Lukens Riley] to JWR, 4 Apr. 1892, Riley Mss., InU-Li; "Summer Home of Mr. Riley in Greenfield," *Hancock Democrat,* 2 Mar. 1893; "His Favorite Longfellow," *Kansas City Journal,* 24 Nov. 1893; JWR, "Poetry and Character"; "Talk with Hoosier Poet"; "Hoosier Poet Comes to Town," *Pittsburgh Chronicle Telegraph,* 26 Oct. 1903.

117. "A Trio of Funnymen," *Indianapolis Journal,* 17 Nov. 1895.

118. Edmund Eitel to Mary (Riley) Payne and Lesley Payne, 21 Jan. 1913, L. Payne, Mss., InU-Li.

119. Edmund Eitel to Mary (Riley) Payne and Lesley Payne, 21 Jan. 1913.

120. Lesley Payne, Summary of Biography of James Whitcomb Riley, n.d., RMA; JWR to Mary (Riley) Payne, 4 May 1908, L. Payne, Mss., InU-Li. The exact date that Mary (Riley) Payne left her husband Frank is unknown. However, it is clear from a letter that she wrote to Riley in Aug. 1900 that Frank Payne was abusive. Mary claimed that Frank "dragged her by her hair," beat her, and threatened to have her committed to a mental institution. In this letter, she pleaded with Riley to come rescue her (Mary [Riley] Payne to JWR, [18 Aug. 1900], Riley Mss., InU-Li).

121. Payne, Summary of Biography of James Whitcomb Riley, n.d., RMA. Riley was probably misled when he bought Lesley this violin. He was told that the violin had been made by a famous eighteenth-century Italian violin maker named Carlos Tononi.

Instead, a German named Johann Gottlieb Ficker probably constructed it ("Depauw Professor Buys Violin Riley Owned for 'Bargain' $900," *Indianapolis Star,* 3 Oct. 1975).

122. JWR to "Saint Lockerbie" [Magdelena Holstein], 15 Feb. 1894, Holstein Mss., InU-Li.

123. JWR to "St. [Magdelena] and Charles Holstein, 24 Feb. 1894, Holstein Mss., InU-Li.

124. JWR to "St. Lockerbie" [Magdelena Holstein], 26–27 Feb. 1894, Holstein Mss., InU-Li; "Readings of Popular Authors, Mark Twain, James Whitcomb Riley, and Douglass Sherley," *New York Sun,* 27 Feb. 1894; Boewe, "On Stage and Off": 22–23.

125. JWR to [Magdelena Holstein], 26–27 Feb. 1894, Holstein Mss., InU-Li.

126. "Readings of Popular Authors, Mark Twain, James Whitcomb Riley, and Douglass Sherley," *New York Sun,* 27 Feb. 1894; Twain quoted in Boewe, "On Stage and Off": 23.

127. JWR to "St. Lockerbie," New York, 5 Mar. 1894, Holstein Mss., InU-Li; JWR to [Louise Chandler] Moulton, 9, 24, Apr. 1894; Receipted Bill, Denison Hotel, 1 May 1892, Riley Mss., InU-Li; Parker and Heiney, eds., "Biographical Notes," *Poets and Poetry of Indiana,* p. 436; Obituary, Charles Holstein, *Indianapolis Journal,* 23 Jan. 1901; James Whitcomb Riley Lockerbie Street Home, Docent Information, n.d., RMA.

128. JWR to [Wilcox], 11 July 1880, Riley III. Mss., InU-Li; Biographical Edition, II: 510–11; JWR, "Lockerbie Street," *Complete Works,* III: 611–12. Theodore Dreiser, *A Hoosier Holiday* (Bloomington: Indiana University Press, 1997), p. 386. 129. JWR to "St. Lockerbie" [Magdelena Holstein], 28 Oct. 1898, Holstein Mss., InU-Li.

130. JWR to Charles Holstein, 5 Mar. 1894, Holstein Mss., InU-Li; Charles Holstein to JWR, 13 Sept. 1894, Riley V. Mss., InU-Li; JWR to Edith M. Thomas, 10 Feb 1902; JWR to Holsteins, 28 Feb. 1892, Holstein Mss., InU-Li; JWR to Joel Chandler Harris, 8 May 1900, Riley Mss., InU-Li.

131. JWR to "Grandpa" [George Smith], 14 Mar. 1893, Riley Mss., InU-Li; Charles Holstein to JWR, 27 Apr. 1898, Riley V. Mss., InU-Li.

132. Magdelena and Riley lived alone in the house at 528 Lockerbie Street in Indianapolis after 5 July 1904 until Riley's death. Magdelena died almost exactly three months after Riley on 18 October 1916. She was seventy-one ("Mrs. Holstein Dies at Lockerbie Street Home," *Indianapolis News,* 18 Oct. 1916; James Whitcomb Riley Lockerbie Street Home, Docent Information, n.d., RMA).

133. JWR to Moulton, 2 Dec. 1895, Riley Mss., InU-Li.

134. "Riley has Retired, Hoosier Poet Leaves the Platform for an Indefinite Time," *Chicago Evening Post,* 22 Feb. 1896.

135. Dickey, Diary entries, 10, 15, Jan. 1891; 4 Feb. 1891; 28 Jan. 1891; 10 June 1891; Dickey Mss., InU-Li; Memorandum of an agreement between JWR and Dickey, 24 Sept. 1896, Riley Mss., InU-Li; "Riley Is Most Loved Man in State," *Marion Daily Chronicle,* 28 Apr. 1910.

136. JWR to Charles Holstein, 10 Oct. 1896, Holstein Mss., InU-Li; "Colorado Springs Lyceum, 1896–1897," no. 49, box 6, PS2700, InU-Li.

137. JWR to Dickey, 11 Dec. 1897, Riley Mss., InU-Li.

138. JWR to Edward S. Van Zile, 7 Nov. 1898, Riley Mss., InU-Li.

139. JWR to St. Lockerbie [Magdelena Holstein], 4, 20 Nov. 1897, Holstein Mss., InU-Li; Dickey, "Gray Days on the Platform" [unpublished manuscript], n.d., p. 16, Dickey Mss., InU-Li.

140. "An Overflowing Welcome to James Whitcomb Riley" [advertising pamphlet]

(Indianapolis: Bowen-Merrill, ca. 1900); Brodhead, *Cultures of Letters,* p. 52; Obituary of William C. Bobbs, *Indianapolis Star,* 12 Feb. 1926. In the second half of the nineteenth century Joe Jefferson (1829–1905) was one of the best known actors on the American stage. His most famous role was Rip Van Winkle (*Webster's New Biographical Dictionary*).

141. "Riley Night Advance Sale," *Atlanta Journal,* 17 Sept. 1898.

142. "Much Interest," *Indianapolis Journal,* 12 May 1899; "JWR': "Amused Immense Audience at the Opera House," *Daily Illinois State Register* [Springfield, Illinois], 4 Dec. 1900; "James Whitcomb Riley," *Boston Beacon,* 5 Nov. 1898.

143. Dickey to JWR, 5 Feb. 1897, Riley Mss., InU-Li; JWR to Debs, 6 Nov. 1898, Riley Mss., InU-Li; JWR to Laughlin, 6, 7, Apr. 1899, Riley Mss., InU-Li; "Eleven Weeks' Tour of James Whitcomb Riley," *Indianapolis News,* 19 Sept. 1903; "Riley Wants to Come Here to Visit," *Detroit Times,* 9 Oct. 1903; Edmund Eitel, Memories of My Uncle, 23 Jan. 1914, M660, InHi.

144. "Riley Wants to Come Here to Visit," *Detroit Times,* 9 Oct. 1903.

145. JWR to Charles [Holstein], 28 Oct. 1898, Holstein Mss., InU-Li; JWR to Albert A. Mason, 14 Feb. 1892, Riley Mss., InU-Li; Katherine Willard to JWR, 26 June 1892, Riley Mss., InU-Li; Dickey to Henry Eitel, [Sept. 1903], M660, InHi; "Riley Will Make Another Reading Tour,"*Indianapolis Journal,* 6 Sept. 1903. Starting in the 1890s, Riley also made at least $150 for each of his poems which were published in magazines (JWR to Edward C. Bok, 1 Apr. 1895, Riley Mss., InU-Li).

146. JWR to [Magdelena Holstein], 20 Nov. 1897.

147. "Dana and Riley," *Milwaukee Sentinel,* 25 July 1888; "Talk with Hoosier Poet," *Chicago Times-Herald,* 22 Oct. 1900; "Riley's Chief Ambition," *New Haven Register,* 16 Nov. 1898.

148. JWR to Charles [Holstein], 2 Oct. 1900, Holstein Mss., InU-Li.

149. JWR, Lists of selections for readings, Riley V. Mss., InU-Li; "Much Interest," *Indianapolis Journal,* 12 May 1899.

150. "Indiana's Poet, Long Silent, Sings Again," *Chicago Times-Herald,* 13 Oct. 1900; "The People's Poet Laureate," *New York World,* 1 Dec. 1911; Meredith Nicholson quoted in *In Honor of James Whitcomb Riley, A Meeting of the Indiana State Teachers' Association,* pp. 34–35.

151. Ziff, *The American 1890s,* p. 3; *Kansas City Star,* 27 Sept. 1893; *James Whitcomb Riley* (Indianapolis: Indianapolis School of Journalism Teachers' Club, 1898); Matthews to JWR, 1 Oct. 1893.

152. JWR to Kahle, 6 Oct. 1880, Brunn Mss., InU-Li.

153. JWR to Edith M. Thomas, 10 Apr. 1902, Riley Mss., InU-Li.

154. Ibid.; Riley quoted in Dickey, "A Quiet Religion," [unpublished manuscript], n.p. n.d., p. 13; JWR, "Thoughts on the Late War," *Complete Works,* V: 1379–80.

155. JWR, "The Soldier: The Dedication of the Soldiers' and Sailors' Monument, Indianapolis, 15 May 1902," *Complete Works,* VIII: 2021.

156. Hendricks, an Indiana Democrat, served in the United States Senate from 1863 to 1869, "was nominated and defeated for the governorship in 1868, and finally elected govenor in 1872." Hendricks was very popular. However, Thornbrough attributes this popularity "to his conciliatory disposition rather than any positive program or profound convictions" (Thornbrough, *Indiana in the Civil War Era,* pp. 185, 226–27). Lawton, who commanded the first American troops to land in Cuba during the Spanish American War, became a famous war hero when he fell in battle in the Philippines

in December 1899. Riley read "The Home-Voyage," which he composed to honor Lawton, at the dedication of a statue in memory of him in 1907 (Philips, *Indiana in Transition*, p. 73; "Roosevelt Receives Ovation; Lawton Statue Unveiled,"*Indianapolis News*, 31 May 1907; JWR, *Complete Works*, VII: 1944–45). "The Veil Is Lifted and the Monument Stands in Hendricks' Memory," *Indianapolis Sentinel*, 2 July 1890; JWR, "Benjamin Harrison," *Complete Works*, IX: 2270–71; Nicholson to JWR, 28 Oct. 1908, Riley II. Mss., InU-Li.

157. "Wallace Statue Unveiled in Capitol," *Indianapolis News*, 12 June 1910; JWR, "General Lew Wallace," *Complete Works*, VIII: 2155–56; "Sousa Music to Riley's Poem," *Indianapolis News*, 19 Apr. 1902; JWR, "America," *Complete Works*, VIII: 2000–1.

158. Robert Burns Wilson to JWR, 23 June 1890, Riley Mss., InU-Li.

159. *Complete Works*, X: 2776–79, 2790–92.

160. "Riley's Recent Poems," *Memphis Commercial*, 27 Oct. 1892. See "Tennyson," *Complete Works*, VI: 1583; "Whittier—At Newburyport," *Complete Works*, VI: 1585; and "Mrs. Benjamin Harrison,"*Complete Works*, VI: 1586.

161. JWR, "Away," *Complete Works*, IV: 1000–1. Riley wrote "Away" in 1884 in memory of General W. H. H. Terrell who rendered distinguished service during the Civil War by devising an efficient method to deliver supplies to Indiana soldiers. Following the Civil War he served as adjutant general (Biographical Editon, III: 520–21).

162. Ramazani, *The Poetry of Mourning*, p. 19.

163. Ibid., pp. 18–19.

164. JWR, "Out to Old Aunt Mary's," *Complete Works*, IV: 1004–8; JWR, "The Old Swimmin'-Hole," *Complete Works*, III: 798–800.

165. JWR, "The Old Swimmin'-Hole," III: 800.

166. Ramazani, *Poetry of Mourning*, p. 36.

167. JWR to Edith M. Thomas, 3 Sept. 1903, Riley Mss., InU-Li; Ramazani, *The Poetry of Mourning*, pp. 13, 18–19.

168. JWR to Thomas, 3 Sept. 1903.

169. JWR to Edith T. Mediary, 26 Nov. 1907, Riley Mss., InU-Li; JWR to Charles W. Stoddard, 28 Nov. 1891, HM6242, CSmH.

170. JWR to Thomas, 3 Sept. 1903; "A Chat with the Poet Riley."

171. "Riley in Omaha," *Omaha World Herald*, 19 Nov. 1897.

172. JWR to Louise Coffin Jones, 3 Apr. 1895, Riley Mss., InU-Li; Thomas W. Symons to JWR, 1 Apr. 1901, Riley Mss., InU-Li; Erasmus Wilson to JWR, 22 Aug. 1896, Riley Mss., InU-Li.

173. "The Hoosier Poet's Illness," *Chicago Times*, 13 Oct. 1889; JWR to Clarence Edmund Stedman, 28 Nov. 1896, Riley Mss., InU-Li; JWR to Frank W. Nye, 25 Dec. 1897, Riley Mss., InU-Li; JWR to R. W. Gilder, 3 Oct. 1899, Riley Mss., InU-Li; JWR to C. C. Buel, 15 Aug. 1900, Riley Mss., InU-Li; Joel Chandler Harris to JWR, 24 Aug. 1901, Riley III. Mss., InU-Li; JWR to Harris, 29 Apr. 1902, Riley Mss., InU-Li; JWR to Edward Bok, 15 Sept. 1902, Riley Mss., InU-Li; JWR to Bliss Carman, [21 Jan. 1904], HM44365, CSmH; JWR to Bliss Carman, 9 June 1905, HM44374, CSmH; JWR to Cawein, 12 Apr. 1906, L135, In; Henry Eitel to Mary (Riley) Payne, 9 June 1907, L. Payne Mss., InU-Li; JWR to Mrs. Riley [Maria Fletcher Berry], 7 Mar. 1908, Riley VI. Mss, InU-Li; JWR to Cawein, 15 June 1910, HM44406, CSmH.

174. Lears, *No Place of Grace*, pp. 49–50; JWR to Dr. S. Weir Mitchell, 14 May 1896, Riley VI. Mss., InU-Li. In addition to being an eminent physician, Mitchell was a successful author of fiction and prose (*Webster's New Biographical Dictionary*).

175. Lears, *No Place of Grace,* pp. 49–52.

176. JWR to Emma Carleton, 11 Jan. 1900, Riley Mss., InU-Li; JWR to Will T. Hale, 30 Jan. 1900, Riley Mss., InU-Li: JWR to Edward Bok, 15 Sept. 1902; JWR to Bliss Carman, [21 Jan. 1904], HM44369, CSmH.

177. JWR to Joel Chandler Harris, 11 Apr. 1900, InU-Li; Joel Chandler Harris to JWR, 24 Aug. 1901, Riley III. Mss., InU-Li.

178. Lears, *No Place of Grace,* p. 53.

179. JWR to Emma Carleton, 11 Jan. 1900; JWR to Will T. Hale, 30 Jan. 1900, Riley Mss., InU-Li.

180. JWR to Cawein, 12 Apr. 1906, L135, In.

181. JWR to Laughlin, 13 June 1899, Riley Mss., InU-Li.

182. Ibid.; R. L. C. White to JWR, 2 Jan. 1891, Riley Mss. InU-Li; Ware to JWR, 15 June 1891, Riley Mss., InU-Li; Laughlin to JWR, 14 June 1899, Riley Mss., InU-Li; Mediary to JWR, 1 Dec. 1907, Riley III. Mss., InU-Li; Leta Billy Blankenship to JWR, 25 Jan. 1916, Riley III. Mss, InU-Li; "Our Bobby Burns," 2 Jan. 1891; "About James Whitcomb Riley. His Simplicity and the Absence of Snobbishness," *Terre Haute Express,* 6 May 1891; JWR to Mediary, 26 Nov. 1907, Riley III. Mss., InU-Li; JWR to Carman, 9 June 1905, HM44374, CSmH; JWR to Bliss Carman, 7 May 1907, Riley VI. Mss., InU-Li; Bliss Carman "Riley Just as He Is," *New York Times,* 16 June 1906; JWR to Cawein, 15 June 1910, HM44406, CSmH; Dickey, Notes on JWR, 1913, Dickey Mss., InU-Li.

183. R[ichard] B[uckner] Gruelle to JWR, 13 Mar. 1900, Riley Mss., InU-Li. R. B. Gruelle, a member of the Hoosier Group of Indiana-based artists which included T. C. Steele and Samuel Richards, was the father of John Barton (Johnny) Gruelle, the creator of Raggedy Ann and Andy. Riley's poems "Little Orphant Annie" and "The Raggedy Man" inspired the name for Gruelle's famous cloth dolls (Patricia Hall, *Johnny Gruelle: Creator of Raggedy Ann and Andy* [Gretna, Louisiana: Pelican, 1998], pp. 18, 107).

184. JWR to Van Dyke, 27 Feburary 1901, Riley Mss., InU-Li.

185. JWR to [Thomas], 17 Apr. 1906, Riley Mss., InU-Li; "Wallace Statue Unveiled in Capitol," *Indianapolis News,* 12 June 1910.

186. JWR to Mrs. Maria Fletcher Berry, 7 Mar. 1908, Riley VI. Mss., InU-Li.

187. JWR to Cawein, 15 June 1910; Henry Eitel to Mary (Riley) Payne, 1 Aug. 1910, L. Payne Mss., InU-Li; Edmund Eitel to Edward Jay Allen, 14 Mar. 1914, M660, InHi.

188. Henry Eitel to Mary (Riley) Payne, 8, 15 Aug. 1910, L. Payne Mss., InU-Li; Thomas to St. Nick [JWR], [26 Dec. 1911], Riley VI., Mss., InU-Li.

189. "Accept Riley Gift: Authorize Bonds," *Indianapolis Star,* 12 July 1911.

190. Edmund Eitel to Edward Jay Allen, 14 Mar. 1914; Eitel to W. D. Nesbit, 19 June 1914, M660, InHi; Carl Fisher to JWR, 23 Aug. 1913, M660, InHi; JWR to Carl G. Fisher, 25 Aug. 1913, M660, InHi; JWR to Robert Burdette, 13 Feb. 1914, M660, InHi. Fisher (1874–1939), a cofounder of the Indianapolis Speedway and owner of Prest-O-Lite Storage Battery Company, was responsible for establishing Miami Beach as a resort area (Bodenhamer and Barrows, eds., *Encyclopedia of Indianapolis,* pp. 572–73).

191. Ade to JWR, 15 Aug. 1911, Riley III. Mss., InU-Li; Thomas to St. Nick [JWR], [26 Dec. 1911]; "Should Dictate," *Indianapolis Star,* 9 Dec. 1911. Between 1911 and 1913, Riley wrote three poems which appear in the *Biographical Edition* (Biographical Edition, V: 492–93). Following the publication of the *Biographical Edition* in 1913, Riley wrote one poem upon the death of his old friend George A. Carr and one for

Cornelia Allison, daughter of the Indianapolis industrialist James A. Allison. This last poem was published two days following the poet's death in July 1916 (Russo, pp. 137, 139).

192. Howland to JWR, 15 Apr. 1915, Riley VI. Mss., InU-Li; JWR to Edmund Eitel, 5 Feb. 1916, Riley VI. Mss., InU-Li; Russo, pp. 119–20, 123–33, 138–39. Howland (1863–1944) was editor-in-chief at Bobbs-Merrill between 1900 and 1925 (Van Allen and Foust, *Keeping the Dream,* p. 109).

193. Permissions Granted for Musical Settings, n.d., Box 145, Riggs to Riley, J. W., Bobbs-Merrill Mss., InU-Li; Motion Picture Rights, Box 145, Riggs to Riley, J. W., Bobbs-Merrill Mss., InU-Li.

194. "Records Taken of Riley's Voice," *Indianapolis Star,* 6 July 1912.

195. Dreiser, *A Hoosier Holiday,* p. 373.

196. Eugene Field to JWR, 20 Apr. 1895, Riley Mss., InU-Li; JWR to "Dear Friends," 1 June 1903, Riley III. Mss., InU-Li.

197. "Gather to Honor Riley's Birthday," *New York Times,* 7 Oct. 1915; Dreiser, *A Hoosier Holiday,* p. 386.

198. T. C. Steele painted Riley for the first time in 1878, at the age of twenty-nine. This portrait was last known to be in the possession of the poet's niece, Lesley Payne. It is not known what happened to it following her death in 1976. Steele painted his second Riley portrait in 1891 for the Indianapolis Literary Club. He made two copies, one of which now hangs in the main atrium of the James Whitcomb Riley Hospital for Children. The Indiana artist completed his last portrait of his friend in 1902. In 1936, J. K. Lilly purchased it, and it now hangs in The Lilly Library, Indiana University, Bloomington. The Indiana State Museum owns a 1916 copy of this painting (Steele and Peat, *The House of the Singing Winds,* p. 154; conversation with Martin Krause, Curator of Works on Paper, Indianapolis Museum of Art, 9 June 1999.)

199. Gary A. Reynolds, "Sargent's Late Portraits," in Patricia Hills, ed., *John Singer Sargent* (New York: Whitney Museum of American Art, 1986), p. 147); R. U. Johnson to JWR, 25 May 1903, Riley V. Mss., InU-Li.

200. JWR to the School Children, [7 Oct. 1912], Riley Mss., InU-Li.

201. Katherine Mannix to Bernard R. DeRemer, 13 May 1968, RMA; "Asks Schools to Honor Riley," *Indianapolis Star,* 23 Sept. 1911; "Mrs. Mitchell's New Book Is Published," *Hancock Democrat,* 10 Sept. 1942; "Entire State Pays Tribute to Riley," *Indianapolis Star,* 7 Oct. 1911; "JWR Receiving Tribute of School Children," *Indianapolis News,* 7 Oct. 1913. Minnie Belle Mitchell was the wife of John F. Mitchell, editor for many years of the *Hancock Democrat.* The Greenfield Mitchells were not related to Silas Weir Mitchell ("Minnie Belle Mitchell, Friend of Riley, Dies," *Indianapolis Star,* 7 Feb. 1956).

202. "Riley Day Celebration Will Be Nationwide."

203. "Childhood of America Greets Poet," *Indianapolis Star,* 8 Oct. 1915.

204. "Program Completed for Riley Celebration," *Indianapolis News,* 4 Sept. 1915.

205. "Indianapolis to Honor James Whitcomb Riley," *Indianapolis News,* 19 Aug. 1915.

206. "Dinner Arrangements Complete," *Indianapolis News,* 4 Oct. 1915; "Those Who Honored Riley at the Banquet," *Indianapolis Star,* 8 Oct. 1915.

207. "Fairbanks Tells of Riley's Early Days."

208. Ibid.; "'Same Jim Riley,' says Senator Kern," *Indianapolis Star,* 8 Oct. 1915; "Divine in Riley Seen by Harvey," *Indianapolis Star,* 8 Oct. 1915; "'Only One Riley, and Thank Goodness We Hoosiers Have Him,' Says Ade," *Indianapolis Star,* 8 Oct. 1915.

209. "'Same Jim Riley,' says Senator Kern."

210. "Fairbanks Tells of Riley's Early Days."

211. Ibid.; "'Same Jim Riley,' says Senator Kern"; Lears, *No Place of Grace,* pp. 17–18.

212. "Fairbanks Tells of Riley's Early Days."

213. "'Only One Riley, and Thank Goodness We Hoosiers Have Him,' Says Ade."

214. "Fairbanks Tells of Riley's Early Days."

215. "Ralston in Welcoming Address, Calls Occasion Red Letter Day in Indiana," *Indianapolis Star,* 8 Oct. 1915.

216. "Divine in Riley Seen by Harvey."

217. "Fairbanks Tells of Riley's Early Days."

218. "Nicholson Calls Him Laird," *Indianapolis Star,* 6 Oct. 1912.

219. "Sunset of Riley's Career Still Far Distant," *New York Times,* 12 Sept. 1912; "Gather to Honor Riley's Birthday"; "Riley Declares That He Feels Like a Boy Again," *Indianapolis News,* 13 Sept. 1915.

Epilogue

1. "Sunset of Riley's Career Still Far Distant."

2. Ibid.

3. Dickey to George Funk, 5 Dec. 1902, Dickey Mss., InU-Li.

4. See Riley Mss., InU-Li and Dickey Mss., InU-Li for the results of Dickey's data gathering efforts.

5. JWR to John R. Nickum, Holstein Mss., InU-Li.

6. Hitt to Dickey, 9 July 1923, Hitt Mss., InU-Li.

7. Dickey—*Youth,* Dickey—*Maturity.*

8. Dickey to JWR, n.d. [ca. 1907], Dickey Mss., InU-Li; "Riley Is Most Loved Man in the State," *Marion Daily Chronicle,* 28 Apr. 1910; Dickey—*Youth;* Dickey—*Maturity;* Dickey, Miscellaneous Notebooks, Scrapbooks, Memories, Dickey Mss., InU-Li.

9. Dickey, Notes on JWR, 1907, Dickey Mss., InU-Li.

10. "The Hoosier Poet Arrives," *Kansas City Star,* 27 Feb. 1892.

11. "About James Whitcomb Riley. His Simplicity and the Absence of Snobbishness," *Terre Haute Express,* 6 May 1891.

12. *Philadelphia Press,* 22 Nov. 1891.

13. *Philadelphia Press,* 21 Nov. 1891; "James Whitcomb Riley's Verse, *Green Fields and Running Brooks,*" *New York Times,* 30 Jan. 1893; "Riley's Recent Poems," *Memphis Commercial,* 27 Oct. 1892.

14. JWR to Charles Holstein, 5 Mar. 1894, Holstein Mss., InU-Li.

15. JWR to Charles Holstein, 28 Jan. 1894, Holstein Mss., InU-Li; Dickey, Notes on JWR, n.d., 1907, Dickey Mss., InU-Li.

16. Lears, *No Place of Grace,* p. 41.

17. "James Whitcomb Riley," *St. Louis Mirror,* 10 Feb. 1898.

18. "James Whitcomb Riley," *Indianapolis Journal,* 5 Feb 1892; "Riley's Recent Poems," *Memphis Commercial,* 27 Oct. 1892; John Clark Ridpath, "James Whitcomb Riley," *Indianapolis Journal,* 6 Sept. 189; "Riley," *Portland* [Indiana] *Commercial-Review,* 27 Nov. 1903; Garland, "Real Conversations," 221–22.

19. "The Apotheosis of Dialect," *Sunday Pioneer Press,* St. Paul Minnesota, 27 Nov 1892; Ambrose Bierce, "Prattle."

20. Ambrose Bierce, "Prattle"; "Poetry of the United States," *The Atheneum,* 3 Mar.

1894; "An American Poet," *Washington, D.C. Evening News,* 8 Mar. 1893; Wilson, "The Quiet Observer."

21. "Received an Ovation," *Scranton Tribune,* 28 Mar. 1899; Garland, "Real Conversations," p. 221.

22. Ibid.

23. Orson Swett Marden, ed., *Little Visits with Great Americans, or Success, Ideals and How to Attain Them* (New York: Success Company, 1905), p. 253.

24. Lears, *No Place of Grace,* p. 18.

25. JWR to [Wilcox], 7 Sept. 1880; JWR to [Wilcox], 11 July 1880; JWR to Jones, 22 Aug. 1880; Lears, *No Place of Grace,* pp. 35–37.

26. [Bottsford] Wambaugh to Mary (Riley) Payne, 23 Sept. 1903.

27. "Sunset of Riley's Career Still Far Distant."

28. "Fairbanks Tells of Riley's Early Days."

29. Trachtenberg, *The Incorporation of America,* pp. 186, 191–92; Ziff, *The American 1890s,* p. 31; "An Evening with a Poet, JWR, the 'Hoosier Poet,' Lectures at the Exchange Hall," *Kansas City Journal,* 2 Feb. 1884.

30. Beers, "The Singer of the Old Swimmin' Hole," p. 36.

31. JWR to Cawein, 25 Feb. 1892, Riley Mss., InU-Li; Elva May (Riley) Eitel to JWR, 26 Dec. 1903, Riley Mss., InU-Li; JWR to Edith T. Mediary, 26 Nov. 1907, Riley Mss., InU-Li.

32. JWR to Bottsford, 24 May 1883, Bottsford Mss., InU-Li.

33. Ibid., 19 Oct. [1880].

34. JWR to Cawein, 5 Feb. 1892, Riley Mss., InU-Li.

35. Beers, "The Singer of the Old Swimmin' Hole," p. 36.

36. "James Whitcomb Riley, A Treasury of Country Tales—His Ideas on Dialect," *Rochester* [New York] *Democrat Chronicle,* 14 Apr. 1888.

37. Brodhead, *Cultures of Letters,* p. 137.

38. "Mr. Riley Here," *Richmond Palladium,* 15 May 1899.

39. JWR to Jones, 8 Jan. 1894, Riley Mss., InU-Li; JWR to Matthews, 12 Oct. 1888, Riley Mss., InU-Li; "Dana and Riley," *Milwaukee Sentinel,* 25 July 1888; "Doesn't Drink Now, 'Jim' Riley Has Turned Over a New Leaf and Started Afresh," *St. Louis Post-Dispatch,* 24 Dec. 1893; JWR to Edith M. Thomas, 10 Aug. 1903, Riley Mss, InU-Li; JWR to Edith T. Mediary, 26 Nov. 1907.

40. "James Whitcomb Riley," *St. Louis Globe Democrat,* 11 Feb. 1898.

41. "James Whitcomb Riley," *New York Sun,* 5 Mar. 1893; Brodhead, *Cultures of Letters,* pp. 136–37; Nicholson, *The Hoosiers,* p. 45; "Mr. Riley in Town."

42. "With the Author," *Rochester* [New York] *Herald,* 15 Mar. 1893; Howells, "The New Poetry," *North American Review,* 168: (May 1899): 588.

43. Bowlby, *Just Looking,* p. 9.

44. *Indianapolis Sentinel,* 19 Feb. 1890.

45. JWR, "Dialect in Literature," *Complete Works,* X: 2687–88.

Index

Index

Index

Elizabeth J. Van Allen is an honors graduate of Indiana University who received her Ph.D. in history from Yale University. She is a former historian of the James Whitcomb Riley Memorial Association where she was Senior Editor for and contributor to the book *Keeping the Dream*, which celebrated the seventy-fifth anniversary of the Association. She is currently historian of the Indiana University School of Medicine in Indianapolis.